PLATO

APOLOGY OF SOCRATES AND CRITO

PLATO

APOLOGY OF SOCRATES AND CRITO

WITH EXTRACTS FROM THE PHAEDO AND SYMPOSIUM
AND FROM XENOPHON'S MEMORABILIA

EDITED BY
LOUIS DYER

REVISED BY
THOMAS DAY SEYMOUR

WITH A VOCABULARY

CARATZAS BROTHERS, PUBLISHERS
New Rochelle, New York — 1979

PLATO, **Apology of Socrates and Crito,** with
extracts from the Phaedo and Symposium and
from Xenophon's Memorabilia.
Edited by Louis Dyer and revised by Thomas
Day Seymour. 246 pages, clothbound.
ISBN 0-89241-000-0

CARATZAS BROTHERS, PUBLISHERS
246 Pelham Road, New Rochelle,
New York 10805

Boston: Ginn, 1908

Printed in U.S.A. by
NOBLE OFFSET PRINTERS, INC.
NEW YORK, N.Y. 10003

PREFACE

This book was first published in 1885 and contained Plato's *Apology* and *Crito*. Its editor, Professor Louis Dyer, subsequently removed his residence to England. When the editors of the College Series of Greek Authors determined last year to issue a new edition, Professor Dyer felt that he was not sufficiently acquainted with the changes in conditions of collegiate instruction in Greek that have occurred in America during the past twenty years to undertake the task, and committed it to Professor Seymour.

The new edition contains, in addition to the *Apology* and *Crito*, extracts from Plato's *Phaedo* and *Symposium* and from Xenophon's *Memorabilia*. Professor Seymour rewrote the introduction and the commentary on the first two dialogues, and added a commentary on the extracts and a vocabulary. The book was practically finished and nearly all in type before his death.

The editors of the College Series had hoped that Professor Dyer, who had long known Professor Seymour intimately, would write the preface to the new edition. His illness and sudden death prevented this, and the sad duty has fallen to me, the friend of both these scholars for many years, to make this simple record of the part borne by each of them in the authorship of this book.

JOHN WILLIAMS WHITE

INTRODUCTION

1. Socrates stands at the very head and source of the history of philosophy in the modern sense. Not that all the ideas and the results of the researches of the earlier sages have come to naught, but for the most part they affect the later world only mediately, through Socrates and Plato.[1] Socrates was the first to introduce scientific inductive argumentation, to form universal conceptions,[2] to require precise definitions, and to study the principles of ethics. Formal logic began with him. Not that men before Socrates did not observe and reason, and define or describe, and take thought for virtue, but they had not studied carefully the laws of thought or the rational foundations of virtuous actions. Socrates was far from simply preaching the morality of his age and city. He insisted on an intellectual basis for moral principles. He would not separate knowledge from right action. The man who knows what is right, according to Socrates, will always do what is right. He who does what is right, however, without clear knowledge, is in danger at any moment of going wrong, and Socrates compares him to a blind man going along the right path. So Socrates contrasted knowledge (ἐπιστήμη) with right opinion (ἀληθὴς δόξα). Before Socrates, thinkers confused many matters which ought to be separated, and vainly hoped to gain one general solution for all problems.

[1] See Zeller's *Geschichte der griechischen Philosophie.* The English translation is convenient : Zeller's *Pre-Socratic Philosophy*, London, 1881, 2 vols. ; *Socrates and the Socratic Schools*, 1885 ; *Plato and the Older Academy*, 1876. See also Burnet's *Early Greek Philosophy* and Bakewell's *Source Book in Ancient Philosophy*, 1907. The most complete collection of the remains of the works of the pre-Socratic philosophers is Diels's *Fragmente der Vorsokratiker*, Berlin, 1903, of which a second edition is appearing. Convenient is Fairbanks's *The First Philosophers of Greece, an edition and translation of the remaining fragments of the pre-Socratic philosophers*, N.Y., 1898. See also Pater's *Plato and Platonism*, 1893.   [2] Aristotle, *Met.* 1078 b.

2. Only by a severe effort can we put ourselves approximately in the place of the pre-Socratic philosophers, so as in a measure to have their point of view and understand their problems. Most of them had no schools and made no propaganda for their beliefs, and left no writings, and we have little definite knowledge of their systems. Many of their sayings which have been preserved seem to us darkly enigmatical, and, as they are stated, most of their investigations and theories appear to us futile, although in some matters they have curiously anticipated the very latest scientific thought. In general, the results of their speculations seem strange to modern minds. Fortunately we do not need to know and understand the views of the pre-Socratic philosophers in order to understand Plato's report of Socrates's defense before his judges. Plato seldom refers distinctly to his predecessors, — not to speak of quoting from them, — and Socrates introduced no philosophical questions in his speech to the court. To determine the indebtedness of Socrates and Plato to their predecessors is an interesting problem, but it does not concern us here. At present we need to remember only that the germs of all later systems of philosophy appear in the thoughts of the Platonic Socrates.

3. The Seven Sages [1] or Wise Men of Greece were not philosophers at all, in the modern sense. They were men of affairs, not of speculation. The traditions which we have in regard to them do not agree in every point, but are harmonious in representing them as rulers filled with practical wisdom. The wise Solon himself was neither a metaphysician nor a psychologist. He was a law-giver, and his thoughts were directed primarily toward means for securing a law-abiding and united spirit in the minds of the people of Athens. All the others of the Seven, according to Cicero, were rulers of their states, with the single exception of Thales, and he also, as Herodotus tells us, gave attention to political measures. The Seven Sages were said to have dedicated to Apollo at Delphi wise sayings, as an offering of their thoughts, — as *Know thyself* (γνῶθι σαυτόν), *Moderation*

---

[1] Τούτων ἦν καὶ Θαλῆς ὁ Μιλήσιος καὶ Πιττακὸς ὁ Μυτιληναῖος καὶ Βίας ὁ Πριηνεὺς καὶ Σόλων ὁ ἡμέτερος καὶ Κλεόβουλος ὁ Λίνδιος καὶ Μύσων ὁ Χηνεύς, καὶ ἕβδομος ἐν τούτοις ἐλέγετο Λακεδαιμόνιος Χίλων, Plato, *Prot.* 343 a. Cf. Hi omnes praeter Milesium Thalem civitatibus suis praefuerunt, Cicero, *de Orat.* iii. 34.

in all things, Nothing to excess (μηδὲν ἄγαν), *Ruin is near to surety-ship* (ἐγγύα, πάρα δ' ἄτα). Of these the last is as severely practical as " He that is surety for a stranger shall smart for it, and he that hateth suretyship is sure " (*Proverbs* xi. 15). The first two seem particularly Athenian, and were attributed to Solon. γνῶθι σαυτόν appears to have been the favorite maxim of Socrates : every man should learn what are his true powers and capacities, in order that he may undertake the work which is best fitted to his nature, — turning aside both from inferior occupations and from undertakings which are beyond his strength. Few faults seemed to Socrates worse than that of thinking one's self to know what he does not know (*Ap.* 21 c, 29 b). When a man has learned what he can do, and what he cannot do, he is already well on the way to become most useful and most happy. These precepts clearly were not philosophical maxims in the modern sense, but wholly practical.

4. The term *philosopher, lover of wisdom* (φιλόσοφος) was not of early use in Greece. It does not appear in extant Greek literature until the fourth century B.C., in the works of Plato and Xenophon, — though the verb derived from it is found earlier in two notable passages, but not in a technical sense.[1] Plato uses his influence to keep φιλόσοφος from becoming a technical term, by employing syno-nyms. In his writings, φιλόσοφος seldom should be translated by *philosopher.* More frequently it means a *seeker after truth.* Wis-dom, truth, and reality are equivalents to Plato. Homer does not use the later adjective for *wise* (σοφοί), and has *wisdom* (σοφία, O 412) but once, and then of the art of a ship-builder. In the poems of Pindar, early in the fifth century B.C., the term *wise* is applied particularly to the poets, and *wisdom* is poetic skill or poesy. This use is continued even in the time of Plato and Xenophon.[2]

---

[1] The Lydian king Croesus has heard much of the wisdom of Solon, and of his extensive travels φιλοσοφέων, Herodotus i. 30. In his *Funeral Oration* (Thucydides ii. 40), Pericles says φιλοσοφοῦμεν ἄνευ μαλακίας, which Jowett trans-lates *We cultivate the mind without loss of manliness.*

[2] Pindar, *Pyth.* iv. 295, ἔν τε σοφοῖς, *among the singers; Pyth.* i. 12, ἀμφί τε Λατοίδα σοφίᾳ, *because of the song of the son of Leto ;* Plato, *Rep.* 365 c, ὡς δηλοῦσί μοι οἱ σοφοί, *as the poets show to me ;* Xen. *An.* i. 2. 8, ἐνταῦθα λέγεται Ἀπόλλων ἐκδεῖ-ραι Μαρσύαν νικήσας ἐρίζοντά οἱ περὶ σοφίας, *when he vied with him in musical skill.*

5. The most noted group of pre-Socratic philosophers is known as the Ionian School, although no one of them had a school or was a teacher in the technical sense. Asia Minor was the home and birthplace of many ideas, as well as of the Homeric poems. Sappho and Alcaeus sung on Lesbos, and Anacreon was born on Teos. Hecataeus, the predecessor of Herodotus and the most important of the logographers or chroniclers, lived at Miletus. Men's minds were active in that whole region, and we are not surprised to find this the home of the earliest Greek philosophy. Thales of Miletus has been recognized as the earliest philosopher. His time is fixed as early in the sixth century, if we accept both the statement of Herodotus (i. 74) that he predicted the eclipse of the sun which occurred at the time of a battle between the Lydians and the Medes, and also the computations of astronomers and chronologists that this was on May 28, 585 B.C. He is reported to have been a man of political and practical sagacity, though an old anecdote is told of a maid-servant's laughing at him for falling into a well while he was occupied with observing the heavens. His chief interest seems to have been in astronomy and the origin of the world. He believed *water* to be the first principle of the universe. — Only a few sayings are preserved of Anaximander of Miletus, who was born about 610 B.C. In his system, no material thing, but the *infinite* and eternal, was the first principle of the universe. "The earth is a heavenly body, controlled by no other power, and keeping its position because it is at the same distance from all things." "Animals came into being through vapors raised by the sun." "Man came into being from another animal, the fish." To Anaximander was ascribed by some the invention of the sun-dial and of maps. — Anaximenes of Miletus, a follower of Anaximander, in the latter part of the sixth century B.C., believed *air* to be the first principle of the universe. — Heraclītus of Ephesus, at the opening of the fifth century B.C., was called "the obscure," and he seems to deserve the name. His sayings are full of apparent contradictions. "All things are in motion" (πάντα ῥεῖ), and yet "All things are one." A man cannot to-day cross the river which he crossed yesterday; the man has changed, and the river has changed, — it is another man who crosses another stream. — The last great philosopher of the Ionian School was Anaxagoras (*Ap.* 26 d) of Clazomenae, near Smyrna, who lived in Athens after the Persian Wars, and was on intimate terms with Pericles and Euripides, but was accused of atheism, probably by the opponents of Pericles. After about thirty years of residence there, he left Athens and went to Lampsacus, on the Hellespont, where he died about 428 B.C. He believed in a primal matter, which formed a sort of chaos, first principles infinite in number, until mind (νοῦς) came and brought order into the universe. The *Apology* refers to his views of the sun and the moon (26 d).

6. Of all pre-Socratic philosophers, no other had so many personal followers, who formed a distinct sect, with peculiar practices as well as peculiar doctrines, as Pythagoras of Samos, who lived in Crotona during the latter half of the sixth century B.C. Of his life and teachings little is known with precision. Not only did he leave no writings of his own, but Philolaus, a contemporary of Socrates (cf. *Phaedo* 61 d), was said to be the first Pythagorean to publish a philosophical work. Plato refers frequently to doctrines which are known to be Pythagorean, but he names Pythagoras but once (*Rep.* 600 a), and Aristotle names him only about ten times. His travels were extensive, and his most important activity was in the Greek colonies (*Magna Graecia*) of Italy. Around no other Greek have more numerous and more curious fables gathered. In later times he was supposed to have had supernatural powers. His followers formed an association for a common life, with many ascetic practices, among which was abstinence from flesh food and from beans. Pythagoras taught the doctrine of *metempsychosis*, or the passing of the soul from one body to another. Thus, tradition said that Pythagoras claimed to have taken part in the Trojan War, in the body of the Trojan Euphorbus. Most notable scientifically, and most difficult for a layman to comprehend, were Pythagoras's studies in numbers as affecting the universe. "Number was the first principle." "The first principles of number are the first principles of all things."

7. The Eleatic School was named from its home, Velia ('Ελέα) in Lucania, in western Italy. Its founder was Xenophanes of Colophon, a somewhat younger contemporary of Pythagoras. Of the didactic poems of Xenophanes considerable fragments are extant, — very largely, however, of a theological character. He did not believe in anthropomorphic gods, and said that if cattle and horses had hands and could paint, they would represent the gods as in the form of cattle or horses. He objected also strenuously to the poems of Homer and Hesiod, as ascribing to the gods deeds which are counted lawless for men. He uttered a noted tirade also against the glory which was given to athletes. To him, earth and water seem to have been first principles, and the source of all things. All things, in his view, are really one. Thus Xenophanes was the original Monist. — But the unity of all Being was apprehended still more definitely by Parmenides, his successor. "The all is alone, unmoved." "The first principle is one, unmoved." More than one hundred and fifty verses are extant of Parmenides's poem on Nature (περὶ Φύσεως), but these, too, are not easy of comprehension. He visited Athens in his old age, when Socrates was a youth, and the two talked together then. — Parmenides's follower Zeno (not the Stoic of that name) was called the inventor of Dialectic. Only four brief quotations from his works are extant, but tradition has preserved the memory of his ingenious arguments to disprove the possibility of motion and to demonstrate that the swift-footed Achilles could never overtake a tortoise. Plato (*Phaedrus* 261 d) makes Socrates refer to Zeno as the Palamedes who can make his hearers believe the same things to be both like and unlike, both one and many, and both at rest and in motion.

8. Empedocles of Agrigentum in Sicily, born early in the fifth century B.C., was the first to assume four primary elements, the "elements" of ordinary modern speech, — earth, water, air, fire. About four hundred and fifty verses remain of his poem on Nature, in quotations made by other authors. In certain matters he was followed by his contemporary Leucippus, the founder of the Atomist philosophy, of whose works only two brief sentences remain, and whose views are best known through his follower, the "laughing philosopher," Democritus of Abdera in Thrace, the birthplace of Protagoras.

9. The gist of pre-Socratic thought on life and the world cannot be condensed satisfactorily into a few paragraphs. But clearly the early thinkers of Greece were striving to solve great problems before the preliminary problems had been solved, before adequate observations had been made or suitable instruments had been prepared. Their studies had slight connection with ordinary life, though Xenophanes and Democritus pronounce admirable maxims. The great achievement of Socrates, as Cicero declared (*Tusc.* v. 4. 10), was in bringing Philosophy down from the skies to dwell among men: Socrates autem primus Philosophiam devocavit e caelo, et in urbibus conlocavit, et in domus etiam introduxit et coëgit de vita et moribus rebusque bonis et malis quaerere. In his youth Socrates seems to have been interested in the problems of natural science (*Phaedo* 96 a), but he was dissatisfied with the failure to attain any definite result. Xenophon (see *Mem.* i. 1. 14 f.) says that Socrates called attention to the wide difference of opinion between the Monists and the Atomists, between Heraclitus, who asserted that all things were in motion, and Zeno who argued that nothing could move, and to the lack of practical results attained by the physicists; and he gives a list of the themes which most interested Socrates, — what is pious, what is impious, what is bravery, what is a city, etc. The answers to these last questions would affect immediately the life of men. The Xenophontic Socrates was intensely pragmatic, to use a modern term. Though his discussions were theoretical, each had a practical bearing. On the other hand, no more than a modern scientist would Plato have accepted as valid the criticism of lack of tangible results. The study of astronomy is not useless because our knowledge does not enable us to regulate the movements of the heavenly bodies, nor can we condemn a science as hopeless because its doctors disagree.

10. The inquiries of the philosophers with regard to the universe were considered by some to have atheistic tendencies, since in early times the Greeks were prone to assign every natural phenomenon to divine agency. The question at the opening of the *Iliad* is characteristic: " Who brought the two together in strife ? " So in the *Clouds*, when the Aristophanic Socrates is made to deny the existence of Zeus, old Strepsiades promptly replies, " Why, *who* sends rain, then ? " — implying the necessity of a personal agent. The scientists left to the gods much less to do than the divinities had done, according to the old beliefs, and thus in a measure they seemed to do away with the gods. Socrates appears to speak as if the theory were absurd that the sun is a stone, and the moon is earth (*Ap.* 26 d), but he is speaking playfully in this passage. How far he agreed with Anaxagoras, no one can say, but he was probably not behind the best physicists of his time.

11. Just as φιλόσοφος was chosen at first, doubtless, as a more modest epithet than σοφός, so *Sophist* seems to have meant originally a *seeker after wisdom*, as a *Hellenist* is one who walks in the ways of the Hellenes, or speaks their language. In the early part of the fifth century B.C., the word had no unpleasant associations, as it appears in literature; certainly it did not have the special meaning of " captious or fallacious reasoner." The Titan Prometheus is called a sophist (*contriver*, Aesch. *Prom.* 62). The term was applied to all poets and musicians (Athenaeus 632 c). The Seven Sages were called sophists by the orator Isocrates (xv. 235). The historian Herodotus calls Solon and Pythagoras sophists. Not only the comic poet Aristophanes but also the orator Aeschines (i. 173) calls Socrates a sophist, and doubtless public opinion justified this epithet. In a notable chapter of his *History of Greece*, Grote showed that the sophists had been maligned, — that they formed a profession rather than a sect, with varied aims and tastes and methods. They were the only professional teachers in Greece above the grade of the elementary schools, and the dignity of their position is shown by their association with the best men of the state. The enormous development of the democratic states of Greece in culture, wealth, and power gave new importance to the arts which fitted men for leadership. The difference between the rhetoricians and the sophists does not seem to have been great or clear, though some of the rhetoricians are represented as despising the sophists. In a playful passage of the *Gorgias*, Socrates says that the art of the sophist is related to that of the legislator as the art of the rhetorician is to that of the judge (*Gorg.* 465 c). Some of the rhetoricians were inclined to include all learning in their art. If they were to teach their pupils to speak they must give them some knowledge of the matters on which they were to speak; and if a man was to be ready, like Gorgias, at a moment's notice to speak on any subject, he must know something about everything. In other words, according to its votaries, rhetoric included all other arts and should be the queen of all. This was essentially the claim which was made by the sophists for their art. Both rhetoricians and sophists took pay for their instruction, and both sought to fit their pupils for public life in Greece. So far as this is concerned, scholars of to-day cannot criticise them. But the sophists, like the rhetoricians, gave more attention to manner than to matter. The chief end of both was to persuade, to please, and to teach how to please. In general they worked for immediate results, and cared less for objective truth than for the subjective appearance of truth, — less to be right than to seem right. To win the suit in the court and to gain the majority of votes in the public Assembly were the ends at which rhetoric aimed, and the sophists were satisfied with teaching the code of morality which existed in Greece. They sought for it no higher or firmer basis than its approval by the people. "Man was the measure of all things" according to Protagoras, and, as in the old Homeric days, custom made right. To them justice was what seemed just to the masses who had never seen justice itself. Their discussions tended to give skill in dialectics rather than to rouse men to search for truth. But we must remember that we have no picture of the work of the Sophists from one of their own number. The student of Plato needs to bear in mind that Gorgias and Protagoras would have appeared to posterity in a better light if they themselves had composed the dialogues in which they are presented.

12. Protagoras of Abdera in Thrace, Prodicus of Ceos, and Hippias of Elis are the best known of the sophists in the narrower sense. Gorgias of Leontini in Sicily and Thrasymachus of Chalcedon, opposite Byzantium, were rhetoricians of high importance in the development of the art of oratory, but were often classed with the sophists. Whether Euenus of Paros (*Ap.* 20 b) was more of a poet or a sophist, we cannot say. These all were contemporaries of Socrates, — Protagoras and Gorgias being about ten years older than he. Though from different lands, all found Athens their most pleasant and profitable place of sojourn. Nowhere else was so much interest shown in their displays of technical skill. Protagoras, as we learn from the Platonic dialogue called by his name (317 c), frankly called himself a sophist, and according to Aristotle (*Rhet.* 1402 a 25) did not shrink from saying that he "made the worse appear the better reason." He might be called the earliest Greek grammarian, for he was the first, so far as we know, to observe critically the genders of nouns and the tenses of verbs. The first distinction of Greek verbal moods of which we learn is his criticism on the first verse of Homer's *Iliad*, — μῆνιν ἄειδε, θεά, — where he said the optative should have been used, to express a wish, a prayer, not a command, which might not be addressed to a divinity. Prodicus, on the other hand, was something of a lexicographer, being particularly nice in his choice of words, and studying to distinguish apparent synonyms. Hippias claimed encyclopedic knowledge, and, like Gorgias, allowed his hearers to choose the theme on which he should speak. He was an astronomer, also, and a diplomat. And once he appeared at Olympia in array which was all the work of his own hands: he had made his ring, and engraved the seal; he had made his strigil and oil-flask, and his shoes, and had woven his clothing, — including a belt which was woven in an intricate Persian pattern. Gorgias came to Athens first as an ambassador from Leontini, in 427 B.C., and his eloquence aroused enthusiastic admiration. That Gorgias not only composed such florid rhetorical exercises as are extant in his *Helene* and *Palamedes*, but also discussed ethical themes, is shown by the question of Meno, the Thessalian, addressed to Socrates on the remark that he had never met any one who knew what virtue is, — "Did you not meet Gorgias when he was here, and did he not seem to you to know what virtue is?" (*Meno* 71 c). In the *Protagoras* (312 a), the youthful Hippocrates, who is greatly interested in Protagoras, and earnestly wishes to learn from him, is represented as blushing at the thought of himself becoming a professional sophist. His admiration for the master shows that he shrinks from becoming a technical sophist chiefly because of the Athenian prejudice against any occupation of wage-earners. The Athenians did not distinguish very clearly and broadly, for instance.

between the social position and pay of a sculptoi and those of an ordinary stone-cutter. British society of a century ago could show analogous prejudices against trade and the profession of a physician.

13. No name of classical antiquity is better known to modern readers than that of Socrates, and his face and form were very familiar to the populace at Athens. He was constantly to be seen in public places, where he would meet as many young men as possible,[1] and he attracted attention apart from his words and his dress. He was not possessed of ideal Greek beauty. He was rather short, and had a bald head, a pot-belly, a broad flat nose, prominent eyes, and large lips. Alcibiades (see *Symp.* 215 b) compares him to such a figure of Silenus as was often sold as a shrine at the statuary shops, — a satyr in form, but when opened disclosing a beautiful figure of a divinity. His baldness was concealed by no hat, and he wore but a single garment, and went barefoot in both summer and winter, — though on occasion he would go to a feast in the garb of a gentleman. He did not object to good food or to good clothes, but he was satisfied with what was convenient. He was neither a mediaeval saint nor a Hebrew prophet. One evening, according to an anecdote, he was observed to be strolling on the street, and was asked what he was doing; he replied that he was collecting sauce for supper, i.e. he was getting an appetite which should serve as sauce. His physical powers were unusual, as is shown clearly by the account of his behavior on the campaign in Thrace (see *Symp.* 219 e), where his comrades watched him stand a whole night through, in meditation on some problem which had come before his mind, and where his bare feet seemed to be less disturbed by snow and ice than were the feet of his comrades, though these were well encased in cloths and skins. According to Alcibiades, he could drink more wine than any one else without being affected by it. Socrates was fortunate in his powers of physical endurance, and he adapted himself easily to all circumstances and all persons. Probably Diogenes the cynic regarded himself as a true follower of Socrates in his disregard of the courtesies and decencies of life, and Epicurus found in the sayings

[1] *Ap.* 17 c, Xen. *Mem.* i. 1. 10.

of Socrates what agreed with his ideas of pleasure, while Plato, keeping the golden mean, was sure that he was maintaining the spirit of his master in his beautiful mansion.

14. Of the family of Socrates we hear very little. He once speaks of himself as of the family of Daedalus, but jestingly, simply as a stone-cutter or sculptor, in which occupation he followed his father Sophroniscus, who was a friend of Lysimachus, son of Aristides the Just, and so of good connections. His mother, Phaenarete, was a midwife, and he compares with her employment his own work in assisting at the birth of ideas. How long he practiced his profession or trade of sculptor, no one knows, for Plato and Xenophon never make him refer to his early life. In it he gained no special repute, and we do not know even whether we should call him a stone-cutter or a sculptor. He nowhere claims or shows special artistic tastes or powers, nor even special fondness for illustrations drawn from the occupation of sculptor. So he mentions none of his own works of this kind. At the entrance to the Athenian Acropolis, Pausanias, in the time of Hadrian, saw a group of draped Graces, said to be the work of Socrates, son of Sophroniscus. Such a group has been found at Athens, but of an earlier period, so that the conjecture is offered that either the group was wrongly ascribed to Socrates, or perhaps he made a copy of the work which has been preserved.[1] We should be greatly interested to know what part, if any, he had in the sculptures of the Parthenon or in the exquisite carving of the Erechtheum. The Parthenon was completed when he was thirty-one years old, and most of the young stone-cutters of Athens in his time must have had part in this work.

15. At the time of his trial, in the spring of 399 B.C., Socrates was seventy years of age (*Ap.* 17 d). So he was born in 469 B.C., — ten years after the battle of Plataea, three years after Aeschylus presented his play of the *Persians*, and eleven years before Aeschylus presented his *Agamemnon*. He was in the strength of his young manhood at the time when Pericles was at the height of his influence and Athens enjoyed her greatest glory of power. We learn that he was at the siege of Potidaea (about 432 B.C.), where he

[1] See Frazer, *Pausanias* ii, p. 268.

saved the life of Alcibiades; in the battle of Amphipolis, ten years later; and in the battle at Delium, 424 B.C. (*Symp.* 221 a). Alcibiades said that the prize for bravery which was awarded to himself was deserved by Socrates, and that Socrates's manner on the retreat from Delium was just that which was his wont on the streets of Athens. Doubtless Socrates had part in many another military affair of the early ten years of the Peloponnesian War, but the records of this military service are lost.

16. The name of Socrates's wife, Xanthippe, is familiar to all. They had three sons (*Ap.* 34 d, *Phaedo* 116 b), — Lamprocles, Sophroniscus (named for the grandfather), and Menexenus, of whom the two latter were still children at the death of their father. Of these sons nothing is known, except that (according to Xenophon, *Mem.* ii. 2), Lamprocles could not endure his mother's temper, and was rebuked for this by Socrates, with a reminder of all that Xanthippe had done and borne for him in the past, as well as of her undoubted present love for her child. Nothing is known of Xanthippe's family, either. She was much younger than her husband, as is made certain by the age of her children at his death, and clearly she was not in sympathy with his vocation. Probably they were not married in 423 B.C., or Aristophanes would have delighted in introducing her in his comedy of the *Clouds.* Not understanding his search for truth, and seeing clearly that he had abandoned his work as a statuary and that he delighted in spending his time with idlers in the market-place, she, like many others, thought him to be a lazy loafer, and was impatient that he did not work as a craftsman and make better provision for his family. In the *Symposium* of Xenophon (ii. 10) she is said to have the worst temper of all the women in the world. That she was the second wife of Socrates, is very probable. Unsupported tradition spoke of Socrates as marrying Myrto, daughter or granddaughter of Aristides the Just, for his second wife. Possibly Myrto may have been his first wife, and on her death he may have married Xanthippe, but of this no exact record remains. What became of Xanthippe and the children on his death is not known. Doubtless Crito, Plato, and his other friends cared for them (cf. *Crito* 54 a).

17. Of the time when Socrates abandoned his craft, no indication is found. That he was interested in philosophical speculations in his youth, we should be ready to believe even without the express statements that he talked with Parmenides on the latter's visit to Athens, and that he early had a great desire to learn the cause of natural phenomena. We read of no young men as specially associated with him before Critias and Alcibiades. Critias took no prominent part in Athenian politics until the latter half of the Peloponnesian War, but then became the leader of the Thirty Tyrants, so that we may suppose him to have been no older than Alcibiades, who was born about the middle of the fifth century B.C. So these two hardly came into connection with him before about 435 B.C. See § 23. But for the last thirty years of his life, at least, Socrates seems to have had no visible means of support. In a conversation reported by Xenophon, he estimates his property as worth about five minas, — in round terms $100 of silver, but with the purchasing power of about $500 in our time. He earnestly repudiates the charge of taking money in return for his instruction, but he must have received gifts from his friends. His only other source of income during the later years of his life, so far as we can see, was the insignificant fees for service as juryman, since fees for attendance on meetings of the popular Assembly seem to have been given first after the Peloponnesian War. For a tenth of one year, he was one of the prytanes, and received a drachma a day, but in purchasing power this amounted to little more than a modern dollar. A possible interpretation of the opening of his speech would declare that he had not served as juryman at all, — but we see no reason why he should have avoided this service, although his statement is more impressive if we suppose that he was a complete stranger to the manner of speaking in court.

18. That Socrates was a brave and faithful citizen-soldier in time of war, we have seen. The only office of state that he ever held was that of senator, for one year (*Ap.* 32 b). In this office he had occasion to show his firm fidelity. He happened to be the presiding officer of the people on the day when (led by demagogues) popular indignation was roused against the naval commanders at Arginusae.

These had gained a notable victory over the Spartan enemy, yet (prevented by a storm, as they said) had not taken up the dead bodies for burial, and the masses desired to sentence these commanders to death, — a trebly irregular procedure. In spite of the noisy threats of the people, Socrates refused to put the question to a vote. In the *Apology*, Socrates distinctly declares that a man at Athens who works for the good of the people must labor in private rather than in public, — thus he excuses himself for taking no part in the public deliberations of the Assembly. In the *Republic* and the *Gorgias* he argues at length to the same end.

19. The fact that Socrates remained in Athens during the eight months' rule of the Thirty Tyrants (405–404 B.C.), doubtless was used against him at his trial to prove that he was not a true friend of the democracy, the established government at Athens, and was brought into connection with his frank criticisms of the constitution of the State, in particular the use of the lot for the selection of public officers, and with the fact that Critias the leader of the Thirty Tyrants had been a follower of his. But Socrates at the time of the Thirty was sixty-five years old, and cannot have been of much importance as a hoplite. To say, as some have said, that Socrates criticised the principles of the democracy, but the leaders of the oligarchy, is epigrammatic, but not based on a firm foundation.

20. The religion of Athens was a state religion, and ritualistic rather than ethical. It was in charge of officials who were selected for no special holiness of character or spiritual ambitions, but simply for excellence as administrators. The religious function was to them much like any other public function, particularly since the Athenians were a very pious people and were inclined to consecrate secular affairs. That the dramatic representations and the athletic games were parts of religious festivals is well known. No body of dogmatic theology existed. The question of orthodoxy or heterodoxy was not raised. Sacrifices were to be paid to the gods after the manner of the fathers, and with this the requirements of religion were satisfied. In this matter, according to both Xenophon and Plato, Socrates was punctilious. Xenophon says that Socrates often was seen sacrificing on the public altars of the city, and often sacrificed at home. So in the charge that Socrates does not believe in the gods in which the city believes, but in other new divinities (*Ap.* 24 b), the stress must have been laid on the former rather than on the latter clause. The introduction of a new divinity might be unpopular, — the worship of Mithras never gained such a footing in Athens as in Rome, — but it does not seem to have been illegal, if it did not interfere with any established worship.

21. Socrates at times seems to speak as a monotheist, of God. More often he uses the language of his contemporaries, and speaks of the gods. Sometimes the change from the singular to the plural is made in a single sentence. God, deity, and the gods are equivalent terms to him. He did not accept the current myths with regard to Zeus, Cronus, and the rest of the Olympian company, in the sense in which the people generally believed them. For instance, he refused to believe that the gods ever warred against each other, and that Zeus dethroned his father Cronus. Such stories he considered both blasphemous against the gods and injurious to the persons who believed them. The gods, he said, were good and truthful, and never could be the cause of evil, nor would they deceive men. In behalf of the gods, he was ready to surrender part of their power, and not to claim omnipotence for them, rather than to allow that evil could proceed from them. His disparaging words of the current stories of the gods, however, may have been understood by the masses as spoken disparagingly of the gods themselves. But his simple confidence in the gods was complete and unfailing. He believed that a good man is ever under the special care of the gods, and that no ill can befall him either in life or in death. The question of life or death was not a very serious matter for him then, since he was not to be separated from the loving presence of the gods. This confidence may account for the tone of the *Apology*, which is lighter than we should expect in the speech of a man on trial for his life.

22. On the δαιμόνιον of Socrates many treatises have been written. The reader should remember (what is often forgotten) that this word is strictly an adjective and not equivalent to *demon* or δαίμων, — a personality. From his boyhood Socrates was conscious of a divine influence within him, frequently checking him, even in minor matters, when he was about to act wrongly or unwisely, but never urging him forward. He calls it a voice (φωνή 31 d, cf. 40 b) from the gods. His accuser seems to have made his language concerning it the ground for the charge of introducing new divinities.[1] Zeller calls it "a profound sense of a not uncommon phenomenon."

23. The earliest definite date that can be set for Socrates's stimulating intercourse with young men is shortly before the death of Pericles (429 B.C.), if the story told by Xenophon is authentic (*Mem.* i. 2. 40). The youthful Alcibiades, then a ward of Pericles, engaged his guardian in a discussion on law, in which he entangled him in inconsistencies, until Pericles laughed and said that he too was skilled in that sort of discussion when he was young, and enjoyed it then. Alcibiades, we are told, finding himself superior in dialectics to the greatest statesman of Athens, no longer thought it necessary to follow Socrates. Plato, however, represents Alcibiades as a warm admirer of Socrates more than a dozen years later, just before the Sicilian Expedition (*Symp.* 215 a). Of the relations between Socrates and Critias much less is said, and these clearly were not friends at the time of the rule of the Thirty.

24. Socrates distinctly disavowed being any man's teacher (*Ap.* 33 a), and never spoke of his *pupils*, but of his *associates* (οἱ συνόντες). He undertook to give no instruction, and disclaimed the possession of any worthy knowledge. In this lay his *irony*, — he claiming to possess less than he really had. His method was not to impart information so much as to rouse his interlocutor to seek this information for himself; by no means to answer the question and solve the difficulty for his friend, but to show him the importance of the question, and to indicate the method by which the problem might be solved. Thus he stimulated and guided thought, but did not teach in the technical sense; he never declared dogmatically what he had learned. He formulated no system of ethics or metaphysics. In

---

[1] καινὰ δαιμόνια may be only *new things about the divinities*, but it was likely to be understood in the other way. The fact that this voice operated only to check from action separates it widely from such visions as those of Joan of Arc, with which it has been compared. The little which Plato says of it is in marked contrast with the space given to it in later discussions.

stimulating men to attain knowledge he must convince them not
only that it was worth having, but also that they lacked it. How
should a man strive to gain what he believes himself to possess ?
So Socrates went about the city, — wherever he would meet men, in
a city where men spent their time in hearing and telling new things,
— and by asking simple questions, which seemed easily answered,
on familiar subjects, engaged men in conversations which ended in
proving that they did not know what they had the reputation of
knowing and what they ought to know. Doubtless many Athenians
considered Socrates not only a lazy, trifling loafer, but also an ill-
bred, exceedingly disagreeable man. They thought his conversations
only a logomachy, a game of draughts with words for counters. He
led the conversation to matters in which they were obliged to contradict themselves or to make admissions against their self-esteem.
But he never wearied men by lectures of his own. In the Platonic
dialogues, Socrates is always represented as treating the conclusions
reached as attained in the conversation by his friend, with whom he
is talking, rather than by himself. The two are seeking for truth
together, as comrades. In the *Republic* they are compared to hunters
in a thicket, with the hare hidden under a bush. Elsewhere Socrates's
office, as we have seen, is chiefly to assist at the birth of ideas, aid-
ing in the expression of what is in his friend's mind, and treating
the new idea properly, when once it is expressed. So, in the *Meno*,
by skillful questions he draws from a slave who knows nothing of
mathematics the proof of the proposition that the square described
on the diagonal of a square is equal to the sum of the squares
described on two sides. The Platonic Socrates shows unfailing
courtesy and tact in his discussions, avoiding all personalities. He
may attract attention by an enigmatic statement or a paradox, but
he never puzzles for long at a time. His humor is marked; in the
Phaedo we are told that on the last day of his life his friends were
" now weeping and now laughing." He is watchful of opportunities
to introduce important discussions. The opening of the *Phaedo*,
which forms a background or setting for the dialogue, shows that
the associates of Socrates did not gather on the last day of his life
to discuss the doctrine of the immortality of the soul, but simply as

sympathetic friends. Step by step, however, by natural transitions, we are led to the philosophical discussion. Similarly at the opening of the *Republic* the company comes to the home of Polemarchus for dinner, but gradually the conversation is led to the theme of justice, and then to the ideal State. But the tact of the Platonic Socrates restrains him from introducing abstruse themes at the banquet of Agatho.

25. Socrates was interested in all matters of human thought, but we have no reason to doubt Xenophon's statement that his chief interest was in questions which directly pertained to man. Whatever might be the starting-point of a discussion, the conclusion was apt to be a practical application to the life of the interlocutor, whether or not he was doing his full duty (*Laches* 187 e). Thus the *Gorgias* begins with a talk on rhetoric, but it closes with a discussion of the question which is the best life to lead, — a life of truth and justice, even with suffering, or a life of false pretense and injustice, even with power.

26. The most noted of Socrates's followers were Alcibiades and Critias, and emphasis was laid upon this in support of the charge that he corrupted the youth.[1] Of these, Critias, as Xenophon says, was the most bloodthirsty and avaricious of the leaders of the oligarchy, while Alcibiades was the most arbitrary, willful, and violent of the leaders of the democracy, — a veritable young lion, whom Athens had reared but could not tame. The two other followers of Socrates whom we know best, and through whom we learn most directly of their master, were Plato and Xenophon — both apparently of like age, but not sympathetic by nature. The practical Xenophon found little for which he cared in Plato's poetic transcendentalism, and Plato probably thought Xenophon hopelessly commonplace. Plato does not mention Xenophon in his dialogues, and Xenophon names Plato but once, and that incidentally. We may count ourselves happy in having accounts of Socrates from two points of view. Scholars have compared these two pictures with the different representations of the Saviour in the gospels of St. Mark and St. John.

[1] Cf. ὑμεῖς, ὦ ἄνδρες Ἀθηναῖοι, Σωκράτην μὲν τὸν σοφιστὴν ἀπεκτείνατε ὅτι Κριτίαν ἐφάνη πεπαιδευκώς, ἕνα τῶν Τριάκοντα τῶν τὸν δῆμον καταλυσάντων, Aeschines i. 173.

27. That the *Apology* was composed soon after the death of Socrates, is a natural supposition, since then it would receive particular attention from others and the subject filled Plato's own mind. An indication of the speedy publication of the *Apology* is found also in the fact that Socrates is made to predict to those who voted for his condemnation, that after his death many would follow him, and rebuke them for paying more attention to wealth and power and reputation than to virtue and their own souls, — a prediction which was not fulfilled, and certainly would not have been invented later. Scholars have never agreed as to the part which Plato had in this work, — whether in writing it he aimed to be merely an accurate reporter of Socrates's words, or rather to present such a speech as Socrates might have made, or to give a free report of the speech. Distinctly in favor of the first view is the fact that Plato tells his reader that he was present at the trial (*Ap.* 34 a, 38 b), while he says that he was not with Socrates on the last day of his life, in the prison (*Phaedo* 59 b). This mention of himself here is the more noticeable since only in these passages does he name himself at all. If Plato was simply imitating the style of his master's conversations, he certainly succeeded in introducing the dialogue-manner throughout, with colloquial freedom in the change of grammatical constructions and in failure to complete sentences. Another indication that the *Apology* is an accurate report of the speech which was actually delivered, is the fact that in the *Apology* Socrates ascribes the popular prejudice against himself largely to his followers' holding dialogues with men, after his own manner, trying to show them that they did not know what they thought they knew, — with no word of intimation that he had endeavored to stop this practice (*Ap.* 23 c), — while both Xenophon in the *Memorabilia* (i. 2. 17) and the Platonic Socrates in the *Republic* (539 b) admit explicitly that young men should not be encouraged in such disputations, and their principles should be well fixed before such edge-tools were furnished them as Socrates put into their hands. If the *Apology* had been written as late as the *Republic*, and out of his own head, Plato would not have thought it necessary to say anything here of the disputations of the pupils of Socrates.

28. Plato was of a wealthy and aristocratic family, claiming descent through his father from Codrus, the last of the line of kings of Athens. His father was *Aristo*. This was the short form of *Aristocles*, the name of Aristo's father, and the name which was given to our philosopher in his infancy; the name *Plato* is said to have been given him later from the breadth (πλατύς) either of his chest, of his forehead, or of his style. His mother was Perictione, sister of Charmides and cousin of Critias. Of his parents, nothing further is known. Aristo seems to have been dead at the time of Socrates's trial, for in the *Apology* (34 a) Adimantus is referred to as the older representative, who might be expected to look after the best interests of his brother Plato.

29. Most of the stories about Plato's youth seem but fables. His birth was probably in 427 B.C., though some authorities would set it two years earlier. He may have been born on the seventh day of the month Thargelion (about May 26), — that was Apollo's day. As an Athenian of military age, at the time when Athens most needed men, we may assume that he served in her armies. But we do not know which side he took in the conflict between the Thirty Tyrants and the party of the democracy. Since his mother's brother Charmides and her cousin Critias were leaders of the Thirty, Plato's remaining in Athens would have been natural. That he was not ashamed of his connection with these kinsmen, is clear from the parts which he assigns to them in his dialogues, naming a dialogue after each. The fate of these men may have had something to do with Plato's disgust for political life at Athens. The youthful Plato is said to have distinguished himself in gymnastics, and even to have entered the Isthmian games in competition for a prize. Entirely probable is another story, — that he had ambitions as a poet, and desired particularly to distinguish himself in tragedy.

30. The occasion and circumstances of Plato's meeting with Socrates are unknown. We suppose Plato to have been twenty-eight years old at the time of his master's death. Very probably he joined the company of Socrates's followers when he was twenty years of age; but in the next eight years of intercourse with Socrates.

many and serious interruptions to the philosophical discussions must have been caused by the wars and disorders of the land.

31. The influence of the master upon the pupil is best shown by the reverence which Plato continued to show to the memory of Socrates during the more than half a century of his life which remained after Socrates's death. That the pupil should continue for fifty years to give his teacher credit for all his best thoughts, shows that Plato ever looked upon his scheme of philosophy as only a development of what he had learned from Socrates. Only in one of his very latest works, the *Laws*, and in two of his minor works, the *Sophistes* and the *Politicus*, does he fail to make Socrates the leading speaker in his dialogues,[1] while he keeps himself entirely in the background, never speaking in his own person.

32. On the death of Socrates, in the spring of 399 B.C., Plato left Athens, and, after a sojourn of uncertain length in Megara, went to Egypt. That he derived knowledge of mathematics, astronomy, and philosophy from the ancient learning of the Egyptians, has often been supposed, but without either external or internal evidence. From Egypt, Plato seems to have returned to Athens, and to have begun his work as a teacher, first in a gymnasium (of Academus), and then in his own neighboring garden, — the "grove of Academe." Plato thrice visited Sicily, and was intimately associated with both the elder and the younger Dionysius, tyrants of Syracuse. But he seems to have offended the one and to have wearied the other, and from each visit he returned to his work at Athens, where he died in 347 B.C.

33. Of Plato's life and work as a teacher we have no authentic detailed picture. He lived apart from the active life of the city. His master had frequented the "full market-place," as well as the palaestra, but Plato was not seen by the banks and in the saddlers' shops. He was soon surrounded by a group of earnest students. That his instruction was chiefly in the form of Socratic dialogues may be inferred from the disparaging remarks made in his written works about harangues.

[1] In the *Parmenides*, which in form is the report of a conversation held in the time of Socrates's young-manhood, Socrates appears only as introducing the discussion.

34. Before the law, Plato's "School," the "Academy," was a religious corporation,[1] formed for the worship of the Muses and Apollo. Corporation law was fully developed at Athens, but this seems to have been the earliest philosophical school to be so incorporated. The members of the School, as of other religious associations, had many common meals, but how frequently is unknown. The expenses of the association were probably borne in common, but nothing indicates that Plato received any salary or fees. He probably had much of Socrates's dislike of receiving pay for giving advice as to virtue, and much of the old Athenian gentleman's prejudice against taking pay for any service. He would not become a hireling ($\mu\iota\sigma\theta\omega\tau\delta$). We know Plato as a writer, and think of him as such. But, although his artistic powers naturally sought expression in the publication of finished works of literature, he was primarily a teacher. In his day few books were written to be read. The written copies of the tragedies of Aeschylus and Sophocles served at first chiefly to assist and correct the memory. The Sophists lectured, rather than wrote for publication. Socrates himself never wrote anything in the way of literature, and cared much more for the living word of personal intercourse than for the more formal and exact written statement which could answer no questions. Plato himself, though the unrivaled master of one branch of literature, calls the writing of treatises a kind of play ($\pi\alpha\iota\delta\iota\acute{\alpha}$).

35. The story of Socrates's life and work does not prepare us for the manner of his death. Prosecuted in his old age, on a most serious charge, he was, after a legal trial, sentenced to death. And this was done, not during any oligarchical or democratic reign of terror, but at the very time when everybody was admiring the moderate spirit of the newly-restored Athenian democracy, after the deposition of the Thirty Tyrants by Thrasybulus.

36. In the spring of 399 B.C., when Socrates had reached the age of threescore years and ten (*Ap.* 17 d), Meletus, seconded by Anytus and Lyco, came forward with his accusation. In Plato's *Euthyphro* Meletus is described as an insignificant youth, and in the

[1] Wilamowitz-Moellendorff, *Antigonos von Karystos*, Excurs 2, 1881 ; Ziebarth, *Das griechische Vereinswesen*, 1896, p. 71.

Apology he is treated with a measure of contempt. He was the son of an unimportant tragic poet, and is said to have been irritated by Socrates's criticisms of the poets (*Ap.* 22 a, 23 e). He led the prosecution, the other two being technically his σvvήγopoɩ. The substantial man of the three, however, was Anytus (*Ap.* 29 c, 31 a), who had property and had repeatedly served as general of the Athenian armies. At this time he was popular because of his recent activity in expelling the Thirty Tyrants. His bitterness was uncompromising toward all sophists, and according to an anonymous ancient writer he was particularly irritated by Socrates's criticism of his putting his son into his works as a tanner, when the youth was capable of better things ([Xen.] *Ap.* 29). Of Lyco, little is known. He was charged by Eupolis, the comic poet, with being of foreign extraction, and his wife was ridiculed by the same poet. His poverty and effeminacy were referred to by the comic poet Cratinus, but he is named by Aristophanes (*Wasps* 1301) with Antiphon, Phrynichus, and other noted aristocrats.

37. The formal terms of the indictment submitted by Meletus to the ἄρχων βασιλεύς, whose jurisdiction covered all cases involving religion, were: "Socrates is guilty of not believing in the gods believed in by the state, and of introducing other new divinities. Moreover, he is guilty of corrupting the youth. The penalty proposed is death." This was an indictment for an offense against the state; so it was technically a γραφή (*public suit*), and, as further qualified by the specific charges, it was a γραφὴ ἀσεβείας (*a public suit on the ground of impiety*).

38. As to the negative clause of the first count (οὓς μὲν ἡ πόλις νομίζει θεοὺς οὐ νομίζων), it certainly is difficult to see any fact to justify such an accusation, inasmuch as Socrates expressly recognized the *law of the land* (νόμος πόλεως) as the final arbiter in all that concerned the worship of the gods, and himself scrupulously observed all its requirements. The terms of the second and affirmative clause (ἕτερα δὲ καινὰ δαιμόνια εἰσηγούμενος) refer to the much-mooted δαιμόνιον, — the mysterious communication from God to Socrates. The first count probably was introduced as a foil to the second, and was primarily intended as a means for giving a legal

foothold to the suit. For among all known provisions of Athenian
law there is none under which Socrates could have been prosecuted
on the second count (ἀδικεῖ δὲ καὶ τοὺς νέους διαφθείρων). This view
is confirmed by the difficulty which even the Thirty Tyrants had in
interfering officially with Socrates's dealings with young men. They
had to pass a special law for the purpose, and that law was doubtless abolished when the democracy was restored. At all events, in
the accuser's mind the second count was the most important. We
remember the prejudices of Anytus, and recall the fact that he was
still smarting under Socrates's sharp criticism of the way in which
he educated his son. The accuser urged that Alcibiades and Critias,
notorious scourges of the body politic, were for some time the companions of Socrates. And, though Xenophon has abundantly shown
the injustice of remembering this against Socrates, the judges could
not forget it. The memory of these men's crimes was still fresh,
and every one was inclined to mistrust the man to whose teaching
many attributed the misdeeds which had so lately made life un-
bearable. This teaching they were therefore determined to stop.
Xenophon himself at this time may have served as an example of
Socrates's evil influence. Having joined the expedition of Cyrus
the Younger, a friend of Sparta, against King Artaxerxes, who was
an ally of Athens, he was already virtually an exile from Athens.

39. Socrates met the charge, and appeared before the court, with
a calm and unruffled spirit. His inward monitor had checked him
from preparing a formal speech in his own defense,[1] and he held
that he had made the best preparation to meet the charges by doing
his duty and shunning evil during all his life. According to Cicero
and Diogenes Laërtius, the orator Lysias composed a speech for him
to deliver at this time, but Socrates declined to use it, — it was a
good speech, he said, but it did not fit him. Socrates made no
"apology" in the English sense. He set forth the reasons for his
reputation as a wise man, and for the prejudice against him, of
which he was well aware. Then he showed that Meletus had no

---

[1] Cf. "But when they deliver you up, take no thought how or what ye shall
speak : for it shall be given you in that same hour what ye shall speak,"
St. Matthew x. 19.

technical right to bring the charge against him, and that the charge was unreasonable in itself and untrue. He refused to follow the custom of the time, to which even Pericles had yielded, and implore the favor of the judges. He spoke to them not as a prisoner at the bar to the men who have his life in their hands, but as a master to men whom he has a right to criticise and rebuke. He told them that he made his defense not on his own account, as some might suppose, but on their account, — in order that they might not put to death the chief benefactor of the city, whom God had given to them, and whose like they would not easily find again. He asked for no favor.

40. And so it came to pass that the judges brought in the verdict of "guilty," but by no large majority (*Ap.* 36 a). In cases of this nature the law did not fix the penalty beforehand, and Socrates had still the right of rating his guilt at his own price, ἀντιτιμᾶσθαι, his accuser having proposed, τιμᾶσθαι, the penalty of death. Just as in his plea Socrates had disdained the ordinary means of working upon the feelings of the court by tears and supplications, so now he scorned the obvious way of safety still open to any man whose guilt had been affirmed by verdict. He absolutely refused to suggest any real counter-penalty, and hence an increased majority [1] sentenced him to death.

41. The same courage which had animated him while speaking his defense, the same rooted conviction that they who love God need fear no evil, supported him now, and prevented him from countenancing any plan for disobeying the laws of the state. Exceptional circumstances (*Phaedo* 58 a) delayed the execution of his sentence for thirty days after it was rendered, and his friends offered him means of escape from prison (*Crito* 44 b). But he was firm in refusing these, just as while on trial he had been firm in rejecting every opportunity to secure either a favorable verdict or a lighter penalty. The tale that shortly after his death the Athenians repented, and actually called the accusers to account, rests on such slender authority that it must not be taken as history.

The works before us in this volume are closely connected with the trial and death of Socrates.

---

[1] It is said that the adverse majority was increased by eighty votes which had previously been cast for a verdict of "not guilty."

THE APOLOGY OF SOCRATES

42. Socrates's address to his judges is in three sections. The first of these is the defense in the strict sense (Chapters I–XXIV); the second is his proposition to set the penalty not at death, but at a fine of thirty minae (Chapters XXV–XXVIII); the third is an informal address to his judges, after the trial is concluded, while the magistrates were busy with making out the warrant for his commitment to prison and his death, — telling those who had voted for his condemnation that he might have been acquitted if he had been willing to flatter and fawn upon them, and saying to those who had voted for his acquittal that death could be no evil for him, or for any other good man.

43. The first of these three divisions, the defense proper, is complete in itself. All the laws of oratorical art are here carefully observed, though the usual practices of oratory are sharply criticised. The five natural heads of the argument are unmistakable.

Analysis of the First Part, or the Defense Proper, cc. I–XXIV

(a) c. i.	**Introduction** (προοίμιον, *exordium*) $= \begin{cases} principium. \\ insinuatio \ (\text{ἔφοδος}). \end{cases}$
(b) c. ii.	**Statement** (πρόθεσις, *propositio*) of the case and of the plan in the plea.
(c) cc. iii–xv.	**Refutation** (λύσις, *confutatio*) of former accusers, cc. iii–x. of Meletus, cc. xi–xv.
(d) cc. xvi–xxii.	**Digression** (παρέκβασις, *digressio*) on Socrates's life.
(e) cc. xxiii, xxiv.	**Peroration** (ἐπίλογος, *peroratio*). This is a criticism of the usual form of peroration, and ends with a confession of trust in God.

An introduction (a) is always intended to prepare the hearers for listening to the speaker's plea. This is especially hard in the face of prejudice against the speaker's person or against his case. The rules of speech-writing here prescribe recourse to *insinuation*, ἔφοδος, a subtle process by which the speaker wins over the sympathies of his audience. He may do this (1) by attacking his opponent, (2) by conciliating his audience, (3) by strongly stating his personal hardship in the case, or (4) by putting concisely the difficulties involved in dealing with the facts. After the introduction follows (*b*) the statement, πρόθεσις. This is commonly a plain unvarnished tale covering the matters of fact involved. If such an account be ur necessary, the statement sets forth simply the plan of the plea This plan is not unfrequently accompanied by a *subdivision* (*partitio*), which is sometimes simply a *summary of heads* (*enumeratio*),[1] and sometimes a *detailed account of topics* (*expositio*).[2] Here, again, Socrates's defense follows the rules of oratory. Next comes the most important part, the proof (πίστις, *probatio*), represented by (*c*) the refutation, which naturally falls, as indicated above, under two heads. In the manner of refutation here given, the genuine Socrates is in his element. After proof or refutation, as the case may be, comes, in the programme of oratorical orthodoxy, (*d*) a digression. This was the orator's opportunity to try his wings. The theme chosen in a digression needed no more than an indirect bearing upon the argument of the case, and the ornamental part which the digression often played has led to the use of another term for it, i.e. *exornatio* or *embellishment*.[3] This, too, can be found in Socrates's speech, and here the laws of school oratory are more than satisfied. Yet, embellishment though it be called, this part of the speech has nothing that is far-fetched or beside the point; in the *Apology* it is the complement of the preceding negative refutation, its positive and required *reënforcement* (*confirmatio*). The transition to (*e*) the peroration is plainly marked. At this point the orator, and more

---

[1] *Rhet. ad Herenn.* i. 10. 17 : Enumeratione utemur, cum dicemus numero, quot de rebus dicturi simus.

[2] Ibid. Expositio est, cum res, quibus de rebus dicturi sumus, exponimus breviter et absolute.

[3] L.c. ii. 29. 46 : Exornatio constat ex similibus et exemplis et rebus iudicatis et amplificationibus et ceteris rebus quae pertinent ad exaugendam et collocu pletandam argumentationem.

than ever if he were on trial for his life, was wont to make a desperate appeal to the feelings of his hearers. No means of moving the judges were left untried. Recourse to such methods Socrates condemned as equally dishonest and dishonorable. Not unmanly subserviency to men, but manly submission to God's will, is heard in the closing words of this defense.

Such was the temper of the *Apology* written for Socrates by Plato, and as such, whether intentionally or unintentionally, it must have been in striking contrast with the drift of the plea which Lysias is said to have elaborated for the same case. The tradition that Plato undertook to plead in the capacity of Socrates's *advocate* (συνήγορος), but was not allowed to do so, rests on very slight authority.

44. The second and third parts, which come respectively after the first and the second votes of the judges, can hardly be expected to answer all the requirements of a set speech. And yet these are symmetrically arranged, and their topics are skillfully set before us. The second part naturally opens with an allusion to the verdict of "guilty" just rendered; any regular peroration would have been out of place before the third, which is the suitable conclusion both for the first part and for the second. And where, indeed, is there a more eloquent and nobly impressive ending than this? That part of it addressed to the judges who voted for Socrates's acquittal is made prominent, and appropriately so. For these judges, they who alone are worthy of that title, are his friends; to them he confides the hopes of happiness after death that are stirring within him, and invites them to be of good cheer and not to fear death.

45. Closely connected with the *Apology* is the dialogue called the

CRITO

This dialogue is a conversation pure and simple, with two speakers only, Socrates and Crito. Their close friendship has been mentioned in the *Apology* (p. 33 d). This intimacy was unbroken, and though Crito was in no sense a philosopher, yet in all the fortunes of Socrates's life Crito had been his firm friend. And now that a sentence which he could not but regard as unjust had been pronounced upon his friend, Crito rebelled against its execution. To prevent this he was willing to risk his fortune and even his civil rights. Apparently, nothing prevented Socrates's escape from prison but Socrates. At this juncture he stands before us as the loyal citizen. Though opposed to many of the principles of the democracy at Athens, he submits without reservation to its laws and exhorts all others to do the like. This, he declares, is the most imperative duty of every citizen. The dramatic picture given of this situation admits of the application of various terms used to designate the development of the plot in a Greek tragedy.

ANALYSIS OF THE CRITO

(*a*) cc. i, ii.   **Prologue** (πρόλογος). The *characters* and their *mental situation* (ἦθός τε καὶ πάθος).

(*b*) cc. iii–x.   **Entanglement** (δέσις or πλοκή) of the logical situation.
 1. c. iii.   The threats of the multitude.
 2. c. iv.   The prayers of friends.
 3. c. v.   The jeers of enemies.
 1. cc. vi, vii.   The threats are many but duty is one.
 2. c. viii.   Nothing should warp our idea of duty.
 3. cc. ix, x.   It is wrong to run away from prison, and wrong should not be done, even in retaliation.

(*c*) cc. xi–xv.   **Clearing up** (λύσις). The laws of Athens require the submission of Socrates, and his death.
 1. cc. xi, xii.   Socrates owes them life, liberty, and happiness.
 2. cc. xiii, xiv.   They require, and he has promised, obedience.
 3. c. xv.   He will gain nothing by disobedience.

(*d*) cc. xvi, xvii.   **Epilogue** (ἐπίλογος). There are laws in Hades which can reach him who disobeys law upon earth.

46. Like the *Apology*, this work bears memorable witness to the nobility of Plato's mind, and it reveals especially his lofty patriotism. As for Socrates, we see in both these works that not words only but deeds prove him a law-abiding citizen. The laws of the land, as well as the example of Socrates submitting to his unjust

sentence of death, declare in no uncertain tones to every Athenian
what true patriotism is and how it is preserved.

47. The *Crito* is by no means simply the chronicle of a conversation actually held; though it is based upon facts, it must still be
recognized as Plato's work. This is proved by the finished skill
both of plan and execution displayed in this dialogue, short and
simple though it is. Plato here has made a step forward in his
notion of duty. For here is the earliest statement of Plato's "silver
rule": "Injustice always is wrong; it is wrong to retaliate for
injustice by injustice." In the *Gorgias* this rule is applied more
universally and put upon its rational basis. Indeed, from a philosophical point of view we may regard the *Crito* and the *Apology*
as a suitable preface to the *Gorgias*, if we do not forget that both
are primarily pictures of the one great master whom Plato in all
his works most delighted to honor.

THE ATHENIAN COURT

48. Six thousand Athenian citizens were intrusted with the
judicial power.[1] Choice was made by lot, every year, of six hundred men from each of the ten tribes (φυλαί), and any citizen
more than thirty years of age was eligible. Every one thus chosen
was liable, after taking a prescribed oath, to be called to act as
a δικαστής. δικασταί, *judges* or *jurymen*, was the official name by
which they were addressed, but they really formed a committee of
the Assembly, and often were addressed as "Men of Athens." Divisions into courts were made. Like the English word court, δικαστήριον may mean a judicial body as well as the place where such a
body sits in judgment. Generally a court was composed of five hundred jurymen, but sometimes of less, as of two or four hundred;
sometimes two or more courts of five hundred sat as one, but seldom
if ever did the whole six thousand sit as one court. The even numbers, 200, 500, 1000, etc., were habitually increased by one, in order
to avoid a tie vote.

[1] The chief authority on Attic courts is Meier und Schömann, *Der attische
Process* (Berlin, 1883–1887), since Lipsius's *Das attische Recht und Rechtsver-
fahren* I, Leipzig, 1905, is still incomplete.

49. On days appointed for holding court, each division was assigned by lot to one of the places used as court-rooms, and there tried the suit appointed for that time and place. Ingenious devices were used that no suitor might know beforehand which court was to try his case, and so be able privately to influence the judges. Each juryman received as the badge of his office a staff (βακτηρία) corresponding in color to a sign over the door of his court. He also received a ticket (σύμβολον), by showing which he secured his fee after his day's service. A fee of one obol (about three cents) for every day's session was introduced by Pericles, and afterwards trebled by Cleon.

50. The most general term to designate an action at law is δίκη, though the same word also has the narrower meaning of a private suit. According as the complaint preferred involved the rights of individuals or of the whole state, δίκαι in the wider sense were subdivided into (1) δίκαι in the narrower sense, *private suits*, and (2) γραφαί, *public suits*.

51. In the ordinary course of procedure, every plaintiff was required to present his charge (γραφή) in writing to the particular magistrate whose department included the matters involved. The first archon, called ὁ ἄρχων *par excellence*, dealt especially with charges involving family rights and inheritance; the second archon, called ἄρχων βασιλεύς, dealt with charges involving the regulations and requirements of religion and public worship; the third archon, called πολέμαρχος, dealt with most cases involving foreign-residents (μέτοικοι) and foreigners; the remaining six archons, called the Thesmothetae, dealt with most cases not specially assigned to the first three.

52. The accusation was made in the presence of the accused, who had previously been served with notice to appear. Legal notice required the presence of two *witnesses to the summons* (κλητῆρες). If the magistrate allowed proceedings in the case, the terms of accusation were copied and posted in some public place, and at the time of this publication a day was fixed, on which both parties were bound to appear before the magistrate for the *preliminary investigation* (ἀνάκρισις). There the plaintiff's charges and the defendant's answer-both of them presented in writing, were reaffirmed under oath, and both parties submitted to the magistrate such evidence as they intended to use. The reaffirmation or *confirmation under oath* was called διωμοσία, sometimes ἀντωμοσία. The evidence submitted consisted in citations from the laws, documentary evidence of various kinds, the depositions of witnesses, and particularly any testimony given under torture (βάσανο;) by slaves, which had been taken and written down in the presence of witnesses. The magistrate fixed his official seal upon all the documents thus submitted, and took charge of them against the day when the case was to be tried. The person charged with an offense was not arrested and put in prison unless he was taken in the very act of crime. Strong efforts were made to settle mere disputes by arbitration.

53. On the day (ἡ κυρία) when a court was to sit upon any case, the magistrate who had presided over the preliminary investigation proceeded to the appointed court-room, where he met the δικασταί *assigned by lot* (ἐπικεκληρωμένοι) to the case. Both parties to the suit, having been previously notified, were required to put in an appearance; if either were absent, the case went by default (δίκη ἐρήμη) against him. Proceedings in court were opened by some religious ceremony; then the *clerk* (γραμματεύς) read aloud the written accusation and the reply, and finally the parties to the suit were successively called to state their case. This was the *opening of the case* (εἰσαγωγὴ τῆς δίκης) by the magistrate (εἰσαγωγεύς). Only one day was allowed for the trial of even a capital case (*Ap.* 37. a); whether two or three unimportant cases, in which the litigants were allowed less time for their speeches, were ever tried by the same court on the same day, is uncertain.

54. The law required that every man should conduct his own case in person, and hence those who were not themselves skillful pleaders often induced others to write for them speeches which they should pronounce. Still, the law permitted a man to appear in court accompanied by *advocates* (συνήγοροι), who came as his friends, and therefore were not supposed to be paid for their trouble. Sometimes, after a short speech from the principal, the most important part of his plea was made by one of his advocates; e.g. Demosthenes's speech *On the Crown* was made by him as Ctesiphon's advocate. The *water-clock* (κλέψυδρα, sometimes called simply τὸ ὕδωρ) was used to measure the time allotted to each for pleading before the court When called for, the written documents offered in evidence were read by the clerk, and meanwhile the flow of water was stopped. By way of precaution, the witnesses whose depositions were read were required to be present in court and acknowledge their testimony; but no opportunity was given for cross-examination. While making his plea a man was protected by law from interruption by his opponent, and the law required his opponent to answer his questions. Such an examination occupied part of the time allotted for the speech. The opponent was not put under oath for this examination, and was not liable to punishment for false statements. The jurymen might interrupt the speaker if in their opinion he was off the point, or if they required fuller explanation on any point, but the extant orations do not show that the judges often did so interrupt the speaker. The presiding magistrate acted simply as a chairman; he did not interpret the law, or even call attention to any misstatements of it. Indeed, Socrates does not appeal to the presiding officer of the court to maintain order, but asks the jurymen not to make a disturbance. In an Athenian court, equity was much more important than justice; harmony with the letter of the law was insufficient to win a case. Of course, frequent attempts were made to prejudice the jurymen instead of enlightening them, and nothing was commoner than to make appeal to their sympathies. A defendant often appeared in court with his wife and children, or with infirm and helpless parents, and sometimes with friends of great popularity or of high character; he depended upon these to act as his intercessors with the court. Such practices, though manifestly tending to disarm the severity of the law and to defeat the ends of justice for which the court was organized, seem not to have been prohibited in any court except that of Areopagus.

No witnesses seem to be introduced in the *Apology*. Possibly the testimony of Chaerephon's brother was read after Chapter V, 21 a; but if this was done, then the opening of the following paragraph has been adapted to the form of Socrates's preceding words and not to the testimony.

55. When the pleas had been made, the jurymen proceeded to decision by a secret vote. In public suits, in general, only one speech was allowed to the plaintiff, and one to the defendant. In private suits, two were allowed to each. The jurors generally voted with bronze disks with axles either solid (to denote acquittal) or perforated (to denote condemnation). These were called ψῆφοι. If the vote was a tie, the case went in favor of the defendant; and, in a public suit, if less than one-fifth of the votes were for the plaintiff, he was fined (1000 drachmas, about $170) and also debarred from ever again acting as plaintiff in a similar suit. In such a case also the plaintiff incurred both these penalties if, without good and sufficient excuse, he failed to appear in court, and thus by his own acts allowed that his case was bad. If the defendant failed to appear, the case went against him by default (see on ἐρήμην κατηγοροῦντες, *Ap.* 18 c), and he was pronounced guilty *in contumaciam*. In most private suits, the plaintiff, under similar circumstances, forfeited one sixth of the sum which he claimed; this forfeiture was called ἐπωβελία, *one obol for every drachma.*

56. Actions were divided into (1) ἀγῶνες τιμητοί, in which, if it decided against the defendant, the court had still to determine the degree of punishment to be inflicted (τίμημα), because no penalty was fixed by law; and (2) ἀγῶνες ἀτίμητοι, in which, after deciding against the defendant, the court had no further decision to make, because the penalty was fixed by law. In cases of the former kind, if they were public suits, — like the γραφὴ ἀσεβείας brought against Socrates, — the accuser proposed the penalty which he considered adequate, and the accused, if convicted, might make a counter-proposition. Probably the judges were not confined to a choice between these two propositions, but could, if they saw fit, impose a third penalty, between the two.

57. The ordinary penalties imposed on citizens for crimes against the state were death, exile, loss of rights of citizenship (ἀτιμία), confiscation of property, and fines. All these are summed up in the formula τί χρὴ παθεῖν ἢ ἀποτεῖσαι, *what must he suffer or pay for his offense.* Imprisonment was comparatively little used by way of punishment. In case the convicted defendant was not an Athenian by birth, he might be sold into slavery.

The commission which had general oversight of all prisons and floggings, and executions generally, was called the Eleven (οἱ Ἔνδεκα). Ten men on this board were chosen by lot every year, one from each of the ten tribes; the eleventh was a *scribe,* γραμματεύς.

ΠΛΑΤΩΝΟΣ ΑΠΟΛΟΓΙΑ
ΣΩΚΡΑΤΟΥΣ

17 a

I. Ὅ τι μὲν ὑμεῖς, ὦ ἄνδρες Ἀθηναῖοι, πεπόνθατε ὑπὸ a
τῶν ἐμῶν κατηγόρων, οὐκ οἶδα· ἐγὼ δ᾽ οὖν καὶ αὐτὸς ὑπ᾽ αὐτῶν ὀλίγου ἐμαυτοῦ ἐπελαθόμην· οὕτω πιθανῶς ἔλεγον· καίτοι ἀληθές γ᾽ ὡς ἔπος εἰπεῖν οὐδὲν εἰρήκασιν. μάλιστα
5 δ᾽ αὐτῶν ἓν ἐθαύμασα τῶν πολλῶν ὧν ἐψεύσαντο, τοῦτο ἐν
ᾧ ἔλεγον ὡς χρὴ ὑμᾶς εὐλαβεῖσθαι μὴ ὑπ᾽ ἐμοῦ ἐξαπατη-

I–II. Introductory, on the manner and arrangement of the defense.

I. *My accusers have spoken very persuasively, but have told very little truth (their most shameless falsehood was that I am eloquent and thus may deceive you); you shall hear the whole truth, however, from me. I beg only that I may tell my story in my own way, for I am not familiar with the manner of courts.*

1. Ὅ τι μὲν ὑμεῖς, ἐγὼ δ᾽: not ὑμεῖς μέν, ἐγὼ δ᾽, because the clauses as wholes, not ὑμεῖς and ἐγώ, are contrasted. — ὦ ἄνδρες Ἀθηναῖοι: instead of the more technical ὦ ἄνδρες δικασταί, which Socrates reserves for his closing words (40 a, to the end), addressed to those who voted for his acquittal. Cf. 26 d, Xen. *Mem.* init. — No hiatus was felt here, for by crasis ὦ ἄνδρες was pronounced as ὦνδρες. — πεπόνθατε: though active in form is passive in meaning. and therefore takes ὑπό

with the genitive. Cf. *Symp.* 215 d. H. 820.

2. δ᾽ οὖν: introduces an asserted fact which is contrasted with the preceding statement of uncertainty, *but at any rate*, Lat. certe. Cf. εἰ μὲν δίκαια ποιήσω οὐκ οἶδα, αἱρήσομαι δ᾽ οὖν ὑμᾶς κτλ. Xen. *An.* i. 3. 5, *whether I shall be doing what is right I do not know, but at any rate I will choose you.* — καὶ αὐτός: *even myself*, which implies "How then may not you have been affected!"

3. ὀλίγου: cf. 22 a b. — ἐμαυτοῦ: i.e. who I was, my own nature.

4. ὡς ἔπος εἰπεῖν: limits a statement which may seem too strong. Cf. 22 b d.

5. αὐτῶν: limiting genitive with τῶν πολλῶν (ψευδέων). — τῶν πολλῶν: the sum of which ἕν is part. — τοῦτο: explains ἕν, and is in apposition with it.

6. ἐν ᾧ: refers to the passage where the statement was made.

17 b

θῆτε, ὡς δεινοῦ ὄντος λέγειν. τὸ γὰρ μὴ αἰσχυνθῆναι ὅτι b
αὐτίκα ὑπ' ἐμοῦ ἐξελεγχθήσονται ἔργῳ, ἐπειδὰν μηδ' ὁπωστιοῦν φαίνωμαι δεινὸς λέγειν, τοῦτό μοι ἔδοξεν αὐτῶν ἀναι-
10 σχυντότατον εἶναι, εἰ μὴ ἄρα δεινὸν καλοῦσιν οὗτοι λέγειν
τὸν τἀληθῆ λέγοντα· εἰ μὲν γὰρ τοῦτο λέγουσιν, ὁμολογοίην
ἂν ἔγωγ' οὐ κατὰ τούτους εἶναι ῥήτωρ. οὗτοι μὲν οὖν, ὥσπερ ἐγὼ λέγω, ἤ τι ἢ οὐδὲν ἀληθὲς εἰρήκασιν· ὑμεῖς δέ
μου ἀκούσεσθε πᾶσαν τὴν ἀλήθειαν. οὐ μέντοι μὰ Δία,
15 ὦ ἄνδρες Ἀθηναῖοι, κεκαλλιεπημένους γε λόγους, ὥσπερ
οἱ τούτων, ῥήμασί τε καὶ ὀνόμασιν οὐδὲ κεκοσμημένους, c
ἀλλ' ἀκούσεσθε εἰκῇ λεγόμενα τοῖς ἐπιτυχοῦσιν ὀνόμασιν·
πιστεύω γὰρ δίκαια εἶναι ἃ λέγω· καὶ μηδεὶς ὑμῶν προσδοκησάτω ἄλλως· οὐδὲ γὰρ ἂν δήπου πρέποι, ὦ ἄνδρες,

---

7. ὅτι κτλ.: object of ἰ'σχυνθῆναι.

8. ἐξελεγχθήσονται: sc. οἱ κατήγοροι,
— convicted of lying in their assertion
that Socrates is δεινὸς λέγειν.

9. αὐτῶν: of them, i.e. of their
statements; this word of theirs. Cf.
Xen. Mem. i. 6. 1.

11. εἰ μὲν κτλ.: the supposition is
restated.

12. οὐ κατὰ τούτους: and not after
their pattern, not in their class. This
is explained by the following words.

13. ἤ τι ἢ οὐδέν: little or nothing.
Cf. ἀναβέβηκε ἤ τις ἢ οὐδείς κω παρ' ἡμέας
αὐτῶν Hdt. iii. 140, hardly a single one
of them has ever been here. — ὑμεῖς δέ
μου ἀκούσεσθε: instead of ἐμοῦ δ' ἀκούσεσθε. The position of ὑμεῖς suggests a
contrast with οὗτοι μέν. The sense
calls for ἐμοῦ δ' ἀκούσεσθε, in contrast
with οὗτος. This collocation brings out
πᾶσαν τὴν ἀλήθειαν with great prominence. For a similar shifting of emphasis, cf. κἀγὼ δέ, εἰ μὲν ὑμεῖς ἐθέλετε

ἐξορμᾶν ἐπὶ ταῦτα, ἕπεσθαι ὑμῖν βούλομαι,
εἰ δ' ὑμεῖς τάττετέ με ἡγεῖσθαι, οὐδὲν προ-
φασίζομαι τὴν ἡλικίαν Xen. An. iii. 1. 25,
now I for one, if you are minded to
bestir yourselves to accomplish this, am
ready to follow your lead; if you, however, appoint me to lead you, I make no
excuse on the score of my age.

16. κεκοσμημένους: arranged in
careful order, contrasted with εἰκῇ, as
the following ἐπιτυχοῦσιν ὀνόμασιν is
opposed to κεκαλλιεπημένους ῥήμασι κτλ.

18. ἃ λέγω: refers to the speech
which follows, my plea. — Socrates had
been preparing for his defense during
all his life, and had been prevented by
his inward monitor from preparing a
formal speech. The Euthyphro represents him just before the trial as with
mind free and ready to enter into any
sort of philosophical discussion.

19. προσδοκησάτω: for the aorist
imperative of "total prohibition," see
GMT. 260; SCG. 417.

17 d

20 τῇδε τῇ ἡλικίᾳ ὥσπερ μειρακίῳ πλάττοντι λόγους εἰς
ὑμᾶς εἰσιέναι. καὶ μέντοι καὶ πάνυ, ὦ ἄνδρες Ἀθηναῖοι,
τοῦτο ὑμῶν δέομαι καὶ παρίεμαι· ἐὰν διὰ τῶν αὐτῶν λόγων
ἀκούητέ μου ἀπολογουμένου δι᾽ ὧνπερ εἴωθα λέγειν καὶ ἐν
ἀγορᾷ ἐπὶ τῶν τραπεζῶν, ἵνα ὑμῶν πολλοὶ ἀκηκόασι, καὶ
25 ἄλλοθι, μήτε θαυμάζειν μήτε θορυβεῖν τούτου ἕνεκα. ἔχει d
γὰρ οὑτωσί· νῦν ἐγὼ πρῶτον ἐπὶ δικαστήριον ἀναβέβηκα,
ἔτη γεγονὼς ἑβδομήκοντα· ἀτεχνῶς οὖν ξένως ἔχω τῆς
ἐνθάδε λέξεως. ὥσπερ οὖν ἄν, εἰ τῷ ὄντι ξένος ἐτύγχανον
ὤν, συνεγιγνώσκετε δήπου ἄν μοι εἰ ἐν ἐκείνῃ τῇ φωνῇ τε

20. τῇδε τῇ ἡλικίᾳ: equivalent to
ἐμοὶ τηλικῷδε, *for me at my age*, as is
shown by πλάττοντι. — μειρακίῳ: attracted into the dative by the construction of the main clause.

21. εἰς ὑμᾶς: *before you*, sc. τοὺς
δικαστάς, equivalent to εἰς τὸ δικαστήριον.
— καὶ μέντοι: a rhetorical *yes*.

22. τῶν αὐτῶν λόγων: this has
respect primarily to the conversation
with Meletus, 27 b, which is prefaced
by the request μὴ θορυβεῖν ἐὰν ἐν τῷ
εἰωθότι τρόπῳ τοὺς λόγους ποιῶμαι.

24. τραπεζῶν: the money-changers'
and bankers' tables, as well as the
shops near the market-place, were
favorite lounging-places at Athens,
and Socrates spent most of his time
where many men were to be met. Cf.
κἀμοὶ μὲν τὰ προειρημένα διείλεκτο ἐπὶ τῇ
Φιλίου τραπέζῃ Lys. ix. 5, *now the
facts just recited I gathered from a conversation at Philius's bank.* Cf. also
Lys. xxiv. 19–20, where, to meet the
charge that his shop is the resort of
evil-minded persons without visible
means of support, the defendant says:
ταῦτα λέγων οὐδὲν ἐμοῦ κατηγορεῖ μᾶλλον
ἢ τῶν ἄλλων ὅσοι τέχνας ἔχουσι (*who

follow trades*), οὐδὲ τῶν ὡς ἐμὲ εἰσιόντων
(*my customers*) μᾶλλον ἢ τῶν ὡς τοὺς
ἄλλους δημιουργούς (*tradesmen*). ἕκαστος
γὰρ ὑμῶν εἴθισται προσφοιτᾶν (*frequent,
lounge in*) ὁ μὲν πρὸς μυροπωλεῖον (*per-
fumer's*), ὁ δὲ πρὸς κουρεῖον (*barber-shop*),
ὁ δὲ πρὸς σκυτοτομεῖον (*cobbler's*), ὁ δ᾽ ὅποι
ἂν τύχῃ, καὶ πλεῖστοι μὲν ὡς τοὺς ἐγγυτάτω
τῆς ἀγορᾶς κατασκευασμένους (*keeping
shop*), ἐλάχιστοι δὲ ὡς τοὺς πλεῖστον
ἀπέχοντας αὐτῆς. On the last point,
cf. Xen. *Mem.* iv. 2. 1, where Socrates
αἰσθανόμενος αὐτὸν (sc. τὸν Εὐθύδημον)
δ:ὰ νεότητα (*because he was so young*)
οὔπω εἰς τὴν ἀγορὰν εἰσιόντα, εἰ δέ τι
βούλοιτο διαπράξασθαι, καθίζοντα εἰς ἡνιο-
ποιεῖόν τι (*a harness-maker's*) τῶν ἐγγὺς
τῆς ἀγορᾶς, εἰς τοῦτο καὶ αὐτὸς ᾔει κτλ.

26. ἐπὶ δικαστήριον: "the preposition has the notion of presenting one's
self to the court; ἀναβέβηκα refers to
the βῆμα" or tribune.

27. ἀτεχνῶς: construe with ξένως
ἔχω, which is equiv. to ξένος εἰμί (cf. 22 a).

28. ἐνθάδε: i.e. ἐν τοῖς δικαστηρίοις.
— λέξεως: genitive with the adverb,
ξένως. G. 1147; H. 756.

29. ἄν: for its repetition, see G.
1312; H. 864.

18 a

30 καὶ τῷ τρόπῳ ἔλεγον ἐν οἷσπερ ἐτεθράμμην, καὶ δὴ καὶ νῦν 18
τοῦτο ὑμῶν δέομαι δίκαιον, ὥς γέ μοι δοκῶ, τὸν μὲν τρόπον
τῆς λέξεως ἐᾶν, — ἴσως μὲν γὰρ χείρων, ἴσως δὲ βελτίων ἂν
εἴη, — αὐτὸ δὲ τοῦτο σκοπεῖν καὶ τούτῳ τὸν νοῦν προσέχειν,
εἰ δίκαια λέγω ἢ μή· δικαστοῦ μὲν γὰρ αὕτη ἀρετή, ῥήτορος
35 δὲ τἀληθῆ λέγειν.

II. πρῶτον μὲν οὖν δίκαιός εἰμι ἀπολογήσασθαι, ὦ ἄνδρες
Ἀθηναῖοι, πρὸς τὰ πρῶτά μου ψευδῆ κατηγορημένα καὶ
τοὺς πρώτους κατηγόρους, ἔπειτα δὲ πρὸς τὰ ὕστερα καὶ
τοὺς ὑστέρους. ἐμοῦ γὰρ πολλοὶ κατήγοροι γεγόνασι πρὸς b
5 ὑμᾶς καὶ πάλαι, πολλὰ ἤδη ἔτη, καὶ οὐδὲν ἀληθὲς λέγοντες,

---

30. ἐτεθράμμην: had been brought
up, belongs to the supposed case. See
on ὃς ἔμελλεν, **20 a.** Foreigners were
allowed to appear in court only in
exceptional cases. Ordinarily their
ξένος, *guest-friend*, or their πρόξενος.
resident consul, represented them in
court and was surety for them. —
καὶ δὴ κτλ.: οὕτω δὴ καὶ νῦν would be
more regular. — **νῦν**: not *now* in contrast to *then*, but *as it is* contrasted
with *as it would have been.* "Now
that I am not a stranger in Athens,
but only a stranger in courts." Lat.
nunc is used in the same way.
31. τοῦτο: cognate accusative. It
refers to what follows.
32. ἴσως: the reason urged is a
general one.
34. αὕτη: in place of τοῦτο, by
assimilation to the gender of the predicate ἀρετή. It refers to the preceding
clause αὐτὸ . . . μή. — The emphasis of
this sentence implies that this doctrine
was needed at Athens.
II. *I have had two sets of accusers,
— not only Anytus. Meletus, and Lycon,*

at present before the court, *with formal
charges, but also a much more numerous company of accusers who years
ago spread abroad the report that I was
pursuing studies not suitable for men,
and was making the worse appear the
better reason. The earlier accusers
must be answered first, particularly because the later accusers base their
hopes of securing a verdict on the prejudice which the old stories have aroused.*
1. δίκαιός εἰμι: the English idiom
generally prefers the impersonal construction, *it is just that*, etc.
4. γάρ: introduces the reason why
Socrates replies first πρὸς τὰ πρῶτα . . .
κατηγόρους. — **πρὸς ὑμᾶς**: construe with
κατήγοροι γεγόνασι, which is equivalent
to κατηγορήκασι.
5. καί: the first καί emphasizes
πάλαι. — **πάλαι, πολλὰ ἤδη ἔτη**: two
parallel statements; πάλαι goes back
to the beginning of the accusations,
while πολλὰ κτλ. follows out their long
continuance. This accusation had been
going on more than twenty years at
the very least, for the *Clouds* was first

18 b

οὓς ἐγὼ μᾶλλον φοβοῦμαι ἢ τοὺς ἀμφὶ Ἄνυτον, καίπερ ὄντας
καὶ τούτους δεινούς· ἀλλ' ἐκεῖνοι δεινότεροι, ὦ ἄνδρες, οἳ
ὑμῶν τοὺς πολλοὺς ἐκ παίδων παραλαμβάνοντες ἔπειθόν τε
καὶ κατηγόρουν ἐμοῦ οὐδὲν ἀληθές, ὡς " ἔστι τις Σωκράτης,
10 σοφὸς ἀνήρ, τά τε μετέωρα φροντιστὴς καὶ τὰ ὑπὸ γῆς

presented in 423, and Socrates was tried in 399 B.C.

6. τοὺς ἀμφὶ Ἄνυτον: Anytus was the most influential of the accusers, though not the technical head of the prosecution.

8. τοὺς πολλούς: this contrasts the majority of the hearers, who were early taught to abhor Socrates, with the few, implied in the partitive genitive, ὑμῶν, to whom this may not have happened. — **παραλαμβάνοντες**: this word is often used of one who takes charge of a child, for its education. But this sense may be too narrow for the present context. — **ἔπειθον κτλ.**: *continually prejudiced you against me by their accusations.* κατηγοροῦντες ἔπειθον is expected, but coördination takes the place of subordination. κατηγόρουν repeats more definitely the thought of ἔπειθον, cf. **18 d.**

9. τις Σωκράτης: τίς with proper names conveys an indefiniteness which is uncomplimentary,—*somebody named Socrates.*

10. σοφὸς ἀνήρ: these words are practically intended to mean a Sophist. "The title σοφὸς ἀνήρ would at once be understood as a class-appellation, cf. **23 a, 27 a**; in it the meaning and associations of Philosopher are uppermost, yet not so distinctly as to exclude those of Sophist." — **τά τε μετέωρα . . . ἀνεζητηκώς**: popular

prejudice coined this phrase, or something like it, to stigmatize all scientific investigation into nature. With such investigation the earliest Greek philosophy began and ended, and even Socrates's contemporaries, the Sophists, — notably Hippias, — were much given to it. — The phrase τὰ ὑπὸ γῆς (where ὑπό has the unusual sense of *beneath and covered by*) is part of a sweeping assertion that nothing is safe from the curiosity of those men This popular view is amusingly exaggerated by Aristophanes in the *Clouds*, 184–234. Here the word ἅπαντα adds a final touch of exaggeration. — Geology and paleontology of course were not studied in the modern sense. — **φροντιστής**: used here with accusative like φροντίζων. For a dative similarly governed, cf. τὴν ἐμὴν τῷ θεῷ ὑπηρεσίαν, **30 a.** — "This 'accusation,' σοφὸς . . . ποιῶν, both as given here, and as repeated with mock formality in **19 b**, is nothing more than a vivid way of representing, for a rhetorical purpose, the popular prejudice, in which the court shared. The charges it contains are two-edged, being borrowed partly from the vulgar representation of the Philosopher, partly from that of the Sophist: the μετέωρα φροντιστής points to the Philosopher, the τὸν . . . ποιῶν to the Sophist." R.

18 b

ἅπαντα ἀνεζητηκὼς καὶ τὸν ἥττω λόγον κρείττω ποιῶν."
οὗτοι, ὦ ἄνδρες Ἀθηναῖοι, οἱ ταύτην τὴν φήμην κατα- c
σκεδάσαντες οἱ δεινοί εἰσί μου κατήγοροι. οἱ γὰρ ἀκούοντες ἡγοῦνται τοὺς ταῦτα ζητοῦντας οὐδὲ θεοὺς νομίζειν.
15 ἔπειτά εἰσιν οὗτοι οἱ κατήγοροι πολλοὶ καὶ πολὺν χρόνον
ἤδη κατηγορηκότες, ἔτι δὲ καὶ ἐν ταύτῃ τῇ ἡλικίᾳ λέγοντες
πρὸς ὑμᾶς ἐν ᾗ ἂν μάλιστα ἐπιστεύσατε (παῖδες ὄντες,
ἔνιοι δ᾽ ὑμῶν καὶ μειράκια), ἀτεχνῶς ἐρήμην κατηγοροῦντες,

11. τὸν ἥττω λόγον κτλ. : any
teaching of rhetoric, as such, must
contain hints as to the most effective
means for making the best of a bad
case by presenting it skillfully. How
far this must be condemned, should be
decided only with reference to circumstances and facts. To-day it is just as
impossible to assert that in all cases a
lawyer is bound not to defend a client
whose cause he knows to be unjust.
Popular opinion at Athens seems to
have been convinced that the Sophist's
single aim in teaching rhetoric was to
communicate the art of proving that
black was white. Cf. the *Clouds*, 889–
1104, where Aristophanes introduces
the Δίκαιος Λόγος and the Ἄδικος Λόγος
respectively. The two have an argument in which the Ἄδικος Λόγος wins.
Cf. Cicero, *Brut.* 8, where the excellent
Claudius says of the Sophists : d o c e r e
s e   p r o f i t e b a n t u r   q u e m a d m o-
d u m   c a u s a   i n f e r i o r   (i t a   e n i m
l o q u e b a n t u r)   d i c e n d o   f i e r i   s u-
p e r i o r   p o s s e t.   H i s   o p p o s u i t
s e s e   S o c r a t e s,   q u i   s u b t i l i t a t e
q u a d a m   d i s p u t a n d i   r e f e l l e r e
e o r u m   i n s t i t u t a   s o l e b a t   v e r b i s.
13. οἱ δεινοὶ κατήγοροι : in the
predicate, — κατ᾽ ἐξοχὴν δεινοί.

14. οὐδὲ θεοὺς κτλ. : the investigations alluded to above, it was charged,
not only were a foolish waste of useful
time, but᾽ also led to atheism. The
gods would have revealed the secrets
of their realm if they had chosen that
man should know these, according to
the Xenophontic Socrates.
16. ἐν τῇ ἡλικίᾳ: logically construed with ὑμᾶς.
17. ἐν ᾗ ἂν ἐπιστεύσατε : for the
potential indicative with ἄν to express
in a guarded way what may have happened, and perhaps did happen, see
GMT. 244 ; SCG. 430.
18. ἐρήμην κατηγοροῦντες : sc. δίκην.
The accusative is cognate with κατηγοροῦντες. Cf. also the common law
phrases διώκειν γραφήν, *prosecute an indictment*, φεύγειν γραφήν, *am defendant
in a suit*. The sense of the whole is repeated in untechnical language by the
appended ἀπολογουμένου οὐδενός. "The
case which they prosecuted always went
by default, with none to speak for the
defendant," i.e. they had a free field
for their accusations. — When either
party to a lawsuit failed to appear, the
court *ent red a default against him*,
ἐρήμην καταγιγνώσκει τινός, and the one
of the two parties to the suit who

18 e
ἀπολογουμένου οὐδενός. ὁ δὲ πάντων ἀλογώτατον, ὅτι οὐδὲ
20 τὰ ὀνόματα οἷόν τ᾽ αὐτῶν εἰδέναι καὶ εἰπεῖν, πλὴν εἴ τις d
κωμῳδοποιὸς τυγχάνει ὤν. ὅσοι δὲ φθόνῳ καὶ διαβολῇ
χρώμενοι ὑμᾶς ἀνέπειθον, — οἱ δὲ καὶ αὐτοὶ πεπεισμένοι ἄλλους πείθοντες, — οὗτοι πάντες ἀπορώτατοί εἰσιν· οὐδὲ γὰρ
ἀναβιβάσασθαι οἷόν τ᾽ ἐστὶν αὐτῶν ἐνταυθοῖ οὐδ᾽ ἐλέγξαι
25 οὐδένα, ἀλλ᾽ ἀνάγκη ἀτεχνῶς ὥσπερ σκιαμαχεῖν ἀπολογού-
μενόν τε καὶ ἐλέγχειν μηδενὸς ἀποκρινομένου. ἀξιώσατε
οὖν καὶ ὑμεῖς, ὥσπερ ἐγὼ λέγω, διττούς μου τοὺς κατηγόρους γεγονέναι, — ἑτέρους μὲν τοὺς ἄρτι κατηγορήσαντας,
ἑτέρους δὲ τοὺς πάλαι οὓς ἐγὼ λέγω, καὶ οἰήθητε δεῖν πρὸς ε

appeared ἐρήμην κρατεῖ or ἐρήμην αἱρεῖ, sc. δίκην. In such a case a plaintiff, if present, ἐρήμην κατηγορεῖ (δίκην) and the absent defendant ἐρήμην ὀφλισκάνει δίκην.

19. ὁ δὲ πάντων κτλ. (ἐστι): appositive with the following sentence. H. 1009 a.

21. κωμῳδοποιός: the *Clouds* of Aristophanes is here especially in mind, since this play contains the specific charges just mentioned. But Cratinus, Ameipsias, and Eupolis also ridiculed Socrates in their comedies. **— ὅσοι δὲ κτλ.** : the clause οἱ δὲ καὶ αὐτοὶ πεπεισμένοι enlarges the scope of φθόνῳ καὶ διαβολῇ χρώμενοι, for οὗτοι 23 includes both classes. Appended as an after-thought, in conversational style, the sense of ἀνέπειθον is casually reiterated in ἄλλους πείθοντες. Strictly speaking, πεπεισμένοι is subordinated to πείθοντες. Logically the sense requires ὅσοι δὲ, οἱ μὲν φθόνῳ . . . χρώμενοι, οἱ δὲ καὶ αὐτοὶ πεπεισμένοι, ὑμᾶς ἀνέπειθον, *whether through envy and malice or through ignorance, being actually*

convinced. In both cases the result was the same.

24. ἀναβιβάσασθαι: contrast **24 d**, where Socrates calls Meletus to come to the bema, and cross-examines him.

25. σκιαμαχεῖν κτλ. : τε καί are used here to connect, not two different ideas, but two statements of the same idea, cf. ἔπειθον κτλ. in b. By thus saying the same thing twice, the speaker expresses his thought the more effectively, without apparent repetition. But the more distinct statement must always follow the figurative expression.

29. οὓς λέγω: sc. in b above. — **οἰήθητε κτλ.** : similarly Demosthenes in his oration *On the Crown* asked the approval of the court for the order of topics which he proposed to follow. — For a fuller description of ἐκείνους, see b above; notice that it refers to ἑτέρους δὲ τοὺς πάλαι. These *old-time accusers*, though the last-mentioned, were the more remote in thought, for Anytus and his crew were actually present, as τῶνδε shows.

18 e

30 ἐκείνους πρῶτόν με ἀπολογήσασθαι· καὶ γὰρ ὑμεῖς ἐκείνων
πρότερον ἠκούσατε κατηγορούντων, καὶ πολὺ μᾶλλον ἢ τῶνδε
τῶν ὕστερον.

εἶεν· ἀπολογητέον δή, ὦ ἄνδρες Ἀθηναῖοι, καὶ ἐπιχειρητέον ὑμῶν ἐξελέσθαι τὴν διαβολήν, ἣν ὑμεῖς ἐν πολλῷ χρόνῳ 19
35 ἔσχετε, ταύτην ἐν οὕτως ὀλίγῳ χρόνῳ. βουλοίμην μὲν οὖν ἂν
τοῦτο οὕτως γενέσθαι, εἴ τι ἄμεινον καὶ ὑμῖν καὶ ἐμοί, καὶ
πλέον τί με ποιῆσαι ἀπολογούμενον· οἶμαι δ᾽ αὐτὸ χαλεπὸν
εἶναι, καὶ οὐ πάνυ με λανθάνει οἷόν ἐστιν. ὅμως δὲ τοῦτο μὲν
ἴτω ὅπῃ τῷ θεῷ φίλον, τῷ δὲ νόμῳ πειστέον καὶ ἀπολογητέον.

III. ἀναλάβωμεν οὖν ἐξ ἀρχῆς, τίς ἡ κατηγορία ἐστὶν
ἐξ ἧς ἡ ἐμὴ διαβολὴ γέγονεν, ᾗ δὴ καὶ πιστεύων Μέλητός με b

34. τὴν διαβολήν: the prejudice produced by the slanders just described.

35. ἔσχετε: acquired. Cf. ἔσχηκα 20 d, and cf. τὴν τυραννίδα οὕτω ἔσχον οἱ Μερμνάδαι Hdt. i. 14. When ἔχω means am in possession, ἔσχον means came into possession. — ταύτην: resumptive after the interrupting clause of explanation introduced by ἥν. — οὕτως: sc. as is allowed, — the trial having to be completed in a single day. Cf. 24 a, 37 a.

36. τοῦτο: refers to ὑμῶν ἐξελέσθαι τὴν διαβολήν.

38. τοῦτο: i.e. the end. For the same spirit of submissive trust in God, cf. 35 d, Crito 54 e.

39. τῷ θεῷ: the article is used without reference to any particular divinity, with a generic or collective force, — the divine will or God. Cf. 35 d, 42 a, 43 d.

III–X. These chapters answer the charges of Socrates's early accusers, and explain how the prejudice against him arose. The counts against him

were given approximately in 18 b; they are repeated more definitely in 19 b. In these counts is implied atheism, as Socrates says in 18 c. The only charges which he directly attempts to disprove in these chapters, however, are his interest in natural science (III) and his teaching for money (IV).

III. *What then are the charges which have commonly been brought against me, whether through ignorance or through malice? (1) That I seek into things which the gods have hidden from men, beneath the earth or in the skies, (2) that I make the worse appear the better reason, by sophistical arguments, and (3) that I teach men to do as I do. — Many of you have heard me talk. Tell each other, if any one of you has heard me talking about any of these things.*

2. ἐξ ἧς: out of which. Cf. ἐκ τούτων 23 e. — ἐμή: equivalent to the objective genitive, against me, about me. — ᾗ: refers to ἡ ἐμὴ διαβολή.

19 c

ἐγράψατο τὴν γραφὴν ταύτην. εἶεν· τί δὴ λέγοντες διέβαλ-
λον οἱ διαβάλλοντες ; ὥσπερ οὖν κατηγόρων τὴν ἀντωμοσίαν
5 δεῖ ἀναγνῶναι αὐτῶν· " Σωκράτης ἀδικεῖ καὶ περιεργάζεται
ζητῶν τά τε ὑπὸ γῆς καὶ οὐράνια καὶ τὸν ἥττω λόγον κρείττω
ποιῶν καὶ ἄλλους ταὐτὰ ταῦτα διδάσκων." τοιαύτη τίς ἐστι.
ταῦτα γὰρ ἑωρᾶτε καὶ αὐτοὶ ἐν τῇ Ἀριστοφάνους κωμῳδίᾳ,
Σωκράτη τινὰ ἐκεῖ περιφερόμενον, φάσκοντά τε ἀεροβατεῖν
10 καὶ ἄλλην πολλὴν φλυαρίαν φλυαροῦντα, ὧν ἐγὼ οὐδὲν οὔτε
μέγα οὔτε μικρὸν πέρι ἐπαΐω. καὶ οὐχ ὡς ἀτιμάζων λέγω

4. ὥσπερ οὖν κτλ. : the formal
charge of the accuser was read at the
beginning of the trial. Since Socrates
proposes to discuss first the informal
charges, a definite statement of these
is in place before his defense.

5. περιεργάζεται : cf. μηδὲν ἐργαζομένους ἀλλὰ περιεργαζομένους 2 *Thess.*
iii. 11.

6. οὐράνια : the article is omitted
because ὑπὸ γῆς and οὐράνια are brought
under one head. Cf. Σωκράτης δὲ πάντα
ἡγεῖτο θεοὺς εἰδέναι, τά τε λεγόμενα καὶ
πραττόμενα καὶ τὰ σιγῇ βουλευόμενα (*the
unuttered plans in man's thought*)
Xen. *Mem.* i. 1. 19. — In *Prot.* 315 c
Plato satirizes the astronomical lore
of Hippias, and in Xenophon's *Memorabilia* (iv. 7. 2) Socrates is represented as advising his friends against
an intensive study of astronomy. —
Aristophanes, in his play, represents
Socrates's friends with heads bending
over, toward the ground, searching
into things below, while the rump, directed upward, is studying astronomy.

7. τοιαύτη τις : sc. ἡ ἀντωμοσία or
διαβολή. Socrates alone is responsible
for the exact words; the accusation
itself was vague

8. ταῦτα γὰρ ἑωρᾶτε : when, in the
Clouds, Aristophanes put before the
Athenians his own feelings against
Socrates, he dramatized an already
existing prejudice.

9. Σωκράτη τινὰ κτλ. : in apposition
with ταῦτα. For the force of τινά, cf.
τις Σωκράτης **18 b**; it implies that
Socrates in the *Clouds* bears no close
resemblance to the real Socrates. Cf.
Clouds 218-225, where Strepsiades
on entering Socrates's thinking-shop
says : " Who is this man up there in
the basket ? " Hearing it is Socrates,
he asks him what he's about. Socrates
answers ἀεροβατῶ καὶ περιφρονῶ τὸν
ἥλιον, *on air I tread and oversee the
sun.* — **φάσκοντα κτλ.** : subordinated
to περιφερόμενον.

10. ὧν : referring to all statements
of the sort above mentioned. — **οὔτε
μέγα οὔτε μικρόν** : a reënforcement of
the οὐδέν, stated disjunctively. Cf.
21 b and **24 a**, and ἤ τι ἤ οὐδέν **17 b**.

11. οὐχ ὡς ἀτιμάζων : cf. in e below,
καὶ τοῦτό γέ μοι δοκεῖ καλὸν εἶναι, "such
knowledge is a fine thing, if any one
has it." Socrates hints his doubt that
any one has it. Cf. Xen. *Mem.* i. 1. 11.
Those who pursued these studies were

19 c
τὴν τοιαύτην ἐπιστήμην, εἴ τις περὶ τῶν τοιούτων σοφός
ἐστι· μή πως ἐγὼ ὑπὸ Μελήτου τοσαύτας δίκας φύγοιμι!
ἀλλὰ γὰρ ἐμοὶ τούτων, ὦ ἄνδρες Ἀθηναῖοι, οὐδὲν μέτεστι.
15 μάρτυρας δ' αὐτοὺς ὑμῶν τοὺς πολλοὺς παρέχομαι, καὶ d
ἀξιῶ ὑμᾶς ἀλλήλους διδάσκειν τε καὶ φράζειν, ὅσοι ἐμοῦ
πώποτε ἀκηκόατε διαλεγομένου· πολλοὶ δ' ὑμῶν οἱ τοιοῦτοί
εἰσι· φράζετε οὖν ἀλλήλοις, εἰ πώποτε ἢ μικρὸν ἢ μέγα
ἤκουσέ τις ὑμῶν ἐμοῦ περὶ τῶν τοιούτων διαλεγομένου· καὶ
20 ἐκ τούτων γνώσεσθε ὅτι τοιαῦτ' ἐστὶ καὶ τἆλλα περὶ ἐμοῦ ἃ
οἱ πολλοὶ λέγουσιν.

IV. ἀλλὰ γὰρ οὔτε τούτων οὐδὲν ἔστιν, οὐδέ γ' εἴ τινος
ἀκηκόατε ὡς ἐγὼ παιδεύειν ἐπιχειρῶ ἀνθρώπους καὶ χρή-

beside themselves, he thought, because
man ought first to know himself (cf. id.
i. 1. 12, and **38 a** below), and because
these physicists looked into questions
which were really beyond the sphere
of man, and therefore arrived at im-
potent conclusions (cf. id. iv. 7. 6–7).

12. εἴ τις κτλ.: the expression of
the condition implies a doubt, though
it is in the logical form. Cf. **19 e**.

13. μή . . . φύγοιμι: *may I never, by
any chance, be accused by Meletus of so
great a wrong as depising such knowledge.* — δίκαι is often best represented
in translation by the singular. — For
ὑπό with φεύγειν, cf. ὑπό with πέπονθα
17 a. φύγοιμι here is used as the passive of διώκω. H. 820.

14. ἀλλὰ γάρ: *but the truth is* that
Socrates does not claim such wisdom
simply because he does not possess it.

17. οἱ τοιοῦτοι: *are in that case,*
sc. the one just mentioned; i.e. "have
heard me."

20. ἐκ τούτων: on ascertaining that
no one had ever heard Socrates talk

on such matters, the judges might infer
reasonably that the other charges
against him also were false. Falsus in
uno, falsus in omnibus. — Xenophon enumerates the subjects chosen
by Socrates for his conversations; cf.
Mem. i. 1. 16. — περὶ ἐμοῦ: the colloquial tone is marked in the position of
these words. Instead of "the other
stories which people tell about me,"
Socrates says, "the other stories about
me, which people tell." The relative
clause is appended as an afterthought.

IV. *Another charge that has been
brought against me is that I teach men,
for money. This is not true, but it
would be no reproach if it were. The
reason why I deny that I teach is simply
that I do not know how to teach.*

1. ἀλλὰ γάρ: in turning to a new
topic, a glance is thrown backward
(οὔτε . . . ἔστιν), and the new departure
begins with the emphatic οὐδέ nor. ἔστιν
is equivalent to the following ἀληθές
(ἔστιν). — εἴ τινος κτλ.: *if any one has
told you.*

20 a

μάτα πράττομαι, οὐδὲ τοῦτο ἀληθές. ἐπεὶ καὶ τοῦτό γέ μοι e
δοκεῖ καλὸν εἶναι, εἴ τις οἷός τ᾽ εἴη παιδεύειν ἀνθρώπους
5 ὥσπερ Γοργίας τε ὁ Λεοντῖνος καὶ Πρόδικος ὁ Κεῖος καὶ
Ἱππίας ὁ Ἠλεῖος. τούτων γὰρ ἕκαστος, ὦ ἄνδρες, οἷός τ᾽ ἐστὶν
ἰὼν εἰς ἑκάστην τῶν πόλεων τοὺς νέους, οἷς ἔξεστι τῶν ἑαυτῶν πολιτῶν προῖκα συνεῖναι ᾧ ἂν βούλωνται, — τούτους
πείθουσι τὰς ἐκείνων συνουσίας ἀπολιπόντας σφίσι συνεῖναι 20
10 χρήματα διδόντας καὶ χάριν προσειδέναι.

ἐπεὶ καὶ ἄλλος ἀνήρ ἐστι Πάριος ἐνθάδε σοφός, ὃν ἐγὼ
ᾐσθόμην ἐπιδημοῦντα· ἔτυχον γὰρ προσελθὼν ἀνδρὶ ὃς τετέ-
λεκε χρήματα σοφισταῖς πλείω ἢ σύμπαντες οἱ ἄλλοι, Καλλίᾳ τῷ Ἱππονίκου· τοῦτον οὖν ἀνηρόμην — ἐστὸν γὰρ αὐτῷ
15 δύο υἱεῖ — "Ὦ Καλλία," ἦν δ᾽ ἐγώ, " εἰ μέν σου τὼ υἱεῖ πώλω

---

3. **χρήματα πράττομαι**: the denial
of this is repeated at **31 c** and **33 b**.—
ἐπεί: *although*. Strictly a connecting
thought must be supplied.

4. **εἴ τις εἴη**: the regular apodosis
καλὸν ἂν εἴη is represented by its equivalent in sense, δοκεῖ καλὸν εἶναι.

6. **τούτων γὰρ κτλ.** : the ironical
surprise of Socrates is reproduced by
the anacoluthon in this sentence. With
οἷός τ᾽ ἐστίν the speaker apparently
leads up to πείθειν, but the emphatic
τούτους (in which the clause τοὺς νέους,
οἷς . . . βούλωνται is summed up) is
followed by πείθουσι instead. (The
plural after ἕκαστος is not uncommon.)
Then comes the statement of a fact
which is surprising, *they pay these men*,
and finally the climax is capped by
their giving them *thanks to boot*. To
make this last point, προσειδέναι, which
might be a participle like διδόντας, is
put on a par with συνεῖναι by being
made an infinitive.

8. **πολιτῶν**: partitive genitive with
ᾧ ἂν βούλωνται. — **συνεῖναι**: Socrates
would not allow that he was a teacher.
His young friends were not his μαθηταί
(cf. **33 a**), but οἱ συνόντες. So he uses
similar language in speaking of others.
Cf. Xen. *Mem.* i. 6. 1.

11. **ἐπεὶ καὶ ἄλλος**: "the men just
named are not the only ones, *for also*,"
etc.

12. **ᾐσθόμην ἐπιδημοῦντα**: for the
supplementary participle, cf. ᾐσθόμην
οἰομένων **22 c**.

13. **Καλλίᾳ**: at Callias's house foreigners, and particularly foreign Sophists, were welcomed. Callias's fondness for Sophists is humorously brought
out in the *Protagoras* (**314 d**), where he
is almost crowded out of house and
home by them. The indulgence of
this and of other tastes exhausted his
resources, and he died in poverty.

15. " Who can do for Callias's sons
what a farmer would do for his calves ? "

20 a

ἢ μόσχω ἐγενέσθην, εἴχομεν ἂν αὐτοῖν ἐπιστάτην λαβεῖν
καὶ μισθώσασθαι, ὃς ἔμελλεν αὐτὼ καλώ τε καὶ ἀγαθὼ
ποιήσειν τὴν προσήκουσαν ἀρετήν· ἦν δ' ἂν οὗτος ἢ τῶν b
ἱππικῶν τις ἢ τῶν γεωργικῶν· νῦν δ' ἐπειδὴ ἀνθρώπω ἐστόν,
20 τίνα αὐτοῖν ἐν νῷ ἔχεις ἐπιστάτην λαβεῖν; τίς τῆς τοιαύτης
ἀρετῆς, τῆς ἀνθρωπίνης τε καὶ πολιτικῆς, ἐπιστήμων ἐστίν ;
οἶμαι γάρ σε ἐσκέφθαι διὰ τὴν τῶν ὑέων κτῆσιν. ἔστι τις,"
ἔφην ἐγώ, " ἢ οὔ;" "Πάνυ γε," ἦ δ' ὅς. "Τίς," ἦν δ' ἐγώ,
" καὶ ποδαπός, καὶ πόσου διδάσκει;" "Εὔηνος," ἔφη, " ὦ
25 Σώκρατες, Πάριος, πέντε μνῶν." καὶ ἐγὼ τὸν Εὔηνον ἐμακάρισα, εἰ ὡς ἀληθῶς ἔχοι ταύτην τὴν τέχνην και ουτως c
ἐμμελῶς διδάσκει. ἐγὼ οὖν καὶ αὐτὸς ἐκαλλυνόμην τε καὶ
ἡβρυνόμην ἂν εἰ ἠπιστάμην ταῦτα· ἀλλ' οὐ γὰρ ἐπίσταμαι,
ὦ ἄνδρες Ἀθηναῖοι.

17. ὃς ἔμελλεν κτλ. : who would, in
the case supposed (εἰ . . . μισθώσασθαι),
proceed to make them, etc., — a present
likelihood not realized. — καλὼ κτλ. :
καλὸς κἀγαθός was a frequent Athenian
designation for a gentleman. Cf. Xen.
Mem. i. 1. 16.

18. ἀρετήν : a cognate accusative,
which was becoming an accusative of
specification. Cf. μέγα σοφὸς ὤν 21 b,
καλὸν εἰδέναι 21 d, σοφὸς σοφίαν 22 e;
but τὰ μέγιστα σοφώτατος 22 a.

19. νῦν : logical, rather than temporal, — "as it is." — Cf. ἔπειτα 20 c.

21. ἀνθρωπίνης κτλ. : the excellence
of a man and a citizen naturally is
different from that befitting (προσήκουσαν, l. 18) a calf. — This clause explains
the preceding τοιαύτης.

24. Εὔηνος κτλ. : not a word is
wasted in this answer. Euenus is
elsewhere mentioned as a teacher of
oratory and a writer of elegiac verses.

(Cf. Phaedo 60 d.) A few such poems
attributed to him still exist. Here he
is introduced as a Sophist and a teacher
of virtue. The smallness of his charge
for instruction probably measures accurately the value attached to it by his
contemporaries, and places him and
his teaching in the second rank. Protagoras charged 100 minas. — Attempts
have been made to distinguish a
younger and an older Euenus, both of
whom came from Paros and wrote
elegiacs. If there were two, allusion
is here made to the elder. — πόσου :
genitive of price.

26. εἰ ἔχοι καὶ διδάσκει : in the
original statement which Socrates may
be supposed to have in mind, both of
these were in the indicative. Both
might change to the optative after
ἐμακάρισα.

27. καὶ αὐτός : implies that Euenus
prided himself on his teaching.

20 d

V. ὑπολάβοι ἂν οὖν τις ὑμῶν ἴσως· " Ἀλλ', ὦ Σώκρατες,
τὸ σὸν τί ἐστι πρᾶγμα; πόθεν αἱ διαβολαί σοι αὗται γεγό-
νασιν; οὐ γὰρ δήπου σοῦ γ' οὐδὲν τῶν ἄλλων περιττότερον
πραγματευομένου ἔπειτα τοσαύτη φήμη τε καὶ λόγος γέγονεν,
5 εἰ μή τι ἔπραττες ἀλλοῖον ἢ οἱ πολλοί· λέγε οὖν ἡμῖν τί
ἐστιν, ἵνα μὴ ἡμεῖς περὶ σοῦ αὐτοσχεδιάζωμεν." ταυτί μοι d
δοκεῖ δίκαια λέγειν ὁ λέγων, κἀγὼ ὑμῖν πειράσομαι ἀπο-
δεῖξαι τί ποτ' ἐστὶ τοῦτο ὃ ἐμοὶ πεποίηκε τό τ' ὄνομα καὶ τὴν
διαβολήν. ἀκούετε δή. καὶ ἴσως μὲν δόξω τισὶν ὑμῶν παίζειν,
10 εὖ μέντοι ἴστε, πᾶσαν ὑμῖν τὴν ἀλήθειαν ἐρῶ.

ἐγὼ γάρ, ὦ ἄνδρες Ἀθηναῖοι, δι' οὐδὲν ἀλλ' ἢ διὰ σοφίαν
τινὰ τοῦτο τὸ ὄνομα ἔσχηκα. ποίαν δὴ σοφίαν ταύτην; ἥπερ
ἐστὶν ἴσως ἀνθρωπίνη σοφία. τῷ ὄντι γὰρ κινδυνεύω ταύτην

V. *But what has caused my reputation, if these stories are untrue? I
will tell you the whole truth. Apollo
himself declared me to be the wisest
of men. Obedience to the god has led
me to disregard the feelings of men.*

1. ἀλλ', ὦ Σώκρατες, κτλ. : objec-
tions dramatized and put in the form
of questions. — "Socrates must have
done something to cause such prejudice." Hence the γάρ in οὐ γὰρ δήπου.

2. τὸ σὸν πρᾶγμα : *what is that
you have been about?* or better, *what
is this about you?* — Cf. τὸ τοῦ Σωκράτους πρᾶγμα *Crito* **53 d**.

3. περιττότερον : what passes the
limits of common men provokes suspicion. — That σοῦ πραγματευομένου
conveys a statement of fact, not a
condition, is shown by οὐδέν, but the
view is restated, in a slightly different
form, as a supposition. "While you
were doing nothing out of the way,
this report did not arise about you, —

if you were doing nothing unusual."
Some explanation of the fame of Socrates is called for, and he has rejected
the ordinary explanation as false.

5. εἰ μὴ κτλ. : a logical condition
referring to continued action in past
time. The conclusion might be expected in the form οὐκ ἂν ἐγένετο κτλ.

8. τὸ ὄνομα καὶ τὴν διαβολήν : i.e.
σοφὸς λέγεσθαι. To be distinguished
from φήμη τε καὶ λόγος, above, only as
bringing out the bad repute which was
their result. The word διαβολήν inter-
prets ὄνομα, and shows that it is no
good name which has been gained.

12. ἔσχηκα : *I have become possessed of and still have.* Cf. ἔσχετε
19 a.— **ποίαν . . . ταύτην** : this question follows the preceding sentence so
closely that διά is not repeated. ποίαν
is in the predicate ; we might expand
to ποία σοφία ἐστὶν αὕτη δι' ἣν τοῦτο . . .
ἔσχηκα. — **ἥπερ** : sc. διὰ ταύτην τοῦτο
. . . ἔσχηκα, ἥπερ κτλ., *just that which*

20 d

εἶναι σοφός· οὗτοι δὲ τάχ᾽ ἂν οὓς ἄρτι ἔλεγον μείζω τινὰ
15 ἢ κατ᾽ ἄνθρωπον σοφίαν σοφοὶ εἶεν, ἢ οὐκ ἔχω τί λέγω· οὐ e
γὰρ δὴ ἔγωγ᾽ αὐτὴν ἐπίσταμαι, ἀλλ᾽ ὅστις φησὶ ψεύδεταί τε
καὶ ἐπὶ διαβολῇ τῇ ἐμῇ λέγει. καί μοι, ὦ ἄνδρες Ἀθηναῖοι,
μὴ θορυβήσητε, μηδ᾽ ἐὰν δόξω τι ὑμῖν μέγα λέγειν· οὐ γὰρ
ἐμὸν ἐρῶ τὸν λόγον ὃν ἂν λέγω, ἀλλ᾽ εἰς ἀξιόχρεων ὑμῖν τὸν
20 λέγοντα ἀνοίσω. τῆς γὰρ ἐμῆς, εἰ δή τίς ἐστι σοφία καὶ
οἵα, μάρτυρα ὑμῖν παρέξομαι τὸν θεὸν τὸν ἐν Δελφοῖς. Χαιρεφῶντα γὰρ ἴστε που. οὗτος ἐμός τ᾽ ἑταῖρος ἦν ἐκ νέου καὶ 21

14. οὗτοι δέ: i.e. Gorgias etc., mentioned in the previous chapter.

15. ἢ οὐκ ἔχω κτλ. : Socrates implies that such wisdom is either superhuman or no wisdom at all. — To be
construed closely with what follows.

17. ἐπί : with dative of purpose.

18. μὴ θορυβήσητε : do not interrupt
me with noise, strictly referring to the
moment fixed by ἐὰν δόξω κτλ. In 21 a
and 30 c the less precise present is
used, make no disturbance. — μέγα
λέγειν : in the sense of μεγαληγορεῖν,
just as μέγα φρονεῖν is equivalent to
μεγαλοφρονεῖν. — οὐ γὰρ ἐμὸν κτλ. : a
compressed form of statement, made
effective with the audience by the allusion to certain Euripidean strains.
Cf. Eur. Frg. 484, κοὐκ ἐμὸς ὁ μῦθος
ἀλλ᾽ ἐμῆς μητρὸς πάρα, not mine the
word, — I heard it from my mother ;
which is parodied in Symp. 177 a, ἡ
μέν μοι ἀρχὴ τοῦ λόγου ἐστὶ κατὰ τὴν
Εὐριπίδου Μελανίππην· "οὐ γὰρ ἐμὸς ὁ
μῦθος ἀλλὰ" Φαιδροῦ τοῦδε. The same
sentiment is found in Eur. Hel. 513,
λόγος γάρ ἐστιν οὐκ ἐμός, σοφῶν δ᾽ ἔπος,
not mine the word; by clerkly men
'twas spoken. Hor. Sat. ii. 2. 2, nec
meus hic sermo est sed quae
praecepit Ofellus. — For a simi-

larly compressed statement, cf. ἱκανὸν
τὸν μάρτυρα 31 c. "A predicate adjective or substantive is often a brief equivalent for one clause of a compound
sentence," H. 618. ἐμόν and ἀξιόχρεων
are both predicate, and special point
is given them by their position.

19. ὃν ἂν λέγω : equivalent to ὃν
μέλλω λέγειν, though it is formally a
hypothetical relative clause with indefinite antecedent. — ἀξιόχρεων κτλ. :
equivalent to ἀξιόχρεώς ἐστιν ὁ λέγων.

20. ἀνοίσω : often used of shifting
responsibility. Cf. εἰς τοὺς τριάκοντα
ἀναφέρειν τὴν αἰτίαν Lys. xii. 28, τὰς
ἀπολογίας εἰς ἐκεῖνον ἀναφερομένας ib.
64. — τῆς γὰρ ἐμῆς, εἰ κτλ. : skill as
well as modesty was required to avoid
blurting out here with τῆς ἐμῆς σοφίας.
The εἰ δή τίς ἐστι interrupts just in time.

21. οἵα : goes back to ποίαν l. 12. —
τὸν θεόν κτλ. : emphatic by its position.

22. Χαιρεφῶντα : certainly, if the
Athenians did not know Chaerephon,
many a joke of Aristophanes at Chaerephon's expense was lost on them; see
below on line 25. He is mentioned by
Xenophon (Mem. i. 2. 48) as one of those
friends of Socrates οἳ ἐκείνῳ συνῆσαν
οὐχ ἵνα δημηγορικοὶ γένοιντο, ἀλλ᾽ ἵνα
καλοί τε κἀγαθοὶ γενόμενοι καὶ οἴκῳ καὶ

21 a

ὑμῶν τῷ πλήθει ἑταῖρός τε καὶ συνέφυγε τὴν φυγὴν ταύτην
καὶ μεθ᾽ ὑμῶν κατῆλθε. καὶ ἴστε δὴ οἷος ἦν Χαιρεφῶν, ὡς
25 σφοδρὸς ἐφ᾽ ὅ τι ὁρμήσειεν. καὶ δή ποτε καὶ εἰς Δελφοὺς
ἐλθὼν ἐτόλμησε τοῦτο μαντεύσασθαι· (καὶ, ὅπερ λέγω, μή
θορυβεῖτε, ὦ ἄνδρες·) ἤρετο γὰρ δὴ εἴ τις ἐμοῦ εἴη σοφώτερος. ἀνεῖλεν οὖν ἡ Πυθία μηδένα σοφώτερον εἶναι. καὶ

οἰκέταις καὶ φίλοις καὶ πόλει καὶ πολίταις
δύναιντο καλῶς χρῆσθαι.

23. ὑμῶν τῷ πλήθει: the ἡλιασταί
are here taken as representing the
whole people ; and here, as often, πλῆθος is equivalent to δῆμος, and means
democratic party. Cf. Lysias xii, xiii,
passim. — **ἑταῖρος**: cf. τῆς ὑπαρχούσης
πολιτείας ἑταῖρον εἶναι *Gorg.* 510 a, *to
be a partisan of the government in
power.* — **τὴν φυγὴν ταύτην**: an allusion, which no hearer could fail of
understanding, to the exile from which
all conspicuous democrats had returned
only four years before (in 403 B.C.).
The Thirty Tyrants were the authors
of this banishment ; cf. προεῖπον μὲν
τοῖς ἔξω τοῦ καταλόγου (*not registered
on their catalogue of 3000 oligarchical
sympathizers*) μὴ εἰσιέναι εἰς τὸ ἄστυ.
φευγόντων δὲ εἰς τὸν Πειραιᾶ, καὶ ἐντεῦθεν
πολλοὺς ἄγοντες ἐνέπλησαν καὶ τὰ Μέγαρα
καὶ τὰς Θήβας τῶν ὑποχωρούντων Xen.
Hell. ii. 4. 1. This allusion here had
the effect of influencing the court in
favor of what they were about to hear.
This was the more important since
Socrates had remained in the city during the rule of the Thirty, and doubtless had been accused by Meletus of
lack of sympathy with the Athenian democracy, — a charge closely connected
with that of corrupting the youth.

25. σφοδρός: Chaerephon was a
born enthusiast. Cf. Χαιρεφῶν δέ, ἅτε

καὶ μανικὸς ὤν, ἀναπηδήσας ἐκ μέσων ἔθει
πρός με *Charm.* 153 b. Aristophanes
calls Chaerephon *a bat* (*Birds* 1564) ;
Chaerephon and Socrates belong to
the jaundiced barefoot brotherhood
(*Clouds* 104). Browning, *Aristophanes's Apology,*

> In me 'twas equal balanced flesh rebuked
> Excess alike in stuff-guts Glauketes
> Or starveling Chaerephon ; I challenge both.

— **ὁρμήσειεν** : the optative indicates indefinite frequency of past action. —
καὶ δή ποτε καὶ κτλ. : cf. **18 a.** A frequent way of introducing a particular
instance of what has been stated generally. What Chaerephon did at Delphi was an instance of his σφοδρότης.

26. τοῦτο : cognate accusative after
μαντεύσασθαι in anticipation of ἤρετο
κτλ. For τοῦτο referring forward, see
H. 696 a. — **μαντεύσασθαι** : the middle
voice is used of the person who con-
sults the oracle. — **ὅπερ λέγω** : *I repeat,*
lit. *just what I am saying.* Cf. **17 c**
and **20 e.**

28. ἀνεῖλεν οὖν ἡ Πυθία : the oracle
in question is lost, but we have a
very fair substitute in σοφὸς Σοφοκλῆς
σοφώτερος δ᾽ Εὐριπίδης, | ἀνδρῶν δὲ πάντων
(or ἁπάντων) Σωκράτης σοφώτατος. —
Socrates must have become well known
from his questionings before such a
question would have been asked. Possibly the prominence given by Socrates
to two precepts of the oracle, made

21 a

τούτων πέρι ὁ ἀδελφὸς ὑμῖν αὐτοῦ οὑτοσὶ μαρτυρήσει, ἐπειδὴ
30 ἐκεῖνος τετελεύτηκεν.

VI. σκέψασθε δὲ ὧν ἕνεκα ταῦτα λέγω· μέλλω γὰρ ὑμᾶς b
διδάξειν ὅθεν μοι ἡ διαβολὴ γέγονεν. ταῦτα γὰρ ἐγὼ ἀκούσας ἐνεθυμούμην οὑτωσί· "Τί ποτε λέγει ὁ θεός, καὶ τί
ποτε αἰνίττεται; ἐγὼ γὰρ δὴ οὔτε μέγα οὔτε σμικρὸν σύνοιδα
5 ἐμαυτῷ σοφὸς ὤν· τί οὖν ποτε λέγει φάσκων ἐμὲ σοφώτατον
εἶναι; οὐ γὰρ δήπου ψεύδεταί γε· οὐ γὰρ θέμις αὐτῷ." καὶ
πολὺν μὲν χρόνον ἠπόρουν τί ποτε λέγει· ἔπειτα μόγις πάνυ
ἐπὶ ζήτησιν αὐτοῦ τοιαύτην τινὰ ἐτραπόμην.

much of at Delphi, γνῶθι σαυτόν and
μηδὲν ἄγαν (self-knowledge and self-
control), which make up Greek σωφροσύνη, may have been the basis of the
story or of the response.

29. ὁ ἀδελφός: i.e. Chaerecrates.

VI. *I did not suppose the words of
Apollo to be strictly and literally true,
but believed them to have some hidden
meaning, which I ought to discover. So
I tried to show that they could not be
true in the ordinary sense.*

1. μέλλω διδάξειν: for μέλλω with
future infinitive, see SCG. 273; GMT.
73. Cf. *Phaedo* **59 a.**

2. ὅθεν: equivalent to ἐξ ἧς, of the
source *out of which* the prejudice arose.
—**ταῦτα:** i.e. the response of the oracle.

3. τί ποτε αἰνίττεται: through
modesty Socrates assumes that this is
"a dark saying." For a genuinely enigmatical oracle, cf. γίνεται δὲ τοῖς βα-
σιλεῦσιν (Temenus and Cresphontes)
αὐτῶν λόγιον τόδε, ἡγεμόνα τῆς καθόδου
ποιεῖσθαι τὸν τριόφθαλμον, Paus. v. 3. 5,
*that they should take "the three-eyed"
as leader of their return home.* The
"three-eyed" turned out to be Oxylus,

son of Andraemon, whom they met
riding on a *one-eyed* mule.

4. σύνοιδα σοφὸς ὤν: for the supplementary participle, cf. **22 d.** GMT. 908.

6. οὐ δήπου: *of course I do not suppose.* — Socrates's perplexity is dramatized. The hearer is reminded of the
speaker's habit of discussion by question and answer. — **οὐ γὰρ θέμις:**
Apollo, being by nature truthful, could
not lie. In Plato's *Republic* the two
primary canons of theology are that
the gods are good and are true. With
this belief, Socrates was much more
pious than many of the old story-
tellers. Homer makes Zeus send a
delusive dream to Agamemnon.

7. μόγις πάνυ: qualifies ἔπειτα ἐτραπόμην, and repeats parenthetically the
idea of πολὺν χρόνον. For a similar
parenthetical qualification, cf. οὐ κατὰ
τούτους **17 b.** For the position of πάνυ,
cf. οὐ πάνυ **19 a.**

8. αὐτοῦ: i.e. τοῦ θεοῦ, equivalent to
τοῦ χρησμοῦ. — **τοιαύτην τινά:** sc. ζήτησιν, purposely vague, "which I began
in some such way as this." Cf. τοιαύτη
τις **19 c.**

21 d

ἦλθον ἐπί τινα τῶν δοκούντων σοφῶν εἶναι, ὡς ἐνταῦθα, c
10 εἴ πέρ που, ἐλέγξων τὸ μαντεῖον καὶ ἀποφανῶν τῷ χρησμῷ
ὅτι "Οὑτοσὶ ἐμοῦ σοφώτερός ἐστι, σὺ δ' ἐμὲ ἔφησθα."
διασκοπῶν οὖν τοῦτον, — ὀνόματι γὰρ οὐδὲν δέομαι λέγειν,
ἦν δέ τις τῶν πολιτικῶν πρὸς ὃν ἐγὼ σκοπῶν τοιοῦτόν τι
ἔπαθον, ὦ ἄνδρες Ἀθηναῖοι, — καὶ διαλεγόμενος αὐτῷ, ἔδοξέ
15 μοι οὗτος ὁ ἀνὴρ δοκεῖν μὲν εἶναι σοφὸς ἄλλοις τε πολλοῖς
ἀνθρώποις καὶ μάλιστα ἑαυτῷ, εἶναι δ' οὔ· κἄπειτα ἐπειρώμην
αὐτῷ δεικνύναι ὅτι οἴοιτο μὲν εἶναι σοφός, εἴη δ' οὔ. ἐντεῦθεν d
οὖν τούτῳ τ' ἀπηχθόμην καὶ πολλοῖς τῶν παρόντων· πρὸς
ἐμαυτὸν δ' οὖν ἀπιὼν ἐλογιζόμην ὅτι "Τούτου μὲν τοῦ ἀν-
20 θρώπου ἐγὼ σοφώτερός εἰμι· κινδυνεύει μὲν γὰρ ἡμῶν οὐδέ-
τερος οὐδὲν καλὸν κἀγαθὸν εἰδέναι, ἀλλ' οὗτος μὲν οἴεταί τι
εἰδέναι οὐκ εἰδώς, ἐγὼ δ', ὥσπερ οὖν οὐκ οἶδα, οὐδ' οἴομαι.
ἔοικά γ' οὖν τούτου γε σμικρῷ τινι αὐτῷ τούτῳ σοφώτερος
εἶναι, ὅτι ἃ μὴ οἶδα οὐδ' οἴομαι εἰδέναι." ἐντεῦθεν ἐπ' ἄλλον
25 ἦα τῶν ἐκείνου δοκούντων σοφωτέρων εἶναι, καί μοι ταῦτα

9. ὡς ἀποφανῶν: *believing that I
should show.* Cf. 22 b.

10. ἀποφανῶν τῷ χρησμῷ: the oracle is personified.

11. ὅτι: often, as here, introduces
a direct quotation.

13. πρὸς ὃν ἔπαθον: cf. ὁμοιότατον
πάσχω πρὸς τοὺς φιλοσοφοῦντας ὥσπερ
πρὸς τοὺς ψελλιζομένους καὶ παίζοντας
Gorg. 485 b, *towards philosophers I feel
just as I do towards people who lisp and
are childish.* Cf. the use of πρός in
such expressions as πρὸς ἐμαυτὸν σκοπῶν,
pondering in my mind ; πρὸς ἀλλήλους
σκοποῦμεν, *we consider among ourselves* ;
πρὸς ἐμαυτὸν ἐλογιζόμην in d below.

14. καὶ διαλεγόμενος αὐτῷ : strictly
speaking, this covers the same ground
as διασκοπῶν τοῦτον. repeating the

idea after the parenthetical remark.
Socrates has no test except by conversing with his man. — ἔδοξέ μοι κτλ. :
the construction is slightly changed.
Cf. καὶ εὐξάμενοι τῇ Ἀρτέμιδι ὁπόσους ἂν
κατακάνοιεν τῶν πολεμίων τοσαύτας χιμαί-
ρας καταθύσειν τῇ θεῷ, ἐπεὶ οὐκ εἶχον
ἱκανὰς εὑρεῖν, ἔδοξεν αὐτοῖς κατ' ἐνιαυτὸν
πεντακοσίας θύειν κτλ. Xen. *An* iii. 2.
12 ; and καὶ ἔδοξεν αὐτοῖς ἀποκτεῖναι . . .
ἐπικαλοῦντες τὴν ἀπόστασιν Thuc. iii. 36,
taxing them with their revolt. SCG. 10.

23. αὐτῷ τούτῳ: *in just this respect.*
This serves to prepare the way for the
clause with ὅτι, which gives a detailed
specification of what is intimated in
σμικρῷ τινι (dative of degree of difference).

25. ἐκείνου: the same as τούτου above

21 e

ταῦτα ἔδοξε· καὶ ἐνταῦθα κἀκείνῳ καὶ ἄλλοις πολλοῖς ε
ἀπηχθόμην.

VII. μετὰ ταῦτ᾿ οὖν ἤδη ἐφεξῆς ᾖα αἰσθανόμενος μὲν καὶ
λυπούμενος καὶ δεδιὼς ὅτι ἀπηχθανόμην, ὅμως δ᾿ ἀναγκαῖον
ἐδόκει εἶναι τὸ τοῦ θεοῦ περὶ πλείστου ποιεῖσθαι. ἰτέον οὖν,
σκοποῦντι τὸν χρησμὸν τί λέγει, ἐπὶ ἅπαντας τούς τι δοκοῦν-
5 τας εἰδέναι. καὶ νὴ τὸν κύνα, ὦ ἄνδρες Ἀθηναῖοι, — δεῖ γὰρ 22
πρὸς ὑμᾶς τἀληθῆ λέγειν, — ἦ μὴν ἐγὼ ἔπαθόν τι τοιοῦτον·
οἱ μὲν μάλιστα εὐδοκιμοῦντες ἔδοξάν μοι ὀλίγου δεῖν τοῦ
πλείστου ἐνδεεῖς εἶναι ζητοῦντι κατὰ τὸν θεόν, ἄλλοι δὲ
δοκοῦντες φαυλότεροι ἐπιεικέστεροι εἶναι ἄνδρες πρὸς τὸ
10 φρονίμως ἔχειν. δεῖ δὴ ὑμῖν τὴν ἐμὴν πλάνην ἐπιδεῖξαι

27. ἀπηχθόμην : cf. ἐμοὶ ὀργίζονται
23 c.

VII. *I found not only the statesmen
but also the poets to have no knowledge.
These composed their poems by a sort
of inspiration, and could give no rational
account of their own works.*

2. Socrates observed his growing
unpopularity with pain and fear. ὅτι
(*that*) after αἰσθάνομαι is a rare construction, and possibly the particle is
affected by the participles. — ὅμως
δ᾿ ἐδόκει : correlative with αἰσθανόμενος
μέν, breaks away from the participial
construction. This gives prominence
to Socrates's determination to do his
duty. Cf. πῶς δύνασθε πιστεῦσαι, δόξαν
παρ᾿ ἀλλήλων λαμβάνοντες, καὶ τὴν δόξαν
τὴν παρὰ τοῦ μόνου θεοῦ οὐ ζητεῖτε St.
John v. 44.

3. τὸ τοῦ θεοῦ: *the interest of the
god*, which required that Socrates
should show the true meaning of the
oracle. — ἰτέον : sc. ἦν μοι.

4. τὸν χρησμὸν τί λέγει : χρησμός
might have been the subject of the

interrogative clause, but is used pro-
leptically. H. 878.

5. νὴ τὸν κύνα : this form of asseveration is a whim of Socrates, upon
which the Scholiast says, Ῥαδαμάνθυος
ὅρκος οὗτος ὁ κατὰ κυνὸς ἢ χηνὸς (*goose*)
ἢ πλατάνου (*plane-tree*) ἢ κριοῦ (*ram*) ἢ
τινος ἄλλου τοιούτου· οἷς ἦν μέγιστος ὅρ-
κος ἅπαντι λόγῳ κύων, | ἔπειτα χὴν· θεοὺς
δ᾿ ἐσίγων (*they named no god*), Κρατῖνος
Χείρωσι (i.e. *in the Chirons*). κατὰ τούτων δὲ νόμος ὀμνύναι ἵνα μὴ κατὰ θεῶν οἱ
ὅρκοι γίγνωνται, τοιοῦτοι δὲ καὶ οἱ Σωκράτους ὅρκοι. A humorous turn is given
to this oath in μὰ τὸν κύνα τὸν Αἰγυπτίων
θεόν *Gorg.* 482 b; Socrates might swear
by the Egyptian god, but seldom by
any of the gods whom he worshiped.
νὴ τὴν Ἥραν **24 e** is a woman's oath ;
πρὸς Διός **25 c** is solemn adjuration.

6. ἦ μήν : the usual formula for beginning any affirmation prefaced by a
solemn oath.

7. ὀλίγου δεῖν: cf. **17 a.** The δεῖν
seems to be used here with a play on
πλείστου ἐνδεεῖς.

22 c

ὥσπερ πόνους τινὰς πονοῦντος ἵνα μοι καὶ ἀνέλεγκτος ἡ
μαντεία γένοιτο. μετὰ γὰρ τοὺς πολιτικοὺς ᾖα ἐπὶ τοὺς
ποιητὰς τούς τε τῶν τραγῳδιῶν καὶ τοὺς τῶν διθυράμβων
καὶ τοὺς ἄλλους, ὡς ἐνταῦθα ἐπ᾽ αὐτοφώρῳ καταληψόμενος b
15 ἐμαυτὸν ἀμαθέστερον ἐκείνων ὄντα. ἀναλαμβάνων οὖν αὐτῶν
τὰ ποιήματα ἅ μοι ἐδόκει μάλιστα πεπραγματεῦσθαι αὐτοῖς,
διηρώτων ἂν αὐτοὺς τί λέγοιεν, ἵν᾽ ἅμα τι καὶ μανθάνοιμι
παρ᾽ αὐτῶν. αἰσχύνομαι οὖν ὑμῖν εἰπεῖν, ὦ ἄνδρες, τἀληθῆ·
ὅμως δὲ ῥητέον. ὡς ἔπος γὰρ εἰπεῖν ὀλίγου αὐτῶν ἅπαντες
20 οἱ παρόντες ἂν βέλτιον ἔλεγον περὶ ὧν αὐτοὶ ἐπεποιήκεσαν.
ἔγνων οὖν αὖ καὶ περὶ τῶν ποιητῶν ἐν ὀλίγῳ τοῦτο, ὅτι οὐ
σοφίᾳ ποιοῖεν ἃ ποιοῖεν, ἀλλὰ φύσει τινὶ καὶ ἐνθουσιάζον- c

11. **ὥσπερ πόνους τινὰς πονοῦντος**:
my Herculean labors, as I may call
them. The genitive agrees with ἐμοῦ
implied in its equivalent ἐμήν. —Socrates compares his own intellectual en-
counters with the physical struggles
of Heracles, and recounts in a half-
tragic vein these "labors" imposed
of God. —**ἵνα μοι καὶ κτλ.**: Socrates,
assuming for the sake of his point an
attitude of opposition, says that he
thought he was refuting the oracle
(cf. **21 c**) while really he was proving
it to be irrefutable. This achievement is stated as his real purpose. —
The optative clause ἵνα γένοιτο depends
upon πονοῦντος, which represents the
imperfect.

14. **καὶ τοὺς ἄλλους**: the κωμῳδο-
ποιοί are hardly included here. The
idea that the true poet was endowed
with exceptional wisdom was common
in ancient times. Cf. φιλοσοφώτερον
(more philosophical) καὶ σπουδαιότερον
(worthier) ποίησις ἱστορίας (prose narrative of facts) ἐστίν Arist. Poet. 9. 3.

In early Greek the poets were preëmi-
nently οἱ σοφοί (see Introduction § 3).

17. **διηρώτων ἄν**: for "the indicative with ἄν of habitual or intermittent
action, ἄν being used without definite
reference," see SCG. 431; GMT. 162;
H. 835. — **καί**: Socrates would thus
not only test the oracle, but also learn
something.

18. **αἰσχύνομαι**: this discovery was
discreditable to the poets, and Socrates
hesitates to mention it, since he feels
shame at the idea of telling what nevertheless must be told, because it is the
truth. When αἰσχύνεσθαι means feel
shame at the thought of an action, it
takes the infinitive, as here, instead of
the participle.

19. **αὐτῶν**: genitive after the comparative βέλτιον.

20. **αὐτοί**: i.e. the poets.

22. **φύσει κτλ.**: the dative of manner (φύσει) and the participle of manner
(ἐνθουσιάζοντες) characterize the same
subject in parallel ways, and so are
appropriately coupled by καί. — **φύσει**:

22 c

τες ὥσπερ οἱ θεομάντεις καὶ οἱ χρησμῳδοί· καὶ γὰρ οὗτοι
λέγουσι μὲν πολλὰ καὶ καλά, ἴσασι δ' οὐδὲν ὧν λέγουσι·
25 τοιοῦτόν τι μοι ἐφάνησαν πάθος καὶ οἱ ποιηταὶ πεπονθότες.
καὶ ἅμα ᾐσθόμην αὐτῶν διὰ τὴν ποίησιν οἰομένων καὶ τᾶλλα
σοφωτάτων εἶναι ἀνθρώπων, ἃ οὐκ ἦσαν. ἀπῇα οὖν καὶ
ἐντεῦθεν τῷ αὐτῷ οἰόμενος περιγεγονέναι ᾧπερ καὶ τῶν
πολιτικῶν.

VIII. τελευτῶν οὖν ἐπὶ τοὺς χειροτέχνας ᾖα. ἐμαυτῷ γὰρ
συνῄδη οὐδὲν ἐπισταμένῳ ὡς ἔπος εἰπεῖν, τούτους δέ γ' ἤδη   d
ὅτι εὑρήσοιμι πολλὰ καὶ καλὰ ἐπισταμένους. καὶ τούτου μὲν
οὐκ ἐψεύσθην, ἀλλ' ἠπίσταντο ἃ ἐγὼ οὐκ ἠπιστάμην, καί μου

by (grace of) nature. Here used to express what Plato elsewhere means by
θείᾳ μοίρᾳ, by the grace of heaven. Acts
done φύσει are done unconsciously, are
inspired by something below the sur-
face of our every-day selves, whereas
conscious acts, if right, are guided by
τέχνη and σοφία, art and wisdom. Cf.
πάντες γὰρ οἵ τε τῶν ἐπῶν ποιηταὶ (epic
poets) οἱ ἀγαθοὶ οὐκ ἐκ τέχνης (out of
knowledge of their art) ἀλλ' ἔνθεοι (inspired) ὄντες καὶ κατεχόμενοι (possessed)
πάντα ταῦτα τὰ καλὰ λέγουσι ποιήματα,
καὶ οἱ μελοποιοὶ (lyric poets) οἱ ἀγαθοὶ
ὡσαύτως . . . ἅτε οὖν οὐ τέχνῃ ποιοῦντες
(writing poetry) ἀλλὰ θείᾳ μοίρᾳ, τοῦτο
μόνον οἷός τε ἕκαστος ποιεῖν καλῶς, ἐφ' ὃ ἡ
Μοῦσα αὐτὸν ὥρμησεν, ὁ μὲν διθυράμβους
(one can write dithyrambs), ὁ δὲ ἐγκώμια
(hymns of praise), ὁ δὲ ὑπορχήματα
(choral songs, accompanied by a lively
dance), ὁ δ' ἔπη (epics), ὁ δ' ἰάμβους
(iambics) . . . διὰ ταῦτα δὲ ὁ θεὸς ἐξαιρού-
μενος τούτων τὸν νοῦν (taking all reason
out of them) τούτοις χρῆται ὑπηρέταις καὶ
τοῖς χρησμῳδοῖς καὶ τοῖς μάντεσι τοῖς θείοις
Ion 533 e–534 c.

26. ᾐσθόμην αὐτῶν οἰομένων: cf.
ἀκούοντες ἐξεταζομένων 23 c. The accusative occurs in ὃν ᾐσθόμην ἐπιδημοῦντα
20 a. — For the supplementary participle, cf. also 21 b.
27. σοφωτάτων: predicate agreeing
with οἰομένων, which contains the subject of εἶναι. Cf. τῶν δοκούντων σοφῶν
εἶναι 21 b. — ἃ οὐκ ἦσαν: sc. σοφοί. Cf.
ὃ ἐπίσταται ἕκαστος, τοῦτο καὶ σοφός ἐστιν
Xen. Mem. iv. 6. 7. E.g. the poet
Sophocles was ready to serve as general; and conversely the generals just
returned from the war were set to be
the judges of the dramatic contest in
which the Antigone was presented.
— ἃ is accusative of specification.
VIII. Finally I went to the crafts-
men. These indeed had knowledge of
their craft, but because of this knowledge they thought themselves wise also
in other matters, and this false conceit
more than outweighed their true wisdom.
1. τελευτῶν: for its adverbial use,
cf. ἀρχόμενος 24 a. — ἐμαυτῷ συνῄδη:
cf. 22 d.
3. τούτου: ablatival genitive. in this.

23 a

5 ταύτῃ σοφώτεροι ἦσαν. ἀλλ', ὦ ἄνδρες Ἀθηναῖοι, ταὐτόν μοι
ἔδοξαν ἔχειν ἁμάρτημα ὅπερ καὶ οἱ ποιηταί, καὶ οἱ ἀγαθοὶ
δημιουργοί· διὰ τὸ τὴν τέχνην καλῶς ἐξεργάζεσθαι ἕκαστος
ἠξίου καὶ τἆλλα τὰ μέγιστα σοφώτατος εἶναι, καὶ αὐτῶν
αὕτη ἡ πλημμέλεια ἐκείνην τὴν σοφίαν ἀπέκρυπτεν, ὥστε με
10 ἐμαυτὸν ἀνερωτᾶν ὑπὲρ τοῦ χρησμοῦ, πότερα δεξαίμην ἂν **e**
οὕτω ὥσπερ ἔχω ἔχειν, μήτε τι σοφὸς ὢν τὴν ἐκείνων σοφίαν
μήτ' ἀμαθὴς τὴν ἀμαθίαν, ἢ ἀμφότερα ἃ ἐκεῖνοι ἔχουσιν
ἔχειν. ἀπεκρινάμην οὖν ἐμαυτῷ καὶ τῷ χρησμῷ ὅτι μοι
λυσιτελοῖ ὥσπερ ἔχω ἔχειν.

IX. ἐκ ταυτησὶ δὴ τῆς ἐξετάσεως, ὦ ἄνδρες Ἀθηναῖοι,
πολλαὶ μὲν ἀπέχθειαί μοι γεγόνασι καὶ οἶαι χαλεπώταται **23**
καὶ βαρύταται, ὥστε πολλὰς διαβολὰς ἀπ' αὐτῶν γεγονέναι,
ὄνομα δὲ τοῦτο λέγεσθαι, σοφὸς εἶναι. οἴονται γάρ με ἑκά-

---

6. **ὅπερ καί, καὶ οἱ** κτλ.: this repetition of καί is idiomatic in correlative
sentences, and both may be represented
by one English word, also. With οἱ
ποιηταί, εἶχον is easily supplied from
the ἔχειν of the leading clause.

7. **διὰ τὸ** κτλ.: here begins the explanation which the preceding clause
demands. — **τὴν τέχνην**: his art.

8. **τἆλλα τὰ μέγιστα**: refers to affairs of state and of the common weal.
Anytus, one of the accusers of Socrates, was a rich and successful tanner,
and entered political life as a practical
man, but was not successful as a general of the army. Similarly a cobbler
needed to be reminded by the painter
Apelles to stick to his last.

10. **δεξαίμην ἄν**: sc. if the choice
were offered.

11. **οὕτω ἔχειν**: is explained by
ὥσπερ ἔχω, and this is explained by the
following clause. — **τι**: at all.

IX. *Now these examinations have
brought me the reputation of wisdom,
but have created also a strong prejudice
against me.*

1. **δή**: marks the close and sum-
ming up of the previous argument.

2. **οἶαι χαλεπώταται**: sc. εἰσί. The
idiom is explained by places where it
is expanded, e.g. ἐμοὶ μὲν δὴ ἐδόκει [Σω-
κράτης] τοιοῦτος εἶναι οἷος ἂν εἴη ἄριστός
τε καὶ εὐδαιμονέστατος Xen. *Mem.* iv. 8.
11.

4. **ὄνομα δὲ τοῦτο λέγεσθαι**: instead
of ὄνομα δὲ τοῦτο ἐλεγόμην, under the
influence of the clause with ὥστε. —
σοφός: introduced to explain precisely
what is meant by ὄνομα τοῦτο. It agrees
with the subject of ἀπέχθημαι, which
is in the speaker's mind, though he
said its equivalent, πολλαὶ ἀπέχθειαί μοι
γεγόνασι. — **εἶναι**: for this idiomatic
use, see SCG. 66, which compares the
English, "Paul, called *to be* an apostle."

23 a

5 στοτε οἱ παρόντες ταῦτα αὐτὸν εἶναι σοφὸν ἃ ἂν ἄλλον ἐξε-
λέγξω· τὸ δὲ κινδυνεύει, ὦ ἄνδρες, τῷ ὄντι ὁ θεὸς σοφὸς εἶναι,
καὶ ἐν τῷ χρησμῷ τούτῳ τοῦτο λέγειν, ὅτι " Ἡ ἀνθρωπίνη
σοφία ὀλίγου τινὸς ἀξία ἐστὶ καὶ οὐδενός." καὶ φαίνεται
τοῦτο λέγειν τὸν Σωκράτη, προσκεχρῆσθαι δὲ τῷ ἐμῷ ὀνό-
10 ματι, ἐμὲ παράδειγμα ποιούμενος, ὥσπερ ἂν εἰ εἴποι ὅτι b
"Οὗτος ὑμῶν, ὦ ἄνθρωποι, σοφώτατός ἐστιν, ὅστις ὥσπερ
Σωκράτης ἔγνωκεν ὅτι οὐδενὸς ἄξιός ἐστι τῇ ἀληθείᾳ πρὸς
σοφίαν."

ταῦτ᾽ οὖν ἐγὼ μὲν ἔτι καὶ νῦν περιιὼν ζητῶ καὶ ἐρευνῶ κατὰ
15 τὸν θεόν, καὶ τῶν ἀστῶν καὶ ξένων ᾽ἄν τινα οἴωμαι σοφὸν
εἶναι· καὶ ἐπειδάν μοι μὴ δοκῇ, τῷ θεῷ βοηθῶν ἐνδείκνυμαι
ὅτι οὐκ ἔστι σοφός. καὶ ὑπὸ ταύτης τῆς ἀσχολίας οὔτε τι
τῶν τῆς πόλεως πρᾶξαί μοι σχολὴ γέγονεν ἄξιον λόγου

5. ἃ ἂν κτλ.: sc. μὴ σοφὸν ὄντα.
6. τὸ δέ: adverbial, " but the fact
is." — τῷ ὄντι: points the contrast between the truth and the popular belief
(οἴονται). It is equivalent to τῇ ἀληθείᾳ
l. 12.
8. καὶ οὐδενός: brought in as a climax after ὀλίγου. Cf. ἡ δὲ διάνοια ταῦτα
πάντα ἡγησαμένη σμικρὰ καὶ οὐδέν Theaet.
173 e, but his (the philosopher's) mind
regarding all this as little or nothing at
all. — φαίνεται: sc. ὁ θεός.
9. τοῦτο λέγειν: sc. ὅτι σοφώτατός
ἐστιν. — The argument runs thus:
"People credit me with knowing all
the things which I convict my neigh-
bors of not knowing. The truth is far
otherwise, for God alone has real
knowledge. The meaning of his dark
saying about my being the wisest of
men is simply that ' human wisdom is
vanity.' He does not mean that Socrates has any other than human wisdom.

He only uses the name ' Socrates ' because he needs a particular instance."
The double accusative with λέγειν
closely resembles the idiom κακὰ λέγειν
τινά. Cf. Crito 48 a.
10. ὥσπερ ἂν εἰ: in this compressed
idiom ἄν alone represents a whole
clause, which the context readily
suggests.
14. ταῦτα: adverb, therefore, as in
Homer.
15. τῶν κτλ.: for the grouping under a single article, cf. 19 b.
16. τῷ θεῷ βοηθῶν: cf. ὑπὲρ τοῦ
χρησμοῦ 22 e. The service which Socrates rendered to Apollo was in proving
his own wisdom, as compared with
that of others, and thus vindicating
the god's truthfulness as shown in the
oracle, and in leading men to obey the
maxim γνῶθι σαυτόν.
17. ἀσχολίας: used here for the
sake of the play on σχολή, below

23 d

οὔτε τῶν οἰκείων, ἀλλ᾽ ἐν πενίᾳ μυρίᾳ εἰμὶ διὰ τὴν τοῦ θεοῦ ◂
20 λατρείαν.

X. πρὸς δὲ τούτοις οἱ νέοι μοι ἐπακολουθοῦντες, οἷς
μάλιστα σχολή ἐστιν, οἱ τῶν πλουσιωτάτων, αὐτόματοι χαίρουσιν ἀκούοντες ἐξεταζομένων τῶν ἀνθρώπων, καὶ αὐτοὶ
πολλάκις ἐμὲ μιμοῦνται, εἶτ᾽ ἐπιχειροῦσιν ἄλλους ἐξετάζειν·
5 κἄπειτ᾽, οἶμαι, εὑρίσκουσι πολλὴν ἀφθονίαν οἰομένων μὲν
εἰδέναι τι ἀνθρώπων, εἰδότων δὲ ὀλίγα ἢ οὐδέν. ἐντεῦθεν οὖν
οἱ ὑπ᾽ αὐτῶν ἐξεταζόμενοι ἐμοὶ ὀργίζονται, ἀλλ᾽ οὐχ αὑτοῖς,
καὶ λέγουσιν ὡς "Σωκράτης τίς ἐστι μιαρώτατος καὶ δια- d
φθείρει τοὺς νέους." καὶ ἐπειδάν τις αὐτοὺς ἐρωτᾷ ὅ τι ποιῶν
10 καὶ ὅ τι διδάσκων, ἔχουσι μὲν οὐδὲν εἰπεῖν, ἀλλ᾽ ἀγνοοῦσιν,

19. ἐν πενίᾳ μυρίᾳ: in Xenophon's
Oecon. ii. 1–4, Socrates says that if he
should find a liberal purchaser, his
property might fetch five minas, or
about $100. The possession of five
minas placed Socrates in the lowest of
the four classes established by Solon,
that of the θῆτες. Originally this lowest
class had few political duties and no
political rights; later on, a law proposed by Aristides gave them the same
rights as the others. — Of course the
purchasing power of money was five
or even ten times as great in Socrates's
time as in our own. — τὴν τοῦ θεοῦ
λατρείαν: in the similar construction
with ὑπηρεσία 30 a, the dative τῷ θεῷ
takes the place of the objective genitive
here. — Another reason for Socrates's
abstention from public life is given in
31 e.

X. *My young friends followed my
example of questioning men who had
the reputation of wisdom, and this increased my unpopularity.*

This chapter shows how the hatred
of the present accusers was developed
from the early prejudice.

2. αὐτόματοι: construe with ἐπακολουθοῦντες.

4. μιμοῦνται, εἶτ᾽ ἐπιχειροῦσιν κτλ.:
*they imitate me, and then they under-
take,* etc. No strict sequence in time
is here marked by εἶτα, although their
readiness to imitate must logically have
preceded the acts in which their imita-
tion consisted. For a lively description
of the symptoms of such imitators, cf.
Rep. vii. 539 b, where Socrates is represented as disapproving of immature
young men's engaging in such dialectics.

6. ὀλίγα ἢ οὐδέν: cf. 17 b, 23 a.

7. ἀλλ᾽ οὐχ : equivalent to *instead
of.*

8. Σωκράτης τις: cf. τις Σωκράτης
18 b.

9. ὅ τι ποιῶν κτλ.: the participle
has the main idea, — " *What does
he do?* "

23 d

ἵνα δὲ μὴ δοκῶσιν ἀπορεῖν, τὰ κατὰ πάντων τῶν φιλοσοφούν-
των πρόχειρα ταῦτα λέγουσιν, ὅτι " τὰ μετέωρα καὶ τὰ ὑπὸ
γῆς " καὶ " θεοὺς μὴ νομίζειν " καὶ " τὸν ἥττω λόγον κρείττω
ποιεῖν." τὰ γὰρ ἀληθῆ, οἶμαι, οὐκ ἂν ἐθέλοιεν λέγειν, ὅτι
15 κατάδηλοι γίγνονται προσποιούμενοι μὲν εἰδέναι, εἰδότες
δ᾽ οὐδέν. ἅτε οὖν, οἶμαι, φιλότιμοι ὄντες καὶ σφοδροὶ καὶ ε
πολλοὶ καὶ συντεταμένως καὶ πιθανῶς λέγοντες περὶ ἐμοῦ,
ἐμπεπλήκασιν ὑμῶν τὰ ὦτα καὶ πάλαι καὶ νῦν σφοδρῶς διαβάλλοντες. ἐκ τούτων καὶ Μέλητός μοι ἐπέθετο καὶ Ἄνυτος
20 καὶ Λύκων, Μέλητος μὲν ὑπὲρ τῶν ποιητῶν ἀχθόμενος,
Ἄνυτος δ᾽ ὑπὲρ τῶν δημιουργῶν καὶ τῶν πολιτικῶν, Λύκων
δ᾽ ὑπὲρ τῶν ῥητόρων· ὥστ᾽, ὅπερ ἀρχόμενος ἐγὼ ἔλεγον, 24
θαυμάζοιμ᾽ ἂν εἰ οἷός τ᾽ εἴην ἐγὼ ὑμῶν ταύτην τὴν διαβολὴν
ἐξελέσθαι ἐν οὕτως ὀλίγῳ χρόνῳ οὕτω πολλὴν γεγονυῖαν.
25 ταῦτ᾽ ἔστιν ὑμῖν, ὦ ἄνδρες Ἀθηναῖοι, τἀληθῆ, καὶ ὑμᾶς οὔτε

11. τὰ κατὰ πάντων κτλ.: ταῦτα
means the familiar well-worn com-
monplaces. These may be found in the
Clouds of Aristophanes. Xenophon,
referring specifically to the λόγων
τέχνη, which is not lost sight of here,
uses almost the words of our text in τὸ
κοινῇ τοῖς φιλοσόφοις ὑπὸ τῶν πολλῶν ἐπι-
τιμώμενον ἐπιφέρων αὐτῷ Mem. i. 2. 31
(Critias) *making against him the charge
made by the many against philosophers
in general.* Cf. 18 b c, 19 b.

12. ὅτι: videlicet.

14. τὸ ἀληθῆ: *the truth,* namely ὅτι
κατάδηλοι κτλ. The English idiom requires the singular of an abstract noun
more frequently than the Greek, e.g.
ταῦτα often means *this.* Cf. *Phaedo* 62 d.

15. γίγνονται: as passive of ποιεῖν.

19. ἐκ τούτων: cf. ἐξ ἧς 19 a.

20. ὑπὲρ τῶν ποιητῶν κτλ.: ὑπέρ
must not be pressed. The accusers

merely represented the feelings of their
respective classes. The ῥήτορες have
not been explicitly mentioned before.
For the ποιηταί, cf. 22 a; for the πολιτικοί, cf. 21 c; for the δημιουργοί, cf.
22 d. The ῥήτορες were included in
πολιτικοί. The line between men who
habitually spoke on public questions,
and what we may call professional
speakers, was not yet clearly drawn at
Athens. All this lends weight to the
suggestion that the words καὶ τῶν πολιτικῶν are a later addition, for which
Plato is not responsible. In favor of
keeping the words, however, is the
fact that Anytus, who, like Cleon, was
a tanner (βυρσοδέψης), came into colli-
sion with the views of Socrates rather
as a πολιτικός than as a δημιουργός.

25. ταῦτ᾽ ἔστιν ὑμῖν: *there you have,*
etc., "just what I promised to tell you
at the beginning of my speech." — The

24 b

μέγα οὔτε μικρὸν ἀποκρυψάμενος ἐγὼ λέγω οὐδ᾽ ὑποστειλά·
μενος. καίτοι οἶδα σχεδὸν ὅτι τοῖς αὐτοῖς ἀπεχθάνομαι· ὃ
καὶ τεκμήριον ὅτι ἀληθῆ λέγω καὶ ὅτι αὕτη ἐστὶν ἡ διαβολὴ
ἡ ἐμὴ καὶ τὰ αἴτια ταῦτά ἐστι. καὶ ἐάν τε νῦν ἐάν ᾽τ᾽ αὖθις b
30 ζητήσητε ταῦτα, οὕτως εὑρήσετε.

XI. περὶ μὲν οὖν ὧν οἱ πρῶτοί μου κατήγοροι κατηγόρουν
αὕτη ἐστὶν ἱκανὴ ἀπολογία πρὸς ὑμᾶς· πρὸς δὲ Μέλητον τὸν
ἀγαθόν τε καὶ φιλόπολιν, ὥς φησι, καὶ τοὺς ὑστέρους, μετὰ
ταῦτα πειράσομαι ἀπολογεῖσθαι. αὖθις γὰρ δή, ὥσπερ ἐτέ-
5 ρων τούτων ὄντων κατηγόρων, λάβωμεν αὖ τὴν τούτων ἀντω-

dative is ethical. "That is true for
you."

27. **τοῖς αὐτοῖς**: i.e. by the very
words which he has uttered before the
court.

28. **τεκμήριον**: this is not a proof,
but it is a clear *indication*. Socrates
would not have told them that which
aroused their antagonism, if it had not
been true. Similarly, in his private
conversations with the Athenians.

28 f. **αὕτη, ταῦτα**: both are predi-
cates. — The two ὅτι-clauses express
the same idea, but the second as usual
is the more precise.

30. **οὕτως εὑρήσετε**: sc. ἔχοντα, —
you will find it as I say. Cf. ταῦτα
μὲν δὴ οὕτως Rep. 360 d, sc. ἔχει. —
Socrates is confident that at last, perhaps after his death, he will be understood.

XI-XV. These chapters answer
the formal charges of the accusers
before the court. Socrates avails himself of his right to examine his chief
accuser, and thus to show (1) that
Meletus had no right to bring the
charge, and (2) that the charge was
unreasonable.

XI. Now I will turn to the charges
of my later accusers. Meletus says
(*1*) that I corrupt the youth, and (*2*) that
I do not believe in the gods of the city.

2. **αὕτη**: viz. what has been said.
The pronoun is attracted to the gender
of the predicate. — **πρὸς ὑμᾶς, πρὸς Μέλητον**: cf. ἀπολογήσασθαι πρὸς τὰ ὕστερα
(sc. κατηγορημένα) καὶ τοὺς ὑστέρους (sc.
κατηγόρους) 18 a. The Greek idiom
is ἀπολογεῖσθαι πρὸς (1) τοὺς δικαστάς,
(2) τοὺς κατηγόρους, (3) τὰ κατηγορημένα.
In English the idiom is to plead (1) be-
fore the court, (2) *against* the accusers,
(3) *against* (*to*) the accusations.

3. **τὸν ἀγαθὸν κτλ.**: the addition of
ὥς φησι suggests that few encourage
Meletus in laying "this flattering unc-
tion" to his soul.

4 f. **αὖθις, αὖ**: once more, in turn.
A clear distinction is made between
the accusation of the first accusers,
who have prejudiced the public mind,
and that of Meletus. — **ὥσπερ ἐτέρων
κτλ.**: understanding that these are a
second set of accusers.

5. **λάβωμεν τὴν ἀντωμοσίαν**: as in
19 b of the accusations of the early
accusers.

24 b

μοσίαν. ἔχει δέ πως ὧδε· Σωκράτη φησὶν ἀδικεῖν τούς τε
νέους διαφθείροντα καὶ θεοὺς οὓς ἡ πόλις νομίζει οὐ νομί-
ζοντα, ἕτερα δὲ δαιμόνια καινά.   c
τὸ μὲν δὴ ἔγκλημα τοιοῦτόν ἐστιν. τούτου δὲ τοῦ ἐγκλή-
10 ματος ἓν ἕκαστον ἐξετάσωμεν. φησὶ γὰρ δὴ τοὺς νέους ἀδικεῖν με διαφθείροντα. ἐγὼ δέ γ᾽, ὦ ἄνδρες Ἀθηναῖοι, ἀδικεῖν
φημι Μέλητον, ὅτι σπουδῇ χαριεντίζεται ῥᾳδίως εἰς ἀγῶνα καθιστὰς ἀνθρώπους, περὶ πραγμάτων προσποιούμενος
σπουδάζειν καὶ κήδεσθαι ὧν οὐδὲν τούτῳ πώποτε ἐμέλησεν.
15 ὡς δὲ τοῦτο οὕτως ἔχει πειράσομαι καὶ ὑμῖν ἐπιδεῖξαι.

XII. καί μοι δεῦρο, ὦ Μέλητε, εἰπέ· ἄλλο τι ἢ περὶ πολλοῦ ποιεῖ ὅπως ὡς βέλτιστοι οἱ νεώτεροι ἔσονται ; "Ἔγωγε." d

The recent charges, at first glance, seem to be entirely different from the former charges, but on closer examination the first count, the corruption of the youth, is seen to be a development of the last count of the earlier charge, — " teaching others these same things "; while the charge of disbelief in the gods may be referred to the first count in 19 b, the pursuit of scientific questions, which were supposed to lead to atheism. The early charge of using sophistical arguments, which was disregarded by Socrates in the first part of his defense (III–X), is now omitted entirely.

Socrates answers the first count now only by showing that Meletus had no right to bring the charge, and that since it was insincere it was also presumably false. He gives a more serious reply in Chapter XXII. The other charge, also, is taken up in a playful way, while he shows his firm belief in the gods at XXIV fin. and XXXIII init.

6. πώς: shows that the quotation is not exact. Cf. Xen. Mem. init. — φησίν: sc. Meletus.

12. σπουδῇ χαριεντίζεται: this is an ὀξύμωρον, for χαριεντίζεσθαι is akin to παίζειν, the substantive to which, παιδιά, is the contradictory of σπουδή. " Meletus treats a serious business (an accusation involving life and death) as playfully as though the whole matter were a joke." Cf. 27 a. — εἰς ἀγῶνα καθιστάς: ἀγών is the usual word for a suit at law; hence the phrase ἀγωνίζεσθαι δίκην, contend in a lawsuit.

14. ὧν: construe with ἐμέλησεν. οὐδέν is adverbial, not at all. — τούτῳ: shows more feeling than αὐτῷ.

15. καὶ ὑμῖν κτλ.: " that you too may see it," " that you may see it as I do."

XII. If Meletus is not interested in the young men of the city, he has no right to bring this charge against me. He makes me out to be so unfortunate as to be the one corrupter of Athenian youth. — The man who has studied the

26 a

Ἴθι δὴ νῦν εἰπὲ τούτοις τίς αὐτοὺς βελτίους ποιεῖ; δῆλον
γὰρ ὅτι οἶσθα, μέλον γέ σοι. τὸν μὲν γὰρ διαφθείροντα
5 ἐξευρών, ὡς φής, ἐμὲ εἰσάγεις τουτοισὶ καὶ κατηγορεῖς· τὸν
δὲ δὴ βελτίους ποιοῦντα ἴθι εἰπέ, καὶ μήνυσον αὐτοῖς τίς
ἐστιν. — ὁρᾷς, ὦ Μέλητε, ὅτι σιγᾷς καὶ οὐκ ἔχεις εἰπεῖν;
καίτοι οὐκ αἰσχρόν σοι δοκεῖ εἶναι καὶ ἱκανὸν τεκμήριον οὗ
δὴ ἐγὼ λέγω, ὅτι σοι οὐδὲν μεμέληκεν; ἀλλ᾽ εἰπέ, ὠγαθέ, τίς
10 αὐτοὺς ἀμείνους ποιεῖ; "Οἱ νόμοι." Ἀλλ᾽ οὐ τοῦτο ἐρωτῶ, e
ὦ βέλτιστε, ἀλλὰ τίς ἄνθρωπος, ὅστις πρῶτον καὶ αὐτὸ τοῦτο
οἶδε, τοὺς νόμους. "Οὗτοι, ὦ Σώκρατες, — οἱ δικασταί." Πῶς
λέγεις, ὦ Μέλητε; οἵδε τοὺς νέους παιδεύειν οἷοί τ᾽ εἰσὶ καὶ
βελτίους ποιοῦσι; "Μάλιστα." Πότερον ἅπαντες, ἢ οἱ μὲν
15 αὐτῶν, οἱ δ᾽ οὔ; "Ἅπαντες." Εὖ γε νὴ τὴν Ἥραν λέγεις καὶ
πολλὴν ἀφθονίαν τῶν ὠφελούντων. τί δὲ δή; οἵδε οἱ ἀκροα-
ταὶ βελτίους ποιοῦσιν ἢ οὔ; "Καὶ οὗτοι." Τί δ᾽ οἱ βουλευταί; 25
"Καὶ οἱ βουλευταί." Ἀλλ᾽ ἄρα, ὦ Μέλητε, μὴ οἱ ἐν τῇ ἐκκλη-

influences which tend to the better-
ment or the corruption of the youth,
can tell what improves as well as what
corrupts. But Meletus does not know
this, and so shows that he has no real
interest in this matter.

4. μέλον: accusative absolute. —
τὸν διαφθείροντα κτλ.: having found out
who corrupts them, you bring me before
this court and make y ur accusation.

5. εἰσάγεις: you summon into court,
commonly with εἰς δικαστήριον or εἰς
τοὺς δικαστάς, instead of which τουτοισὶ
is used. Sometimes also εἰσάγειν is
found with the genitive of the charge.
Cf. 26 a. The word is used strictly of
the magistrates, but not infrequently
it is said of the plaintiff, whose charge
causes the magistrate εἰσάγειν, to bring
into court, the suit.

8. τεκμήριον: one may presume
that if Meletus knew, he would tell.
Though his silence is not absolute
proof, for he may have other motives,
yet it is an indication of his ignorance.

10. οὐ τοῦτο ἐρωτῶ: that is not my
question.

12. οὗτοι, οἱ δικασταί: these men,
the judges. The οἵδε which follows,
strictly speaking, includes only the
ἡλιασταί who were present at the trial;
but evidently they are taken as representing all δικασταί.

15. λέγεις: is modified by εὖ, and
its force is continued as the governing
verb for ἀφθονίαν.

18. ἀλλ᾽ ἄρα μή: questions with μή
take a negative answer for granted.
The use of ἄρα here marks the last
stage in Socrates's enumeration. Only

25 a

σίᾳ, οἱ ἐκκλησιασταί, διαφθείρουσι τοὺς νεωτέρους ; ἢ κἀκεῖ-
20 νοι βελτίους ποιοῦσιν ἅπαντες ; "Κἀκεῖνοι." Πάντες ἄρα, ὡς
ἔοικεν, Ἀθηναῖοι καλοὺς κἀγαθοὺς ποιοῦσι πλὴν ἐμοῦ, ἐγὼ δὲ
μόνος διαφθείρω. οὕτω λέγεις ; "Πάνυ σφόδρα ταῦτα λέγω."
Πολλήν γ' ἐμοῦ κατέγνωκας δυστυχίαν. καί μοι ἀπόκριναι·
ἦ καὶ περὶ ἵππους οὕτω σοι δοκεῖ ἔχειν· οἱ μὲν βελτίους b
25 ποιοῦντες αὐτοὺς πάντες ἄνθρωποι εἶναι, εἷς δέ τις ὁ διαφθείρων ; ἢ τοὐναντίον τούτου πᾶν εἷς μέν τις ὁ βελτίους οἷός
τ' ὢν ποιεῖν ἢ πάνυ ὀλίγοι, οἱ ἱππικοί· οἱ δὲ πολλοί, ἐάνπερ
συνῶσι καὶ χρῶνται ἵπποις, διαφθείρουσιν ; οὐχ οὕτως ἔχει,
ὦ Μέλητε, καὶ περὶ ἵππων καὶ τῶν ἄλλων ἁπάντων ζῴων;
30 πάντως δήπου, ἐάν τε σὺ καὶ Ἄνυτος οὐ φῆτε ἐάν τε φῆτε·
πολλὴ γὰρ ἄν τις εὐδαιμονία εἴη περὶ τοὺς νέους, εἰ εἷς μὲν
μόνος αὐτοὺς διαφθείρει, οἱ δ' ἄλλοι ὠφελοῦσιν. ἀλλὰ γάρ, c
ὦ Μέλητε, ἱκανῶς ἐπιδείκνυσαι ὅτι οὐδεπώποτε ἐφρόντισας
τῶν νέων, καὶ σαφῶς ἀποφαίνεις τὴν σαυτοῦ ἀμέλειαν, ὅτι
35 οὐδέν σοι μεμέληκε περὶ ὧν ἐμὲ εἰσάγεις.

the ἐκκλησιασταί are left. "Somebody
in Athens is corrupting the youth.
We have seen that it is nobody else,
I hope it is not these gentlemen!"
But this suggestion is absurd, hence
πάντες ἄρα Ἀθηναῖοι κτλ.

19. οἱ ἐκκλησιασταί : all Athenians,
twenty years of age, in full standing
(ἐπίτιμοι), were members of the public
assembly (ἐκκλησία) at Athens.

24. περὶ ἵππους : this question
doubtless surprised Meletus, but it
was entirely in the manner of Socrates,
who found analogies for his arguments
in very familiar things. For the
thought, cf. Crito 47 b. — οἱ ποιοῦντες :
sc. δοκοῦσιν.

26. τοὐναντίον πᾶν : adverbial accusative. — In Crito 47 b, Socrates appeals

from the many and ignorant to the
few, or the one, who has special
knowledge.

27. οἱ δὲ κτλ. : here the δέ-clause is
subordinate, and δέ may be translated while.

30. πάντως δήπου : before this,
Socrates waits a moment in order to
give Meletus opportunity to answer.
— οὐ φῆτε : is used as one word,
deny, and so the οὐ need not become
μή in a condition. GMT. 384. — The
answer no is made prominent by the
order of clauses.

35. ὅτι οὐδέν σοι κτλ. : appended to
explain τὴν σαυτοῦ ἀμέλειαν. These
words take us back neatly to the close
of the preceding chapter, where Socrates said he would try to prove the

25 d

XIII. ἔτι δ' ἡμῖν εἰπέ, ὦ πρὸς Διὸς Μέλητε, πότερόν ἐστιν
οἰκεῖν ἄμεινον ἐν πολίταις χρηστοῖς ἢ πονηροῖς; ὦ τάν,
ἀπόκριναι· οὐδὲν γάρ τοι χαλεπὸν ἐρωτῶ. οὐχ οἱ μὲν πονη-
ροὶ κακόν τι ἐργάζονται τοὺς ἀεὶ ἐγγυτάτω ἑαυτῶν ὄντας,
5 οἱ δ' ἀγαθοὶ ἀγαθόν τι; "Πάνυ γε." Ἔστιν οὖν ὅστις βούλεται ὑπὸ τῶν συνόντων βλάπτεσθαι μᾶλλον ἢ ὠφελεῖσθαι; d
ἀποκρίνου, ὦ ἀγαθέ· καὶ γὰρ ὁ νόμος κελεύει ἀποκρίνεσθαι.
ἔσθ' ὅστις βούλεται βλάπτεσθαι; "Οὐ δῆτα." Φέρε δή,
πότερον ἐμὲ εἰσάγεις δεῦρο ὡς διαφθείροντα τοὺς νεωτέρους,
10 καὶ πονηροτέρους ποιοῦντα, ἑκόντα ἢ ἄκοντα; "Ἑκόντα
ἔγωγε." Τί δῆτα, ὦ Μέλητε; τοσοῦτον σὺ ἐμοῦ σοφώτερος

indifference of Meletus, and thus that
he had no right to bring this suit.
Here at last is the pun upon Meletus's
name (cf. also **26 b**), for which the
constant recurrence of the idea of
μεμέληκε (variously expressed, ἐμέλησεν
and περὶ πολλοῦ ποιεῖ in **24 c**, μέλον γέ
σοι and μεμέληκεν in **24 d**) has paved
the way. For similar plays upon
words, cf. ὁ μηδὲν εἰδὼς Οἰδίπους Soph.
O. T. 397, Παυσανίου δὲ παυσαμένου
Symp. **185 c**,

Old Gaunt indeed, and gaunt in being
old, ...
Within me grief hath kept a tedious fast;
Gaunt am I for the grave; gaunt as a
grave

Rich. II ii. 1. — περὶ ὧν: i.e. τούτων
περὶ ὧν.

XIII. *The charge that I willingly
corrupt my young associates cannot be
true. I am experienced enough to know
that if I should make them bad, I should
myself suffer ill from them. So, if I
corrupt them, I corrupt them unwillingly. In that case I should receive
instruction, not punishment.*

1. **ὦ πρὸς Διὸς Μέλητε**: this order
of words gives prominence to the name,
which Meletus does not seem to deserve.
(Strictly Μέλητος was one for whom
care or love was felt, not one who
felt care; but in puns men are not
over particular as to minor matters.)

4. **τοὺς ἐγγυτάτω ἑαυτῶν ὄντας**:
i.e. those who were most continually
associating with them.

7. **ἀπόκρινου**: this imperative implies a pause. The reluctance of Meletus in answering is manifest. From
his observation of Socrates's conversations, he may suspect that he is to be
led into an absurdity. At any rate, he
might reasonably claim that such questions had nothing to do with the case
before the court, and that he was not
required to answer. So at **27 b** Meletus declined to answer questions which
seemed very remote from the case.

10. **ἑκόντα**: construe with διαφθείροντα.

11. **τοσοῦτον σὺ** κτλ.: τηλικοῦτος
and τηλικόσδε, according to the context, mean indifferently *so young* or *so*

25 d

εἰ τηλικούτου ὄντος τηλικόσδε ὤν, ὥστε σὺ μὲν ἔγνωκας ὅτι
οἱ μὲν κακοὶ κακόν τι ἐργάζονται ἀεὶ τοὺς μάλιστα πλησίον
ἑαυτῶν, οἱ δ᾽ ἀγαθοὶ ἀγαθόν· ἐγὼ δὲ δὴ εἰς τοσοῦτον ἀμα- e
15 θίας ἥκω, ὥστε καὶ τοῦτο ἀγνοῶ, ὅτι, ἐάν τινα μοχθηρὸν
ποιήσω τῶν συνόντων, κινδυνεύσω κακόν τι λαβεῖν ἀπ᾽ αὐτοῦ,
ὥστε τοῦτο τὸ τοσοῦτον κακὸν ἑκὼν ποιῶ, ὡς φῂς σύ; ταῦτα
ἐγώ σοι οὐ πείθομαι, ὦ Μέλητε, οἶμαι δ᾽ οὐδ᾽ ἄλλον ἀνθρώπων οὐδένα· ἀλλ᾽ ἢ οὐ διαφθείρω, ἤ, εἰ διαφθείρω, ἄκων, 26
20 ὥστε σύ γε κατ᾽ ἀμφότερα ψεύδει. εἰ δ᾽ ἄκων διαφθείρω,
τῶν τοιούτων καὶ ἀκουσίων ἁμαρτημάτων οὐ δεῦρο νόμος
εἰσάγειν ἐστίν, ἀλλ᾽ ἰδίᾳ λαβόντα διδάσκειν καὶ νουθετεῖν·
δῆλον γὰρ ὅτι ἐὰν μάθω παύσομαι ὅ γ᾽ ἄκων ποιῶ. σὺ δὲ
συγγενέσθαι μέν μοι καὶ διδάξαι ἔφυγες καὶ οὐκ ἠθέλησας,

---

old. Cf. below, 26 e fin., and νέος γάρ
τίς μοι φαίνεται καὶ ἀγνώς· ὀνομάζουσι
μέντοι αὐτὸν, ὡς ἐγῷμαι, Μέλητον, ἔστι δὲ
τὸν δῆμον Πιτθεύς, εἴ τιν᾽ ἐν νῷ ἔχεις Πιτθέα
Μέλητον, οἷον τετανότριχα καὶ οὐ πάνυ
εὐγένειον, ἐπίγρυπον δέ Euthyphro 2 b,
a young person who, I conceive, is not
much known: his name is Meletus and
Pithos is his deme. — perhaps you remember a Meletus of Pithos, who has
rather a beak, a scrubby beard, and lank
long hair. — Notice the chiastic order :

$$\sigma\acute{\upsilon} \diagdown \acute{\epsilon}\mu o\hat{\upsilon}$$
$$\tau\eta\lambda\iota\kappa o\acute{\upsilon}\tau o\upsilon \diagup \tau\eta\lambda\iota\kappa\acute{o}\sigma\delta\epsilon$$

12. σὺ μὲν κτλ. : this clause is subordinate in thought, — "while you
have learned." Cf. εἰς μὲν κτλ. 25 b,
ὅτε μὲν κτλ. 28 e.

14. ἀμαθίας : partitive genitive of
degree, with τοσοῦτον.

15. ὅτι κτλ. : explains τοῦτο. Cf.
26 b.—μοχθηρόν: masculine,—a predicate object; not a cognate accusative
like κακόν τι l. 13.

18. οἶμαι οὐδένα : sc. πείθεσθαι.

19. ἤ, ἄκων : the verb is supplied
from its subordinate clause, εἰ διαφθείρω.
Socrates believed that all sin was involuntary, οὐδεὶς ἑκὼν ἁμαρτάνει. No
man, in his view, would do wrong if
he really knew what was right. Here
the matter is treated from a strictly
practical point of view.

21. καὶ ἀκουσίων : this explains
τοιούτων. Cf. ἀδικεῖ καὶ περιεργάζεται
19 b, τῷ δὲ νόμῳ πειστέον καὶ ἀπολογητέον
19 a, in which καί introduces a more
distinct statement of the former idea.
—ἁμαρτημάτων : genitive of the charge,
with εἰσάγω. — οὐ δεῦρο κτλ. : for οὐ
νόμος ἐστὶν δεῦρο εἰσάγειν.

23. παύσομαι κτλ. : from ποιῶ supply ποιῶν. Such an ellipsis as this is
obvious, and therefore not uncommon.

24. συγγενέσθαι : see on συνεῖναι
20 a. — ἔφυγες κτλ. : you declined.
Socrates offered Meletus every opportunity for such an effort.

26 c

25 δεῦρο δ' εἰσάγεις, οἷ νόμος ἐστὶν εἰσάγειν τοὺς κολάσεως
δεομένους, ἀλλ' οὐ μαθήσεως.

XIV. ἀλλὰ γάρ, ὦ ἄνδρες Ἀθηναῖοι, τοῦτο μὲν δῆλον ὅ
ἐγὼ ἔλεγον, ὅτι Μελήτῳ τούτων οὔτε μέγα οὔτε μικρὸν πώ- b
ποτ' ἐμέλησεν· ὅμως δὲ δὴ λέγε ἡμῖν, πῶς με φῂς διαφθείρειν, ὦ Μέλητε, τοὺς νεωτέρους; ἢ δῆλον δὴ ὅτι, κατὰ τὴν
5 γραφὴν ἣν ἐγράψω, θεοὺς διδάσκοντα μὴ νομίζειν οὓς ἡ πόλις
νομίζει, ἕτερα δὲ δαιμόνια καινά. οὐ ταῦτα λέγεις ὅτι διδάσκων διαφθείρω; "Πάνυ μὲν οὖν σφόδρα ταῦτα λέγω." Πρὸς
αὐτῶν τοίνυν, ὦ Μέλητε, τούτων τῶν θεῶν ὧν νῦν ὁ λόγος
ἐστίν, εἰπὲ ἔτι σαφέστερον καὶ ἐμοὶ καὶ τοῖς ἀνδράσι του-
10 τοισί. ἐγὼ γὰρ οὐ δύναμαι μαθεῖν πότερον λέγεις διδάσκειν c
με νομίζειν εἶναί τινας θεούς, καὶ αὐτὸς ἄρα νομίζω εἶναι
θεούς, καὶ οὐκ εἰμὶ τὸ παράπαν ἄθεος οὐδὲ ταύτῃ ἀδικῶ, — οὐ
μέντοι οὕσπερ γ' ἡ πόλις, ἀλλ' ἑτέρους, καὶ τοῦτ' ἔστιν ὅ μοι
ἐγκαλεῖς, ὅτι ἑτέρους· ἢ παντάπασί με φῂς οὔτ' αὐτὸν νομί-

XIV. *Clearly Meletus has paid no
attention to this subject, and I might
demand that the case be thrown out of
court on this plea. Yet, Meletus, how
do you say that I corrupt the youth?
By teaching them not to believe in the
gods? You seem to forget that you have
brought not Anaxagoras but Socrates to
the bar of this court.*

Socrates does not discuss the charge
as stated in the indictment, that he
does not believe in the city's gods, but
in order that his accuser may be involved in an inconsistency he leads
Meletus to say that Socrates believes
in no gods at all.

1. **ἀλλὰ γάρ** : marks a transition.

2. **ὅτι Μελήτῳ** κτλ. : cf. 24 c, 25 c.
— **τούτων** : for the genitive, cf. 24 c. —
οὔτε μέγα κτλ. : cf. 19 d, 21 b.

4. **ἢ δῆλον ὅτι** κτλ. : Socrates an-
ticipates the answer.

5. **διδάσκοντα** : construe with μέ as
subject of διαφθείρειν νεωτέρους.

6. **ταῦτα** : construe with διδάσκων
though ταῦτα in l. 7 is object of λέγω.

7. **πάνυ μὲν οὖν** κτλ. : Meletus
agrees, and asserts it with all energy.

8. **ὧν ὁ λόγος** : that is, οὓς λέγομεν.
A preposition is more usual, but compare τὸ Μεγαρέων ψήφισμα Thuc. i. 140.
3 with τὸ περὶ Μεγαρέων ψήφισμα id.
139. 1. In many cases the genitive is
used without a preposition, especially
where περί would seem appropriate.

10. **πότερον** : the second member
of the sentence begins with ἢ παντάπασι
l. 14.

13. **τοῦτο** : explained by ὅτι ἑτέρους
(νομίζω).

26 c
15 ζειν θεοὺς τούς τ᾽ ἄλλους ταῦτα διδάσκειν. "Ταῦτα λέγω, ὡς
τὸ παράπαν οὐ νομίζεις θεούς." Ὦ θαυμάσιε Μέλητε, ἵνα τί
ταῦτα λέγεις; οὐδ᾽ ἥλιον οὐδὲ σελήνην ἄρα νομίζω θεοὺς d
εἶναι, ὥσπερ οἱ ἄλλοι ἄνθρωποι: "Μὰ Δί᾽, ὦ ἄνδρες δικασταί, ἐπεὶ τὸν μὲν ἥλιον λίθον φησὶν εἶναι, τὴν δὲ σελήνην
20 γῆν." Ἀναξαγόρου οἴει κατηγορεῖν, ὦ φίλε Μέλητε, καὶ
οὕτω καταφρονεῖς τῶνδε καὶ οἴει αὐτοὺς ἀπείρους γραμμάτων εἶναι, ὥστ᾽ οὐκ εἰδέναι ὅτι τὰ Ἀναξαγόρου βιβλία τοῦ

15. τί: correlative with οὔτε.

17. οὐδὲ ... οὐδέ: not even ... nor
yet. — ἄρα: the statement of Meletus
is met by Socrates in a tone of playful
irony. Every religious-minded Greek
reverenced the sun. No appeal was
more solemn and sincere than that to
ἥλιος πανόπτης. Accordingly this appeal is constantly met with in the most
moving situations created by tragedy.
Ajax, when in despair he falls upon
his sword, and outraged Prometheus
from his rock, both cry out to the sun.
Ion, before entering upon his peaceful
duties in the temple, looks first with
gladness toward the sun. Both Heracles and Agaue are saved from madness when they once more can clearly
recognize the sun. That Socrates
habitually paid reverence to this divinity not made by human hands is here
suggested, and is still more plainly
shown in *Symp.* **220 d.**

18. ὦ ἄνδρες δικασταί: Meletus uses
this form of address, which Plato does
not put into the mouth of Socrates in
the first two divisions of his speech.
See on ὦ ἄνδρες κτλ. **17 a.**

20. Ἀναξαγόρου: Diogenes Laërtius, ii. 3. 4, reports that Anaxagoras
declared τὸν ἥλιον μύδρον εἶναι διάπυρον

(*a red-hot mass of stone or iron*) καὶ
μείζω τῆς Πελοποννήσου ... τὴν δὲ σελήνην
οἰκήσεις ἔχειν καὶ λόφους καὶ φάραγγας
(*ravines*). From this last apparently
the public inferred that Anaxagoras
held the belief which Meletus attrib-
utes to Socrates, τὴν δὲ σελήνην γῆν.
The real view of Socrates in regard to
such an account of the "all-seeing
sun" as was attributed to Anaxagoras
is represented, perhaps, by the parenthetical refutation introduced by Xenophon in *Mem.* iv. 7. 7. For a criticism
of Anaxagoras which is more worthy
of Socrates himself, see the one attributed to him in the *Phaedo,* **97 c–
99 d.** The capital objection there made
to Anaxagoras is that he unfolds his
dogmatic views ἀμελήσας τὰς ὡς ἀληθῶς
αἰτίας λέγειν, and really makes much
less use of νοῦς than one would expect
from his professions.

21. οὕτω: qualifying ἀπείρους below
as well as καταφρονεῖς. — γραμμάτων:
γράμματα stand in the same relation to
μαθήματα as litterae to disciplinae.

22. οὐκ εἰδέναι: οὐ is used because
Socrates wishes to suggest the most
positive form of statement, οὕτως ἄπειροι
γραμμάτων εἰσὶν ὥστε οὐκ ἴσασι ὅτι κτλ.
This vivid use of οὐ for μή in infinitive

27 a

Κλαζομενίου γέμει τούτων τῶν λόγων; καὶ δὴ καὶ οἱ νέοι
ταῦτα παρ' ἐμοῦ μανθάνουσιν, ἃ ἔξεστιν ἐνίοτε, εἰ πάνυ πολ-
25 λοῦ, δραχμῆς ἐκ τῆς ὀρχήστρας πριαμένοις Σωκράτους κατα- e
γελᾶν, ἐὰν προσποιῆται ἑαυτοῦ εἶναι, ἄλλως τε καὶ οὕτως
ἄτοπα ὄντα. ἀλλ' ὦ πρὸς Διός, οὑτωσί σοι δοκῶ οὐδένα
νομίζειν θεὸν εἶναι; " Οὐ μέντοι μὰ Δί', οὐδ' ὁπωστιοῦν."
Ἄπιστός γ' εἶ, ὦ Μέλητε, καὶ ταῦτα μέντοι, ὡς ἐμοὶ δοκεῖς,
30 σαυτῷ. ἐμοὶ μὲν γὰρ δοκεῖ οὑτοσί, ὦ ἄνδρες Ἀθηναῖοι, πάνυ
εἶναι ὑβριστὴς καὶ ἀκόλαστος, καὶ ἀτεχνῶς τὴν γραφὴν
ταύτην ὕβρει τινὶ καὶ ἀκολασίᾳ καὶ νεότητι γράψασθαι.
ἔοικε γὰρ ὥσπερ αἴνιγμα συντιθέντι διαπειρωμένῳ· "Ἆρα 27
γνώσεται Σωκράτης ὁ σοφὸς δὴ ἐμοῦ χαριεντιζομένου καὶ

clauses after ὥστε is not uncommon
where it is indifferent whether the indicative or infinitive is used.

23. καὶ δὴ καί: *and now you expect people to believe that it is from
me,* etc.

24. ἃ . . . ἐκ τῆς ὀρχήστρας πριαμένοις: this passage has been inter-
preted by some scholars as referring
to the philosophical utterances of some
of the choral odes of tragedy (and the
drachme then would be the price of a
season-ticket to the theatre), but it is
more naturally understood as meaning
that Anaxagoras's book Περὶ Φύσεως
was to be purchased not infrequently,
very likely second-hand, for a moderate sum. It was not always in stock,
and the prices may have varied.
Then the ὀρχήστρα in mind, probably,
was not the orchestra of the great
theatre of Dionysus, but a part of the
agora. (See Dörpfeld, *Das griechische
Theater.* p. 8.)

25. For the use of ἐκ, instead of
ἐν τῇ ὀρχήστρᾳ, cf. **32 b.**

26. ἄλλως τε καὶ κτλ.: "without taking even their singularity into account,
the youths must know well enough
that these are not my doctrines."

27. ἀλλ' ὦ πρὸς Διός: cf. ὦ πρὸς
κτλ. **25 c.** Socrates does not complete
his clause, being seemingly at a loss
for a suitable epithet. — This marks the
transition to a second argument against
the charge of atheism, and hence Meletus is made to repeat the charge.
Socrates has called attention to the
absurdity of the charge viewed as a
statement of fact. Now he considers
it as a statement of opinion (οὑτωσί σοι
δοκῶ;), and urges that Meletus cannot
really hold such an opinion because
it conflicts with another of Meletus's
own views.

29. ἄπιστος κτλ.: alludes to οὐ πείθομαι **25 e.**

33. ὥσπερ . . . συντιθέντι: explains
διαπειρωμένῳ.

34. σοφὸς δή: δή marks irony. —
χαριεντιζομένου: for the participle in
the genitive, cf. οἰομένων **22 c.**

27 a
35 ἐναντί' ἐμαυτῷ λέγοντος, ἢ ἐξαπατήσω αὐτὸν καὶ τοὺς ἄλλους τοὺς ἀκούοντας;" οὗτος γὰρ ἐμοὶ φαίνεται τὰ ἐναντία λέγειν αὐτὸς ἑαυτῷ ἐν τῇ γραφῇ, ὥσπερ ἂν εἰ εἴποι
" Ἀδικεῖ Σωκράτης θεοὺς οὐ νομίζων, ἀλλὰ θεοὺς νομίζων."
καίτοι τοῦτό ἐστι παίζοντος.

XV. συνεπισκέψασθε δή, ὦ ἄνδρες, ᾗ μοι φαίνεται ταῦτα
λέγειν· σὺ δ' ἡμῖν ἀπόκριναι, ὦ Μέλητε· ὑμεῖς δ', ὅπερ
κατ' ἀρχὰς ὑμᾶς παρῃτησάμην, μέμνησθέ μοι μὴ θορυβεῖν, b
ἐὰν ἐν τῷ εἰωθότι τρόπῳ τοὺς λόγους ποιῶμαι.

5 ἔστιν ὅστις ἀνθρώπων, ὦ Μέλητε, ἀνθρώπεια μὲν νομίζει
πράγματ' εἶναι, ἀνθρώπους δ' οὐ νομίζει; — ἀποκρινέσθω,
ὦ ἄνδρες, καὶ μὴ ἄλλα καὶ ἄλλα θορυβείτω· ἔσθ' ὅστις
ἵππους μὲν οὐ νομίζει, ἱππικὰ δὲ πράγματα; ἢ αὐλητὰς μὲν
οὐ νομίζει εἶναι, αὐλητικὰ δὲ πράγματα; οὐκ ἔστιν, ὦ ἄριστε
10 ἀνδρῶν· εἰ μὴ σὺ βούλει ἀποκρίνασθαι, ἐγὼ σοὶ λέγω,
καὶ τοῖς ἄλλοις τουτοισί. ἀλλὰ τὸ ἐπὶ τούτῳ γ' ἀπόκριναι·

38. θεοὺς οὐ νομίζων κτλ. : Socrates here states the absurdity which he makes clear in the next following chapter.

39. παίζοντος: the part of a man in jest, predicate genitive of characteristic.

XV. Meletus acknowledges, and even charges, that I believe in divine things, — but in that case I must believe in divine beings and gods.

1. ταῦτα: i.e. ἀδικεῖ Σωκράτης . . . θεοὺς νομίζων.

3. παρῃτησάμην: in 17 c.

4. τοὺς λόγους: the article here has nearly the force of a possessive.

5. Here again Socrates employs the inductive method; but, while at 25 a the case was so clear that he was satisfied with a single example, here

he uses three before he applies the principle to the case in hand.

7. ἄλλα καὶ ἄλλα κτλ. : be always disturbing in one way or another. The accusative is after the analogy of θόρυβον θορυβεῖν, i.e. cognate. — Here Meletus makes no answer. Cf. 25 d. The words in c below, ὑπὸ τουτωνὶ ἀναγκαζόμενος, suggest that the court indicated its desire that Meletus should reply, — but this was informal, many of the judges shouting "Answer," rather than by a decision of the presiding magistrate. Of course, many "waits" of one kind or another may have occurred during such an examination as is here reported.

9. ἄριστε: cf. βέλτιστε 24 e.

11. τὸ ἐπὶ τούτῳ κτλ. : answer at least the next question.

27 d

ἔσθ' ὅστις δαιμόνια μὲν νομίζει πράγματ' εἶναι, δαίμονας c
δ' οὐ νομίζει; "Οὐκ ἔστιν." Ὡς ὤνησας ὅτι μόγις ἀπεκρίνω
ὑπὸ τουτωνὶ ἀναγκαζόμενος. οὐκοῦν δαιμόνια μὲν φῄς με
15 καὶ νομίζειν καὶ διδάσκειν, εἴτ' οὖν καινὰ εἴτε παλαιά·
ἀλλ' οὖν δαιμόνιά γε νομίζω κατὰ τὸν σὸν λόγον, καὶ ταῦτα
καὶ διωμόσω ἐν τῇ ἀντιγραφῇ. εἰ δὲ δαιμόνια νομίζω, καὶ
δαίμονας δήπου πολλὴ ἀνάγκη νομίζειν μέ ἐστιν· οὐχ οὕτως
ἔχει; ἔχει δή· τίθημι γάρ σε ὁμολογοῦντα, ἐπειδὴ οὐκ ἀπο-
20 κρίνει. τοὺς δὲ δαίμονας οὐχὶ ἤτοι θεούς γ' ἡγούμεθα ἢ d
θεῶν παῖδας; φῂς ἢ οὔ; "Πάνυ γε." Οὐκοῦν εἴ περ δαίμονας
ἡγοῦμαι, ὡς σὺ φῄς, εἰ μὲν θεοί τινές εἰσιν οἱ δαίμονες,
τοῦτ' ἂν εἴη ὃ ἐγώ φημί σε αἰνίττεσθαι καὶ χαριεντίζεσθαι,

16. κατὰ τὸν σὸν λόγον: merely
repeats φῄς above.

17. τῇ ἀντιγραφῇ: in its stricter
use, this means the written affidavit
put in as a rejoinder by the accused;
rarely, as here, the accusation or the
written affidavit of the accuser.

19. ἔχει: repeated by way of answering yes, after οὕτως ἔχει. Similarly the simple verb is often repeated
after a compound. Cf. Crito 44 d.

20. τοὺς δαίμονας κτλ.: the definition here given is consistent with Greek
usage from Homer to Plato. In Homer
θεός and δαίμων, applied to any divinity
in particular or to divinity in general,
are all but interchangeable terms. The
distinction between them, if distinction
there is, suggests itself rather in the
adjectives derived from them than in
the two nouns themselves. Hesiod,
Op. 108–125, calls the guardian spirits
that watch over men δαίμονες: to the
rank of δαίμονες he says those were
raised who lived on earth during the
golden age. He distinguishes between

θεοί, δαίμονες, and ἥρωες, and this same
distinction is attributed to Thales. On
this Plato based the fancy expressed
in the Symposium (202 e): πᾶν τὸ δαιμόνιον μεταξύ (intermediate) ἐστι θεοῦ τε
καὶ θνητοῦ . . . ἑρμηνεῦον καὶ διαπορθμεῦον
(interpreting and convoying) θεοῖς τὰ
παρ' ἀνθρώπων καὶ ἀνθρώποις τὰ παρὰ θεῶν
τῶν μὲν τὰς δεήσεις καὶ θυσίας, τῶν δὲ τὰς
ἐπιτάξεις τε καὶ ἀμοιβὰς (commands and
rewards) τῶν θυσιῶν.

21. φῂς ἢ οὔ: yes or no? — εἴ περ
δαίμονας κτλ.: a protasis with two
subordinate alternative conditions, (1)
εἰ μὲν θεοί εἰσιν οἱ δαίμονες and (2) εἰ
δ' αὖ οἱ δαίμονες θεῶν παῖδές εἰσι. The
apodosis for the group is, θεοὺς ἡγοῦμαι
εἶναι. — "If I believe in δαίμονες, I must
believe in θεοί, for δαίμονες are either
θεοί or παῖδες θεῶν."

23. τοῦτ' ἂν εἴη: to τοῦτο ὃ σε . . .
χαριεντίζεσθαι is appended φάναι, which
explains it, and has the same subject.
All this points back to θεοὺς οὐ νομίζων
ἀλλὰ θεοὺς νομίζων 27 a. — ὃ: cognate
accusative with αἰνίττεσθαι.

27 d

θεοὺς οὐχ ἡγούμενον φάναι ἐμὲ θεοὺς αὖ ἡγεῖσθαι πάλιν,
25 ἐπειδήπερ γε δαίμονας ἡγοῦμαι· εἰ δ' αὖ οἱ δαίμονες θεῶν
παῖδές εἰσι νόθοι τινὲς ἢ ἐκ νυμφῶν ἢ ἔκ τινων ἄλλων, ὧν
δὴ καὶ λέγονται, τίς ἂν ἀνθρώπων θεῶν μὲν παῖδας ἡγοῖτο
εἶναι, θεοὺς δὲ μή; ὁμοίως γὰρ ἂν ἄτοπον εἴη, ὥσπερ ἂν
εἴ τις ἵππων μὲν παῖδας ἡγοῖτο [ἢ] καὶ ὄνων, τοὺς ἡμι- e
30 όνους, ἵππους δὲ καὶ ὄνους μὴ ἡγοῖτο εἶναι. ἀλλ', ὦ Μέλητε,
οὐκ ἔστιν ὅπως σὺ [ταῦτα] οὐχὶ ἀποπειρώμενος ἡμῶν
ἐγράψω τὴν γραφὴν ταύτην ἢ ἀπορῶν ὅ τι ἐγκαλοῖς ἐμοὶ
ἀληθὲς ἀδίκημα· ὅπως δὲ σύ τινα πείθοις ἂν καὶ σμικρὸν
νοῦν ἔχοντα ἀνθρώπων, ὡς τοῦ αὐτοῦ ἐστὶ καὶ δαιμόνια καὶ
35 θεῖα ἡγεῖσθαι, καὶ αὖ τοῦ αὐτοῦ μήτε δαίμονας μήτε θεοὺς
μήθ' ἥρωας, οὐδεμία μηχανή ἐστιν.

28

26. ὧν: equivalent to ἐξ ὧν, for
"when the antecedent stands before
the relative, a preposition belonging to
both usually appears only with the
first."

27. δή: *you know.*

31. ἡμῶν: i.e. Socrates and the
judges.

32. ἢ ἀπορῶν ὅ τι κτλ.: this no
doubt was Socrates's real view of the
case of Meletus (cf. 23 d), whereas all
that precedes is only to bring home to
the court how foolish and self-contra-
dictory the charge is. — ἐγκαλοῖς: the
optative represents Meletus's original
reflection τί ἐγκαλῶ; The subjunctive
might have been retained.

33. ὅπως δὲ σὺ κτλ.: here Socrates
closes his argument to the effect that
it is a contradiction in terms to say
of one and the same man (1) that he
is an out-and-out atheist, and (2) that
he believes in δαιμόνια. Whoever believes in δαιμόνια must believe also in

θεοί. The second τοῦ αὐτοῦ must be regarded as redundant. — ὅπως means
how or *by which*, with μηχανή.

XVI–XXII. A digression, on Socrates's life. The key-note of chapters
XVI–XX is, "Injustice is worse than
death." This note is struck in **28 b, 29 b,
32 a d, 33 a.** Cf. *Crito* 48 c; μέγιστον
τῶν κακῶν τυγχάνει ὂν τὸ ἀδικεῖν *Gorg.*
469 b; and αὐτὸ μὲν γὰρ τὸ ἀποθνῄσκειν
οὐδεὶς φοβεῖται, ὅστις μὴ παντάπασιν ἀλόγιστός τε καὶ ἄνανδρός ἐστιν, τὸ δ' ἀδικεῖν
φοβεῖται *Gorg.* **522 e.** Socrates shows
how his life has been ruled by this
principle, and gives examples of his
conduct in obedience to it. Chapters
XIX, XX, and part of XXI account
for his general abstention from public
affairs. Then he takes up once more
Meletus's charge, that he is a corrupter of youth, and expresses surprise that none of the sufferers or
their relatives have appeared to aid in
his prosecution.

28 b

XVI. Ἀλλὰ γάρ, ὦ ἄνδρες Ἀθηναῖοι, ὡς μὲν ἐγὼ οὐκ ἀδικῶ κατὰ τὴν Μελήτου γραφήν, οὐ πολλῆς μοι δοκεῖ εἶναι
ἀπολογίας, ἀλλὰ ἱκανὰ καὶ ταῦτα· ὃ δὲ καὶ ἐν τοῖς ἔμπροσθεν
ἔλεγον, ὅτι πολλή μοι ἀπέχθεια γέγονε καὶ πρὸς πολλούς,
5 εὖ ἴστε ὅτι ἀληθές ἐστι. καὶ τοῦτ' ἔστιν ὃ ἐμὲ αἱρήσει, ἐάν περ
αἱρῇ, οὐ Μέλητος οὐδ' Ἄνυτος, ἀλλ' ἡ τῶν πολλῶν διαβολή
τε καὶ φθόνος. ἃ δὴ πολλοὺς καὶ ἄλλους καὶ ἀγαθοὺς ἄνδρας
ᾕρηκεν, οἶμαι δὲ καὶ αἱρήσειν· οὐδὲν δὲ δεινὸν μὴ ἐν ἐμοὶ στῇ. **b**
ἴσως δ' ἂν οὖν εἴποι τις· " Εἶτ' οὐκ αἰσχύνει, ὦ Σώκρατες,
10 τοιοῦτον ἐπιτήδευμα ἐπιτηδεύσας, ἐξ οὗ κινδυνεύεις νυνὶ ἀποθανεῖν ;" ἐγὼ δὲ τούτῳ ἂν δίκαιον λόγον ἀντείποιμι, ὅτι "Οὐ
καλῶς λέγεις, ὦ ἄνθρωπε, εἰ οἴει δεῖν κίνδυνον ὑπολογίζεσθαι

XVI. *What has been said suffices as
a reply to the charges of Meletus. If I
am convicted, it will be because of the
prejudice of the masses. Does any one
say that I ought to be ashamed of having
incurred this ill-will? No. For in a
matter of duty a man ought not to
take into consideration the chance of
death.*

1. ἀλλὰ γὰρ κτλ.: this marks a
transition, — dismissing one topic in
order to make room for the next.

3. ἐν τοῖς ἔμπροσθεν: viz. at **18 a,
23 e**.

5. ὃ ἐμὲ αἱρήσει, ἐάν περ αἱρῇ: *will
be the condemnation of me, if condemnation it is to be.* αἱρεῖν and ἁλίσκεσθαι
are technical terms of the law, as
is the case with φεύγειν and διώκειν. —
Socrates's feeling that it is the prejudice
against him which will cause his conviction, accounts for his giving more
time to the explanation of this prejudice (chapters III–X) than to the reply
to the formal charges (chapters XI–
XV).

7. δή: *certainly.* The allusion is
to facts generally known and acknowl-
edged, cf. **31 d**. — πολλοὺς καὶ ἄλλους
καὶ ἀγαθούς: instead of καὶ ἄλλους πολλοὺς καὶ ἀγαθούς. The second καί is idiomatic, and joins πολλούς with a second
adjective. Cf. πολλοὶ καὶ σοφοὶ ἄνδρες.

8. οὐδὲν δὲ δεινὸν μὴ ἐν ἐμοὶ στῇ: *the
rule is in no danger of stopping with
me ;* "I shall not be the last." Cf.
οὐδὲν δεινὸν μὴ φοβηθῇ Phaedo **84 b**, *we
need not apprehend that the soul will
have to fear.*

9. εἶτ' οὐκ αἰσχύνει κτλ.: a question of an imaginary interlocutor.
εἶτα indicates impatience. The per-
versity of Socrates, in view of the fact
just recited, seems unreasonable.

11. ἀποθανεῖν: passive of ἀποκτείνω.
— ἐγὼ δὲ κτλ.: cf. *Crito* **48 d** for the
same thought, and Xen. *An.* iii. 1. 43
for its application to the risks of war.

12. κίνδυνον τοῦ ζῆν ἢ τεθνάναι:
*the question of life or death, danger to
one's life.* For the use and omission
of the article, cf. **23 e, 24 b**.

28 b

τοῦ ζῆν ἢ τεθνάναι ἄνδρα ὅτου τι καὶ σμικρὸν ὄφελός ἐστιν,
ἀλλ᾽ οὐκ ἐκεῖνο μόνον σκοπεῖν, ὅταν πράττῃ, πότερα δίκαια
15 ἢ ἄδικα πράττει καὶ ἀνδρὸς ἀγαθοῦ ἔργα ἢ κακοῦ. φαῦλοι
γὰρ ἂν τῷ γε σῷ λόγῳ εἶεν τῶν ἡμιθέων ὅσοι ἐν Τροίᾳ τετε- c
λευτήκασιν, οἵ τ᾽ ἄλλοι καὶ ὁ τῆς Θέτιδος υἱός, ὃς τοσοῦτον
τοῦ κινδύνου κατεφρόνησε παρὰ τὸ αἰσχρόν τι ὑπομεῖναι,
ὥστ᾽ ἐπειδὴ εἶπεν ἡ μήτηρ αὐτῷ προθυμουμένῳ Ἕκτορα
20 ἀποκτεῖναι, θεὸς οὖσα, οὑτωσί πως, ὡς ἐγὼ οἶμαι· ᾽Ω παῖ,
εἰ τιμωρήσεις Πατρόκλῳ τῷ ἑταίρῳ τὸν φόνον καὶ Ἕκτορα ἀποκτενεῖς, αὐτὸς ἀποθανεῖ· αὐτίκα γάρ τοι,᾽ φησί,
᾽μεθ᾽ Ἕκτορα πότμος ἑτοῖμος·᾽ ὁ δὲ ταῦτα ἀκούσας τοῦ
μὲν θανάτου καὶ τοῦ κινδύνου ὠλιγώρησε, πολὺ δὲ μᾶλλον
25 δείσας τὸ ζῆν κακὸς ὢν καὶ τοῖς φίλοις μὴ τιμωρεῖν, ᾽Αὐτίκα,᾽ d
φησί, ᾽τεθναίην, δίκην ἐπιθεὶς τῷ ἀδικοῦντι, ἵνα μὴ ἐνθάδε
μένω καταγέλαστος παρὰ νηυσὶ κορωνίσιν ἄχθος ἀρούρης.᾽
μὴ αὐτὸν οἴει φροντίσαι θανάτου καὶ κινδύνου ; "

14. ἀλλ᾽ οὐκ : i.e. and not rather.
16. ἂν εἶεν : "must have been," or
"must be considered." SCG. 437, 442.
— τῶν ἡμιθέων : i.e. τῶν ἡρώων. Hesiod,
Op. 158, calls the fourth race ἀνδρῶν
ἡρώων θεῖον γένος οἳ καλέονται | ἡμίθεοι
κτλ., and he counts among their
number the heroes that laid siege to
Thebes and Troy.
17. ὁ τῆς Θέτιδος υἱός : any appeal
to the example of Achilles was always
telling. The enthusiasm with which
the Greeks regarded this hero was
shown by countless works of art in
which he appeared.
20. θεὸς οὖσα : added in an unusual
way, because the circumstance has
unusual weight. The utterance of
Thetis not only was prompted by the
natural anxiety of a mother for her

son, but also was inspired by the un-
erring wisdom of a goddess. The passage from Hom. Σ 70 ff. is quoted
rather loosely in part (οὑτωσί πως).
23. ὁ δὲ ταῦτα ἀκούσας κτλ. : at
this point ὥστε is forgotten. The long
speech and explanation given to Thetis
makes this shift in the construction
very natural. In fact, this clause is as
independent as if a coördinate clause
(with or without μέν) had preceded it. —
τοῦ θανάτου : notice the exceptional use
of the article. Cf. 28 e, 29 a, 32 c,
38 c, 39 a b, Crito 52 c. For the article
used as here, cf. 29 a, 40 d, 41 c, in
each instance as a weak demonstrative.
25. τὸ ζῆν : for the use of the
article, cf. GMT. 800. — καὶ τοῖς φίλοις
κτλ. : explains κακὸς ὤν.
28. μή. . . οἴει : see on ἀλλ᾽ ἄρα, 25 a.

28 e

οὕτω γὰρ ἔχει, ὦ ἄνδρες Ἀθηναῖοι, τῇ ἀληθείᾳ· οὗ ἄν τις
30 ἑαυτὸν τάξῃ, ἡγησάμενος βέλτιστον εἶναι, ἢ ὑπ᾽ ἄρχοντος
ταχθῇ, ἐνταῦθα δεῖ, ὡς ἐμοὶ δοκεῖ, μένοντα κινδυνεύειν
μηδ᾽ ὑπολογιζόμενον μήτε θάνατον μήτ᾽ ἄλλο μηδὲν πρὸ
τοῦ αἰσχροῦ.

XVII. ἐγὼ οὖν δεινὰ ἂν εἴην εἰργασμένος, ὦ ἄνδρες Ἀθηναῖοι, εἰ, ὅτε μέν με οἱ ἄρχοντες ἔταττον, οὓς ὑμεῖς εἵλεσθε ε
ἄρχειν μου, καὶ ἐν Ποτειδαίᾳ καὶ ἐν Ἀμφιπόλει καὶ ἐπὶ Δηλίῳ,

XVII. *At the risk of my life I obeyed
the military commanders whom the
Athenians set over me, and should I not
obey God rather than man? Even now,
if you should offer to release me on
condition of my abandoning my wonted
occupations, I would say that I must
continue to obey God.*

1. δεινὰ ἂν εἴην κτλ. : the protasis
(limiting the apodosis δεινὰ ἂν εἴην κτλ.,
I should have done a dreadful thing)
includes various acts in the past which
are looked upon from a supposed time
in the future. It falls into two parts :
one, marked off by μέν, states (in the
form of a supposition) well-known
facts in the past; the other, distinguished by δέ, states a supposed future
case in connection with certain present
circumstances. The outrageous conduct for Socrates would be with this
combination of facts and convictions,
after his past fidelity to human trusts,
at some future time to desert his
divinely appointed post of duty, — *if
while then I stood firm I should now
desert my post.* The repetition of μέν
and δέ respectively is for the sake of
clearness. Cf. **32 d.** This repetition
would not be natural if the antecedent
had preceded its relative. — The main

stress is laid upon the δέ-clause. Cf.
25 b d.

2. ἔταττον : takes up τάξῃ and ταχθῇ
above. — **ὑμεῖς εἵλεσθε** : the δικασταί
are taken as representatives of the
δῆμος, — of which they were a sort of
committee. The generals were elected
by show of hands (χειροτονία) by the
ἐκκλησιασταί.

3. ἐν Ποτειδαίᾳ κτλ. : Potidaea, a
Corinthian colony on the peninsula
Chalcidice, became a tributary ally of
Athens without wholly abandoning its
earlier connection with Corinth. Per-
diccas, king of Macedonia, took advantage of this divided allegiance to
persuade the Potidaeans to revolt
from Athens, which they did in
432 B.C. The Potidaeans, with the
reënforcements sent them by the Pel-
oponnesians, were defeated by the
Athenian force under Callias. For two
whole years the town was invested by
land and blockaded by sea, and finally
made favorable terms with the be-
leaguering force. In the engagement
before Potidaea, Socrates is said to
have saved Alcibiades's life. Cf. *Symp.*
219 e–220 e. Alcibiades says that
Socrates ought to have had the prize
which was given to himself. — The

28 e

τότε μὲν οὐ ἐκεῖνοι ἔταττον ἔμενον ὥσπερ καὶ ἄλλος τις, καὶ
5 ἐκινδύνευον ἀποθανεῖν, τοῦ δὲ θεοῦ τάττοντος, ὡς ἐγὼ ᾠήθην
τε καὶ ὑπέλαβον, φιλοσοφοῦντά με δεῖν ζῆν καὶ ἐξετάζοντα
ἐμαυτὸν καὶ τοὺς ἄλλους, ἐνταῦθα δὲ φοβηθεὶς ἢ θάνατον ἢ
ἄλλο ὁτιοῦν πρᾶγμα λίποιμι τὴν τάξιν. δεινόν τἂν εἴη, καὶ 29
ὡς ἀληθῶς τότ᾿ ἄν με δικαίως εἰσάγοι τις εἰς δικαστήριον,
10 ὅτι οὐ νομίζω θεοὺς εἶναι, ἀπειθῶν τῇ μαντείᾳ καὶ δεδιὼς
θάνατον καὶ οἰόμενος σοφὸς εἶναι οὐκ ὤν. τὸ γάρ τοι θάνατον δεδιέναι, ὦ ἄνδρες, οὐδὲν ἄλλο ἐστὶν ἢ δοκεῖν σοφὸν εἶναι
μὴ ὄντα· δοκεῖν γὰρ εἰδέναι ἐστὶν ἃ οὐκ οἶδεν. οἶδε μὲν γὰρ
οὐδεὶς τὸν θάνατον οὐδ᾿ εἰ τυγχάνει τῷ ἀνθρώπῳ πάντων μέ-

battle at Amphipolis took place in the
year 422. The Athenians were defeated, and their general, Cleon, perished in the rout, while Brasidas, the
Spartan general, paid for victory with
his life. — Delium was an inclosure
and a temple sacred to Apollo near
Oropus, a border town sometimes held
by the Athenians and sometimes by
the Boeotians. The battle, which was
a serious check to the power of Athens,
resulted in the defeat and death of
their general, Hippocrates. — ἐπὶ Δηλίῳ: for the gallantry of Socrates on
the retreat, see *Symp.* 221 a. — In the
Laches (181 b), the general who gives
his name to that dialogue says that if
the rest had been as brave as Socrates
at Delium their city would not have
been worsted.

4. ὥσπερ καὶ ἄλλος τις : "like a good
soldier, Socrates speaks modestly of
his service." The repeated allusions
which are scattered through Plato's
dialogues to the brave conduct of Socrates in these battles show that it was
well known at Athens.

5. τοῦ δὲ θεοῦ τάττοντος : i.e. *now
that my post is assigned me by the god*,
a circumstance of the supposition εἰ
λίποιμι, which is repeated in ἐνταῦθα. —
ὡς ἐγὼ ᾠήθην τε καὶ ὑπέλαβον : *as I
thought and understood*, — perhaps with
special reference to the oracle which
was given to Chaerephon.

6. δεῖν: depends on the force of
saying implied in τάττοντος, and repeats the notion of commanding. —
ἐξετάζοντα κτλ. : explains φιλοσοφοῦντα.
Cf. ἀδικεῖν καὶ ἀπειθεῖν l. 21.

8. λίποιμι τὴν τάξιν : so worded as
to suggest λιποταξίου γραφή, a technical
phrase of criminal law. Any one
convicted of λιποταξία suffered ἀτιμία,
i.e. forfeited his civil rights.

10. ὅτι οὐ νομίζω κτλ. : refers to
the charge in 24 b.

11. οἰόμενος σοφὸς κτλ. : refers to
chapters VI–VIII. — This explains the
preceding clause, δεδιὼς θάνατον, and both
are subordinate to ἀπειθῶν τῇ μαντείᾳ.

13. οἶδε μὲν κτλ. : cf. 37 b, 40 c.

14. τὸν θάνατον οὐδ᾿ εἰ: by prolepsis for οὐδ᾿ εἰ ὁ θάνατος, *not even*

29 c

15 γιστον ὂν τῶν ἀγαθῶν, δεδίασι δ' ὡς εὖ εἰδότες ὅτι μέγιστον
τῶν κακῶν ἐστι. καὶ τοῦτο πῶς οὐκ ἀμαθία ἐστὶν αὕτη ἡ b
ἐπονείδιστος ἡ τοῦ οἴεσθαι εἰδέναι ἃ οὐκ οἶδεν; ἐγὼ δ', ὦ
ἄνδρες, τούτῳ καὶ ἐνταῦθα ἴσως διαφέρω τῶν πολλῶν ἀνθρώπων, καὶ εἰ δή τῳ σοφώτερός του φαίην εἶναι, τούτῳ ἄν,
20 ὅτι οὐκ εἰδὼς ἱκανῶς περὶ τῶν ἐν Ἅιδου, οὕτω καὶ οἴομαι
οὐκ εἰδέναι· τὸ δ' ἀδικεῖν καὶ ἀπειθεῖν τῷ βελτίονι, καὶ θεῷ
καὶ ἀνθρώπῳ, ὅτι κακὸν καὶ αἰσχρόν ἐστιν οἶδα. πρὸ οὖν
τῶν κακῶν ὧν οἶδα ὅτι κακά ἐστιν, ἃ μὴ οἶδα εἰ ἀγαθὰ ὄντα
τυγχάνει οὐδέποτε φοβήσομαι οὐδὲ φεύξομαι.
25 ὥστ' οὐδ' εἰ με νῦν ὑμεῖς ἀφίετε, Ἀνύτῳ ἀπιστήσαντες, ὃς ς
ἔφη ἢ τὴν ἀρχὴν οὐ δεῖν ἐμὲ δεῦρο εἰσελθεῖν ἤ, ἐπειδὴ εἰσῆλ-

whether, i.e. whether death may not
actually be. Thus he is as far as possible from knowing that death is the
greatest of ills. See on τοῦ θανάτου 28 c
for the use of the article.

15. ὄν: here, as usual, in the gender
of its predicate, μέγιστον τῶν ἀγαθῶν.

16. τοῦτο: not in the gender of
ἀμαθία. This makes a smoother sentence than αὕτη πῶς οὐκ ἀμαθία ἐστὶν
αὕτη ἡ κτλ., which was the alternative.
— αὕτη ἡ ἐπονείδιστος: limits ἀμαθία
and recalls the whole statement made
above, 21 b–23 e, — falling in a sort
of apposition.

18 f. τούτῳ, τούτῳ ἄν: repeated for
the greater effect. Both represent the
same point of superiority, i.e. ὅτι κτλ.
Notice the cleverness of the ellipsis
after ἄν. Socrates thus evades any
too circumstantial praise of himself, as
in 20 e. For the ellipsis in the leading
clause, cf. ἢ . . . ἄκων 25 e.

19. δή: viz. as the oracle says.

20. οὐκ εἰδὼς, οὕτω: i.e. ὥσπερ οὐκ
οἶδα, οὕτω. οὕτω sums up a previous

participial clause, and its force is nearly
so likewise. Cf. παντὸς μᾶλλον αὐτὸς
ἀπορῶν οὕτω καὶ τοὺς ἄλλους ἀπορεῖν ποιῶ
Meno 80 c.

23. κακῶν ὧν: a notable instance
of assimilation, for τούτων ἃ οἶδα.
Cf. ἄν εὖ οἶδ' ὅτι κακῶν ὄντων 37 b. κακά
is related to ὧν as ἀγαθά in the next
line is related to ἅ. — οἶδα εἰ: see on
τὸν θάνατον l. 14.

25. οὐδέ: not even. This implies a
conclusion in the form "would I accept it," — but this appears in l. 33, in
changed form. — εἰ ἀφίετε, εἰ οὖν ἀφίοιτε
(34), εἴποιμ' ἄν: the speaker adds the
explanatory detail of εἴ μοι εἴποιτε and
various reiterations of the conditions
upon which this release may be granted,
until the weaker clause εἰ ἀφίοιτε comes
of itself to his lips, — less of a merely
logical condition than he began with,
and presenting his acquittal as a mere
possibility.

26. οὐ δεῖν, οὐχ οἷόν τ' εἶναι: in the
original form this would be οὐκ ἔδει and
οὐχ οἷόντ' ἐστιν. — δεῦρο: i.e. into court.

29 c

θον, οὐχ οἷόν τ᾽ εἶναι τὸ μὴ ἀποκτεῖναί με, λέγων πρὸς ὑμᾶς
ὡς, εἰ διαφευξοίμην, "ἤδη ἂν ὑμῶν οἱ ὑεῖς ἐπιτηδεύοντες ἃ
Σωκράτης διδάσκει πάντες παντάπασι διαφθαρήσονται," —
30 εἴ μοι πρὸς ταῦτα εἴποιτε· "᾽Ω Σώκρατες, νῦν μὲν ᾽Ανύτῳ οὐ
πεισόμεθα, ἀλλ᾽ ἀφίεμέν σε, ἐπὶ τούτῳ μέντοι ἐφ᾽ ᾧτε μηκέτι
ἐν ταύτῃ τῇ ζητήσει διατρίβειν μηδὲ φιλοσοφεῖν· ἐὰν δ᾽ ἁλῷς
ἔτι τοῦτο πράττων, ἀποθανεῖ." εἰ οὖν με, ὅπερ εἶπον, ἐπὶ τού- c
τοις ἀφίοιτε, εἴποιμ᾽ ἂν ὑμῖν ὅτι "᾽Εγὼ ὑμᾶς, ἄνδρες ᾽Αθηναῖοι,
35 ἀσπάζομαι μὲν καὶ φιλῶ, πείσομαι δὲ μᾶλλον τῷ θεῷ ἢ ὑμῖν,
καὶ ἕωσπερ ἂν ἐμπνέω καὶ οἷός τ᾽ ὦ, οὐ μὴ παύσωμαι φιλο-
σοφῶν καὶ ὑμῖν παρακελευόμενός τε καὶ ἐνδεικνύμενος ὅτῳ
ἂν ἀεὶ ἐντυγχάνω ὑμῶν, λέγων οἷάπερ εἴωθα, ὅτι ᾽Ω ἄριστε
ἀνδρῶν, ᾽Αθηναῖος ὤν, πόλεως τῆς μεγίστης καὶ εὐδοκιμωτά-
40 της εἰς σοφίαν καὶ ἰσχύν, χρημάτων μὲν οὐκ αἰσχύνει ἐπιμε-
λούμενος (ὅπως σοι ἔσται ὡς πλεῖστα) καὶ δόξης καὶ τιμῆς, c
φρονήσεως δὲ καὶ ἀληθείας καὶ τῆς ψυχῆς (ὅπως ὡς βελτίστη

—εἰσελθεῖν: used as the passive of
εἰσάγω 24 d.   Cf. φύγοιμι 19 c.—
Anytus argues: "If Socrates had not
been prosecuted, his evil communica-
tions might have been ignored; once
in court, his case allows but one verdict. To acquit him would be to sanc-
tion all his heresies."

28. εἰ διαφευξοίμην: future optative
in indirect discourse. — ἂν διαφθαρήσονται: a shift of construction, — when
he said ἄν, the speaker expected to
use the optative, but changed to the
future. SCG. 432.

31. ἐφ᾽ ᾧτε: for construction with
infinitive, see GMT. 610; H. 999 a.

33. οὖν: resumes after a digression.

35. πείσομαι: cf. ὁ δὲ Πέτρος καὶ
᾽Ιωάννης ἀποκριθέντες εἶπον πρὸς αὐτούς·
εἰ δίκαιόν ἐστιν ἐνώπιον (in the sight)

τοῦ θεοῦ, ὑμῶν ἀκούειν μᾶλλον ἢ τοῦ θεοῦ
κρίνατε Acts iv. 19, πειθαρχεῖν (obey)
δεῖ θεῷ μᾶλλον ἢ ἀνθρώποις ib. v. 29.
Also Soph. Ant. 450 ff.

36. οὐ μὴ παύσωμαι: for οὐ μὴ with
the subjunctive in strong denials, see
GMT. 295; H. 1032. Cf. 28 b.

39. πόλεως: is in apposition with
᾽Αθηνῶν, which is implied in ᾽Αθηναῖος.
Cf. πονοῦντος in agreement with μού
implied in ἐμήν 22 a.

40. χρημάτων μὲν κτλ.: here,
again, the μέν-clause is subordinate in
thought. Cf. 25 b d. The point is not
that care for property and strength of
body is shameful, but that to neglect
the soul while one cares for these is
a disgrace.

42. φρονήσεως δέ: while, etc., as if
opposed to an ἐπιμελεῖ, — a departure

30 b
ἔσται) οὐκ ἐπιμελεῖ οὐδὲ φροντίζεις·' καὶ ἐάν τις ὑμῶν ἀμφισ-
βητῇ καὶ φῇ ἐπιμελεῖσθαι, οὐκ εὐθὺς ἀφήσω αὐτὸν οὐδ' ἄπειμι,
45 ἀλλ' ἐρήσομαι αὐτὸν καὶ ἐξετάσω καὶ ἐλέγξω, καὶ ἐάν μοι
μὴ δοκῇ κεκτῆσθαι ἀρετήν, φάναι δ', ὀνειδιῶ ὅτι τὰ πλείστου
ἄξια περὶ ἐλαχίστου ποιεῖται, τὰ δὲ φαυλότερα περὶ πλείο- 30
νος. ταῦτα καὶ νεωτέρῳ καὶ πρεσβυτέρῳ, ὅτῳ ἂν ἐντυγχάνω,
ποιήσω, καὶ ξένῳ καὶ ἀστῷ, μᾶλλον δὲ τοῖς ἀστοῖς, ὅσῳ μου
50 ἐγγυτέρω ἐστὲ γένει. ταῦτα γὰρ κελεύει ὁ θεός, εὖ ἴστε, καὶ
ἐγὼ οἴομαι οὐδέν πω ὑμῖν μεῖζον ἀγαθὸν γενέσθαι ἐν τῇ πόλει
ἢ τὴν ἐμὴν τῷ θεῷ ὑπηρεσίαν. οὐδὲν γὰρ ἄλλο πράττων
ἐγὼ περιέρχομαι ἢ πείθων ὑμῶν καὶ νεωτέρους καὶ πρεσβυ-
τέρους μήτε σωμάτων ἐπιμελεῖσθαι μήτε χρημάτων πρότερον
55 μηδ' οὕτω σφόδρα ὡς τῆς ψυχῆς, ὅπως ὡς ἀρίστη ἔσται, b
λέγων· 'Οὐκ ἐκ χρημάτων ἀρετὴ γίγνεται, ἀλλ' ἐξ ἀρετῆς

from the participial construction. Cf.
21 e.
45. ἐρήσομαι, ἐξετάσω, ἐλέγξω:
these words represent the process by
which Socrates disconcerted his fel-
low-countrymen. Beginning with a
harmless *question* or two, his method
soon proved uncomfortably *scrutiniz-
ing* (ἐξετάσω), and generally ended by
convicting (ἐλέγξω) of ignorance.
46. φάναι δέ: *while he claims it.*
49. ὅσῳ . . . ἐστε: Socrates insen-
sibly returns in thought to his hearers,
in whom he sees embodied the whole
people of Athens. The correlative of
ὅσῳ readily suggests itself with μᾶλλον.
50. κελεύει ὁ θεός: cf. τοῦ δὲ θεοῦ τάττοντος l. 5, 28 e. In the earlier chapters
Socrates seems to speak of his service
of God as a quest in proof of the oracle
(23 b), but here it is rather a reference
to his vocation in general, as a teacher
and admonisher of what is right.

52. τῷ θεῷ: dative of interest with
the verbal idea in ὑπηρεσίαν. Cf. τὴν
τοῦ θεοῦ δόσιν ὑμῖν in d below, and τὰ
μετέωρα φροντιστής 18 b.
54. πρότερον: sc. ἢ τῆς ψυχῆς,
which has to be supplied out of ὡς τῆς
ψυχῆς, and which is governed by ἐπιμελεῖσθαι.
55. μηδέ: is not a third specification with μήτε . . . μήτε. It serves only
to connect οὕτω σφόδρα with πρότερον,
and is negative only because the whole
idea is negative.
56. ἐξ ἀρετῆς χρήματα: the foundation of real prosperity is laid in the
character; the best of windfalls is
natural good sense sharpened by expe-
riénce; this is the making of your
successful man's character, and the
mending of his fortunes; this is ἀρετή
(*skill in the art of right living*), i.e.
wisdom (σοφία). Such in substance is
Socrates's theory of getting on in the

30 b

χρήματα καὶ τὰ ἄλλα ἀγαθὰ τοῖς ἀνθρώποις ἅπαντα καὶ
ἰδίᾳ καὶ δημοσίᾳ.' εἰ μὲν οὖν ταῦτα λέγων διαφθείρω τοὺς
νέους, ταῦτ' ἂν εἴη βλαβερά· εἰ δέ τίς μέ φησιν ἄλλα λέγειν
60 ἢ ταῦτα, οὐδὲν λέγει. πρὸς ταῦτα," φαίην ἄν, "ὦ 'Αθηναῖοι,
ἢ πείθεσθε 'Ανύτῳ ἢ μή, καὶ ἢ ἀφίετε ἢ μὴ ἀφίετε, ὡς ἐμοῦ
οὐκ ἂν ποιήσαντος ἄλλα, οὐδ' εἰ μέλλω πολλάκις τεθνάναι." c
XVIII. μὴ θορυβεῖτε, ἄνδρες 'Αθηναῖοι, ἀλλ' ἐμμείνα-
τέ μοι οἷς ἐδεήθην ὑμῶν, μὴ θορυβεῖν ἐφ' οἷς ἂν λέγω,
ἀλλ' ἀκούειν· καὶ γάρ, ὡς ἐγὼ οἶμαι, ὀνήσεσθε ἀκούοντες.
μέλλω γὰρ οὖν ἄττα ὑμῖν ἐρεῖν καὶ ἄλλα, ἐφ' οἷς ἴσως
5 βοήσεσθε· ἀλλὰ μηδαμῶς ποιεῖτε τοῦτο. εὖ γὰρ ἴστε, ἐὰν
ἐμὲ ἀποκτείνητε ϊ οιοῦτον ὄντα οἷον ἐγὼ λέγω, οὐκ ἐμὲ μείζω

world which may be gathered from Xenophon's *Memorabilia* in many places.

57. τοῖς ἀνθρώποις: construed with γίγνεται.

58. εἰ μὲν οὖν κτλ.: "If this corrupts the youth, I am guilty of the charge against me. But the truth cannot corrupt them, therefore my speaking it can do no harm, and I am not guilty as charged."

61. ὡς ἐμοῦ κτλ.: assured that I should never alter my ways.

62. τεθνάναι: the absolute contradictory of ζῆν, here used rather than the somewhat less emphatic ἀποθνήσκειν, — a thousand times a dead man. This distinction, however, is not strictly maintained. Cf. **39 e**, *Crito* **43 d**; and τεθνάναι δὲ μυριάκις κρεῖττον ἢ κολακείᾳ τι ποιῆσαι Φιλίππου Dem. ix. 65.

XVIII. *You, gentlemen, should listen quietly, — for it is to your advantage to listen. I am making my defense not in my own behalf, but for the sake of the*

city, that you may not make the great mistake of putting to death one whom God has given to be your benefactor. I clearly have been under divine influence, for otherwise I should not have neglected that for which most men care, and devoted my life to the persuasion of men to care for virtue.

2. οἷς ἐδεήθην: cf. 17 d, 20 e. This is explained by μὴ θορυβεῖν.

3 ff. καὶ γάρ, μέλλω γάρ, εὖ γὰρ ἴστε: the first γάρ is closely connected with ἀκούειν, the second goes back to the leading clause μὴ θορυβεῖν and accounts for the renewal of a request which the speaker has made three times already. The third γάρ, now, is explanatory rather than causal, and merely points the new statement for which Socrates has been preparing the court. γάρ with this force is especially frequent after ὁ δὲ (τὸ δὲ) μέγιστον, δεινότατον, also after σημεῖον δέ, τεκμήριον δέ, and other favorite idioms of like import in Plato and the orators.

6. οἷον: sc. ἐμὲ εἶναι.

30 e

βλάψετε ἢ ὑμᾶς αὐτούς· ἐμὲ μὲν γὰρ οὐδὲν ἂν βλάψειεν οὔτε
Μέλητος οὔτ᾽ Ἄνυτος· οὐδὲ γὰρ ἂν δύναιντο· οὐ γὰρ οἴομαι
θεμιτὸν εἶναι ἀμείνονι ἀνδρὶ ὑπὸ χείρονος βλάπτεσθαι. ἀπο- d
10 κτείνειε μεντἂν ἴσως ἢ ἐξελάσειεν ἢ ἀτιμώσειεν· ἀλλὰ ταῦτα
οὗτος μὲν ἴσως οἴεται καὶ ἄλλος τίς που μεγάλα κακά, ἐγὼ
δ᾽ οὐκ οἴομαι, ἀλλὰ πολὺ μᾶλλον ποιεῖν ἃ οὗτος νυνὶ ποιεῖ,
ἄνδρα ἀδίκως ἐπιχειρεῖν ἀποκτεινύναι.

νῦν οὖν, ὦ ἄνδρες Ἀθηναῖοι, πολλοῦ δέω ἐγὼ ὑπὲρ ἐμαυτοῦ
15 ἀπολογεῖσθαι, ὥς τις ἂν οἴοιτο, ἀλλ᾽ ὑπὲρ ὑμῶν, μή τι ἐξα-
μάρτητε περὶ τὴν τοῦ θεοῦ δόσιν ὑμῖν ἐμοῦ καταψηφισάμενοι.
ἐὰν γὰρ ἐμὲ ἀποκτείνητε, οὐ ῥᾳδίως ἄλλον τοιοῦτον εὑρήσετε, e
ἀτεχνῶς, εἰ καὶ γελοιότερον εἰπεῖν, προσκείμενον τῇ πόλει
[ὑπὸ τοῦ θεοῦ], ὥσπερ ἵππῳ μεγάλῳ μὲν καὶ γενναίῳ, ὑπὸ
20 μεγέθους δὲ νωθεστέρῳ καὶ δεομένῳ ἐγείρεσθαι ὑπὸ μύωπός
τινος· οἷον δή μοι δοκεῖ ὁ θεὸς ἐμὲ τῇ πόλει προστεθεικέναι,

7. οὔτε Μέλητος κτλ. : this is more
courteous than to continue the use of
the second person.

10. ἀτιμώσειεν: civil ἀτιμία involved the forfeiture of some or of all
the rights of citizenship. In the latter
case the ἄτιμος was looked upon by the
state as dead, i.e. he had suffered
"civil death," and his property, having no recognized owner, might be
confiscated.

16. τὴν τοῦ θεοῦ δόσιν: explained
in 31 a. — ὑμῖν: with the verbal idea
in δόσιν. Cf. 30 a. — καταψηφισάμενοι:
by condemning me. Coincident in time
with the principal verb. Cf. Phaedo
60 c. GMT. 150.

18. εἰ καὶ γελοιότερον εἰπεῖν: "if I
may use such a ludicrous figure of
speech." This is thrown in to prepare
his hearers for the humorous treatment
of a serious subject which follows. A

close scrutiny of the simile shows that
Socrates mistrusted the sovereign people. See below (21) for the same idea
put actively.

20. ὑπὸ μύωπος: the situation is
met humorously (γελοιότερον). First
the Athenians are compared to a horse
bothered out of inaction by a buzzing
horse-fly. The metaphor of the horse
is not pressed, but that of the μύωψ
is ingeniously elaborated: "Socrates
gives them no rest but teases them all
day long (προσκαθίζων), and does not allow them even a nap; he bothers them
incessantly when they are drowsing (οἱ
νυστάζοντες). Then they make an impatient slap (κρούσαντες) at him which
deprives them forever of his company."

21. οἷον δή μοι κτλ. : lit. in which
capacity God seems to me to have fas-
tened me upon the state, — such a one

82   ΠΛΑΤΩΝΟΣ ΑΠΟΛΟΓΙΑ ΣΩΚΡΑΤΟΥΣ

τοιοῦτόν τινα ὃς ὑμᾶς ἐγείρων καὶ πείθων καὶ ὀνειδίζων ἕνα
ἕκαστον οὐδὲν παύομαι τὴν ἡμέραν ὅλην πανταχοῦ προσ- 31
καθίζων. τοιοῦτος οὖν ἄλλος οὐ ῥᾳδίως ὑμῖν γενήσεται, ὦ
25 ἄνδρες, ἀλλ᾽ ἐὰν ἐμοὶ πείθησθε, φείσεσθέ μου· ὑμεῖς δ᾽ ἴσως
τάχ᾽ ἂν ἀχθόμενοι, ὥσπερ οἱ νυστάζοντες ἐγειρόμενοι, κρούσαντες ἄν με, πειθόμενοι Ἀνύτῳ, ῥᾳδίως ἂν ἀποκτείναιτε,
εἶτα τὸν λοιπὸν βίον καθεύδοντες διατελοῖτ᾽ ἄν, εἰ μή τινα
ἄλλον ὁ θεὸς ὑμῖν ἐπιπέμψειε κηδόμενος ὑμῶν.

30   ὅτι δ᾽ ἐγὼ τυγχάνω ὢν τοιοῦτος, οἷος ὑπὸ τοῦ θεοῦ τῇ πόλει δεδόσθαι, ἐνθένδ᾽ ἂν κατανοήσαιτε· οὐ γὰρ ἀνθρωπίνῳ b
ἔοικε τὸ ἐμὲ τῶν μὲν ἐμαυτοῦ ἀπάντων ἠμεληκέναι καὶ
ἀνέχεσθαι τῶν οἰκείων ἀμελουμένων τοσαῦτα ἤδη ἔτη, τὸ
δ᾽ ὑμέτερον πράττειν ἀεί, ἰδίᾳ ἑκάστῳ προσιόντα ὥσπερ
35 πατέρα ἢ ἀδελφὸν πρεσβύτερον, πείθοντα ἐπιμελεῖσθαι ἀρετῆς. καὶ εἰ μέντοι τι ἀπὸ τούτων ἀπέλαυον καὶ μισθὸν
λαμβάνων ταῦτα παρεκελευόμην, εἶχον ἄν τινα λόγον· νῦν
δ᾽ ὁρᾶτε δὴ καὶ αὐτοί, ὅτι οἱ κατήγοροι, τἄλλα πάντα ἀναι-
σχύντως οὕτω κατηγοροῦντες, τουτὸ γ᾽ οὐχ οἷοί τ᾽ ἐγένοντο

(in fact) as never ceases, etc., a repetition of προσκείμενον [ὑπὸ τοῦ θεοῦ].
Avoid the awkwardness of too literal
translation. Notice that οἷον really refers not to the μύωψ simply, but to it
as engaged in enlivening the horse.
μύωψ also means spur, and in part of
the passage this meaning seems to be
in mind.
  26 f. ἄν, ἄν, ἄν: for the repetition,
cf. 17 d, 41 a. — ἐγειρόμενοι: i.e. ἐὰν
ἐγείρωνται.
  30. οἷος δεδόσθαι: for the construction, cf. Crito 46 b.
  31. γάρ: introduces the explanation of ὑπὸ τοῦ θεοῦ, l. 30. It needs no
translation.

33. ἀμελουμένων: for the participle,
cf 23 c, 22 c.
  35. πείθοντα: to persuade him.
  37. εἶχον ἄν κτλ.: then at least I
should have some reason. Cf. ἀνθρωπίνῳ
ἔοικε l. 31. It was not according to
human nature that he should devote
himself to others, neglecting his own
affairs, particularly as he was not paid
for it; so such a man must have been
under divine influence. — Probably
many Athenians thought that Socrates
neglected his work because he was
lazy, and that he delighted in showing
men that they knew nothing simply because of his mischievous, spiteful spirit.
  39. κατηγοροῦντες: concessive.

31 c

40 ἀπαναισχυντῆσαι, παρασχόμενοι μάρτυρα, ὡς ἐγώ ποτέ τινα
ἢ ἐπραξάμην μισθὸν ἢ ῄτησα. ἱκανὸν γάρ, οἶμαι, ἐγὼ παρέχομαι τὸν μάρτυρα, ὡς ἀληθῆ λέγω, τὴν πενίαν.
XIX. ἴσως ἂν οὖν δόξειεν ἄτοπον εἶναι ὅτι δὴ ἐγὼ ἰδίᾳ
μὲν ταῦτα συμβουλεύω περιιὼν καὶ πολυπραγμονῶ, δημοσίᾳ
δ' οὐ τολμῶ ἀναβαίνων εἰς τὸ πλῆθος τὸ ὑμέτερον συμβου-
λεύειν τῇ πόλει. τούτου δ' αἴτιόν ἐστιν ὃ ὑμεῖς ἐμοῦ πολ-
5 λάκις ἀκηκόατε πολλαχοῦ λέγοντος, ὅτι μοι θεῖόν τι καὶ

40. ἀπαναισχυντῆσαι κτλ. : the
reading idea is in the participle, not in
the infinitive. Cf. **28 b, 29 d**, *Crito* **53 c.**
42. τὸν μάρτυρα : i.e. παρέχομαι
μάρτυρα καὶ ὁ μάρτυς ὃν παρέχομαι ἱκανός
ἐστιν. Cf. **20 e.** No special witness
is needed on this point. — ἱκανόν is
used predicatively, and the necessity
of the article is obvious. — πενίαν :
see on **23 b.**
XIX. *Why have I not served the
city in public life?* *Why have I been so
ready to offer advice in private, and yet
never have addressed the assembly of
the people?* *My inward monitor, my
daemonion, has checked me,* — *and
wisely; for I should not have been long-
lived if I had entered public life and
opposed the unjust desires of the people.*
1. ἴσως ἂν οὖν δόξειεν κτλ. : that
Socrates did not regard abstention
from the public service as in itself
commendable, is proved by his conversation with Charmides (Xen. *Mem.*
iii. 7), ἀξιόλογον μὲν ἄνδρα ὄντα, ὀκνοῦντα
δὲ προσιέναι τῷ δήμῳ (*to address the
people*) καὶ τῶν τῆς πόλεως πραγμάτων ἐπιμελεῖσθαι. He pointedly asks Charmides : εἰ δέ τις, δυνατὸς ὢν τῶν τῆς πόλεως
πραγμάτων ἐπιμελόμενος τήν τε πόλιν
αὔξειν (*advance the common weal*) καὶ

αὐτὸς διὰ τοῦτο τιμᾶσθαι, ὀκνοίη δὴ τοῦτο
πράττειν, οὐκ ἂν εἰκότως δειλὸς νομίζοιτο ;
See also ib. i. 6. 15. — For Socrates's
small experience in public life, cf.
32 b, *Gorgias* **473** fin.
2. πολυπραγμονῶ : *am a busybody.*
Cf. περιεργάζεται **19 b**, τὰ ἐμοῦ πράττοντος **33 a.** Nothing short of a divine
mission could justify this. Plato in-
variably uses the word in an unfavor-
able sense. Cf. ἀνδρὸς φιλοσόφου τὰ αὑτοῦ
πράξαντος καὶ οὐ πολυπραγμονήσαντος ἐν
τῷ βίῳ *Gorg.* **526 c.** There is a subtle
irony in πολυπραγμονῶ as here used by
Socrates. It was his business to mind
other people's business, therefore he
was far from being really πολυπράγμων.
Cf. Xen. *Mem.* iii. 11. 16, καὶ ὁ Σωκράτης ἐπισκώπτων (*making fun of*) τὴν
αὑτοῦ ἀπραγμοσύνην (*abstention from
business*), "Ἀλλ', ὦ Θεοδότη," ἔφη, "οὐ
πάνυ μοι ῥᾴδιόν ἐστι σχολάσαι (*be at
leisure*)· καὶ γὰρ ἴδια πράγματα πολλὰ
καὶ δημόσια παρέχει μοι ἀσχολίαν (*keep
me busy*)." Cf. **33 a b.**
3. ἀναβαίνων : as in **17 d** the preposition refers to ascending the tribune,
— although at this time the assembly
regularly met on the Pnyx hill, and
doubtless men spoke of going up to its
meetings.

31 d

δαιμόνιον γίγνεται, [φωνή], ὃ δὴ καὶ ἐν τῇ γραφῇ ἐπικωμῳ- d
δῶν Μέλητος ἐγράψατο· ἐμοὶ δὲ τοῦτο ἔστιν ἐκ παιδὸς
ἀρξάμενον φωνή τις γιγνομένη, ἢ ὅταν γένηται ἀεὶ ἀπο-
τρέπει με τοῦτο ὃ ἂν μέλλω πράττειν, προτρέπει δ' οὔποτε·
10 τοῦτο ἔστιν ὅ μοι ἐναντιοῦται τὰ πολιτικὰ πράττειν. καὶ
παγκάλως γέ μοι δοκεῖ ἐναντιοῦσθαι· εὖ γὰρ ἴστε, ὦ ἄνδρες
Ἀθηναῖοι, εἰ ἐγὼ [πάλαι] ἐπεχείρησα πράττειν τὰ πολιτικὰ
πράγματα, πάλαι ἂν ἀπολώλη καὶ οὔτ' ἂν ὑμᾶς ὠφελήκη
οὐδὲν οὔτ' ἂν ἐμαυτόν. καί μοι μὴ ἄχθεσθε λέγοντι τἀ- e
15 ληθῆ· οὐ γὰρ ἔστιν ὅστις ἀνθρώπων σωθήσεται οὔθ' ὑμῖν
οὔτ' ἄλλῳ πλήθει οὐδενὶ γνησίως ἐναντιούμενος καὶ διακωλύων πολλὰ ἄδικα καὶ παράνομα ἐν τῇ πόλει γίγνεσθαι,
ἀλλ' ἀναγκαῖόν ἐστι τὸν τῷ ὄντι μαχούμενον ὑπὲρ τοῦ δι- 32
καίου, καὶ εἰ μέλλει ὀλίγον χρόνον σωθήσεσθαι, ἰδιωτεύειν,
20 ἀλλὰ μὴ δημοσιεύειν.

XX. μεγάλα δ' ἔγωγ' ὑμῖν τεκμήρια παρέξομαι τούτων,
οὐ λόγους, ἀλλ' ὃ ὑμεῖς τιμᾶτε, ἔργα. ἀκούσατε δή μου τὰ

---

6. δαιμόνιον: perhaps sc. σημεῖον.
Cf. τὸ δαιμόνιον σημεῖον Rep. 476 c, referring to this inward monitor.— ἐπι-
κωμῳδῶν: a reminder of the remark
that Meletus was not in earnest.
8. φωνή: in apposition with τοῦτο.
9. τοῦτο: object of πράττειν.
13. ἀπολώλη: Plato used the old
Attic forms of the pluperfect. Cf.
ὠφελήκη and ἦ.
15 f. οὐ, οὔτε, κτλ. : a remarkable
sequence of negatives. — This thought
is resumed in **32 e**.
16. διακωλύων: conative.
19. καὶ εἰ: introduces an extreme
form of supposition, implying that
even then the conclusion is unassail-
able; εἰ καί (cf. **30 e**) introduces a
condition which implies that in that

case, as in many others, the conclusion
remains.
20. ἀλλὰ μή: and not. The English idiom avoids the Greek abruptness.
XX. *Facts substantiate my last assertion. I opposed the democracy once,
and the oligarchy on another occasion,
— and on both occasions had right on
my side, as all now agree, — and yet I
nearly lost my life on each occasion.*
1. τούτων: i.e. the assertion that for
him persistence in public life would
have meant early death or exile ; see
the beginning of the next chapter.
Socrates desires also to make clear
the manner of his public services.
2. ὑμεῖς: i.e. the hearers, as representing the Athenians in general.
Here appears what amounts to the

32 b

ἐμοὶ συμβεβηκότα, ἵνα εἰδῆτε ὅτι οὐδ' ἂν ἑνὶ ὑπεικάθοιμι
παρὰ τὸ δίκαιον δείσας θάνατον, μὴ ὑπείκων δ' ἄμ' ἂν
5 ἀπολοίμην. ἐρῶ δ' ὑμῖν φορτικὰ μὲν καὶ δικανικά, ἀληθῆ
δέ. ἐγὼ γάρ, ὦ 'Αθηναῖοι, ἄλλην μὲν ἀρχὴν οὐδεμίαν πώ- b
ποτ' ἦρξα ἐν τῇ πόλει, ἐβούλευσα δέ· καὶ ἔτυχεν ἡμῶν ἡ
φυλὴ 'Αντιοχὶς πρυτανεύουσα, ὅθ' ὑμεῖς τοὺς δέκα στρατη-

common rhetorical τόπος of rehearsing
a man's services, in his own defense.
Cf. **28 e.**

3. **οὐδ' ἂν ἑνί:** more emphatic than
οὐδενὶ ἄν.

7. **ἐβούλευσα:** before the senate of
500 came, in the first instance, the
questions to be dealt with by the ἐκκλησία (assembly). A preliminary decree (προβούλευμα) from this senate was
the regular form in which matters came
before the assembly, i.e. the senate
had the initiative ; but the assembly
at times evaded this by directing the
senate to bring in a measure to a certain end. — **ἔτυχεν . . . πρυτανεύουσα :**
the fifty representatives in the senate
of each of the ten tribes (each φυλή taking its turn in an order yearly determined by lot) had the general charge
of the business of the senate, and
directed the meetings both of the
senate and of the popular assembly,
for 35 or 36 days, i.e. one tenth of the
lunar year of 354 days, or in leap-
years for 38 or 39 days. Of this board
of fifty (whose members were called
πρυτάνεις during its term of office) one
member was chosen every day by lot
as ἐπιστάτης, or president. The ἐπιστάτης held the keys of the public
treasury and of the public repository
of records, also the seal of the commonwealth, and, further. presided at

the meetings of the senate and of the
assembly. In Socrates's time, the
φυλὴ πρυτανεύουσα, and the ἐπιστάτης
of the day, had the responsibility of
putting to the vote (ἐπιψηφίζειν) any
question that arose, or of refusing to
allow a vote. According to Xenophon,
Socrates was the ἐπιστάτης on the occasion in question. He was of the
δῆμος 'Αλωπεκή, in the φυλὴ 'Αντιοχίς.
Notice the addition of 'Αντιοχίς here
without the article, and as an after-
thought ; ἡμῶν ἡ φυλή would have been
sufficient, though less circumstantial.

8. **ὅθ' ὑμεῖς κτλ :** i.e. after the
Athenian success off the Arginusae
islands, in 406 B.C. This battle is also
spoken of as ἡ περὶ Λέσβον ναυμαχία,
Xen. Hell. ii. 3. 32–35. The victorious
generals were promptly prosecuted for
remissness in the performance of their
duty. Accused of having shown criminal neglect in failing to gather up the
dead and save those who, at the end
of the engagement, were floating about
on wrecks, they pleaded "not guilty."
The ships and men detailed for this
duty had been hindered, they said, by
stress of weather. The main fleet went
in pursuit of the worsted enemy. The
details of the case for and against them
cannot satisfactorily be made out,
though the reasons are many and
strong for thinking them innocent.

32 b

γοὺς τοὺς οὐκ ἀνελομένους τοὺς ἐκ τῆς ναυμαχίας ἐβούλεσθε
10 ἀθρόους κρίνειν, παρανόμως, ὡς ἐν τῷ ὑστέρῳ χρόνῳ πᾶσιν
ὑμῖν ἔδοξε. τότ᾿ ἐγὼ μόνος τῶν πρυτάνεων ἠναντιώθην μηδὲν
ποιεῖν παρὰ τοὺς νόμους [καὶ ἐναντία ἐψηφισάμην], καὶ ἑτοί-

The illegality of the procedure by
which they were condemned is undoubted. The condemnation was ἀνό-
μως (1) because judgment was passed
upon them ἀθρόους, i.e. μιᾷ ψήφῳ ἅπαντας, —this was irregular, since not only
the general practice at Athens, but
the decree of Cannonus (τὸ Καννω-
νοῦ ψήφισμα) provided δίχα (apart)
ἕκαστον κρίνειν, — (2) because they had
not reasonable time allowed them for
preparing and presenting their defense,
cf. βραχέα ἕκαστος ἀπελογήσατο, οὐ γὰρ
προὐτέθη σφίσι λόγος κατὰ τὸν νόμον
Xen. Hell. i. 7. 5, and (3) because the
popular assembly in strictness was
not a court and had no right to condemn to death. See Xen. Hell. i.
6. 33 ff. and 7; Mem. i. 1. 18; iv. 4. 2.
Xenophon says that the Athenians
soon repented of their rash and illegal
action : καὶ οὐ πόλλῳ χρόνῳ ὕστερον
μετέμελε τοῖς Ἀθηναίοις καὶ ἐψηφίσαντο,
οἵτινες τὸν δῆμον ἐξηπάτησαν (deceived)
προβολὰς αὐτῶν εἶναι (their case was
thus prejudiced by an informal vote
of the assembly) καὶ ἐγγυητὰς κατα-
στῆσαι, ἕως ἂν κριθῶσιν Hell. i. 7. 35.
The fate of these generals was remembered thirty years afterward by the
Athenian admiral Chabrias. He won
a great victory off Naxos (B.C. 376),
but neglected the pursuit of the enemy,
in order to save the men on the wrecks
and bury the dead. — τοὺς δέκα στρα-
τηγούς: the round number of all the
generals is given here. One of the

ten, Archestratus, died at Mytilene,
where Conon, another of them, was
still blockaded when the battle was
fought. Of the remaining eight who
were in the battle, two, Protomachus
and Aristogenes, flatly refused to obey
the summons to return to Athens.
Thus only six reached Athens, and
these, Pericles, Lysias, Diomedon,
Erasinides, Aristocrates, and Thrasyllus, were put to death.

9. τοὺς ἐκ τῆς ναυμαχίας : not only
the dead but those who were floating
about in danger of their lives. Cf.
Xen. Hell. i. 7. 11, παρῆλθε δέ τις εἰς
τὴν ἐκκλησίαν φάσκων ἐπὶ τεύχους ἀλφίτων
(on a meal-barrel) σωθῆναι· ἐπιστέλλειν
(enjoined upon) δ᾿ αὐτῷ τοὺς ἀπολλυμένους
(those who were drowning), ἐὰν σωθῇ
ἀπαγγεῖλαι τῷ δήμῳ, ὅτι οἱ στρατηγοὶ οὐκ
ἀνείλοντο (rescued) τοὺς ἀρίστους ὑπὲρ
τῆς πατρίδος γενομένους. — For the use
of ἐκ, cf. Xen. An. i. 2. 3, where
τοὺς ἐκ τῶν πόλεων is equivalent to ἐκ
τῶν πόλεων τοὺς ἐν ταῖς πόλεσιν ὄντας.
Here the fuller expression might be
οὐκ ἀνελομένους ἐκ τῆς θαλάσσης τοὺς
ἐν τῇ ναυμαχίᾳ ἀπολωλότας.

10. ἀθρόους: Xenophon's expression is μιᾷ ψήφῳ.

11. μηδὲν ποιεῖν : after the negative
idea in ἠναντιώθην the negative is repeated, according to Greek idiom.

12. καὶ ἐναντία ἐψηφισάμην : and I
voted against it, i.e. allowing the question to be put. Socrates as ἐπιστάτης
τῶν πρυτάνεων on this day followed up

32 d

μων ὄντων ἐνδεικνύναι με καὶ ἀπάγειν τῶν ῥητόρων, καὶ
ὑμῶν κελευόντων καὶ βοώντων, μετὰ τοῦ νόμου καὶ τοῦ δικαίου c
15 ὤμην μᾶλλόν με δεῖν διακινδυνεύειν ἢ μεθ' ὑμῶν γενέσθαι
μὴ δίκαια βουλευομένων, φοβηθέντα δεσμὸν ἢ θάνατον.

καὶ ταῦτα μὲν ἦν ἔτι δημοκρατουμένης τῆς πόλεως· ἐπειδὴ
δ' ὀλιγαρχία ἐγένετο, οἱ Τριάκοντα αὖ μεταπεμψάμενοί με
πέμπτον αὐτὸν εἰς τὴν θόλον προσέταξαν ἀγαγεῖν ἐκ Σα-
20 λαμῖνος Λέοντα τὸν Σαλαμίνιον ἵνα ἀποθάνοι· οἷα δὴ καὶ
ἄλλοις ἐκεῖνοι πολλοῖς πολλὰ προσέταττον βουλόμενοι ὡς
πλείστους ἀναπλῆσαι αἰτιῶν· τότε μέντοι, ἐγὼ οὐ λόγῳ d
ἀλλ' ἔργῳ αὖ ἐνεδειξάμην, ὅτι ἐμοὶ θανάτου μὲν μέλει, εἰ
μὴ ἀγροικότερον ἦν εἰπεῖν, οὐδ' ὁτιοῦν, τοῦ δὲ μηδὲν ἄδικον
25 μηδ' ἀνόσιον ἐργάζεσθαι, τούτου δὲ τὸ πᾶν μέλει. ἐμὲ γὰρ
ἐκείνη ἡ ἀρχὴ οὐκ ἐξέπληξεν οὕτως ἰσχυρὰ οὖσα, ὥστ' ἄδι-
κόν τι ἐργάσασθαι, ἀλλ' ἐπειδὴ ἐκ τῆς θόλου ἐξήλθομεν, οἱ
μὲν τέτταρες ᾤχοντο εἰς Σαλαμῖνα καὶ ἤγαγον Λέοντα, ἐγὼ
δ' ᾠχόμην ἀπιὼν οἴκαδε. καὶ ἴσως ἂν διὰ ταῦτ' ἀπέθανον,

this opposition, — manifested when in
consultation with the other πρυτάνεις,
— by absolutely refusing to put the
question to vote. — Cf. ὅτε ἐν ταῖς ἐκ-
κλησίαις ἐπιστάτης γενόμενος οὐκ ἐπέτρεψε
τῷ δήμῳ παρὰ τοὺς νόμους ψηφίσασθαι,
Xen Mem. iv. 4. 2.

13 f. ῥητόρων, ὑμῶν: observe the
chiasmus.

14. βοώντων: in his account of this
incident Xenophon says, τὸ δὲ πλῆθος
ἐβόα δεινὸν εἶναι, εἰ μή τις ἐάσει τὸν δῆμον
πράττειν ὃ ἂν βούληται Hell. i. 7. 12.

18. αὖ: in turn. Both democracy
and oligarchy, however opposed in
other respects, agreed in resenting the
independence of Socrates.

22. ἀναπλῆσαι κτλ. : those who
served the Thirty in such a matter, thus

becoming their accomplices, would
dread the restoration of the democracy,
which would mean punishment for
them.

24. εἰ μὴ ἀγροικότερον κτλ : cf. 30 e.
A supposition contrary to fact, with
suppressed apodosis, is used by way of
showing hesitation.

25. τούτου δέ: summarizes the
preceding clause. For the repetition
of δέ, cf. 28 e.

26 ὥστ' : construe with ἐξέπληξεν.

28 f. ᾤχοντο, ᾠχόμην : the recurrence of the same word only makes
more distinct the contrast between the
courses pursued. — According to Dio-
dorus xiv. 5, Socrates opposed actively
the execution of Theramenes by the
Thirty.

32 e

30 εἰ μὴ ἡ ἀρχὴ διὰ ταχέων κατελύθη· καὶ τούτων ὑμῖν ἔσονται e
πολλοὶ μάρτυρες.

XXI. ἆρ' οὖν ἄν με οἴεσθε τοσάδε ἔτη διαγενέσθαι, εἰ
ἔπραττον τὰ δημόσια καὶ πράττων ἀξίως ἀνδρὸς ἀγαθοῦ
ἐβοήθουν τοῖς δικαίοις καί, ὥσπερ χρή, τοῦτο περὶ πλείστου
ἐποιούμην; πολλοῦ γέ δεῖ, ὦ ἄνδρες Ἀθηναῖοι· οὐδὲ γὰρ
5 ἂν ἄλλος ἀνθρώπων οὐδείς. ἀλλ' ἐγὼ διὰ παντὸς τοῦ βίου 33
δημοσίᾳ τε, εἴ πού τι ἔπραξα, τοιοῦτος φανοῦμαι, καὶ ἰδίᾳ
ὁ αὐτὸς οὗτος, οὐδενὶ πώποτε συγχωρήσας οὐδὲν παρὰ τὸ
δίκαιον οὔτ' ἄλλῳ οὔτε τούτων οὐδενί, οὓς οἱ διαβάλλοντες ἐμέ φασιν ἐμοὺς μαθητὰς εἶναι. ἐγὼ δὲ διδάσκαλος
10 μὲν οὐδενὸς πώποτ' ἐγενόμην· εἰ δέ τίς μου λέγοντος καὶ
τὰ ἐμαυτοῦ πράττοντος ἐπιθυμεῖ ἀκούειν, εἴτε νεώτερος εἴτε
πρεσβύτερος, οὐδενὶ πώποτ' ἐφθόνησα, οὐδὲ χρήματα μὲν

---

30. διὰ ταχέων: the Thirty were
only eight months in power, and the
arrest of Leon was one of their later
acts.

31. μάρτυρες: possibly proceedings
were here interrupted for these witnesses, though it seems quite as likely
that Socrates is appealing to the δικασταί themselves to be his witnesses.

XXI. *In all my life, whether in
public or in private, I have never
yielded the cause of right, and in particular I have never made concessions to
gratify those whom my accusers call my
pupils; I have never been any man's
teacher, but have been ready to talk
with rich and poor alike.*

1. The first lines sum up the two
preceding chapters, while at l. 9 comes
the transition to the question of Socrates's teaching.

2. ἔπραττον: contrary to fact in
past time, of continued action.

3. τοῖς δικαίοις: neuter, *whatever
was just,* — a concrete way of express-
ing an abstraction.

5. οὐδεὶς ἄν: sc. διεγένετο. — **ἀλλ' ἐ-
γώ**: i.e. "however it may be with
others, as for me, I, etc."

6. τοιοῦτος: sc. as has been stated,
— explained by συγχωρήσας.

8. οὔτ' ἄλλῳ κτλ.: perhaps draws
attention to the fact that in the incident of **32 c d**, Socrates had not been
influenced by his former association
with Critias. — That the accusers laid
stress on the charge of evil teachings
and lack of restraint by Socrates, is
shown by the defense offered by Xenophon in his *Memorabilia.*

9. μαθητάς: see Introduction § 38.

11. τὰ ἐμαυτοῦ πράττοντος: cf. 31 c.
— People generally gave it a different
name.

12. οὐδέ: negatives the combination of μέν- and δέ-clauses.

33 b

λαμβάνων διαλέγομαι, μὴ λαμβάνων δ' οὔ, ἀλλ' ὁμοίως καὶ ὶ
πλουσίῳ καὶ πένητι παρέχω ἐμαυτὸν ἐρωτᾶν, καὶ ἐάν τις
15 βούληται ἀποκρινόμενος ἀκούειν ὧν ἂν λέγω. καὶ τούτων
ἐγὼ εἴτε τις χρηστὸς γίγνεται εἴτε μή, οὐκ ἂν δικαίως τὴν
αἰτίαν ὑπέχοιμι, ὧν μήθ' ὑπεσχόμην μηδενὶ μηδὲν πώποτε
μάθημα μήτ' ἐδίδαξα· εἰ δέ τίς φησι παρ' ἐμοῦ πώποτέ τι
μαθεῖν ἢ ἀκοῦσαι ἰδίᾳ ὅ τι μὴ καὶ ἄλλοι πάντες, εὖ ἴστε ὅτι
20 οὐκ ἀληθῆ λέγει.

XXII. ἀλλὰ διὰ τί δή ποτε μετ' ἐμοῦ χαίρουσί τινες πολὺν

13. οὔ: sc. διαλέγομαι. Cf. Chapter IV init. This has the main stress : " I do not refuse to converse, if I receive no money."

14. πένητι: the accuser seems to have made much of Socrates's association with rich young men. Cf. 23 c.

15. ἀποκρινόμενος ἀκούειν: characteristic of the Socratic συνουσία. — ἀκούειν: after παρέχω, this, like ἐρωτᾶν above, expresses purpose. — " I am ready for questions, but if any so wishes he may answer, and hear what I then have to say." — τούτων ἐγὼ κτλ. : ἐγώ is placed next to τούτων for the sake of contrast, while τούτων, though it is governed by τὶς, adheres to τὴν αἰτίαν ὑπέχοιμι. This last corresponds, as a passive, to αἰτίαν ἐπιφέρειν or προστιθέναι. The notion of responsibility is colored, like the English " have to answer for," with the implication of blame.

17. ὧν: partitive genitive with μηδενί. — ὑπεσχόμην: is meant probably as a side thrust at imposing promises like the one attributed to Protagoras about his own teaching in Prot. 319 a. Socrates himself followed no profession strictly so called; he had no ready-made art, or rules of art, to

communicate. His field of instruction was so wide that he could truly say that, in the accepted sense of διδάσκειν and μανθάνειν at Athens, his pupils got no learning from him. From him they learned no μάθημα and acquired no useful (professional) knowledge; he put them in the way of getting this for themselves. Plato makes him decline to become the tutor of Nicias's son (Lach. 200 d). Socrates taught nothing positive, but by his searching questions he removed the self-deception which prevented men from acquiring the knowledge of which they were capable. See his successful treatment of the conceited Εὐθύδημος ὁ καλός, in Xen. Mem. iv. 2.

19. ἄλλοι πάντες: a complete antithesis to ἰδίᾳ, taking the place of the more usual δημοσίᾳ. Socrates calls attention to the publicity of the places where he talks (cf. 17 c) and to the opportunity of conversing with him offered to all alike.

XXII. Why, then, do some young men like to spend much time with me? They enjoy listening to the examination of those who think themselves to be wise, though they are not. But if I have

33 c

χρόνον διατρίβοντες; ἀκηκόατε, ὦ ἄνδρες Ἀθηναῖοι· πᾶσαν c
ὑμῖν τὴν ἀλήθειαν· ἐγὼ εἶπον, ὅτι ἀκούοντες χαίρουσιν ἐξετα-
ζομένοις τοῖς οἰομένοις μὲν εἶναι σοφοῖς, οὖσι δ᾽ οὔ· ἔστι
5 γὰρ οὐκ ἀηδές. ἐμοὶ δὲ τοῦτο, ὡς ἐγώ φημι, προστέτακται
ὑπὸ τοῦ θεοῦ πράττειν καὶ ἐκ μαντείων καὶ ἐξ ἐνυπνίων καὶ
παντὶ τρόπῳ, ᾧπέρ τίς ποτε καὶ ἄλλη θεία μοῖρα ἀνθρώπῳ
καὶ ὁτιοῦν προσέταξε πράττειν.
     ταῦτα, ὦ Ἀθηναῖοι, καὶ ἀληθῆ ἐστι καὶ εὐέλεγκτα. εἰ γὰρ
10 δὴ ἔγωγε τῶν νέων τοὺς μὲν διαφθείρω, τοὺς δὲ διέφθαρ- d
κα, χρῆν δήπου, εἴτε τινὲς αὐτῶν πρεσβύτεροι γενόμενοι
ἔγνωσαν ὅτι νέοις οὖσιν αὐτοῖς ἐγὼ κακὸν πώποτέ τι συνεβούλευσα, νυνὶ αὐτοὺς ἀναβαίνοντας ἐμοῦ κατηγορεῖν καὶ
τιμωρεῖσθαι· εἰ δὲ μὴ αὐτοὶ ἤθελον, τῶν οἰκείων τινὰς τῶν
15 ἐκείνων, πατέρας καὶ ἀδελφοὺς καὶ ἄλλους τοὺς προσήκοντας, εἴ περ ὑπ᾽ ἐμοῦ τι κακὸν ἐπεπόνθεσαν αὐτῶν οἱ οἰκεῖοι,
νῦν μεμνῆσθαι [καὶ τιμωρεῖσθαι]. πάντως δὲ πάρεισιν αὐτῶν
πολλοὶ ἐνταυθοῖ οὓς ἐγὼ ὁρῶ, πρῶτον μὲν Κρίτων οὑτοσί,

corrupted the youth, then some of these
men, — or their friends, — on becoming
older and wiser, and learning that the
influence which they received from me
was bad, ought to join in the accusation
which Meletus brings.

**2 f. διατρίβοντες, ἀκούοντες, ἐξετα-
ζομένοις**: in close relation with χαίρουσι.
Cf. the construction of the participles
in **23 c**. GMT. 881.

3. εἶπον κτλ.: the ὅτι-clause really
answers διὰ τί . . . διατρίβοντες, but
grammatically is an appended explanation of τὴν ἀλήθειαν, and is governed by εἶπον.

6. ἐκ μαντείων: cf. **21 b**. — **ἐξ ἐνυπνίων** : cf. *Crito* 44 a, *Phaedo* 60 e.

9. ταῦτα : i.e. the statement of his
relation to the young men of Athens.

11. χρῆν: the conclusion states an
unfulfilled obligation. The protasis is
elaborated in two parallel clauses,
(1) εἴτε ἔγνωσαν, (2) εἰ δὲ μὴ αὐτοὶ ἤθελον.
See on εἴπερ κτλ. **27 d**. Instead of εἴτε . . .
εἴτε we have εἴτε . . . εἰ δέ (like οὔτε . . .
οὐδέ), which gives a certain independence to the second member. Hence
this is treated as a condition by itself,
and the leading protasis, εἰ διαφθείρω,
is substantially repeated in εἴπερ ἐπεπόνθεσαν.

13. ἀναβαίνοντας : cf. **17 d**, **31 c**.

15. τοὺς προσήκοντας : after the detailed enumeration this is introduced
appositively, to sum up, and therefore
the article is used.

18. ἐνταυθοῖ: construed with πάρεισιν, which denotes the result of

33 e

20

ἐμὸς ἡλικιώτης καὶ δημότης, Κριτοβούλου τοῦδε πατήρ· e
ἔπειτα Λυσανίας ὁ Σφήττιος, Αἰσχίνου τοῦδε πατήρ· ἔτι Ἀντιφῶν ὁ Κηφισιεὺς οὑτοσί, Ἐπιγένους πατήρ· ἄλλοι τοίνυν
οὗτοι ὧν οἱ ἀδελφοὶ ἐν ταύτῃ τῇ διατριβῇ γεγόνασι, Νικό-
στρατος ὁ Θεοζοτίδου, ἀδελφὸς Θεοδότου, — καὶ ὁ μὲν Θεό-
δοτος τετελεύτηκεν, ὥστ' οὐκ ἂν ἐκεῖνός γ' αὐτοῦ καταδεηθείη,

παριέναι, and which might be called here the perfect of παριέναι. Cf. καὶ λαβόντες τὰ ὅπλα παρῆσαν εἰς Σάρδεις Xen. *An.* i. 2. 2.

19. Κριτοβούλου: although his father Crito modestly declares (*Euthyd.* 271 b) that he is thin (σκληφρός) in comparison with his exquisite play-mate Clinias (cousin of Alcibiades), Critobulus was famous for his beauty. See Xen. *Symp.* iv. 12 ff. He was one of Socrates's most constant compan-ions. The *Oeconomicus* of Xenophon is a conversation between Socrates and Critobulus. The affection between Soc-rates and Crito is best shown by the pains taken by the former in furthering Critobulus's education. In the *Mem-orabilia* (i. 3. 8 ff.), Socrates indirectly reproves Critobulus by a conversation in his presence held with Xenophon. The same lesson he reënforces (ii. 6, esp. 31 and 32). That it was needed appears from the impetuous character shown by Critobulus in Xenophon's *Symposium.* Cf. iii. 7, τί γὰρ σύ, ἔφη, ὦ Κριτόβουλε, ἐπὶ τίνι μέγιστον φρονεῖς (*of what are you proudest ?*) ; ἐπὶ κάλλει, ἔφη. That Critobulus perplexed his father is shown in *Euthyd.* 306 d, where, speaking of his sons, Crito says : Κριτόβουλος δ' ἤδη ἡλικίαν ἔχει (*is getting on*) καὶ δεῖταί τινος ὅστις αὐ-τὸν ὀνήσει.

20. Αἰσχίνου: like Plato, Xeno-phon, and Antisthenes, Aeschines (sur-named ὁ Σωκρατικός) carefully wrote down the sayings of Socrates after the master's death. Three dialogues preserved among the writings of Plato have been attributed to Aeschines the Socratic. The *Eryxias* possibly is by him, but hardly either the *Axiochus* or the treatise περὶ ἀρετῆς. Aeschines was unpractical, if we can trust the amusing account given by Lysias (Frg. 1) of his attempt to establish, with bor-rowed money, a τέχνη μυρεψική (*salve-shop*). His failure in this venture may have led him to visit Syracuse, where, according to Lucian (*Parasit.* 32), he won the favor of Dionysius.

21. Ἐπιγένους: the same whom Socrates saw νέον τε ὄντα καὶ τὸ σῶμα κακῶς ἔχοντα (Xen. *Mem.* iii. 12), and reproached for not doing his duty to himself and to his country by taking rational exercise. — τοίνυν: marks a transition. The fathers of some have been named, now Socrates passes to the case of brothers.

24. ἐκεῖνός γε: *he at least,* i.e. ὁ ἐκεῖ = ὁ ἐν "Αιδου, Θεόδοτος, named last, but the more remote. — αὐτοῦ: Νικό-στρατος, of whom he is speaking. His brother being dead, Nicostratus will give an unbiased opinion. — κατα-δεηθείη : sc. not to accuse Socrates.

33 c

25 — καὶ Παράλιος ὅδε ὁ Δημοδόκου οὗ ἦν Θεάγης ἀδελφός·
ὅδε δ' Ἀδείμαντος ὁ Ἀρίστωνος οὗ ἀδελφὸς οὑτοσὶ Πλά- 34
των, καὶ Αἰαντόδωρος οὗ Ἀπολλόδωρος ὅδ' ἀδελφός. καὶ
ἄλλους πολλοὺς ἐγὼ ἔχω ὑμῖν εἰπεῖν, ὧν τινα ἐχρῆν μάλιστα
μὲν ἐν τῷ ἑαυτοῦ λόγῳ παρασχέσθαι Μέλητον μάρτυρα· εἰ
30 δὲ τότε ἐπελάθετο, νῦν παρασχέσθω, ἐγὼ παραχωρῶ, καὶ
λεγέτω, εἴ τι ἔχει τοιοῦτον. ἀλλὰ τούτου πᾶν τοὐναντίον
εὑρήσετε, ὦ ἄνδρες, — πάντας ἐμοὶ βοηθεῖν ἑτοίμους τῷ
διαφθείροντι, τῷ κακὰ ἐργαζομένῳ τοὺς οἰκείους αὐτῶν, ὥς
φασι Μέλητος καὶ Ἄνυτος. αὐτοὶ μὲν γὰρ οἱ διεφθαρμένοι b

25. Θεάγης : this brother of Paralius is known through *Rep.* vi. 496 b,
where Plato uses the now proverbial
expression, ὁ τοῦ Θεάγους χαλινός, *the
bridle of Theages,* i.e. ill health. Such
was the providential restraint which
made Theages, in spite of political
temptations, faithful to philosophy ;
otherwise, like Demodocus, his father,
he would have gone into politics.
Demodocus is one of the speakers in
the *Theages,* a dialogue attributed to
Plato, but now regarded as spurious.

26. Ἀδείμαντος : son of Aristo and
brother of Plato and of Glauco (Xen.
Mem. iii. 6. 1) ; both of Plato's brothers were friends of Socrates. Glauco
and Adimantus are introduced in
the *Republic,* as the chief actors, after
Socrates.

27. Ἀπολλόδωρος : surnamed ὁ μανικός because of his excitability. Cf.
Symp. **173 d.** This is nowhere better
shown than in the *Phaedo,* **117 d,** where
he gives way to uncontrollable grief
as soon as Socrates drinks the fatal
hemlock. In the *Symposium,* **172 c,** he
describes with almost religious fervor

his first association with Socrates. In
the Ἀπολογία Σωκράτους (28), attributed to Xenophon, he is mentioned as
ἐπιθυμητὴς μὲν ἰσχυρῶς αὐτοῦ (Σωκράτους),
ἄλλως δ' εὐήθης (a *simpleton*). Of the
persons here mentioned, Nicostratus,
Theodotus, Paralius, and Aeantodorus
are not elsewhere mentioned by Plato ;
of the eleven named as certainly present at the trial (there is doubt about
Epigenes) only four (or five with
Epigenes), Apollodorus, Crito, Critobulus, and Aeschines, are named as
present at the death of Socrates.

30. ἐγὼ παραχωρῶ : parenthetical.
Cf. παραχωρῶ σοι τοῦ βήματος, ἕως ἂν
εἴπῃς Aeschi. iii. 165. Socrates offers
to Meletus the opportunity to present
such evidence, and to use part of the
time allotted to him, — but the offer
was futile on every account. No formal
evidence could be introduced at the
trial that was not presented at the preliminary hearing.

34. μέν : the μέν-clause is subordinate. Cf. **34 c, 28 e.** — γάρ : "this
fact proves innocence, *for* how can
you account for this ? "

34 c

35 τάχ' ἂν λόγον ἔχοιεν βοηθοῦντες· οἱ δ' ἀδιάφθαρτοι, πρεσβύτεροι ἤδη ἄνδρες, οἱ τούτων προσήκοντες, τίνα ἄλλον ἔχουσι
λόγον βοηθοῦντες ἐμοὶ ἀλλ' ἢ τὸν ὀρθόν τε καὶ δίκαιον, ὅτι
συνίσασι Μελήτῳ μὲν ψευδομένῳ, ἐμοὶ δ' ἀληθεύοντι;

XXIII. Εἶεν δή, ὦ ἄνδρες· ἃ μὲν ἐγὼ ἔχοιμ' ἂν ἀπολογεῖσθαι, σχεδόν ἐστι ταῦτα καὶ ἄλλα ἴσως τοιαῦτα. τάχα
δ' ἄν τις ὑμῶν ἀγανακτήσειεν ἀναμνησθεὶς ἑαυτοῦ, εἰ ὁ μὲν
καὶ ἐλάττω τουτουὶ τοῦ ἀγῶνος ἀγῶνα ἀγωνιζόμενος ἐδεήθη
5 τε καὶ ἱκέτευσε τοὺς δικαστὰς μετὰ πολλῶν δακρύων, παιδία
θ' αὑτοῦ ἀναβιβασάμενος, ἵνα ὅτι μάλιστα ἐλεηθείη, καὶ ἄλλους τῶν οἰκείων καὶ φίλων πολλούς, ἐγὼ δ' οὐδὲν ἄρα τούτων

---

35. λόγον ἔχοιεν: cf. 31 b.—They
might not like to acknowledge that
they had been corrupted.

36. οἱ τούτων προσήκοντες: this
participle, like ἄρχων and συνάρχων,
by usage has become substantially a
noun. The poets apparently were the
first to use participles in this way. Cf.
ἰόντων τοῖς τεκοῦσι Aesch. Pers. 245,
ὁ ἐκείνου τεκών Eur. El. 335. The participial use and the use as a noun sub-
sisted side by side.

37. ἀλλ' ἤ: cf. 20 d.

XXIII–XXIV.   Peroration.   Instead of making the usual personal
appeal to the judges' feelings, Socrates
dilates on the lack of dignity, the injustice, and the impiety of making such
an appeal.

XXIII. *I have said all that I care
to say in reply to the charges against
me. I will not do what is customary,
and close my defense with an appeal for
pity and mercy. Such an appeal would
not be for my honor or for that of the
city. I have the reputation of surpassing
the other Athenians at least in some*

respects, and the best of the citizens
ought not to be womanish. The court,
too, should not favor those who bring
forward their children in order to excite
pity, and thus introduce a pitiable
spectacle.

1. εἶεν δή: marks the close of the
argument.

3. ἀναμνησθεὶς ἑαυτοῦ: i.e. remembering how he himself had striven to
arouse the sympathy and pity of his
judges. In so large a court were
doubtless many δικασταί who had been
defendants. — ὁ μὲν κτλ.: here again
the μέν-clause is subordinate in importance. Cf. 33 b, 35 a.

4. ἐλάττω ἀγῶνα: the μέγιστος ἀγών
was the one involving a man's fran-
chise and his life. Cf. παιδία γὰρ παρα-
στήσεται καὶ κλαήσει καὶ τούτοις αὐτὸν
ἐξαιτήσεται Dem. xxi. 99, and οἶδα
τοίνυν ὅτι τὰ παιδία ἔχων ὀδυρεῖται (the
defendant will bring his children and
burst into lamentations) καὶ πολλοὺς
λόγους καὶ ταπεινοὺς ἐρεῖ, δακρύων καὶ ὡς
ἐλεινότατον ποιῶν αὑτόν ib. 186.

6. ἐλεηθείη: awaken pity.

34 c

ποιήσω, καὶ ταῦτα κινδυνεύων, ὡς ἂν δόξαιμι, τὸν ἔσχατον
κίνδυνον. τάχ᾽ οὖν τις ταῦτα ἐννοήσας αὐθαδέστερον ἂν πρός
10 με σχοίη, καὶ ὀργισθεὶς αὐτοῖς τούτοις θεῖτο ἂν μετ᾽ ὀργῆς
τὴν ψῆφον. εἰ δή τις ὑμῶν οὕτως ἔχει, — οὐκ ἀξιῶ μὲν γὰρ d
ἔγωγε· εἰ δ᾽ οὖν, — ἐπιεικῆ ἄν μοι δοκῶ πρὸς τοῦτον λέγειν
λέγων ὅτι "Ἐμοί, ὦ ἄριστε, εἰσὶν μέν πού τινες καὶ οἰκεῖοι· καὶ
γὰρ τοῦτο αὐτὸ τὸ τοῦ Ὁμήρου, οὐδ᾽ ἐγὼ ' ἀπὸ δρυὸς οὐδ᾽ ἀπὸ
15 πέτρης' πέφυκα, ἀλλ᾽ ἐξ ἀνθρώπων, ὥστε καὶ οἰκεῖοί μοί εἰσι
καὶ ὑεῖς, ὦ ἄνδρες Ἀθηναῖοι, τρεῖς, εἷς μὲν μειράκιον ἤδη,
δύο δὲ παιδία· ἀλλ᾽ ὅμως οὐδένα αὐτῶν δεῦρο ἀναβιβασάμενος δεήσομαι ὑμῶν ἀποψηφίσασθαι." τί δὴ οὖν οὐδὲν τούτων
ποιήσω; οὐκ αὐθαδιζόμενος, ὦ ἄνδρες Ἀθηναῖοι, οὐδ᾽ ὑμᾶς
20 ἀτιμάζων, ἀλλ᾽ εἰ μὲν θαρραλέως ἐγὼ ἔχω πρὸς θάνατον ἢ μή, e
ἄλλος λόγος, πρὸς δ᾽ οὖν δόξαν καὶ ἐμοὶ καὶ ὑμῖν καὶ ὅλῃ τῇ
πόλει οὔ μοι δοκεῖ καλὸν εἶναι ἐμὲ τούτων οὐδὲν ποιεῖν καὶ

8. ὡς ἂν δόξαιμι: of course Socrates himself is far from believing that the risk he runs is desperate.

9. οὖν: marks the resumption of the thought of l. 3. — αὐθαδέστερον σχοίη: might be too easily offended, more literally represented by more (than otherwise) self-willed. The δικασταί might be too proud to submit to even tacit criticism of their own conduct in like cases.

10. αὐτοῖς τούτοις: causal. — ὀργῆς: the state of mind which results from ὀργισθείς.

11. γάρ: "(I say if), for, though I do not expect it of you, yet (making the supposition) if it should be so."

12. εἰ δ᾽ οὖν: resumptive.

13. καὶ οἰκεῖοι: "I am not alone in the world; I too have relatives."

14. τοῦτο αὐτὸ τὸ τοῦ Ὁμήρου: this idiom (with the genitive of the proper name) is common in quotations. No verb is expressed, and the quotation is in apposition with τοῦτο etc. Cf. *Symp.* **221 b.** — The reference is to οὐ γὰρ ἀπὸ δρυός ἐσσι παλαιφάτου οὐδ᾽ ἀπὸ πέτρης Hom. τ 163, — an old proverb used by Penelope in questioning the disguised Odysseus.

15 f. καί, καί: not correlative. The first καί means also, while the second introduces a particular case under οἰκεῖοι — yes, and sons.

16. τρεῖς: appositively, three of them. See Introduction § 16.

17. οὐδένα: the negative applies to both the participle and δεήσομαι.

20. εἰ μὲν θαρραλέως ἔχω κτλ.: whether I can look death in the face or not. Grammatical consistency would require that ἀλλά should be followed by a participle, but the construction is shifted. Cf. ἐδόκει **21 e.**

35 b

τηλικόνδε ὄντα καὶ τοῦτο τοὔνομα ἔχοντα, εἴτ᾽ οὖν ἀληθὲς
εἴτ᾽ οὖν ψεῦδος· ἀλλ᾽ οὖν δεδογμένον γ᾽ ἐστὶ τὸ Σωκράτη
25 διαφέρειν τινὶ τῶν πολλῶν ἀνθρώπων. εἰ οὖν ὑμῶν οἱ δο- 35
κοῦντες διαφέρειν εἴτε σοφίᾳ εἴτ᾽ ἀνδρείᾳ εἴτ᾽ ἄλλῃ ᾑτινιοῦν
ἀρετῇ τοιοῦτοι ἔσονται, αἰσχρὸν ἂν εἴη· οἷούσπερ ἐγὼ πολλάκις ἑώρακά τινας, ὅταν κρίνωνται, δοκοῦντας μέν τι εἶναι,
θαυμάσια δ᾽ ἐργαζομένους, ὡς δεινόν τι οἰομένους πείσεσθαι
30 εἰ ἀποθανοῦνται, ὥσπερ ἀθανάτων ἐσομένων, ἂν ὑμεῖς αὐτοὺς
μὴ ἀποκτείνητε· οἳ ἐμοὶ δοκοῦσιν αἰσχύνην τῇ πόλει περι-
άπτειν, ὥστ᾽ ἄν τινα καὶ τῶν ξένων ὑπολαβεῖν ὅτι οἱ διαφέροντες Ἀθηναίων εἰς ἀρετήν, οὓς αὐτοὶ ἑαυτῶν ἔν τε ταῖς b
ἀρχαῖς καὶ ταῖς ἄλλαις τιμαῖς προκρίνουσιν, οὗτοι γυναικῶν
35 οὐδὲν διαφέρουσι. ταῦτα γάρ, ὦ ἄνδρες Ἀθηναῖοι, οὔθ᾽ ἡμᾶς
χρὴ ποιεῖν τοὺς δοκοῦντας καὶ ὁτιοῦν εἶναι, οὔτ᾽ ἂν ἡμεῖς
ποιῶμεν ὑμᾶς ἐπιτρέπειν, ἀλλὰ τοῦτο αὐτὸ ἐνδείκνυσθαι, ὅτι

23. τοῦτο τοὔνομα : cf. 23 a.
24. ψεῦδος : used as the contrary
of the adjective ἀληθές. — ἀλλ᾽ οὖν
κτλ. : however that may be, people have
come to believe. — τό : indicates that
what follows is quoted.
25. ὑμῶν : partitive with οἱ δοκοῦντες. — οἱ δοκοῦντες : here Socrates may
have had Pericles in mind, if Plutarch's
gossip is truth. Cf. Ἀσπασίαν μὲν οὖν
ἐξῃτήσατο, πολλὰ πάνυ παρὰ τὴν δίκην,
ὡς Αἰσχίνης φησίν, ἀφεὶς ὑπὲρ αὐτῆς
δάκρυα καὶ δεηθεὶς τῶν δικαστῶν Pericl.
32. 3, he begged Aspasia off, though
Aeschines says it was by a flagrant disregard of justice, by weeping for her
and beseeching the jurymen.
27. τοιοῦτοι : i.e. such as are described in 34 c, and below.
30. ἀθανάτων ἐσομένων : the subject of this genitive absolute is the
same as that of ἀποθανοῦνται. This is

not the regular construction, for usually the genitive absolute expresses
a subordinate limitation, and clearness demands an independent subject.
Here, and in many cases where it introduces an independent idea, it depends on the leading clause for its
subject. Cf. καὶ οὐκ ἔφασαν ἰέναι, ἐὰν μή
τις αὐτοῖς χρήματα διδῷ, ὥσπερ καὶ τοῖς
προτέροις μετὰ Κύρου ἀναβᾶσι . . . καὶ
ταῦτα οὐκ ἐπὶ μάχην ἰόντων Xen. An. i.
4. 12. — For the thought, cf. ὦ πέπον,
εἰ μὲν γὰρ πόλεμον περὶ τόνδε φυγόντε |
αἰεὶ δὴ μέλλοιμεν ἀγήρω τ᾽ ἀθανάτω τε | ἔσ-
σεσθ᾽, οὔτε κεν αὐτὸς ἐνὶ πρώτοισι μαχοί-
μην Hom. M 322.
33 ἐν ταῖς ἀρχαῖς : i.e. in bestow-
ing offices.
34. οὗτοι : a pointed reiteration.
35. ἡμᾶς : i.e. defendants.
36. δοκοῦντας κτλ. : cf. l. 28.
37. ὑμᾶς : i.e. the δικασταί.

35 b

πολὺ μᾶλλον καταψηφιεῖσθε τοῦ τὰ ἐλεεινὰ ταῦτα δράματα
εἰσάγοντος καὶ καταγέλαστον τὴν πόλιν ποιοῦντος ἢ τοῦ
40 ἡσυχίαν ἄγοντος.

XXIV. χωρὶς δὲ τῆς δόξης, ὦ ἄνδρες, οὐδὲ δίκαιόν μοι
δοκεῖ εἶναι δεῖσθαι τοῦ δικαστοῦ οὐδὲ δεόμενον ἀποφεύγειν, c
ἀλλὰ διδάσκειν καὶ πείθειν. οὐ γὰρ ἐπὶ τούτῳ κάθηται ὁ δικαστής, ἐπὶ τῷ καταχαρίζεσθαι τὰ δίκαια, ἀλλ᾽ ἐπὶ τῷ κρί-
5 νειν ταῦτα· καὶ ὀμώμοκεν οὐ χαριεῖσθαι οἷς ἂν δοκῇ αὐτῷ,
ἀλλὰ δικάσειν κατὰ τοὺς νόμους. οὔκουν χρὴ οὔθ᾽ ἡμᾶς ἐθί-
ζειν ὑμᾶς ἐπιορκεῖν οὔθ᾽ ὑμᾶς ἐθίζεσθαι· οὐδέτεροι γὰρ ἂν
ἡμῶν εὐσεβοῖεν. μὴ οὖν ἀξιοῦτέ με, ὦ ἄνδρες Ἀθηναῖοι,
τοιαῦτα δεῖν πρὸς ὑμᾶς πράττειν, ἃ μήθ᾽ ἡγοῦμαι καλὰ εἶναι
10 μήτε δίκαια μήθ᾽ ὅσια, ἄλλως τε μέντοι νὴ Δία [πάντως] καὶ d

39. **εἰσάγοντος**: a word borrowed
from the theatre.

XXIV. But, *reputation aside, it
is not just that the accused should ask
for pity. The court sits to dispense justice, not to award favors. If I should
urge you to acquit me contrary to your
oath, I should show that I do not believe
the gods to exist and punish perjurers.
But I believe in the gods, and am ready
to leave the decision of my case to them
and my judges.*

1. **χωρὶς δὲ τῆς δόξης κτλ.** : after the
unseemly practice has been condemned
by reference to τὸ καλόν (δόξα), it is
found inconsistent also with τὸ δίκαιον,
and this is conclusive against it. The
second οὐδέ (with ἀποφεύγειν) is merely
the correlative of the first ; in the positive form of statement, καί would be
used.

3. **διδάσκειν καὶ πείθειν**: perhaps
the full idea would be, διδάσκειν καὶ
διδάσκοντα πείθειν.

4. **ἐπὶ τῷ καταχαρίζεσθαι** : this explains ἐπὶ τούτῳ. For ἐπί, cf. ἐπὶ διαβολῇ 20 e, ἐπὶ παρακελεύσει 36 d. Notice
the implication of κατά in composition,
and cf. καταδεηθείη 33 e.

5. **ὀμώμοκεν** : part of the oath taken
by the δικασταί was ψηφιοῦμαι κατὰ τοὺς
νόμους . . . καὶ οὔτε χάριτος ἕνεκ᾽ οὔτ᾽ ἔχ-
θρας. . . . καὶ ἀκροάσομαι τοῦ τε κατηγόρου
καὶ τοῦ ἀπολογουμένου ὁμοίως ἀμφοῖν. The
orators often refer to this oath. οὐ is
used, not μή, in keeping the form of
the oath in indirect discourse.

7. **ἐθίζεσθαι** : *allow yourselves to be
habituated.*

8. **ἡμῶν**: includes both the speaker
and the court, referred to above by
ἡμᾶς and ὑμᾶς respectively.

9. **ἃ μήθ᾽ ἡγοῦμαι**: notice the order.
Socrates adds μήθ᾽ ὅσια last because
he remembers the ἐπιορκεῖν above.

10. **ἄλλως . . . καί**: the hyperbaton (H. 1062) consists in interrupting
the familiar phrase ἄλλως τε καί, in

36 a

ἀσεβείας φεύγοντα ὑπὸ Μελήτου τουτουΐ. σαφῶς γὰρ ἄν, εἰ
πείθοιμι ὑμᾶς καὶ τῷ δεῖσθαι βιαζοίμην ὀμωμοκότας, θεοὺς
ἂν διδάσκοιμι μὴ ἡγεῖσθαι ὑμᾶς εἶναι, καὶ ἀτεχνῶς ἀπολο-
γούμενος κατηγοροίην ἂν ἐμαυτοῦ ὡς θεοὺς οὐ νομίζω. ἀλλὰ
15 πολλοῦ δεῖ οὕτως ἔχειν· νομίζω τε γάρ, ὦ ἄνδρες Ἀθηναῖοι,
ὡς οὐδεὶς τῶν ἐμῶν κατηγόρων, καὶ ὑμῖν ἐπιτρέπω καὶ τῷ θεῷ
κρῖναι περὶ ἐμοῦ ὅπῃ μέλλει ἐμοί τ' ἄριστα εἶναι καὶ ὑμῖν.

XXV. Τὸ μὲν μὴ ἀγανακτεῖν, ὦ ἄνδρες Ἀθηναῖοι, ἐπὶ e
τούτῳ τῷ γεγονότι, ὅτι μου κατεψηφίσασθε, ἄλλα τέ μοι 36
πολλὰ συμβάλλεται, καὶ οὐκ ἀνέλπιστόν μοι γέγονε τὸ γεγο-

order to make room for μέντοι νὴ Δία,
after which ἄλλως is forgotten and
πάντως is brought in with καί.
12. πείθοιμι κτλ. : this gives in brief
Socrates's objection to the practice of
appeals for pity and mercy. — θεοὺς
εἶναι : widely separated, giving great
emphasis to both. This arrangement
of words is intended to arrest the
attention and thus prevent their
meaning from being slighted. Here,
of course, Socrates refers to Meletus's
charge of atheism, 24 b, 26 c.
16. ἐπιτρέπω : Socrates concludes
his plea with words of submission.
XXV–XXVIII. Now that Socrates
has been convicted what penalty is to
be imposed ? For a γραφὴ ἀσεβείας no
definite penalty was prescribed by the
law, but it was to be determined in
each case by the court (Introd. § 56).
— Since Chapter XXIV the judges
have voted, and declared Socrates
guilty, by a vote of 281 to 220; and
Meletus has spoken, proposing and
urging a sentence of death.

XXV. I was prepared for the decision against me. Indeed I thought the
majority would be much larger. A
change of thirty votes would have
given me acquittal. Clearly, then, if
Anytus and Lycon had not joined
Meletus in the prosecution, he would
have failed.
1. τὸ μὴ ἀγανακτεῖν : the infinitive
with the article is placed at the beginning of the clause, and amounts to an
accusative of specification, instead of
being construed with συμβάλλεται.
" Many things contribute toward my
not grieving," i e. prevent me from
grieving ; "the fact that I feel no dis-
position to be indignant results from
many causes."
2. ὅτι μου κατεψηφίσασθε : a definition of τούτῳ τῷ γεγονότι.
3. καὶ . . . γέγονε : the important
fact detaches itself from any connect-
ive like ὅτι. This is often the case in
clauses connected with τέ . . . καί, οὔτε
. . . οὔτε, μέν . . . δέ. Cf. ὅμως δ' ἐδόκει
21 e, and διαφθείρουσιν 25 b.

36 a

νὸς τοῦτο, ἀλλὰ πολὺ μᾶλλον θαυμάζω ἑκατέρων τῶν ψήφων
5 τὸν γεγονότα ἀριθμόν. οὐ γὰρ ᾠόμην ἔγωγ᾽ οὕτω παρ᾽ ὀλίγον ἔσεσθαι, ἀλλὰ παρὰ πολύ· νῦν δ᾽, ὡς ἔοικεν, εἰ τριάκοντα
μόναι μετέπεσον τῶν ψήφων, ἀποπεφεύγη ἄν. Μέλητον μὲν
οὖν, ὡς ἐμοὶ δοκῶ, καὶ νῦν ἀποπέφευγα, καὶ οὐ μόνον ἀποπέφευγα, ἀλλὰ παντὶ δῆλον τοῦτό γε, ὅτι, εἰ μὴ ἀνέβη Ἄνυτος
10 καὶ Λύκων κατηγορήσοντες ἐμοῦ, κἂν ὦφλε χιλίας δραχμὰς
οὐ μεταλαβὼν τὸ πέμπτον μέρος τῶν ψήφων.   b

XXVI. τιμᾶται δ᾽ οὖν μοι ὁ ἀνὴρ θανάτου. εἶεν· ἐγὼ δὲ
δὴ τίνος ὑμῖν ἀντιτιμήσομαι, ὦ ἄνδρες Ἀθηναῖοι; ἢ δῆλον
ὅτι τῆς ἀξίας; τί οὖν; τί ἄξιός εἰμι παθεῖν ἢ ἀποτεῖσαι, ὅ τι
μαθὼν ἐν τῷ βίῳ οὐχ ἡσυχίαν ἦγον, ἀλλ᾽ ἀμελήσας ὧνπερ

5. οὕτω παρ᾽ ὀλίγον: so close. οὕτω
is separated from ὀλίγον by παρά, a
case of apparent hyperbaton. See on
ἄλλως τε κτλ. **35 d.** The combination
παρ᾽ ὀλίγον is treated as inseparable,
because the whole of it is required to
express the idea "a little beyond," i.e.
close. The whole idea of by a small
majority is qualified by οὕτω. The
ὀλίγον was sixty-one votes. — The subject of ἔσεσθαι, of course, is to be supplied from τὸν γεγονότα ἀριθμόν.

6. εἰ τριάκοντα κτλ.: strictly speaking, thirty-one. Socrates probably reck-
oned roughly, as he heard the numbers,
and said that thirty votes would have
turned the scale.

8 ἀποπέφευγα: the argument (which
Socrates could not have pressed seriously) is that Meletus alone could not
have won 100 votes, since with two
helpers he failed to get 300. His
share of 281 votes would not be more
than ninety-four!

11. τὸ πέμπτον μέρος: the accuser
must convince at least one fifth of the

judges, or pay 1000 drachmae, — a
fine intended to discourage false and
malicious accusations. The article is
used here, since the reference is to a
well-known fraction; and the accusative is used, since the whole fifth is
needed.

XXVI. *Meletus proposes a sentence
of death for me. What shall I propose? What do I deserve? I really
deserve to be invited to dine in the
Prytaneum, as a guest of the city.*

2. ὑμῖν: ethical dative. — ἤ: cf.
26 b.

3. παθεῖν κτλ.: see Introduction
§ 57. — ὅ τι μαθών: strictly speaking, this is the indirect form of τί
μαθών, which hardly differs from τί
παθών. GMT. 839 ; H. 968 c. Both
idioms ask with surprise for the reason
of an act. They resemble two English ways of asking "why?" "what
possessed (μαθών) you?" "what came
over (παθών) you?"

4. ἀμελήσας: more fully explained
below by ἐνταῦθα οὐκ ἦα. For Socrates's

36 d

5 οἱ πολλοί, χρηματισμοῦ τε καὶ οἰκονομίας καὶ στρατηγιῶν
καὶ δημηγοριῶν καὶ τῶν ἄλλων ἀρχῶν καὶ συνωμοσιῶν καὶ
στάσεων τῶν ἐν τῇ πόλει γιγνομένων, ἡγησάμενος ἐμαυτὸν
τῷ ὄντι ἐπιεικέστερον εἶναι ἢ ὥστ᾽ εἰς ταῦτ᾽ ἰόντα σῴζεσθαι, c
ἐνταῦθα μὲν οὐκ ᾖα, οἷ ἐλθὼν μήθ᾽ ὑμῖν μήτ᾽ ἐμαυτῷ ἔμελλον
10 μηδὲν ὄφελος εἶναι, ἐπὶ δὲ τὸ ἰδίᾳ ἕκαστον [ἰὼν] εὐεργετεῖν
τὴν μεγίστην εὐεργεσίαν, ὡς ἐγώ φημι, ἐνταῦθα ᾖα, ἐπιχειρῶν ἕκαστον ὑμῶν πείθειν μὴ πρότερον μήτε τῶν ἑαυτοῦ
μηδενὸς ἐπιμελεῖσθαι, πρὶν ἑαυτοῦ ἐπιμεληθείη ὅπως ὡς βέλτιστος καὶ φρονιμώτατος ἔσοιτο, μήτε τῶν τῆς πόλεως πρὶν
15 αὐτῆς τῆς πόλεως, τῶν τ᾽ ἄλλων οὕτω κατὰ τὸν αὐτὸν τρόπον
ἐπιμελεῖσθαι· τί οὖν εἰμι ἄξιος παθεῖν τοιοῦτος ὤν; ἀγαθόν d
τι, ὦ ἄνδρες Ἀθηναῖοι, εἰ δεῖ γε κατὰ τὴν ἀξίαν τῇ ἀληθείᾳ
τιμᾶσθαι· καὶ ταῦτά γ᾽ ἀγαθὸν τοιοῦτον, ὅ τι ἂν πρέποι ἐμοί.

neglect of his private interests, cf.
31 b; for his abstention from public
life, cf. **31 c**. — ὧνπερ οἱ πολλοί : sc.
ἐπιμελοῦνται from ἀμελήσας. — Socrates
excuses himself for not taking part
with the democracy against the Thirty.

6. ἄλλων ἀρχῶν κτλ. : ἀρχῶν κτλ.
are in apposition with τῶν ἄλλων. —
Socrates means to include all per-
formances which bring a citizen into
public life; he talks of responsible
public offices as on a par with irre-
sponsible participation in public affairs.
Of course στρατηγία is a public office,
and among the most important; but
δημηγορία is not so, even in the case of
the ῥήτορες.

10. ἐπὶ δὲ τὸ ἰδίᾳ κτλ. : *but to bene-
fiting privately individuals.* This is
strictly the completion of the thought
introduced by ἀλλ᾽ ἀμελήσας, which,
though ἐνταῦθα μὲν οὐκ ᾖα furnishes its
verb, still requires a positive expression

to explain οὐχ ἡσυχίαν ἦγον. ἐνταῦθα, as
is often the case with οὗτος, is resumptive, and restates ἐπὶ τὸ ἰδίᾳ ἕκαστον κτλ.
11. ἐπιχειρῶν : explains εὐεργετεῖν.
12. μὴ πρότερον κτλ. : cf. **30 a b.**
13. μηδενός : neuter. — πρὶν ἐπιμεληθείη : πρίν takes the optative on the
principle of *oratio obliqua*, since the
tense of the leading verb (ᾖα) is
secondary.
15. τῶν τ᾽ ἄλλων : not a third specification in line with μήτε . . . μήτε,
but connected with the whole μὴ πρότερον . . . πόλεως. — κατὰ τὸν αὐτὸν τρόπον : repeats ἐκ παραλλήλου the thought
conveyed by οὕτω, which points back
to μὴ πρότερον . . . πρίν, i.e. so that what
was essential might not be neglected
in favor of what is unessential.
16. τί οὖν κτλ. : a return to the question asked above, with omission of what
does not suit the new connection.
"What recompense should be given?"

36 d

τί οὖν πρέπει ἀνδρὶ πένητι εὐεργέτῃ, δεομένῳ ἄγειν σχολὴν
20 ἐπὶ τῇ ὑμετέρᾳ παρακελεύσει ; _οὐκ_ ἔσθ' ὅ τι μᾶλλον, ὦ
ἄνδρες Ἀθηναῖοι, πρέπει οὕτως, ὡς τὸν τοιοῦτον ἄνδρα ἐν
πρυτανείῳ σιτεῖσθαι, πολύ γε μᾶλλον ἢ εἴ τις ὑμῶν ἵππῳ ἢ
συνωρίδι ἢ ζεύγει νενίκηκεν Ὀλυμπίασιν. ὁ μὲν γὰρ ὑμᾶς
ποιεῖ εὐδαίμονας δοκεῖν εἶναι, ἐγὼ δ' εἶναι· καὶ ὁ μὲν τρο- e
25 φῆς οὐδὲν δεῖται, ἐγὼ δὲ δέομαι. εἰ οὖν δεῖ με κατὰ τὸ
δίκαιον τῆς ἀξίας τιμᾶσθαι, τούτου τιμῶμαι, ἐν πρυτανείῳ 37
σιτήσεως.

XXVII. ἴσως οὖν ὑμῖν καὶ ταυτὶ λέγων παραπλησίως
δοκῶ λέγειν ὥσπερ περὶ τοῦ οἴκτου καὶ τῆς ἀντιβολήσεως,

---

19. ἀνδρὶ πένητι εὐεργέτῃ : a poor
man who has well served the state.
He is poor, and therefore needs the
σίτησις, and he deserves this, because
he is a εὐεργέτης.

20. ἐπί : cf. **35 c.** — **μᾶλλον πρέπει
οὕτως** : with colloquial freedom Socrates combines two idioms οὐκ ἔσθ' ὅ
τι μᾶλλον πρέπει ἤ and ὅ τι πρέπει οὕτως ὡς.

22. ἐν πρυτανείῳ σιτεῖσθαι : those
entertained by the state (1) were invited once, or (2) were maintained
permanently. Socrates is speaking of
(2), i.e. maintenance in the prytaneum.
The nine archons dined in the θεσμοθέ-
σιον, the prytanes in the rotunda or
θόλος, but the public guests had plain
fare in the prytaneum. Some of these
guests attained the distinction by winning victories in the national games;
others received it on account of their
forefathers' services to the state, e.g.
the oldest living descendants of Har-
modius and of Aristogeiton were thus
honored. — **ἵππῳ κτλ.** : since a victory
in the great pan-Hellenic festivals was

glorious for the country from which
the victor came, he received on his
return the greatest honors, and even
substantial rewards.

24. εὐδαίμονας κτλ. : according to
Thucydides (vi. 16), Alcibiades claimed
that his appearance at the Olympian
games in the time of the Peloponnesian
War (420 B.C.) with seven four-horse
chariots to compete for prizes, — and
winning the first, second, and fourth
prizes, — made a great impression on
the other Greeks, and convinced them
that the power of Athens was not, as
they thought, nearly exhausted by the
war.

25. οὐδὲν δεῖται : only rich men
could afford to compete in such con-
tests, since horses in Greece were not
kept and used for menial labor, but
were "the delight of proud luxury."

XXVII. Some may think that I have
spoken thus in a self-willed spirit of
bravado. Not at all. Being convinced
that I have wronged no one else, I am
not disposed to wrong myself. As for
living in prison or in exile, — I might

37 c

ἀπαυθαδιζόμενος. τὸ δ' οὐκ ἔστιν, ὦ 'Αθηναῖοι, τοιοῦτον,
ἀλλὰ τοιόνδε μᾶλλον· πέπεισμαι ἐγὼ ἑκὼν εἶναι μηδένα
5 ἀδικεῖν ἀνθρώπων, ἀλλὰ ὑμᾶς τοῦτο οὐ πείθω· ὀλίγον γὰρ
χρόνον ἀλλήλοις διειλέγμεθα· ἐπεί, ὡς ἐγῷμαι, εἰ ἦν ὑμῖν
νόμος, ὥσπερ καὶ ἄλλοις ἀνθρώποις, περὶ θανάτου μὴ μίαν
ἡμέραν μόνον κρίνειν, ἀλλὰ πολλάς, ἐπείσθητε ἄν· νῦν δ' οὐ b
ῥᾴδιον ἐν χρόνῳ ὀλίγῳ μεγάλας διαβολὰς ἀπολύεσθαι. πε-
10 πεισμένος δὴ ἐγὼ μηδένα ἀδικεῖν πολλοῦ δέω ἐμαυτόν γ' ἀδικήσειν καὶ κατ' ἐμαυτοῦ ἐρεῖν αὐτός, ὡς ἄξιός εἰμί του κακοῦ,
καὶ τιμήσεσθαι τοιούτου τινὸς ἐμαυτῷ. τί δείσας; ἢ μὴ πάθω
τοῦτο οὗ Μέλητός μοι τιμᾶται, ὃ φημι οὐκ εἰδέναι οὔτ' εἰ ἀγαθὸν οὔτ' εἰ κακόν ἐστιν; ἀντὶ τούτου δὴ ἕλωμαι ὧν εὖ οἶδ' ὅτι
15 κακῶν ὄντων, τούτου τιμησάμενος; πότερον δεσμοῦ; καὶ τί με c
δεῖ ζῆν ἐν δεσμωτηρίῳ, δουλεύοντα τῇ ἀεὶ καθισταμένῃ ἀρχῇ,
τοῖς Ἕνδεκα; ἀλλὰ χρημάτων, καὶ δεδέσθαι ἕως ἂν ἐκτείσω;

as well submit to the sentence proposed
by Meletus.

3. ἀπαυθαδιζόμενος: explains παρα-
πλησίως κτλ. — For the facts, cf. **34 d**.
— **τὸ δέ**: ὁ δέ, οἱ δέ, τὸ δέ are used without a preceding μέν when they introduce some person or topic in contrast
to what has just been dwelt upon, here
περὶ τοῦ οἴκτου κτλ. For a different use
of τὸ δέ, cf. τὸ δὲ κινδυνεύει **23 a**.

4. ἑκὼν εἶναι: with subject of ἀδικεῖν. — **μηδένα**: object of ἀδικεῖν. Cf.
l. 10.

5. ὀλίγον: i.e. only a short time.

6. ὡς ἐγῷμαι: belongs to the principal clause.

7. ὥσπερ καὶ ἄλλοις. for instance
the Lacedaemonians.

9. χρόνῳ ὀλίγῳ: cf. **19 a**.

10. πεπεισμένος: resumes l. 4. —
ἀδικήσειν: for the future cf. GMT. 113.

13. φημι: cf. **28 e–30 b**.

14. ἕλωμαι ὧν... ὄντων: a remarkable construction, arising from ἕλωμαί
τι τούτων ἃ εὖ οἶδα κακὰ ὄντα, by the
assimilation of τούτων ἃ to ὧν and of
κακὰ ὄντα to κακῶν ὄντων, and the inser-
tion of ὅτι after οἶδα. εὖ οἶδ' ὅτι and
οἶδ' ὅτι occur frequently (in parenthe-
sis) where ὅτι is superfluous. Cf. δῆλον
ὅτι Crito **53 a**. — ἕλωμαι is subjunctive
of deliberation.

15. τούτου κτλ.: a part (τι) of ὧν,
by proposing a penalty of that.

16. δουλεύοντα: as a man in prison,
who ceases to be his own master. —
ἀεί: the eleven were chosen annually.

17. τοῖς Ἕνδεκα: cf. οἱ ἄρχοντες
39 e. — ἀλλὰ χρημάτων: a negative
answer to the preceding rhetorical
question is here implied; otherwise ἤ
might equally well have been used.
The second ἀλλά introduces an objection, which answers the question

37 c

ἀλλὰ ταὐτόν μοί ἐστιν ὅπερ νυνδὴ ἔλεγον· οὐ γὰρ ἔστι μοι
χρήματα ὁπόθεν ἐκτείσω. ἀλλὰ δὴ φυγῆς τιμήσωμαι; ἴσως
20 γὰρ ἄν μοι τούτου τιμήσαιτε. πολλὴ μεντἄν με φιλοψυχία
ἔχοι, εἰ οὕτως ἀλόγιστός εἰμι ὥστε μὴ δύνασθαι λογίζεσθαι,
ὅτι ὑμεῖς μὲν ὄντες πολῖταί μου οὐχ οἷοί τ᾽ ἐγένεσθε ἐνεγκεῖν
τὰς ἐμὰς διατριβὰς καὶ τοὺς λόγους, ἀλλ᾽ ὑμῖν βαρύτεραι γεγό- d
νασι καὶ ἐπιφθονώτεραι, ὥστε ζητεῖτε αὐτῶν νυνὶ ἀπαλλαγῆ-
25 ναι· ἄλλοι δ᾽ ἄρα αὐτὰς οἴσουσι ῥᾳδίως; πολλοῦ γε δεῖ, ὦ
Ἀθηναῖοι. καλὸς οὖν ἄν μοι ὁ βίος εἴη ἐξελθόντι τηλικῷδε ἀνθρώπῳ ἄλλην ἐξ ἄλλης πόλεως ἀμειβομένῳ καὶ ἐξελαυνομένῳ
ζῆν. εὖ γὰρ οἶδ᾽ ὅτι, ὅποι ἂν ἔλθω, λέγοντος ἐμοῦ ἀκροάσον-
ται οἱ νέοι ὥσπερ ἐνθάδε· κἂν μὲν τούτους ἀπελαύνω, οὗτοι
30 ἐμὲ αὐτοὶ ἐξελῶσι πείθοντες τοὺς πρεσβυτέρους· ἐὰν δὲ μὴ
ἀπελαύνω, οἱ τούτων πατέρες τε καὶ οἰκεῖοι δι᾽ αὐτοὺς τούτους. e

immediately preceding it. — καὶ δεδέσθαι κτλ.: to remain in prison.—Punishment by long imprisonment was rare
at Athens, but occasionally a man was
kept in prison for failure to pay a fine
(cf. Ant. v. 63).

18. ταὐτόν: i.e. this proposition
amounts to the other, — perpetual
imprisonment.

19. ἐκτείσω: for the future with
relative, to denote purpose, see GMT.
565, H. 911.

21. εἰ . . . εἰμί: cf. 30 b, 25 b.

22. ὅτι ὑμεῖς μέν: that (while) you,
my fellow-citizens, proved unable to
bear my company. After this we look
for something like this, "others will
prove still less able to bear it." But
instead, we find a question with ἄρα,
will others then, etc., answered by πολλοῦ γε δεῖ. The dependence of the
whole upon ὅτι is forgotten, because
of the intervening detailed statement.

23. βαρύτεραι: feminine because
τὰς ἐμὰς διατριβάς is the more important idea, τοὺς λόγους being incidentally
added by way of explanation.

26. ὁ βίος: the article as here used
has something of its original demonstrative force; accordingly ἐξελθόντι
. . . ζῆν is appended as if to a demonstrative pronoun, that would be a fine
life for me, — to be banished at my time
of life, and wander from city to city.
— Manifestly ironical. — Notice that
ἐξέρχεσθαι means go into exile; φεύγειν,
live in exile; and κατιέναι, come back
from exile. — τηλικῷδε ἀνθρώπῳ: the
common idiom would be τηλικῷδε ὄντι.
But cf. τηλικοίδε ἄνδρες Crito 49 a.

31. δι᾽ αὐτοὺς τούτους: the involuntary cause in contrast to οὗτοι αὐτοί.
Since Socrates attracts the young men,
he will be considered a corrupter of
youth in other cities also, and will be
banished on their account.

38 b

XXVIII. ἴσως οὖν ἄν τις εἴποι· "Σιγῶν δὲ καὶ ἡσυχίαν ἄγων, ὦ Σώκρατες, οὐχ οἷός τ᾽ ἔσει ἡμῖν ἐξελθὼν ζῆν;" τουτὶ δή ἐστι πάντων χαλεπώτατον πεῖσαί τινας ὑμῶν. ἐάν τε γὰρ λέγω ὅτι τῷ θεῷ ἀπειθεῖν τοῦτ᾽ ἔστι καὶ διὰ τοῦτ᾽ ἀδύνατον

5 ἡσυχίαν ἄγειν, οὐ πείσεσθέ μοι ὡς εἰρωνευομένῳ· ἐάν τ᾽ αὖ 38 λέγω ὅτι καὶ τυγχάνει μέγιστον ἀγαθὸν ὂν ἀνθρώπῳ τοῦτο, ἑκάστης ἡμέρας περὶ ἀρετῆς τοὺς λόγους ποιεῖσθαι καὶ τῶν ἄλλων περὶ ὧν ὑμεῖς ἐμοῦ ἀκούετε διαλεγομένου καὶ ἐμαυτὸν καὶ ἄλλους ἐξετάζοντος, ὁ δ᾽ ἀνεξέταστος βίος οὐ βιωτὸς

10 ἀνθρώπῳ, — ταῦτα δ᾽ ἔτι ἧττον πείσεσθέ μοι λέγοντι. τὰ δ᾽ ἔχει μὲν οὕτως ὡς ἐγώ φημι, ὦ ἄνδρες, πείθειν δ᾽ οὐ ῥᾴδιον. καὶ ἐγὼ ἅμ᾽ οὐκ εἴθισμαι ἐμαυτὸν ἀξιοῦν κακοῦ οὐδενός. εἰ μὲν γὰρ ἦν μοι χρήματα, ἐτιμησάμην ἂν χρημάτων ὅσα b

XXVIII. *I cannot change the order of my life. I am ready, however, to pay as large a fine as my means allow; this would not injure me. And I might pay a mina of silver. But Plato and others urge me to propose a fine of 30 minae, and they — responsible men — will be my sureties for the payment.*

2 ἡμῖν: ethical dative. — **ἐξελθὼν ζῆν**: to live on in exile. This forms a unit to which σιγῶν and ἡσυχίαν ἄγων are added by way of indicating the manner of life he will lead. The meaning of ἡσυχίαν ἄγων is plain from **36 b**. It is the opposite of πολυπραγμονῶν. If Socrates would so live, he would be unmolested at Thebes or at Corinth. — **τουτὶ δή**: that is the thing of which, viz. that I cannot be silent.

3. χαλεπώτατον: two reasons follow in the form of a dilemma, — ἐάν τε (3) and ἐάν τε (5). — **πεῖσαι**: explanatory infinitive. — **τινάς**: Socrates probably means most of the Athenians.

6. καὶ τυγχάνει μέγιστον ἀγαθόν: to speak of virtue and seek truth is not duty only; it is the highest good and gives the greatest pleasure.

9. ἀνεξέταστος: in which case a man examines neither himself nor others, that is, his life is unthinking. Verbal adjectives in -τος, especially with a- privative, occur with both an active and a passive sense. Here the active meaning substantially includes the passive in so far as it involves self-examination (καὶ ἐμαυτὸν καὶ ἄλλους ἐξετάζοντος).

10. ταῦτα δέ: this is the apodosis to ἐάν τ᾽ αὖ λέγω, with a shift of construction. — **τὰ δέ**: cf. τὸ δέ **37 a.**

12 f. εἰ μὲν γὰρ ἦν κτλ.: γάρ is related to the thought which lies unuttered in the previous explanation, — "not from love of money do I refuse to make a proposition." The apodosis includes ὅσα ἔμελλον κτλ. Cf. ὃς ἔμελλεν **20 a.**

38 b

ἔμελλον ἐκτείσειν· οὐδὲν γὰρ ἂν ἐβλάβην· νῦν δὲ — οὐ γὰρ
15 ἔστιν, εἰ μὴ ἄρα ὅσον ἂν ἐγὼ δυναίμην ἐκτεῖσαι τοσούτου
βούλεσθέ μοι τιμῆσαι. ἴσως δ᾽ ἂν δυναίμην ἐκτεῖσαι ὑμῖν
μνᾶν ἀργυρίου· τοσούτου οὖν τιμῶμαι.

Πλάτων δ᾽ ὅδε, ὦ ἄνδρες Ἀθηναῖοι, καὶ Κρίτων καὶ Κριτό-
βουλος καὶ Ἀπολλόδωρος κελεύουσί με τριάκοντα μνῶν τιμή-
20 σασθαι, αὐτοὶ δ᾽ ἐγγυᾶσθαι· τιμῶμαι οὖν τοσούτου, ἐγγυηταὶ
δ᾽ ὑμῖν ἔσονται τοῦ ἀργυρίου οὗτοι, ἀξιόχρεῳ.

XXIX. Οὐ πολλοῦ γ᾽ ἕνεκα χρόνου, ὦ ἄνδρες Ἀθηναῖοι, c
ὄνομα ἕξετε καὶ αἰτίαν ὑπὸ τῶν βουλομένων τὴν πόλιν λοιδορεῖν, ὡς "Σωκράτη ἀπεκτόνατε, ἄνδρα σοφόν·" φήσουσι γὰρ

14. νῦν δὲ, οὐ γάρ: but as it is (I
cannot propose a fine), *for money I
have none*. The connection is similar
to ἀλλὰ γάρ (**19 d, 20 c**), where the unexpressed thought alluded to by γάρ
is easily supplied. Doubtless this was
indicated here by a shrug of the
shoulders or some other gesture.

17. μνᾶνἀργυρίου: about seventeen
dollars. This is certainly small compared with the fines of fifty talents
($50,000) imposed in other cases, e.g.
upon Miltiades, Pericles, Timotheus,
and Demosthenes.

20. αὐτοὶ δ᾽ ἐγγυᾶσθαι: sc. φασίν,
to be supplied from κελεύουσι (cf. δεῖν
28 e). Their surety would relieve
Socrates from imprisonment.

Here ends Socrates's ἀντιτίμησις,
which was followed by the final vote
of the court determining the penalty.
The majority was much larger than
before, — 360 to 141. With this the
case ends. Socrates has only to be led
away to prison.

In the address that follows, Socrates is entirely out of order. He takes
advantage of a slight delay to say his
last words both to those who had voted
for his condemnation and to those who
had voted for his acquittal.

XXIX. *You Athenians have not
gained much by putting me to death.
You have gained only a brief respite by
doing a great wrong. I should soon
have died in the natural course of events.
I might have been acquitted, if I had
been ready to fawn upon you, and to
say what you like to hear. But I am
satisfied with the decision.*

2. ὄνομα κτλ.: cf. τὸ ὄνομα καὶ τὴν
διαβολήν **20 d**.— ὑπό: as if with ὀνο-
μασθήσεσθε and αἰτιασθήσεσθε. See on
πεπόνθατε **17 a**, φύγοιμι **19 c**. Some
periphrasis like ὄνομα ἕξετε κτλ. was
often preferred by the Greeks to their
somewhat cumbrous future passive. —
λοιδορεῖν: Athens was not popular in
Greece, and many were ready to criticise her.

38 e

δὴ σοφὸν εἶναι, εἰ καὶ μὴ εἰμί, οἱ βουλόμενοι ὑμῖν ὀνειδίζειν.
5 εἰ οὖν περιεμείνατε ὀλίγον χρόνον, ἀπὸ τοῦ αὐτομάτου ἂν
ὑμῖν τοῦτο ἐγένετο· ὁρᾶτε γὰρ δὴ τὴν ἡλικίαν ὅτι πόρρω ἤδη
ἐστὶ τοῦ βίου, θανάτου δ' ἐγγύς. λέγω δὲ τοῦτο οὐ πρὸς πάντας ὑμᾶς, ἀλλὰ πρὸς τοὺς ἐμοῦ καταψηφισαμένους θάνατον. d
λέγω δὲ καὶ τόδε πρὸς τοὺς αὐτοὺς τούτους. ἴσως με
10 οἴεσθε, ὦ ἄνδρες, ἀπορίᾳ λόγων ἑαλωκέναι τοιούτων, οἷς
ἂν ὑμᾶς ἔπεισα, εἰ ᾤμην δεῖν ἅπαντα ποιεῖν καὶ λέγειν
ὥστ' ἀποφυγεῖν τὴν δίκην. πολλοῦ γε δεῖ. ἀλλ' ἀπορίᾳ μὲν
ἑάλωκα, οὐ μέντοι λόγων, ἀλλὰ τόλμης καὶ ἀναισχυντίας καὶ
τοῦ ἐθέλειν λέγειν πρὸς ὑμᾶς τοιαῦτα, οἷ' ἂν ὑμῖν ἥδιστα ἦν
15 ἀκούειν, θρηνοῦντός τέ μου καὶ ὀδυρομένου καὶ ἄλλα ποιοῦντος καὶ λέγοντος πολλὰ καὶ ἀνάξια ἐμοῦ, ὡς ἐγώ φημι· οἷα e
δὴ καὶ εἴθισθε ὑμεῖς τῶν ἄλλων ἀκούειν. ἀλλ' οὔτε τότ' ᾤθην
δεῖν ἕνεκα τοῦ κινδύνου πρᾶξαι οὐδὲν ἀνελεύθερον, οὔτε νῦν
μοι μεταμέλει οὕτως ἀπολογησαμένῳ, ἀλλὰ πολὺ μᾶλλον
20 αἱροῦμαι ὧδ' ἀπολογησάμενος τεθνάναι ἢ ἐκείνως ζῆν· οὔτε
γὰρ ἐν δίκῃ οὔτ' ἐν πολέμῳ οὔτ' ἐμὲ οὔτ' ἄλλον οὐδένα δεῖ

5. εἰ οὖν: resumes l. 1.

6. .ὅτι πόρρω κτλ.: explains ἡλικίαν.
— πόρρω τοῦ βίου: *far on in life.* The
genitive is local, not ablatival.

7. θανάτου δ' ἐγγύς: *and near unto
death.* The contrast introduced by δέ
is often so slight that *but* overtranslates
it; it here marks the contrast with βίου,
with which μέν might have been used.

13. τόλμης: in its worst sense, like
the Latin audacia. Cf. ἐάν τις τολμᾷ
39 a, below, and *Crito* 53 e.

15. θρηνοῦντος κτλ.: a development
of the idea in τοιαῦτα, οἷ' ἂν κτλ. Here
is a transition from the accusative of
the thing heard (θρήνους καὶ ὀδυρμούς) to
the genitive of the person heard. —The
thought refers to 34 c. — Cf. also *Gorg.*

522 d, where (evidently with reference
to the point here made) Plato puts the
following words into Socrates's mouth:
εἰ δὲ κολακικῆς ῥητορικῆς (*rhetorical flat-
tery*) ἐνδείᾳ τελευτῴην ἔγωγε, εὖ οἶδα ὅτι
ῥᾳδίως ἴδοις ἄν με φέροντα τὸν θάνατον.

17. τότε: i.e. at the time of his
defense.

20. ὧδ' ἀπολογησάμενος: *in this
way,* etc., i.e. after such a defense.
οὕτως above means *as I have,* and that
idea is vividly repeated by ὧδε. Thus
its contrast with ἐκείνως (sc. ἀπολογησάμενος) is made all the more striking.
— τεθνάναι: because of the contrast
with ζῆν. Cf. τεθνάναι 30 c.

21. οὔτε, οὔτε κτλ.: a double set of
disjunctives in a single sentence.

τοῦτο μηχανᾶσθαι, ὅπως ἀποφεύξεται πᾶν ποιῶν θάνατον. **39**
καὶ γὰρ ἐν ταῖς μάχαις πολλάκις δῆλον γίγνεται ὅτι τό
γ' ἀποθανεῖν ἄν τις ἐκφύγοι καὶ ὅπλα ἀφεὶς καὶ ἐφ' ἱκετείαν
25 τραπόμενος τῶν διωκόντων· καὶ ἄλλαι μηχαναὶ πολλαί εἰσιν
ἐν ἑκάστοις τοῖς κινδύνοις ὥστε διαφεύγειν θάνατον, ἐάν τις
τολμᾷ πᾶν ποιεῖν καὶ λέγειν. ἀλλὰ μὴ οὐ τοῦτ' ᾖ χαλεπόν,
ὦ ἄνδρες, θάνατον ἐκφυγεῖν, ἀλλὰ πολὺ χαλεπώτερον πονη-
ρίαν· θᾶττον γὰρ θανάτου θεῖ. καὶ νῦν ἐγὼ μὲν ἅτε βραδὺς **b**
30 ὢν καὶ πρεσβύτης ὑπὸ τοῦ βραδυτέρου ἑάλων, οἱ δ' ἐμοὶ
κατήγοροι ἅτε δεινοὶ καὶ ὀξεῖς ὄντες ὑπὸ τοῦ θάττονος, τῆς
κακίας. καὶ νῦν ἐγὼ μὲν ἄπειμι ὑφ' ὑμῶν θανάτου δίκην
ὀφλών, οὗτοι δ' ὑπὸ τῆς ἀληθείας ὠφληκότες μοχθηρίαν καὶ
ἀδικίαν. καὶ ἐγώ τε τῷ τιμήματι ἐμμένω καὶ οὗτοι. ταῦτα μέν
35 που ἴσως οὕτω καὶ ἔδει σχεῖν, καὶ οἶμαι αὐτὰ μετρίως ἔχειν.
XXX. τὸ δὲ δὴ μετὰ τοῦτο ἐπιθυμῶ ὑμῖν χρησμῳδῆσαι,

22. **μηχανᾶσθαι**: cf. **28 b**.

27. **μὴ . . . ᾖ**: substituted rhetor-
ically for a statement of fact. Cf. μὴ
σκέμματα ᾖ *Crito* **48 c**. For the idea
of fearing implied, see GMT. 265;
H. 867.

28. **ἀλλὰ πολὺ** κτλ.: fully expressed
we should have ἀλλὰ μὴ πολὺ χαλεπώτερον ἢ πονηρίαν ἐκφυγεῖν.

29. **θᾶττον θανάτου θεῖ**: *flies faster
than death*, to preserve the alliteration,
which here, as often, is picturesque.
— For the thought, cf. *Henry V* iv. 1,
" Now, if these men have defeated the
law and outrun native punishment,
though they can outstrip men, they
have no wings to fly from God." —
καὶ νῦν: introduces a particular instance of the general remark.

32. **θανάτου δίκην ὀφλών**: with
ὀφλισκάνειν, whether used technically
(as a law term) or colloquially, the

crime or the penalty is named either
(1) in the accusative or (2) in the genitive with or without δίκην.

33. **ἀληθείας**: contrasted with ὑμῶν.

34. **καὶ ἐγὼ** κτλ.: i.e. they will escape their punishment just as little as
I escape mine. The καί before ἔδει
makes a climax : " it may well be that
all this had to come just so, and I
have no fault to find with it."

35. **σχεῖν**: cf. ἔσχετε **19 a**.

XXX. *Y u Athenians who have
voted for my condemnat on th nk that
you will be freed henceforth from my
reproaches. But others will arise to
reproach you. The only honorable and
effectual way to escape reproach, is by
leading an upright life.*

1. **τὸ μετὰ τοῦτο**: adverbial, like
τὸ πρῶτον, τὸ νῦν, κτλ. — **χρησμῳδῆσαι**:
The Greek oracles were ordinarily in
verse. Cf. χρησμῳδός **22 c**.

39 d

ὦ καταψηφισάμενοί μου. καὶ γάρ εἰμι ἤδη ἐνταῦθα, ἐν ᾧ
μάλιστ᾽ ἄνθρωποι χρησμῳδοῦσιν, ὅταν μέλλωσιν ἀποθα-
νεῖσθαι. φημὶ γάρ, ὦ ἄνδρες, οἳ ἐμὲ ἀπεκτόνατε, τιμωρίαν
5 ὑμῖν ἥξειν εὐθὺς μετὰ τὸν ἐμὸν θάνατον πολὺ χαλεπωτέραν
νὴ Δία ἢ οἵαν ἐμὲ ἀπεκτόνατε· νῦν γὰρ τοῦτο εἰργάσασθε
οἰόμενοι ἀπαλλάξεσθαι τοῦ διδόναι ἔλεγχον τοῦ βίου, τὸ
δ᾽ ὑμῖν πολὺ ἐναντίον ἀποβήσεται, ὡς ἐγώ φημι. πλείους
ἔσονται ὑμᾶς οἱ ἐλέγχοντες, οὓς νῦν ἐγὼ κατεῖχον, ὑμεῖς
10 δ᾽ οὐκ ᾐσθάνεσθε· καὶ χαλεπώτεροι ἔσονται ὅσῳ νεώτεροί ἱ
εἰσι, καὶ ὑμεῖς μᾶλλον ἀγανακτήσετε. εἰ γὰρ οἴεσθε ἀπο-

3. **ἄνθρωποι χρησμῳδοῦσιν κτλ.**:
Socrates has in mind such instances as
Homer Il 852 f., where Patroclus as
he dies prophesies truly to Hector, οὔ
θην οὐδ᾽ αὐτὸς δηρὸν βέῃ, ἀλλά τοι ἤδη |
ἄγχι παρέστηκεν θάνατος καὶ μοῖρα κρα-
ταιή, and X 358 ff., where Hector's
last words foretell the killing of Achilles by Paris and Phoebus Apollo. Cf.
Verg. Aen. x. 739, —

Ille autem expirans: Non me, quicumque es,
inulto,
Victor,nec longum laetabere; te quoque fata
Prospectant paria, atque eadem mox arva
tenebis.

Cf. also Xen. Cyr. viii. 7. 21, ἡ δὲ τοῦ
ἀνθρώπου ψυχὴ τότε (at the hour of death)
δήπου θειοτάτη καταφαίνεται καὶ τότε τι
τῶν μελλόντων προορᾷ· τότε γάρ, ὡς ἔοικε,
μάλιστα ἐλευθεροῦται. The same idea is
found in many literatures. The dying
patriarch Jacob "called unto his sons,
and said, 'Gather yourselves together
that I may tell you that which shall
befall you in the last days.'" Genesis
xlix. 1. Cf. Brunhild in the song of
Siegfried (Edda), —

I prithee, Gunther, sit thee here by me,
For death is near and bids me prophesy.

See also John of Gaunt's dying speech,
Richard II ii. 1, —

Methinks I am a prophet new inspired,
And thus expiring do foretell of him :
His rash fierce blaze of riot cannot last,
For violent fires soon burn out themselves.

4. **ἀπεκτόνατε** : sc. by their verdict,
and by the penalty which they voted.
6. **οἵαν ἐμὲ ἀπεκτόνατε** : equivalent
to "than the death which you have
voted for me," "the sentence which
you have imposed." This is after the
analogy of τιμωρίαν τιμωρεῖσθαί τινα,
without some reminiscence of which it
would hardly occur to any one to say
θάνατον or τιμωρίαν ἐμὲ ἀπεκτόνατε. ἀπεκτόνατε is substituted, as more vivid
and concrete, for the expected τετιμώ-
ρησθε. Similarly we have μάχην νικᾶν
or ἡττᾶσθαι as more specific equivalents
of μάχην μάχεσθαι. — **νῦν** : expresses
reality. This use of νῦν is akin to its
very frequent use in contrast to a supposition contrary to fact (cf. 38 b), but
here it is connected with a false notion of what will come to pass, in
contrast with the truth as foretold by
Socrates.

39 d
κτείνοντες ἀνθρώπους ἐπισχήσειν τοῦ ὀνειδίζειν τινὰ ὑμῖν
ὅτι οὐκ ὀρθῶς ζῆτε, οὐκ ὀρθῶς διανοεῖσθε. οὐ γὰρ ἔσθ᾽ αὕτη
ἡ ἀπαλλαγὴ οὔτε πάνυ δυνατὴ οὔτε καλή, ἀλλ᾽ ἐκείνη καὶ
15 καλλίστη καὶ ῥᾴστη, μὴ τοὺς ἄλλους κολούειν, ἀλλ᾽ ἑαυτὸν
παρασκευάζειν ὅπως ἔσται ὡς βέλτιστος. ταῦτα μὲν οὖν
ὑμῖν τοῖς καταψηφισαμένοις μαντευσάμενος ἀπαλλάττομαι.

XXXI. Τοῖς δ᾽ ἀποψηφισαμένοις ἡδέως ἂν διαλεχθείην e
ὑπὲρ τοῦ γεγονότος τουτουὶ πράγματος, ἐν ᾧ οἱ ἄρχοντες
ἀσχολίαν ἄγουσι καὶ οὔπω ἔρχομαι οἷ ἐλθόντα με δεῖ τεθνάναι. ἀλλά μοι, ὦ ἄνδρες, παραμείνατε τοσοῦτον χρόνον·
5 οὐδὲν γὰρ κωλύει διαμυθολογῆσαι πρὸς ·ἀλλήλους ἕως ἔξ-
εστιν· ὑμῖν γὰρ ὡς φίλοις οὖσιν ἐπιδεῖξαι ἐθέλω τὸ νυνί μοι 40
συμβεβηκὸς τί ποτε νοεῖ. ἐμοὶ γάρ, ὦ ἄνδρες δικασταί, —
ὑμᾶς γὰρ δικαστὰς καλῶν ὀρθῶς ἂν καλοίην, — θαυμάσιόν

13. ἔσθ᾽ αὕτη: the position of ἔστι
near οὐ at the beginning of the clause
justifies the accent.

17. μαντευσάμενος κτλ.: the main
thought is in the participle, though I
take my leave is in place at the close.

XXXI–XXXIII. Socrates now ad-
dresses the judges who voted for his
acquittal.

XXXI. To you who voted for my
acquittal, I should like to show the
meaning of what has happened. Death
must be a good thing for me. In nothing connected with this case has my inward monitor checked or opposed my
act or word, yet it surely would have
done so if I had not been about to act
for my best good.

2. ὑπέρ: here equals περί. Socrates speaks about what has befallen him,
which he looks upon as for the best
since it is the will of Divine Provi-
dence.

3. ἀσχολίαν ἄγουσι: the officials
were occupied with preparing the
formal record of the judgment and
the warrant for the death of Socrates.

4. ἀλλά: used frequently, for the
sake of vivacity, before the imperative or subjunctive of command. Cf.
ἀλλ᾽ ἐμοὶ κτλ. Crito 45 a.

5. οὐδὲν γὰρ κωλύει κτλ.: indicates
the calm self-possession of Socrates,
contrasted with the ordinary attitude
of those under sentence of death. - -
διαμυθολογῆσαι: more familiar than
διαλέγεσθαι. Thus Socrates prepares to
open his heart upon matters which only
those who care for him need hear. Cf.
Phaedo 61 e.

7. τί νοεῖ: Socrates always sought
the inner meaning of an event.

8. ὑμᾶς κτλ.: here, for the first
time Socrates calls his hearers judges;
until now he has addressed them simply as Athenian citizens.

40 c

τι γέγονεν. ἡ γὰρ εἰωθυῖά μοι μαντικὴ ἡ τοῦ δαιμονίου ἐν
10 μὲν τῷ πρόσθεν χρόνῳ παντὶ πάνυ πυκνὴ ἀεὶ ἦν καὶ πάνυ
ἐπὶ σμικροῖς ἐναντιουμένη, εἴ τι μέλλοιμι μὴ ὀρθῶς πράξειν·
νυνὶ δὲ συμβέβηκέ μοι, ἅπερ ὁρᾶτε καὶ αὐτοί, ταυτὶ ἅ γε
δὴ οἰηθείη ἄν τις καὶ νομίζεται ἔσχατα κακῶν εἶναι, ἐμοὶ
δ' οὔτ' ἐξιόντι ἕωθεν οἴκοθεν ἠναντιώθη τὸ τοῦ θεοῦ σημεῖον, ὶ
15 οὔθ' ἡνίκα ἀνέβαινον ἐνταυθοῖ ἐπὶ τὸ δικαστήριον, οὔτ' ἐν
τῷ λόγῳ οὐδαμοῦ μέλλοντί τι ἐρεῖν· καίτοι ἐν ἄλλοις λόγοις
πολλαχοῦ δή με ἐπέσχε λέγοντα μεταξύ· νῦν δ' οὐδαμοῦ
περὶ ταύτην τὴν πρᾶξιν οὔτ' ἐν ἔργῳ οὐδενὶ οὔτ' ἐν λόγῳ
ἠναντίωταί μοι. τί οὖν αἴτιον εἶναι ὑπολαμβάνω; ἐγὼ ὑμῖν
20 ἐρῶ· κινδυνεύει γάρ μοι τὸ συμβεβηκὸς τοῦτο ἀγαθὸν γεγονέναι, καὶ οὐκ ἔσθ' ὅπως ἡμεῖς ὀρθῶς ὑπολαμβάνομεν ὅσοι
οἰόμεθα κακὸν εἶναι τὸ τεθνάναι. μέγα μοι τεκμήριον τούτου c
γέγονεν· οὐ γὰρ ἔσθ' ὅπως οὐκ ἠναντιώθη ἄν μοι τὸ εἰωθὸς
σημεῖον, εἰ μή τι ἔμελλον ἐγὼ ἀγαθὸν πράξειν.

9. γάρ: introduces not the single statement but the combination of statements. The θαυμάσιόν τι is that now, when Socrates has such a fate before him, the voice is silent, while previously, etc.—ἡ τοῦ δαιμονίου: cf. 31 d.

10. πάνυ ἐπὶ σμικροῖς: see on οὕτω παρ' ὀλίγον 36 a.

13. οἰηθείη, νομίζεται: change of voice and of mood, — from possibility to actuality, — νομίζεται being almost a correction of οἰηθείη.

14. ἐξιόντι κτλ: Socrates did not suffer the indignity of a technical "arrest," but was simply summoned to appear before the court. If he had chosen to leave the court-room at the close of the first division of his speech (35 d), without waiting for the verdict, probably no officer of the law

would have been authorized to detain him.

18. ταύτην τὴν πρᾶξιν: the trial, including everything that led up to it.

19. ἠναντίωται: ἠναντιώθη was used above. Here the whole is included. — ὑπολαμβάνω: not subjunctive, since there is no question of doubt. The question is only a vivid fashion of speech, of which Plato is fond.

21. ἡμεῖς: to be connected immediately with ὅσοι, all we, — even though strictly Socrates was not included in this number. The first person gives a courteous color to the whole. In English we might use a partitive expression, all of us.

24. ἔμελλον: refers definitely to past time but still contains the idea of continued action.

40 c

XXXII. ἐννοήσωμεν δὲ καὶ τῇδε ὡς πολλὴ ἐλπίς ἐστιν
ἀγαθὸν αὐτὸ εἶναι. δυοῖν γὰρ θάτερόν ἐστι τὸ τεθνάναι· ἢ
γὰρ οἷον μηδὲν εἶναι μηδ' αἴσθησιν μηδεμίαν μηδενὸς ἔχειν
τὸν τεθνεῶτα, ἢ κατὰ τὰ λεγόμενα μεταβολή τις τυγχάνει
5 οὖσα καὶ μετοίκησις τῇ ψυχῇ τοῦ τόπου τοῦ ἐνθένδε εἰς
ἄλλον τόπον. καὶ εἴτε μηδεμία αἴσθησίς ἐστιν, ἀλλ' οἷον
ὕπνος ἐπειδάν τις καθεύδων μηδ' ὄναρ μηδὲν ὁρᾷ, θαυμάσιον
κέρδος ἂν εἴη ὁ θάνατος. ἐγὼ γὰρ ἂν οἶμαι, εἴ τινα ἐκλεξά-

Chapters XXXII and XXXIII are
translated by Cicero, *Tusculan Disputations* i. 41.

XXXII. *But a general argument
may be presented to show that death is
a good: Death is either unending sleep,
or it is a departure of the soul to a new
home, where it will meet with the just
and honored men of old,— with Minos
and Rhadamanthys, with Orpheus and
Homer. I in particular shall find
pleasure in comparing my experiences
with those of Palamedes and Telamonian Ajax, who also died because of an
unjust judgment, and in questioning
Agamemnon and Odysseus. In either
case, then, death is a blessing.*

1. τῇδε: *the following.* After the
argument based upon the silence of
his inner voice, Socrates considers the
question upon its merits.

2. αὐτό: i.e. what has befallen
Socrates. — τεθνάναι: subject.

3. οἷον μηδὲν εἶναι: without definitely expressed subject (cf. οἷον ἀποδη-
μῆσαι in e below), — *to be dead is as to
be nothing,* i.e. its nature is such that
a man when dead is nothing.

4. τὸν τεθνεῶτα: the subject of ἔχειν,
which is an afterthought; not of εἶναι.

— κατὰ τὰ λεγόμενα: Socrates asso-

ciates his idea of the life hereafter
with stories and traditions whose early
stages are represented by Homer's
utterances about the Ἠλύσιον πεδίον and
Hesiod's account of the μακάρων νῆσοι.
The later poets, e.g. Pindar, continued
what Homer and Hesiod began. And
Pindar incorporates into his descrip-
tions of life after death Orphic and
Pythagorean accounts of metempsychosis. Here and in the *Phaedo* (70 c–
72 a) Socrates appeals to a παλαιὸς
λόγος. — τυγχάνει οὖσα: the subject is
τεθνάναι, but the gender of the participle is attracted to that of the predicate,
μεταβολή.

5. τῇ ψυχῇ: dative of interest. —
τοῦ τόπου: limiting genitive with μετα-
βολὴ καὶ μετοίκησις. Of these, the latter
repeats the former in more specific
form. — τοῦ ἐνθένδε: cf. τοὺς ἐκ τῆς ναυμαχίας 32 b.

6. καὶ εἴτε κτλ.: takes up in detail
ἢ γὰρ οἷον κτλ. of l. 3. The second alternative is introduced by εἰ δ' αὖ l. 18.
— οἷον ὕπνος: cf. καὶ τῷ ἥδυμος ὕπνος
ἐπὶ βλεφάροισιν ἔπιπτε | νήγρετος ἥδιστος,
θανάτῳ ἄγχιστα ἐοικώς Hom. ν 79 f.

8. κέρδος: not ἀγαθόν, because Socrates does not consider such a condition as in itself a good. — ἂν οἶμαι: ἄν

41 a

μενον δέοι ταύτην τὴν νύκτα, ἐν ᾗ οὕτω κατέδαρθεν ὥστε
10 μηδ' ὄναρ ἰδεῖν, καὶ τὰς ἄλλας νύκτας τε καὶ ἡμέρας τὰς τοῦ
βίου τοῦ ἑαυτοῦ ἀντιπαραθέντα ταύτῃ τῇ νυκτὶ δέοι σκεψάμενον εἰπεῖν πόσας ἄμεινον καὶ ἥδιον ἡμέρας καὶ νύκτας
ταύτης τῆς νυκτὸς βεβίωκεν ἐν τῷ ἑαυτοῦ βίῳ, οἶμαι ἂν μὴ
ὅτι ἰδιώτην τινά, ἀλλὰ τὸν μέγαν βασιλέα εὐαριθμήτους ἂν e
15 εὑρεῖν αὐτὸν ταύτας πρὸς τὰς ἄλλας ἡμέρας καὶ νύκτας. εἰ
οὖν τοιοῦτον ὁ θάνατός ἐστι, κέρδος ἔγωγε λέγω· καὶ γὰρ
οὐδὲν πλείων ὁ πᾶς χρόνος φαίνεται οὕτω δὴ εἶναι ἢ μία
νύξ. εἰ δ' αὖ οἷον ἀποδημῆσαί ἐστιν ὁ θάνατος ἐνθένδε εἰς
ἄλλον τόπον, καὶ ἀληθῆ ἐστι τὰ λεγόμενα ὡς ἄρα ἐκεῖ εἰσιν
20 ἅπαντες οἱ τεθνεῶτες, τί μεῖζον ἀγαθὸν τούτου εἴη ἄν, ὦ
ἄνδρες δικασταί; εἰ γάρ τις ἀφικόμενος εἰς Ἅιδου, ἀπαλ-
λαγεὶς τούτων τῶν φασκόντων δικαστῶν εἶναι, εὑρήσει τοὺς 41
ἀληθῶς δικαστάς, οἵπερ καὶ λέγονται ἐκεῖ δικάζειν, Μίνως

belongs to εὑρεῖν, and on account of the
length of the protasis is repeated first
with οἶμαι in l. 13, and again just before
the infinitive; similarly δέοι is twice
used in the protasis. See on ἴσως τάχ' ἂν
31 a.—εἴ τινα ἐκλεξάμενον δέοι . . . εἰπεῖν,
εὐαριθμήτους ἂν εὑρεῖν κτλ.—ἐκλεξάμενον
καὶ ἀντιπαραθέντα σκεψάμενον: the first
two participles coupled by καὶ are
subordinated to σκεψάμενον, just as
this in turn is subordinated to εἰπεῖν.
Cf. 21 e.

14. μὴ ὅτι, ἀλλὰ κτλ.: not to speak
of any one in private station, no, not the
Great King, etc. ἀλλά here introduces
a climax. See H. 1035 a.

15. αὐτόν: this gives a final touch
of emphasis to βασιλέα. Socrates here
talks of the king of Persia in the strain
which was common among Greeks in
his day. Polus, in the Gorgias (470 e),

is surprised because Socrates refuses
to take it for granted that the king of
Persia is happy.

16. τοιοῦτον: predicate to θάνατος.
— κέρδος λέγω: sc. αὐτόν. — καὶ γὰρ
κτλ.: for thus the whole of time appears
no more than a single night, etc.

18. εἰ δ' αὖ: refers to l. 6.

19. ἄρα: as they say, marks this as
the popular view.

22. δικαστῶν: predicate ablatival
genitive.

23 f. Μίνως κτλ.: attracted from
the accusative in apposition with δικαστάς to the construction of the relative clause. — According to ordinary
Greek belief, a man's occupations after
death were much the same as before.
So Socrates assumes that Minos is a
ruler and judge, and that he himself
will continue his questionings.

41 a

τε καὶ Ῥαδάμανθυς καὶ Αἰακὸς καὶ Τριπτόλεμος καὶ ἄλλοι
25 ὅσοι τῶν ἡμιθέων δίκαιοι ἐγένοντο ἐν τῷ ἑαυτῶν βίῳ, ἆρα
φαύλη ἂν εἴη ἡ ἀποδημία; ἢ αὖ Ὀρφεῖ συγγενέσθαι καὶ Μου-
σαίῳ καὶ Ἡσιόδῳ καὶ Ὁμήρῳ ἐπὶ πόσῳ ἄν τις δέξαιτ᾽ ἂν
ὑμῶν; ἐγὼ μὲν γὰρ πολλάκις ἐθέλω τεθνάναι, εἰ ταῦτά ἐστιν
ἀληθῆ· ἐπεὶ ἔμοιγε καὶ αὐτῷ θαυμαστὴ ἂν εἴη ἡ διατριβὴ
30 αὐτόθι, ὁπότ᾽ ἐντύχοιμι Παλαμήδει καὶ Αἴαντι τῷ Τελαμῶ- b
νος καὶ εἴ τις ἄλλος τῶν παλαιῶν διὰ κρίσιν ἄδικον τέθνη-
κεν. ἀντιπαραβάλλοντι τὰ ἐμαυτοῦ πάθη πρὸς τὰ ἐκείνων,
ὡς ἐγὼ οἶμαι, οὐκ ἂν ἀηδὲς εἴη. καὶ δὴ τὸ μέγιστον, τοὺς
ἐκεῖ ἐξετάζοντα καὶ ἐρευνῶντα ὥσπερ τοὺς ἐνταῦθα διάγειν,
35 τίς αὐτῶν σοφός ἐστι καὶ τίς οἴεται μέν, ἔστι δ᾽ οὔ. ἐπὶ
πόσῳ δ᾽ ἄν τις, ὦ ἄνδρες δικασταί, δέξαιτο ἐξετάσαι τὸν ἐπὶ
Τροίαν ἄγοντα τὴν πολλὴν στρατιὰν ἢ Ὀδυσσέα ἢ Σίσυφον, c
ἢ ἄλλους μυρίους ἄν τις εἴποι καὶ ἄνδρας καὶ γυναῖκας, οἷς

25. ἐγένοντο: as aorist of εἰμί.

27. ἐπὶ πόσῳ κτλ.: i.e. how much
would one give ? — ἄν, ἄν: the repetition of ἄν has an effect comparable
to the repeated negation. The first
ἄν is connected with the most important word of the clause, while the
second takes the place naturally belonging to ἄν in the sentence. Cf.
31 a.

30. ὁπότε: *when (if at any time) I
might meet.*

31. εἴ τις ἄλλος: i.e. whoever else.

32. ἀντιπαραβάλλοντι: asyndeton
(H. 1039), which occurs not infrequently where, as here, a sentence is
thrown in by way of explanation, virtually in apposition with the preceding. μοί is easily supplied from the
preceding ἔμοιγε. The action would be
οὐκ ἀηδές. — For the participle, cf.
Phaedo 114 d, and see GMT. 901.

33. οὐκ ἀηδές: repeats θαυμαστή
l. 29. — καὶ δὴ τὸ μέγιστον: *and what
after all is the greatest thing.* Then
follows, in the form of an appositive
clause, an explanation of the μέγιστον.
The whole is equivalent to τὸ μέγιστόν
ἐστι τοῦτο, ἐξετάζοντα διάγειν (with an
indefinite personal subject). See on
οἷον μηδὲν εἶναι 40 c.

37. ἄγοντα: represents ὃς ἦγε. This
use of the imperfect instead of the
aorist is not uncommon where extreme
accuracy is not aimed at.

38. μυρίους ἄν τις εἴποι: escapes
from the grammatical construction, —
a not uncommon irregularity. — οἷς
διαλέγεσθαι καὶ συνεῖναι καὶ ἐξετάζειν:
when verbs governing different cases
have the same object, the Greek idiom
usually expresses the object once only,
and then in the case governed by the
nearest verb.

41 d

ἐκεῖ διαλέγεσθαι καὶ συνεῖναι καὶ ἐξετάζειν ἀμήχανον ἂν
40 εἴη εὐδαιμονίας! πάντως οὐ δήπου τούτου γ᾽ ἕνεκα οἱ ἐκεῖ
ἀποκτείνουσι· τά τε γὰρ ἄλλα εὐδαιμονέστεροί εἰσιν οἱ
ἐκεῖ τῶν ἐνθάδε, καὶ ἤδη τὸν λοιπὸν χρόνον ἀθάνατοί εἰσιν,
εἴ πέρ γε τὰ λεγόμενα ἀληθῆ.

XXXIII. ἀλλὰ καὶ ὑμᾶς χρή, ὦ ἄνδρες δικασταί, εὐέλπι-
δας εἶναι πρὸς τὸν θάνατον, καὶ ἕν τι τοῦτο διανοεῖσθαι ἀληθές, ὅτι οὐκ ἔστιν ἀνδρὶ ἀγαθῷ κακὸν οὐδὲν οὔτε ζῶντι οὔτε d
τελευτήσαντι, οὐδ᾽ ἀμελεῖται ὑπὸ θεῶν τὰ τούτου πράγματα·
5 οὐδὲ τὰ ἐμὰ νῦν ἀπὸ τοῦ αὐτομάτου γέγονεν, ἀλλά μοι δῆλόν
ἐστι τοῦτο, ὅτι ἤδη τεθνάναι καὶ ἀπηλλάχθαι πραγμάτων
βέλτιον ἦν μοι. διὰ τοῦτο καὶ ἐμὲ οὐδαμοῦ ἀπέτρεψε τὸ

39. ἀμήχανον εὐδαιμονίας: *more
blessed than tongue can tell.*

40. πάντως οὐ δήπου κτλ.: *in any
event, I am sure that they put no man
to death there,* etc. — **τούτου γ᾽ ἕνεκα:**
spoken humorously and with a thrust
at those who voted for his death.

XXXIII. *All should have good
heart as regards death, and believe that
no ill befalls a good man, either while
he lives or on his death. So I am
not very angry with my accusers and
those who voted for my death, — though
they thought to injure me, and for
this they are blameworthy. But if they
will treat my sons as I have treated
my fellow-citizens, and rebuke them if
they take no care for virtue, I shall be
satisfied.*

2. ἕν τι τοῦτο: *this one thing above
all.* The position of τοῦτο, coming as
it does after instead of before ἕν τι, is
emphatic.

3. The same thought is expressed
distinctly also in the *Republic* **613 a.**
Cf. also *Phaedo* **58 e, 64 a.**

6. τεθνάναι καὶ ἀπηλλάχθαι: the
perfect is used, because to speak of the
completion of the change, i.e. *to be
dead,* is the most forcible way of putting the idea. The second infinitive
explains the first. πράγματα applies to
the trouble and the unrest of a busy
life.

7. βέλτιον ἦν: Socrates considers
the whole complication of circumstances in which he is already involved, or in which he must, if he
lives, sooner or later be involved.
Deliverance from this he welcomes.
— **διὰ τοῦτο κτλ.:** cf. **40 a c.** Socrates
argued from the silence of τὸ δαιμόνιον
that no evil was in store for him when
he went before the court. This led
him to conclude that his death could
be no harm. On further consideration,
he is confirmed in this, because death
is never a harm. Applying this principle to his own actual circumstances,
its truth becomes the more manifest,
so that, finally, he can explain why the
divine voice was silent. The Homeric

41 d

σημεῖον, καὶ ἔγωγε τοῖς καταψηφισαμένοις μου καὶ τοῖς
κατηγόροις οὐ πάνυ χαλεπαίνω. καίτοι οὐ ταύτῃ τῇ δια-
10 νοίᾳ κατεψηφίζοντό μου καὶ κατηγόρουν, ἀλλ᾽ οἰόμενοι βλά-
πτειν· τοῦτο αὐτοῖς ἄξιον μέμφεσθαι. τοσόνδε μέντοι δέομαι ε
αὐτῶν· τοὺς ὑεῖς μου ἐπειδὰν ἡβήσωσι τιμωρήσασθε, ὦ ἄνδρες, ταὐτὰ ταῦτα λυποῦντες ἅπερ ἐγὼ ὑμᾶς ἐλύπουν, ἐὰν
ὑμῖν δοκῶσιν ἢ χρημάτων ἢ ἄλλου του πρότερον ἐπιμε-
15 λεῖσθαι ἢ ἀρετῆς, καὶ ἐὰν δοκῶσί τι εἶναι μηδὲν ὄντες, ὀνειδίζετε αὐτοῖς ὥσπερ ἐγὼ ὑμῖν, ὅτι οὐκ ἐπιμελοῦνται ὧν δεῖ,
καὶ οἴονταί τι εἶναι ὄντες οὐδενὸς ἄξιοι. καὶ ἐὰν ταῦτα
ποιῆτε, δίκαια πεπονθὼς ἐγὼ ἔσομαι ὑφ᾽ ὑμῶν, αὐτός τε καὶ 42
οἱ ὑεῖς.

20 ἀλλὰ γὰρ ἤδη ὥρα ἀπιέναι, ἐμοὶ μὲν ἀποθανουμένῳ, ὑμῖν
δὲ βιωσομένοις· ὁπότεροι δ᾽ ἡμῶν ἔρχονται ἐπὶ ἄμεινον
πρᾶγμα, ἄδηλον παντὶ πλὴν ἢ τῷ θεῷ.

Achilles in Hades is represented as
holding a different view (λ 489 ff.), and
Euripides makes Iphigenia say κακῶς
ζῆν κρεῖσσον ἢ καλῶς θανεῖν (*Iph. Aul.*
1252).

10. βλάπτειν : used intransitively,
without accusative of the person or of
the thing, because the abstract idea of
doing harm is alone required.

11. τοῦτο . . . ἄξιον μέμφεσθαι : *so
far it is fair to blame them.* Cf. τοῦτό
μοι ἔδοξεν αὐτῶν 17 b, *this . . . about
them.* They deserve blame for their
malicious intention. — ἄξιον : *it is fair.*
— τοσόνδε μέντοι : "although they
certainly are far from wishing me
well, yet I ask so much as a favor,"

i.e. so little that they can well afford
to grant it. Then follows an explanation of τοσόνδε.

12. ἡβήσωσι : for the aorist, see on
ἔσχετε 19 a. Cf. Hes. *Op.* 132, ἀλλ᾽ ὅταν
ἡβήσειε καὶ ἥβης μέτρον ἵκοιτο.

15. ὀνειδίζετε : cf. ὀνειδίζων 30 e.

18. δίκαια πεπονθώς : *fairly treated*,
to be understood in the light of Chapters XVIII and XXVI. Socrates deserves what is good, — but death is
good. — αὐτός τε κτλ. : for ἐγὼ αὐτὸς
κτλ. Cf. *Crito* 50 e.

20. ἀλλὰ γὰρ κτλ. : serves to close
the speech, giving at the same time the
reason for coming to an end.

22. πλὴν ἤ : cf. ἀλλ᾽ ἤ 20 d.

ΠΛΑΤΩΝΟΣ ΚΡΙΤΩΝ

ΣΩΚΡΑΤΗΣ, ΚΡΙΤΩΝ

43 b

I. ΣΩΚΡΑΤΗΣ. Τί τηνικάδε ἀφῖξαι, ὦ Κρίτων; ἢ οὐ πρῷ a
ἔτι ἐστίν;

ΚΡΙΤΩΝ. Πάνυ μὲν οὖν.

ΣΩ. Πηνίκα μάλιστα;

5 ΚΡ. Ὄρθρος βαθύς.

ΣΩ. Θαυμάζω ὅπως ἠθέλησέ σοι ὁ τοῦ δεσμωτηρίου φύλαξ
ὑπακοῦσαι.

ΚΡ. Συνήθης ἤδη μοί ἐστιν, ὦ Σώκρατες, διὰ τὸ πολλάκις
δεῦρο φοιτᾶν, καί τι καὶ εὐεργέτηται ὑπ' ἐμοῦ.

10 ΣΩ. Ἄρτι δὲ ἥκεις ἢ πάλαι;

ΚΡ. Ἐπιεικῶς πάλαι.

ΣΩ. Εἶτα πῶς οὐκ εὐθὺς ἐπήγειράς με, ἀλλὰ σιγῇ παρα- b
κάθησαι;

I. Crito has come to Socrates's cell in the prison very early in the morning, and has wondered at the peaceful slumber of his friend. He brings the tidings that the festival boat, which has been at Delos, has reached Sunium on its return, and is expected to reach the harbor of Athens to-day, and so Socrates will die on the morrow.

4. πηνίκα: in the prison, Socrates could have slight indication of the time of day.

5. ὄρθρος βαθύς: the expression means rather the end of night than the beginning of day. Cf. the time when the *Protagoras* begins (**310 a**), τῆς παρελθούσης νυκτὸς ταυτησί, ἔτι

βαθέος ὄρθρου. The description of young Hippocrates feeling his way through the dark to Socrates's bedside, in the same dialogue, shows that ὄρθρος βαθύς means *just before daybreak*. Cf. Xen. *An.* iv. 3. 8 ff., where Xenophon dreams a dream, ἐπεὶ δὲ ὄρθρος ἦν . . . διηγεῖται . . . καὶ ὡς τάχιστα ἕως ὑπέφαινεν ἐθύοντο. Here ὄρθρος means the dark before the dawn. Cf. also τῇ δὲ μιᾷ τῶν σαββάτων ὄρθρου βαθέως ἐπὶ τὸ μνῆμα ἦλθον St. Luke xxiv. 1.

9. τι: equivalent to εὐεργεσίαν τινά (a tip).

12. εἶτα: refers to ἐπιεικῶς πάλαι in a vein of slight wonder or perhaps of gentle reproof.

43 b
ΚΡ. Οὐ μὰ τὸν Δία, ὦ Σώκρατες, οὐδ' ἂν αὐτὸς ἤθελον ἐν
15 τοσαύτῃ τ' ἀγρυπνίᾳ καὶ λύπῃ εἶναι. ἀλλὰ καὶ σοῦ πάλαι
θαυμάζω αἰσθανόμενος ὡς ἡδέως καθεύδεις· καὶ ἐπίτηδές σε
οὐκ ἤγειρον, ἵνα ὡς ἥδιστα διάγῃς. καὶ πολλάκις μὲν δή
σε καὶ πρότερον ἐν παντὶ τῷ βίῳ ηὐδαιμόνισα τοῦ τρόπου,
πολὺ δὲ μάλιστα ἐν τῇ νῦν παρεστώσῃ συμφορᾷ, ὡς ῥᾳδίως
20 αὐτὴν καὶ πρᾴως φέρεις.
ΣΩ. Καὶ γὰρ ἄν, ὦ Κρίτων, πλημμελὲς εἴη ἀγανακτεῖν
τηλικοῦτον ὄντα, εἰ δεῖ ἤδη τελευτᾶν.
ΚΡ. Καὶ ἄλλοι, ὦ Σώκρατες, τηλικοῦτοι ἐν τοιαύταις συμ- c
φοραῖς ἁλίσκονται, ἀλλ' οὐδὲν αὐτοὺς ἐπιλύεται ἡ ἡλικία τὸ
25 μὴ οὐχὶ ἀγανακτεῖν τῇ παρούσῃ τύχῃ.
ΣΩ. Ἔστι ταῦτα. ἀλλὰ τί δὴ οὕτω πρῷ ἀφῖξαι;
ΚΡ. Ἀγγελίαν, ὦ Σώκρατες, φέρων — χαλεπὴν οὐ σοί, ὡς
ἐμοὶ φαίνεται, ἀλλ' ἐμοὶ καὶ τοῖς σοῖς ἐπιτηδείοις πᾶσιν καὶ
χαλεπὴν καὶ βαρεῖαν, ἣν ἐγὼ ὡς ἐμοὶ δοκῶ ἐν τοῖς βαρύ-
30 τατ' ἂν ἐνέγκαιμι.

14. οὐ μὰ τὸν Δία: sc. ἐπήγειρα. —
The answer to Socrates's question
becomes categorical in καὶ ἐπίτηδες
κτλ.
15. ἐν τοσαύτῃ τ' ἀγρυπνίᾳ κτλ.:
sc. as I am. τέ is placed after τοσαύτῃ,
since this belongs to both substantives.
This position of τέ is very common
after the article or a preposition.
17. ἤγειρον: the imperfect indicates
the length of time that Crito sat by
Socrates without waking him.
18. τοῦ τρόπου: genitive of cause.
At the end of the sentence, a clause
with ὡς (equivalent to ὅτι οὕτω) is introduced in place of the genitive.
21. πλημμελές: cf. Ap. 22 d and
ἐμμελῶς Ap. 20 c.

22. τηλικοῦτον: cf. τηλικόνδε 34 e.
25. τὸ μὴ οὐχὶ ἀγανακτεῖν: ἐπιλύεται is here qualified by οὐδέν, and is
used in the sense of preventing. Hence
the doubled negative.
29. καὶ χαλεπὴν καὶ βαρεῖαν: an
effective and almost pathetic reiteration
of the first χαλεπήν, — made all the
stronger by the doubled καί. — ἐν τοῖς
βαρύτατ' ἂν ἐνέγκαιμι: Herodotus,
Thucydides, Plato, and later writers
use ἐν τοῖς, about, idiomatically to limit
the superlative. Originally in such an
expression the participle was used, e.g.
ἐν τοῖς βαρέως φέρουσι κτλ. Thus ἐν
τοῖς becomes an adverb, which describes not absolute precedence but a
general superiority.

44 a

ΣΩ. Τίνα ταύτην; ἢ τὸ πλοῖον ἀφῖκται ἐκ Δήλου, οὗ δεῖ ἀφικομένου τεθνάναι με;   **d**

ΚΡ. Οὗτοι δὴ ἀφῖκται, ἀλλὰ δοκεῖ μέν μοι ἥξειν τήμερον ἐξ ὧν ἀπαγγέλλουσιν ἥκοντές τινες ἀπὸ Σουνίου καὶ καταλι-
35 πόντες ἐκεῖ αὐτό. δῆλον οὖν ἐκ τούτων [τῶν ἀγγέλων] ὅτι ἥξει τήμερον, καὶ ἀνάγκη δὴ εἰς αὔριον ἔσται, ὦ Σώκρατες, τὸν βίον σε τελευτᾶν.

ΙΙ. ΣΩ. Ἀλλ', ὦ Κρίτων, τύχῃ ἀγαθῇ. εἰ ταύτῃ τοῖς θεοῖς φίλον, ταύτῃ ἔστω. οὐ μέντοι οἶμαι ἥξειν αὐτὸ τήμερον.

ΚΡ. Πόθεν τοῦτο τεκμαίρει;   **44**

ΣΩ. Ἐγώ σοι ἐρῶ. τῇ γάρ που ὑστεραίᾳ δεῖ με ἀποθνή-
5 σκειν ἢ ᾗ ἂν ἔλθῃ τὸ πλοῖον.

ΚΡ. Φασί γέ τοι δὴ οἱ τούτων κύριοι.

ΣΩ. Οὐ τοίνυν τῆς ἐπιούσης ἡμέρας οἶμαι αὐτὸ ἥξειν, ἀλλὰ τῆς ἑτέρας. τεκμαίρομαι δ' ἔκ τινος ἐνυπνίου ὃ ἑώ-ρακα ὀλίγον πρότερον ταύτης τῆς νυκτός· καὶ κινδυνεύεις
10 ἐν καιρῷ τινι οὐκ ἐγεῖραί με.

31. τίνα ταύτην: the construction of the previous clause is continued. Cf. ποίαν σοφίαν ταύτην Ap. **20 d.** — τὸ πλοῖον: cf. Phaedo **58 a.**
32. τεθνάναι: cf. Ap. **30 c** fin.
33. δοκεῖ μέν: with no following δέ. In such cases the original affinity of μέν with μήν is usually apparent. Its meaning is indeed, surely.
36. εἰς αὔριον: construe with τελευτᾶν.
ΙΙ. Socrates does not think that the boat will arrive to-day, for a dream has intimated to him that he is to reach home on the third day.
1. ἀλλά: introduces the cheerful hope of Socrates in vivid contrast to Crito's despondency.

4. τῇ γάρ που κτλ.: this is the first premise that follows the conclusion stated above in οὐ μέντοι ἥξειν τήμερον; the second is contained in the account of the dream.
6. οἱ κύριοι: i.e. οἱ Ἕνδεκα.
7. τῆς ἐπιούσης ἡμέρας: means the same as τήμερον, for Socrates is now thinking of the fact that day has not yet dawned. See on ὄρθρος βαθύς **43 a.**
9. ταύτης τῆς νυκτός: temporal genitive, explaining πρότερον. The vision came after midnight, a circumstance of the greatest importance according to Moschus, Idyll. ii. 2, νυκτὸς ὅτε τρίτατον λάχος ἵσταται, ἐγγύθι δ' ἠώς ... εὖτε καὶ ἀτρεκέων ποιμαίνεται

44 a

ΚΡ. Ἦν δὲ δὴ τί τὸ ἐνύπνιον;

ΣΩ. Ἐδόκει τίς μοι γυνὴ προσελθοῦσα καλὴ καὶ εὐειδής, λευκὰ ἱμάτια ἔχουσα, καλέσαι με καὶ εἰπεῖν· "Ὦ Σώκρατες, **b** 'ἤματί κεν τριτάτῳ Φθίην ἐρίβωλον ἵκοιο.'"

15 ΚΡ. Ἄτοπον τὸ ἐνύπνιον, ὦ Σώκρατες.

ΣΩ. Ἐναργὲς μὲν οὖν ὥς γέ μοι δοκεῖ, ὦ Κρίτων.

III. ΚΡ. Λίαν γε, ὡς ἔοικεν. ἀλλ', ὦ δαιμόνιε Σώκρατες, ἔτι καὶ νῦν ἐμοὶ πείθου καὶ σώθητι· ὡς ἐμοί, ἐὰν σὺ ἀποθά- νῃς, οὐ μία συμφορά ἐστιν, ἀλλὰ χωρὶς μὲν τοῦ ἐστερῆσθαι τοιούτου ἐπιτηδείου, οἷον ἐγὼ οὐδένα μή ποτε εὑρήσω, ἔτι δὲ 5 καὶ πολλοῖς δόξω, οἳ ἐμὲ καὶ σὲ μὴ σαφῶς ἴσασιν, ὡς οἷός τ' ὢν σε σῴζειν, εἰ ἤθελον ἀναλίσκειν χρήματα, ἀμελῆσαι. **c** καίτοι τίς ἂν αἰσχίων εἴη ταύτης δόξα — ἢ δοκεῖν χρήματα περὶ πλείονος ποιεῖσθαι ἢ φίλους; οὐ γὰρ πείσονται οἱ πολλοὶ ὡς σὺ αὐτὸς οὐκ ἠθέλησας ἀπιέναι ἐνθένδε, ἡμῶν 10 προθυμουμένων.

ΣΩ. Ἀλλὰ τί ἡμῖν, ὦ μακάριε Κρίτων, οὕτω τῆς τῶν πολ-

ἔθνος ὀνείρων. Cf. Hor. Sat. i. 10. 32 ff.—

Atque ego cum Graecos facerem, natus mare citra,
Versiculos, vetuit me tali voce Quirinus
Post mediam noctem visus, cum somnia vera.

14. ἤματι κτλ.: quoted from Homer I 363, ἤματί κε τριτάτῳ Φθίην ἐρίβωλον ἱκοίμην, in which Achilles tells Odysseus that he expects to sail from Troy, and to reach his home in Phthia on the third day.

15. ἄτοπον κτλ.: sc. ἐστί, an ex- clamation which nearly approaches the form of a regular sentence. Cf. δημο- βόρος βασιλεύς, ἐπεὶ οὐτιδανοῖσιν ἀνάσσεις Homer A 231.

III. Crito not only mourns the loss of his best friend but also fears the shameful repute of not caring to use his

money for his friend's safety, and he begs Socrates to escape from the prison.

2. ἔτι καὶ νῦν: this gives a hint as to what Crito has planned. It is devel- oped later. — ὡς: causal, since.

3. ἐστίν: more vivid and natural than ἔσται. — ἐστερῆσθαι: construed with χωρίς.

4. οὐδένα μή ποτε: equivalent to οὐ μή ποτέ τινα, and so here with the future indicative, I certainly shall never, etc. Cf. Ap. **28 b.** GMT. 295; H. 1032.

5. ὡς οἷός τ' ὢν κτλ.: many will think that though I was able to save you, I neglected you. οἷός τ' ὢν σῴζειν represents οἷός τ' ἦν σῴζειν, I might have saved you, if I had wished.

7. ἢ δοκεῖν . . . φίλους: explains ταύτης.

44 e

λῶν δόξης μέλει; οἱ γὰρ ἐπιεικέστατοι, ὧν μᾶλλον ἄξιον
φροντίζειν, ἡγήσονται αὐτὰ οὕτω πεπρᾶχθαι ὥσπερ ἂν
πραχθῇ.

15 ΚΡ. Ἀλλ᾿ ὁρᾷς δὴ ὅτι ἀνάγκη, ὦ Σώκρατες, καὶ τῆς τῶν **d**
πολλῶν δόξης μέλειν. αὐτὰ δὲ δῆλα τὰ παρόντα νυνί, ὅτι
οἷοί τ᾿ εἰσὶν οἱ πολλοὶ οὐ τὰ σμικρότατα τῶν κακῶν ἐξεργάζεσθαι, ἀλλὰ τὰ μέγιστα σχεδόν, ἐάν τις ἐν αὐτοῖς
διαβεβλημένος ᾖ.

20 ΣΩ. Εἰ γὰρ ὤφελον, ὦ Κρίτων, οἷοί τ᾿ εἶναι οἱ πολλοὶ
τὰ μέγιστα κακὰ ἐργάζεσθαι, ἵνα οἷοί τ᾿ ἦσαν καὶ ἀγαθὰ τὰ
μέγιστα, καὶ καλῶς ἂν εἶχεν· νῦν δ᾿ οὐδέτερα οἷοί τε· οὔτε
γὰρ φρόνιμον οὔτ᾿ ἄφρονα δυνατοὶ ποιῆσαι, ποιοῦσι δὲ τοῦτο
ὅ τι ἂν τύχωσιν.

IV. ΚΡ. Ταῦτα μὲν δὴ οὕτως ἐχέτω. τάδε δ᾿, ὦ Σώκρα- **e**

---

13. ὥσπερ ἂν πράχθῃ: the aorist
subjunctive is used with the force of
the future perfect.

15. ὁρᾷς δή: Crito means to point
at the case in hand. "The fact is that
the many are really able, etc." Crito
has profited little by what Socrates
has said in the court-room. Cf. *Ap.*
30 d, 40 b.

16. δῆλα κτλ : i.e. show clearly.

20. εἰ γὰρ ὤφελον κτλ.: a wish the
object of which is not attained; and
ἵνα οἷοί τ᾿ ἦσαν expresses an unattained
purpose depending on the preceding
unfulfilled wish. SCG. 367; GMT.
333; H. 884.

21. ἐργάζεσθαι: serves as a repetition of ἐξεργάζεσθαι above. Such repetition of the simple verb is common.
Cf. 49 c d.

22. καλῶς κτλ : indeed (i.e. in this
case) *it would be well.* — **νῦν δέ**: introduces the fact. Supply ἐργάζεσθαι

here, and ποιοῦντες with ὅ τι ἂν τύχωσιν. In hypothetical and relative sentences, τυγχάνειν may be used without
the participle, which is always suggested by the leading clause.

IV. *Perhaps Socrates hesitates to
escape from prison because of his fear
lest his friends should be brought into
trouble for their connivance with his
escape. But not very much money is
required both to hire assistance for the
escape, and to buy off the malicious
accusers who might present themselves.
Crito's means are sufficient, but if Socrates does not want to use these, Simmias
has brought from Thebes enough for the
purpose. Provision can be made easily,
also, for a comfortable home for Socrates in Thessaly.*

1. ταῦτα κτλ.: Crito cannot stop
to discuss this point, and so is ready
to grant it. — A like clause is often
used to mark a transition.

44 e

τες, εἰπέ μοι· ἆρά γε μὴ ἐμοῦ προμηθεῖ καὶ τῶν ἄλλων ἐπιτηδείων, μή, ἐὰν σὺ ἐνθένδ' ἐξέλθῃς, οἱ συκοφάνται ἡμῖν
πράγματα παρέχωσιν ὡς σὲ ἐνθένδε ἐκκλέψασιν, καὶ ἀναγ-
5 κασθῶμεν ἢ καὶ πᾶσαν τὴν οὐσίαν ἀποβαλεῖν ἢ συχνὰ
χρήματα, ἢ καὶ ἄλλο τι πρὸς τούτοις παθεῖν; εἰ γάρ τι
τοιοῦτον φοβεῖ, ἔασον αὐτὸ χαίρειν· ἡμεῖς γάρ που δί- 45
καιοί ἐσμεν σώσαντές σε κινδυνεύειν τοῦτον τὸν κίνδυνον
καὶ ἐὰν δέῃ ἔτι τούτου μείζω. ἀλλ' ἐμοὶ πείθου καὶ μὴ
10 ἄλλως ποίει.

ΣΩ. Καὶ ταῦτα προμηθοῦμαι, ὦ Κρίτων, καὶ ἄλλα πολλά.

ΚΡ. Μήτε τοίνυν ταῦτα φοβοῦ· καὶ γὰρ οὐδὲ πολὺ τἀργύ-
ριόν ἐστιν, ὃ θέλουσι λαβόντες τινὲς σῶσαί σε καὶ ἐξαγα-
γεῖν ἐνθένδε. ἔπειτα οὐχ ὁρᾷς τούτους τοὺς συκοφάντας ὡς
15 εὐτελεῖς, καὶ οὐδὲν ἂν δέοι ἐπ' αὐτοὺς πολλοῦ ἀργυρίου; σοὶ
δ' ὑπάρχει μὲν τὰ ἐμὰ χρήματα, — ὡς ἐγὼ οἶμαι, ἱκανά· b
ἔπειτα καὶ εἴ τι ἐμοῦ κηδόμενος οὐκ οἴει δεῖν ἀναλίσκειν

2. ἆρά γε μή: like μή alone (Ap.
25 a), ἆρα μή looks for a negative
answer, but the connection may con-
vey an insinuation that in spite of the
expected denial the facts really would
justify an affirmative answer. You
surely don't, though I imagine you do,
is Crito's meaning. — The μή which
follows προμηθεῖ is obviously connected
with the notion of anxiety in that
verb. The same idea is again presented in φοβεῖ (are fearful) below.
The subjunctive παρέχωσιν conveys an
idea of action indefinitely continued,
whereas ἐξέλθῃς and ἀναγκασθῶμεν denote simply the occurrence of the
action.

9. ἀλλ' ἐμοὶ πείθου, μή . . . ποίει:
no, no! do as I say. ἀλλά with the
imperative introduces a demand or a

request made in opposition to an expressed refusal, or to some unwilling-
ness merely implied or feared. This
vigorous request is reënforced by the
negative μὴ ποίει, do this and do not do
that. Cf. 46 a.

12. μήτε: the second clause, which
we miss here, appears below (b) in
the resumptive statement ὅπερ λέγω,
μήτε κτλ. — φοβοῦ: reiterates φοβεῖ
above.

13. ὅ: object of λαβόντες.

14. τούτους: said with some contempt.

16. ὡς ἐγὼ οἶμαι: said with reference to the appositive ἱκανά.

17. οὐκ οἴει: Crito recollects what
Socrates had said (45 a, in connection with 44 e). See on οὐ φῆτε Ap
25 b.

45 d

τἀμά, ξένοι οὗτοι ἐνθάδ' ἕτοιμοι ἀναλίσκειν· εἷς δὲ καὶ κεκό-
μικεν ἐπ' αὐτὸ τοῦτο ἀργύριον ἱκανόν, Σιμμίας ὁ Θηβαῖος·
20 ἕτοιμος δὲ καὶ Κέβης καὶ ἄλλοι πολλοὶ πάνυ. ὥστε, ὅπερ
λέγω, μήτε ταῦτα φοβούμενος ἀποκάμῃς σαυτὸν σῶσαι,
μήθ' ὃ ἔλεγες ἐν τῷ δικαστηρίῳ δυσχερές σοι γενέσθω, ὅτι
οὐκ ἂν ἔχοις ἐξελθὼν ὅ τι χρῷο σαυτῷ. πολλαχοῦ μὲν γὰρ
καὶ ἄλλοσε ὅποι ἂν ἀφίκῃ ἀγαπήσουσί σε· ἐὰν δὲ βούλῃ c
25 εἰς Θετταλίαν ἰέναι, εἰσὶν ἐμοὶ ἐκεῖ ξένοι, οἵ σε περὶ πολλοῦ
ποιήσονται καὶ ἀσφάλειάν σοι παρέξονται ὥστε σε μηδένα
λυπεῖν τῶν κατὰ Θετταλίαν.

V. ἔτι δ', ὦ Σώκρατες, οὐδὲ δίκαιόν μοι δοκεῖς ἐπιχειρεῖν
πρᾶγμα, σαυτὸν προδοῦναι, ἐξὸν σωθῆναι· καὶ τοιαῦτα
σπεύδεις περὶ σαυτὸν γενέσθαι, ἅπερ ἂν καὶ οἱ ἐχθροί σου
σπεύσαιέν τε καὶ ἔσπευσαν σὲ διαφθεῖραι βουλόμενοι. πρὸς
5 δὲ τούτοις καὶ τοὺς υἱεῖς τοὺς σαυτοῦ ἔμοιγε δοκεῖς προδιδό-
ναι, οὓς σοι ἐξὸν καὶ ἐκθρέψαι καὶ ἐκπαιδεῦσαι οἰχήσει d
καταλιπών, καὶ τὸ σὸν μέρος, ὅ τι ἂν τύχωσι, τοῦτο πράξου-

18. ξένοι οὗτοι: cf. ἄλλοι τοίνυν
οὗτοι Ap. 33 e. The pronoun calls up
the ξένοι as present in Athens, and,
for rhetorical purposes, within sight.
20. Κέβης: he also was from
Thebes, and Cebes and Simmias play
very important parts in the Phaedo. —
ἄλλοι πολλοὶ πάνυ: the English idiom
reverses the order.
21. μήτε ταῦτα: repeated from
l. 12. — ἀποκάμῃς σαυτὸν σῶσαι: get
tired of trying, etc. Here is no implication that Socrates has already tried
to get away. Crito only hints that
any other course is nothing short of
cowardice.
22. ὃ ἔλεγες: cf. Ap. 37 c d.
23. χρῷο: the optative represents
the subjunctive of doubt.

24. ἄλλοσε: for ἄλλοθι, which we
expect after πολλαχοῦ, on account of
ὅποι. This is attraction, or inverse
assimilation. — The μέν-clause seems
here less important than the δέ-clause.
V. Crito urges that Socrates is not
doing his duty either to himself or to his
sons, in abandoning himself to his sentence. Having children, Socrates ought
to care for them. The whole course of
his case is likely to bring reproach as
well as ill upon him and his friends.
4. σὲ διαφθεῖραι: σέ is accented
for emphasis and to disconnect it from
ἔσπευσαν.
7. ὅ τι ἂν τύχωσι: sc. πράττοντες.
Cf. 44 d. — τοῦτο πράξουσιν: cf. εὖ,
κακῶς, and even ἀγαθόν (used adverbially) with πράττειν (Ap. 40 c)

45 d

σιν· τεύξονται δ' ὡς τὸ εἰκὸς τοιούτων οἷάπερ εἴωθε γίγνεσθαι ἐν ταῖς ὀρφανίαις περὶ τοὺς ὀρφανούς. ἢ γὰρ οὐ χρὴ
10 ποιεῖσθαι παῖδας, ἢ συνδιαταλαιπωρεῖν καὶ τρέφοντα καὶ
παιδεύοντα· σὺ δέ μοι δοκεῖς τὰ ῥᾳθυμότατα αἱρεῖσθαι·
χρὴ δ', ἅπερ ἂν ἀνὴρ ἀγαθὸς καὶ ἀνδρεῖος ἕλοιτο, ταῦτα
αἱρεῖσθαι, φάσκοντά γε δὴ ἀρετῆς διὰ παντὸς τοῦ βίου ἐπι-
μελεῖσθαι· ὡς ἔγωγε καὶ ὑπὲρ σοῦ καὶ ὑπὲρ ἡμῶν τῶν σῶν e
15 ἐπιτηδείων αἰσχύνομαι, μὴ δόξῃ ἅπαν τὸ πρᾶγμα τὸ περὶ σὲ
ἀνανδρίᾳ τινὶ τῇ ἡμετέρᾳ πεπρᾶχθαι, καὶ ἡ εἴσοδος τῆς δίκης
εἰς τὸ δικαστήριον ὡς εἰσῆλθεν ἐξὸν μὴ εἰσελθεῖν, καὶ αὐτὸς
ὁ ἀγὼν τῆς δίκης ὡς ἐγένετο, καὶ τὸ τελευταῖον δὴ τουτὶ

9. **ἢ γὰρ** κτλ.: the γάρ is connected
with an unexpressed reproof.

13. **φάσκοντά γε δή**: *particularly
when one claims that he has*, etc. Cf.
ἅ γε δή *Ap.* **40 a.**

15. **μή**: see on ἆρα γε μή **44 e.**
The notion of fear is remotely implied. This construction is common
in Plato. — **ἅπαν τὸ πρᾶγμα**: in three
divisions, — the entry of the suit, the
conduct of the case, and the neglect of
the opportunity to escape.

16. **ἀνανδρίᾳ τινὶ** κτλ.: *some lack
of manliness on our part.* Notice here
the emphasis given to τῇ ἡμετέρᾳ, *for
which we are responsible.* If Crito and
the rest, by showing more energy, by
using all possible influence against
Meletus and his abettors, had carried
the day, they would have been more
genuinely ἄνδρες in Crito's sense. —
καὶ ἡ εἴσοδος, καὶ ὁ ἀγών: in apposition with ἅπαν τὸ πρᾶγμα τὸ περὶ σέ.
On the meaning of the technical
terms, see Introduction § 50 f. — Precisely how the trial of Socrates could
have been avoided except by his

flight from Athens is not clear. A
wholly untrustworthy tradition says
that Anytus offered him terms of
compromise. Socrates's friends might
have brought pressure to bear on the
prosecutors to let the charge fall, even
if these could not be bought off.
The state had no regular prosecutor.
Probably abundant means were at
hand for raising legal technicalities,
and for securing thus an indefinite delay. All that Crito necessarily suggests, however, is that flight was open
to Socrates. At Athens, as at Rome,
the law allowed a man to go into
voluntary exile.

17. **εἰσῆλθεν**: cf. *Ap.* **29 c.**

18. **ὁ ἀγών**: the management of the
case, when it came to trial, — that
Socrates did not properly conciliate
his judges. — **τὸ τελευταῖον τουτί**: the
scene of this act is laid in the prison.
The expression at first is indefinite, —
whether death or escape from death,
but at last refers to the present opportunity to leave the prison by the connivance of some official.

46 b

ὥσπερ κατάγελως τῆς πράξεως κακίᾳ τινὶ καὶ ἀνανδρίᾳ τῇ
20 ἡμετέρᾳ διαπεφευγέναι ἡμᾶς δοκεῖν, οἵτινές σε οὐχὶ ἐσώ- **46**
σαμεν οὐδὲ σὺ σαυτόν, οἷόν τ' ὂν καὶ δυνατόν, εἴ τι καὶ μικρὸν ἡμῶν ὄφελος ἦν. ταῦτα οὖν, ὦ Σώκρατες, ὅρα μὴ ἅμα
τῷ κακῷ καὶ αἰσχρὰ ᾖ σοί τε καὶ ἡμῖν. ἀλλὰ βουλεύου,
μᾶλλον δ' οὐδὲ βουλεύεσθαι ἔτι ὥρα, ἀλλὰ βεβουλεῦσθαι.
25 μία δὲ βουλή· τῆς γὰρ ἐπιούσης νυκτὸς πάντα ταῦτα δεῖ
πεπρᾶχθαι. εἰ δέ τι περιμενοῦμεν, ἀδύνατον καὶ οὐκέτι
οἷόν τε. ἀλλὰ παντὶ τρόπῳ, ὦ Σώκρατες, πείθου μοι καὶ
μηδαμῶς ἄλλως ποίει.

VI. ΣΩ. Ὦ φίλε Κρίτων, ἡ προθυμία σου πολλοῦ ἀξία, **b**
εἰ μετά τινος ὀρθότητος εἴη· εἰ δὲ μή, ὅσῳ μείζων, τοσούτῳ

19. κατάγελως: in Crito's opinion,
all who were involved made themselves
a laughing-stock by their negligence
and irresolution. In Crito's phrase-
ology, the notion of acting a part on
the stage before the Athenian public
is prominent. — **κακίᾳ κτλ.**: in Crito's
eyes this is the culmination of disgrace
(connect with τὸ τελευταῖον) in a matter
that has been disgracefully misman-
aged. Here is a return to the leading
thought and a departure from the regular grammatical sequence. The anacoluthon is most obvious in the repetition of δοκεῖν after δόξῃ.

20. διαπεφευγέναι ἡμᾶς: people will
think that Socrates's friends allowed
every opportunity, especially the possibility of escape, to pass unimproved.
ἡμᾶς is the object.

21. οὐδὲ σὺ σαυτόν: sc. ἔσωσας.
Crito hints at Socrates's part, then
recurs to his own. The interjection
of such a clause in a relative sentence
is irregular, but not unnatural.

22. ἅμα τῷ κακῷ: equivalent to οὐ
μόνον κακά, or the adverbial πρός, besides.

23. ἀλλά: cf. line 27, below, and
ἀλλ' ἐμοὶ πείθου 45 a.

25. τῆς ἐπιούσης: cf. 44 a. Crito
shows no faith in Socrates's dream as
a prediction, but his plans had been
made before he heard it.

26. εἰ δέ τι περιμενοῦμεν: this adverbial use of τι is developed out of the
cognate accusative (kindred significa-
tion). Cf. the English idiom, "to
delay somewhat (a bit)."

VI. "Let us be sure that we are
right, before we go ahead," Socrates
says. "I am ready to obey that principle which seems best. Now were we
right in saying that we should pay
attention to some opinions, and not to
others?"

1. ὦ Κρίτων: note the "prepositive
vocative." — ἀξία: sc. ἐστίν, in spite of
the optative in the protasis.

2. εἰ εἴη: not if it should be, but
if it should prove to be. Cf. δεινὰ ἂν εἴην

46 D

χαλεπωτέρα. σκοπεῖσθαι οὖν χρὴ ἡμᾶς εἴτε ταῦτα πρακτέον
εἴτε μή· ὡς ἐγὼ οὐ νῦν πρῶτον ἀλλὰ καὶ ἀεὶ τοιοῦτος οἷος
5 τῶν ἐμῶν μηδενὶ ἄλλῳ πείθεσθαι ἢ τῷ λόγῳ ὃς ἄν μοι λογι-
ζομένῳ βέλτιστος φαίνηται. τοὺς δὲ λόγους οὓς ἐν τῷ ἔμπροσθεν ἔλεγον οὐ δύναμαι νῦν ἐκβαλεῖν, ἐπειδή μοι ἥδ᾽ ἡ τύχη
γέγονεν, ἀλλὰ σχεδόν τι ὅμοιοι φαίνονταί μοι, καὶ τοὺς αὐτοὺς πρεσβεύω καὶ τιμῶ οὕσπερ καὶ πρότερον· ὧν ἐὰν μὴ c
10 βελτίω ἔχωμεν λέγειν ἐν τῷ παρόντι, εὖ ἴσθι ὅτι οὐ μή σοι
συγχωρήσω, οὐδ᾽ ἂν πλείω τῶν νῦν παρόντων ἡ τῶν πολλῶν
δύναμις ὥσπερ παῖδας ἡμᾶς μορμολύττηται, δεσμοὺς καὶ
θανάτους ἐπιπέμπουσα καὶ χρημάτων ἀφαιρέσεις. πῶς οὖν
ἂν μετριώτατα σκοποίμεθα αὐτά; εἰ πρῶτον μὲν τοῦτον
15 τὸν λόγον ἀναλάβοιμεν, ὃν σὺ λέγεις περὶ τῶν δοξῶν, πό-

εἰργασμένος *Ap.* 28 d. For the present,
Socrates does not decide whether
Crito's zeal is right or wrong.

3. σκοπεῖσθαι: takes up the βουλεύεσθαι, for which Crito says there is
no time.

4. οὐ νῦν κτλ. : Socrates maintains
that "truth is truth to the end of
reckoning." He has always held the
view which he maintains now. For a
collocation similar to this combination of νῦν and ἀεί, cf. 49 e.

5. τῶν ἐμῶν : τὰ ἐμά includes all the
faculties and functions both of body
and of mind, but very likely *friends*,
as well. Among these λόγος is included
as his wisest counselor. Cf. εἰς τί τῶν
τοῦ ἀπειθοῦντος 47 c and ὅ τί ποτ᾽ ἐστὶ τῶν
ἡμετέρων 47 e. — πείθεσθαι : for the infinitive with οἷος, cf. *Ap.* 31 a.

8. σχεδόν τι : is used courteously,
instead of some word like ἀτεχνῶς
or παντάπασι. — ὅμοιοι: not very different in sense from οἱ αὐτοί, and to be

understood in the light of what immediately follows. Cf. καὶ πρότερον
48 b. "They seem like what they
formerly were." Supply οἷοί περ καὶ
πρότερον (from what follows) with ὅμοιοι.

11. πλείω μορμολύττηται : μορμολύτ-
τεσθαι has the double accusative like
βλάπτειν τινά τι. Μορμώ was one of
the fictitious terrors of the Greek
nursery. — τῶν παρόντων: i.e. ἤ τὰ
παρόντα.

12. δεσμοὺς καὶ θανάτους κτλ. :
these are the usual punishments, to
the harshest of which Socrates has
been condemned. The plural is used
to put an abstract idea vividly by a
process of multiplication. Cf. the use
of *mortes, neces*, and the common
poetical use of θάνατοι to describe a
violent and premature death.

14. πρῶτον μέν : the second point is
taken up at 48 b.

15. εἰ . . . ἀναλάβοιμεν: *I think, if
we should begin by taking up your point*

47 a

τερον καλῶς ἐλέγετο ἑκάστοτε ἢ οὔ, ὅτι ταῖς μὲν δεῖ τῶν
δοξῶν προσέχειν τὸν νοῦν, ταῖς δ' οὔ· ἢ πρὶν μὲν ἐμὲ δεῖν d
ἀποθνῄσκειν καλῶς ἐλέγετο, νῦν δὲ κατάδηλος ἄρα ἐγένετο
ὅτι ἄλλως ἕνεκα λόγου ἐλέγετο, ἦν δὲ παιδιὰ καὶ φλυαρία ὡς
20 ἀληθῶς; ἐπιθυμῶ δ' ἔγωγ' ἐπισκέψασθαι, ὦ Κρίτων, κοινῇ
μετὰ σοῦ, εἴ τί μοι ἀλλοιότερος φανεῖται, ἐπειδὴ ὧδ' ἔχω, ἢ
ὁ αὐτός, καὶ ἐάσομεν χαίρειν ἢ πεισόμεθα αὐτῷ. ἐλέγετο δέ
πως ὡς ἐγῷμαι ἑκάστοτε ὧδ' ὑπὸ τῶν οἰομένων τι λέγειν,
ὥσπερ νυνδὴ ἐγὼ ἔλεγον, ὅτι τῶν δοξῶν ἃς οἱ ἄνθρωποι
25 δοξάζουσι δέοι τὰς μὲν περὶ πολλοῦ ποιεῖσθαι, τὰς δὲ μή. e
τοῦτο πρὸς θεῶν, ὦ Κρίτων, οὐ δοκεῖ καλῶς σοι λέγεσθαι;
σὺ γὰρ ὅσα γε τἀνθρώπεια ἐκτὸς εἶ τοῦ μέλλειν ἀποθνῄσκειν αὔριον, καὶ οὐκ ἄν σε παρακρούοι ἡ παροῦσα συμ- 47
φορά· σκόπει δή, οὐχ ἱκανῶς δοκεῖ σοι λέγεσθαι, ὅτι οὐ
30 πάσας χρὴ τὰς δόξας τῶν ἀνθρώπων τιμᾶν, ἀλλὰ τὰς μέν,
τὰς δ' οὔ; τί φῄς; ταῦτα οὐχὶ καλῶς λέγεται;

ΚΡ. Καλῶς.

etc. That is, such thorough consideration of Crito's point (ὃν σὺ λέγεις,
44 b, 45 e) involves considering the
whole question *whether*, etc.

16. ἑκάστοτε: i.e. whenever they
came to speak on this subject.

17. ἢ πρὶν μὲν κτλ.: with ἢ (an) a
second question is superadded, which
substantially forestalls the answer to
the first. Cf. *Ap.* 26 b. Cf. also 47 e,
below, and especially 50 e and 51 a,
where we find ἢ πρὸς μὲν ἄρα σοι τὸν
πατέρα . . . πρὸς δὲ τὴν πατρίδα ἄρα.—
δεῖν ἀποθνῄσκειν: *was condemned to
die.*

19. ἄλλως: explained by what
follows. Cf. *Phaedo* 115 d.

21. ὧδ' ἔχω: i.e. am in prison under
condemnation of death.

23. τὶ λέγειν: the contradictory of
οὐδὲν λέγειν. Cf. *Ap.* 30 b. It means
"to say something that can be depended upon, that amounts to something." Cf. τί δοκεῖ Λάχης λέγειν, ὦ
Νικία; ἔοικε μέντοι λέγειν τι *Laches*
195 c, to which Nicias humorously
responds, καὶ γὰρ λέγει γέ τι, οὐ μέντοι
ἀληθές γε.

27. ὅσα: cf. ὅσα γε τὰ νῦν ἐμοὶ
δοκοῦντα 54 d.— Since Crito is not condemned to death, he should have the
same view as before, or at least should
be less biased than Socrates.

28. αὔριον: Socrates's dream is
forgotten, or he is arguing from Crito's
position (cf. 46 a).

32. καλῶς: Crito's answers are
brief. He cares for no discussion.

47 a

ΣΩ. Οὐκοῦν τὰς μὲν χρηστὰς τιμᾶν, τὰς δὲ πονηρὰς μή;

ΚΡ. Ναί.

35 ΣΩ. Χρησταὶ δ' οὐχ αἱ τῶν φρονίμων, πονηραὶ δ' αἱ τῶν
ἀφρόνων;

ΚΡ. Πῶς δ' οὔ;

VII. ΣΩ. Φέρε δή, πῶς αὖ τὰ τοιαῦτα ἐλέγετο; γυμναζό-
μενος ἀνὴρ καὶ τοῦτο πράττων πότερον παντὸς ἀνδρὸς ἐπαίνῳ b
καὶ ψόγῳ καὶ δόξῃ τὸν νοῦν προσέχει, ἢ ἑνὸς μόνου ἐκείνου
ὃς ἂν τυγχάνῃ ἰατρὸς ἢ παιδοτρίβης ὤν;

5 ΚΡ. Ἑνὸς μόνου.

ΣΩ. Οὐκοῦν φοβεῖσθαι χρὴ τοὺς ψόγους καὶ ἀσπάζεσθαι
τοὺς ἐπαίνους τοὺς τοῦ ἑνὸς ἐκείνου, ἀλλὰ μὴ τοὺς τῶν πολλῶν.

ΚΡ. Δῆλα δή.

ΣΩ. Ταύτῃ ἄρα αὐτῷ πρακτέον καὶ γυμναστέον καὶ ἐδε-

VII. If a man devotes himself to gymnastics, he must fear the blame and welcome the praise of the physician or the gymnastic trainer, and disregard the opinions of the masses, — or he will ruin his body. So in questions of what is just and honorable and good, a man must disregard the opinions of the masses, or he will ruin his soul.

1. πῶς αὖ ἐλέγετο: the imperfect because the new question (αὖ) involves a matter which has already been discussed. — τὰ τοιαῦτα: refers to what follows. The definite instance given is only one of many possible illustrations of the kind. For further examples of the inductive method, cf. Ap. 25 b. Cf. also Laches 184 c–185 b, where the same example is elaborated to establish the same principle, that approval and instruction alike, if we are to heed them, should come from the one man who has made himself

an authority, ὁ μαθὼν καὶ ἐπιτηδεύσας, while the praise and the blame of the many are to be neglected.

2. τοῦτο πράττων: a man who makes this his work, and hence is earnest about it, one who wishes to make an athlete of himself.

4. ἰατρὸς ἢ παιδοτρίβης: often coupled together as having special charge of bodily vigor and health. The ἰατρός was expected to cure disease; the παιδοτρίβης professed and was expected (Gorg. 452 b) καλούς τε καὶ ἰσχυροὺς ποιεῖν τοὺς ἀνθρώπους τὰ σώματα, i.e. to prevent disease. Thus ἡ γυμναστική had a higher aim than ἡ ἰατρική. — For the thought, cf. also Ap. 25 b.

9. καὶ ἐδεστέον γε: γέ serves, where various points are enumerated, to mark a new departure; i.e. a fact different in kind from the preceding, and thus belonging to a new class.

47 d

10 στέον γε καὶ ποτέον, ᾗ ἂν τῷ ἑνὶ δοκῇ τῷ ἐπιστάτῃ καὶ
ἐπαΐοντι, μᾶλλον ἢ ᾗ σύμπασι τοῖς ἄλλοις.

ΚΡ. Ἔστι ταῦτα.

ΣΩ. Εἶεν. ἀπειθήσας δὲ τῷ ἑνὶ καὶ ἀτιμάσας αὐτοῦ τὴν c
δόξαν καὶ τοὺς ἐπαίνους, τιμήσας δὲ τοὺς τῶν πολλῶν λόγους
15 καὶ μηδὲν ἐπαϊόντων, ἆρα οὐδὲν κακὸν πείσεται;

ΚΡ. Πῶς γὰρ οὔ;

ΣΩ. Τί δ' ἐστὶ τὸ κακὸν τοῦτο καὶ ποῖ τείνει καὶ εἰς τί τῶν
τοῦ ἀπειθοῦντος;

ΚΡ. Δῆλον ὅτι εἰς τὸ σῶμα. τοῦτο γὰρ διόλλυσιν.

20 ΣΩ. Καλῶς λέγεις. οὐκοῦν καὶ τἆλλα, ὦ Κρίτων, οὕτως,
ἵνα μὴ πάντα διίωμεν, καὶ δὴ καὶ περὶ τῶν δικαίων καὶ ἀδίκων καὶ αἰσχρῶν καὶ καλῶν καὶ ἀγαθῶν καὶ κακῶν, περὶ ὧν
νῦν ἡ βουλὴ ἡμῖν ἐστιν, πότερον τῇ τῶν πολλῶν δόξῃ δεῖ
ἡμᾶς ἕπεσθαι, καὶ φοβεῖσθαι αὐτήν, ἢ τῇ τοῦ ἑνός, εἴ τίς d
25 ἐστιν ἐπαΐων, ὃν δεῖ καὶ αἰσχύνεσθαι καὶ φοβεῖσθαι μᾶλλον
ἢ σύμπαντας τοὺς ἄλλους; ᾧ εἰ μὴ ἀκολουθήσομεν, διαφθε-
ροῦμεν ἐκεῖνο καὶ λωβησόμεθα ὃ τῷ μὲν δικαίῳ βέλτιον ἐγίγνετο, τῷ δ' ἀδίκῳ ἀπώλλυτο. ἢ οὐδέν ἐστι τοῦτο;

ΚΡ. Οἶμαι ἔγωγε, ὦ Σώκρατες.

14. τοὺς λόγους: states collectively
what has been subdivided into δόξα,
ψόγος, ἔπαινος. — **πολλῶν . . . ἐπαϊόντων**:
of the masses, who have no special
knowledge whatever. — καί is explica-
tive, as in the second line above.

17. εἰς τί κτλ.: cf. τῶν ἐμῶν 46 b.

19. διόλλυσιν: sc. ὁ ἀπειθῶν.

21. καὶ δὴ καί: introducing the
particular point for the sake of which
the illustration has been made. Cf.
καὶ δὴ καί 18 a. Socrates has at last
reached his goal; his point has been
established by induction. Cf. 27 b. —
Notice the doubly chiastic arrangement,

δικαίων   αἰσχρῶν   ἀγαθῶν
      ╳   ╳
ἀδίκων   καλῶν   κακῶν.

28. ἐγίγνετο, ἀπώλλυτο: i.e. γίγνεσθαι, ἀπόλλυσθαι ἐλέγετο, the so-called
philosophical imperfect, which carries
a statement of the admitted results of
a previous discussion back to the well-
remembered time when the facts stated
were established in argument. "We
saw that the soul is made better by
justice." Cf. ἀλλ' ἦν ἐκείνη γ' (sc. ἡ
μουσική) ἀντίστροφος τῆς γυμναστικῆς, εἰ
μέμνησαι Rep. 522 a, ἐν μέσῳ γὰρ αὐτῶν
ὁ δημοτικὸς ἦν (sc. as we saw) Rep.
587 c. See GMT. 40; SCG. 218.

47 d

VIII. ΣΩ. Φέρε δή, ἐὰν τὸ ὑπὸ τοῦ ὑγιεινοῦ μὲν βέλτιον
γιγνόμενον, ὑπὸ τοῦ νοσώδους δὲ διαφθειρόμενον διολέσω-
μεν, πειθόμενοι μὴ τῇ τῶν ἐπαϊόντων δόξῃ, ἆρα βιωτὸν ἡμῖν
ἐστι διεφθαρμένου αὐτοῦ; ἔστι δέ που τοῦτο τὸ σῶμα· ἢ e
5 οὐχί;

ΚΡ. Ναί.

ΣΩ. ᾽Αρ᾽ οὖν βιωτὸν ἡμῖν ἐστιν μετὰ μοχθηροῦ καὶ διεφθαρμένου σώματος;

ΚΡ. Οὐδαμῶς.

10 ΣΩ. ᾽Αλλὰ μετ᾽ ἐκείνου ἆρα ἡμῖν βιωτὸν διεφθαρμένου,
ᾧ τὸ ἄδικον μὲν λωβᾶται τὸ δὲ δίκαιον ὀνίνησιν; ἢ φαυλό-
τερον ἡγούμεθα εἶναι τοῦ σώματος ἐκεῖνο, ὅ τί ποτ᾽ ἐστὶ τῶν
ἡμετέρων, περὶ ὃ ἥ τ᾽ ἀδικία καὶ ἡ δικαιοσύνη ἐστίν; 48

ΚΡ. Οὐδαμῶς.

15 ΣΩ. ᾽Αλλὰ τιμιώτερον;

ΚΡ. Πολύ γε.

ΣΩ. Οὐκ ἄρα, ὦ βέλτιστε, πάνυ ἡμῖν οὕτω φροντιστέον,

VIII. *Life is not worth living if a
man has a diseased body, and so a man
must obey the directions of a physician,
an expert, and not follow the opinions
of the masses. Is life worth living with
a diseased soul? Should a man heed
the opinions of the masses as to what is
right and honorable?*

3. πειθόμενοι μὴ κτλ. : by its position μή contradicts τῇ . . . δόξῃ, but
not πειθόμενοι, and implies ἀλλὰ τῇ τῶν
μὴ ἐπαϊόντων δόξῃ. The effect of writing πειθόμενοι μή instead of μὴ πειθόμενοι is to lay greater stress on both
words, and the failure to say distinctly
whose opinion it is which is obeyed
leaves all the more stress on μή. —
ἆρα βιωτὸν κτλ. : cf. ἀνεξέταστος βίος
Δp. 38 a.

10. ἀλλὰ . . . ἆρα : ironically opposed to the preceding negative statement, but at the same time expecting
no for its answer. This last must be
indicated by the tone in which the
question is asked. — The argument is
a minore ad maius.

11. ᾧ : with both verbs, though
ὀνινάναι does not govern the dative.
Cf. οἷς . . . ἐξετάζειν *Ap.* 41 c. Even
λωβᾶσθαι usually takes the accusative.

12. ὅ τί ποτ᾽ ἐστί : it was not specified above (d), and consequently there
is no reason for arguing about its
name here.

17. οὐκ ἄρα οὕτω : here again Socrates takes the last step in a long induction.

48 b

τί ἐροῦσιν οἱ πολλοὶ ἡμᾶς, ἀλλ' ὅ τι ὁ ἐπαΐων περὶ τῶν δικαίων καὶ ἀδίκων, ὁ εἷς, καὶ αὐτὴ ἡ ἀλήθεια. ὥστε πρῶτον
20 μὲν ταύτῃ οὐκ ὀρθῶς εἰσηγεῖ, εἰσηγούμενος τῆς τῶν πολλῶν
δόξης δεῖν ἡμᾶς φροντίζειν περὶ τῶν δικαίων καὶ καλῶν καὶ
ἀγαθῶν καὶ τῶν ἐναντίων. " Ἀλλὰ μὲν δή," φαίη γ' ἄν τις,
" οἷοί τ' εἰσὶν ἡμᾶς οἱ πολλοὶ ἀποκτεινύναι."
   ΚΡ. Δῆλα δὴ καὶ ταῦτα· φαίη γὰρ ἄν, ὦ Σώκρατες.   b
25 ΣΩ. Ἀληθῆ λέγεις. ἀλλ', ὦ θαυμάσιε, οὗτός τ' ὁ λόγος
ὃν διεληλύθαμεν ἔμοιγε δοκεῖ ἔτι ὅμοιος εἶναι καὶ πρότερον·
καὶ τόνδ' αὖ σκόπει εἰ ἔτι μένει ἡμῖν ἢ οὔ, ὅτι οὐ τὸ ζῆν περὶ
πλείστου ποιητέον, ἀλλὰ τὸ εὖ ζῆν.
   ΚΡ. Ἀλλὰ μένει.
30 ΣΩ. Τὸ δ' εὖ καὶ καλῶς καὶ δικαίως ὅτι ταὐτόν ἐστι, μένει
ἢ οὐ μένει;
   ΚΡ. Μένει.
   IX. ΣΩ. Οὐκοῦν ἐκ τῶν ὁμολογουμένων τοῦτο σκεπτέον,
πότερον δίκαιον ἐμὲ ἐνθένδε πειρᾶσθαι ἐξιέναι μὴ ἀφιέντων

18. τί, ὅ τι: a not unusual combination of the direct and indirect
forms of question. — The double accusative is as in κακὰ (κακῶς) λέγειν τινά.
— ἀλλά: a shift of construction, instead of ὡς, correlative with οὕτω.
19. αὐτὴ ἡ ἀλήθεια: i.e. *Truth*,
speaking with the lips of ὁ ἐπαΐων, or
appearing as the result of strict and
patient inquiry. The Laws are introduced later as the final authority in
such matters. — ὥστε κτλ.: again Socrates reproves Crito, this time for his
appeal to the Athenian public (44 d).
22. μὲν δή: nearly equivalent to
μήν.
25. οὗτός τ' ὁ λόγος κτλ.: corresponds to καὶ τόνδ' αὖ, which might
have been καὶ ὅδ' αὖ δοκεῖ κτλ. — The

connection of thought would not hinder us from subordinating the first
clause: " as our discussion just closed
agrees with what we argued formerly
(when dealing with the same matter),
so, etc."
27. ὅτι οὐ τὸ ζῆν κτλ.: cf. *Ap.*
28 b ff.
30. τὸ δ' εὖ κτλ.: this is needed
because of the confused ideas which
many associate with εὖ ζῆν, e.g. (1) plain
living and high thinking, or (2) high
living and no thinking.
IX. " *In this case, then.*" says Socrates, " *we are to disregard the opinions
of the masses, and to consider only
whether it is just or unjust, right or
wrong, for me to leave the prison without the consent of the Athenians.*"

48 c

'Αθηναίων, ἢ οὐ δίκαιον· καὶ ἐὰν μὲν φαίνηται δίκαιον, πει- c
ρώμεθα, εἰ δὲ μή, ἐῶμεν. ἃς δὲ σὺ λέγεις τὰς σκέψεις περὶ
5 τ' ἀναλώσεως χρημάτων καὶ δόξης καὶ παίδων τροφῆς, μὴ
ὡς ἀληθῶς ⸍ταῦτα, ὦ Κρίτων, σκέμματα ᾖ τῶν ῥᾳδίως ἀπο-
κτεινύντων καὶ ἀναβιωσκομένων γ' ἄν, εἰ οἷοί τ' ἦσαν, οὐδενὶ
σὺν νῷ, τούτων τῶν πολλῶν. ἡμῖν δ', ἐπειδὴ ὁ λόγος οὕτως
αἱρεῖ, μὴ οὐδὲν ἄλλο σκεπτέον ᾖ ἢ ὅπερ νυνδὴ ἐλέγομεν,
10 πότερον δίκαια πράξομεν καὶ χρήματα τελοῦντες τούτοις τοῖς
ἐμὲ ἐνθένδ' ἐξάξουσι καὶ χάριτας, καὶ αὐτοὶ ἐξάγοντές τε καὶ d
ἐξαγόμενοι, ἢ τῇ ἀληθείᾳ ἀδικήσομεν πάντα ταῦτα ποιοῦντες·
κἂν φαινώμεθα ἄδικα αὐτὰ ἐργαζόμενοι, μὴ οὐ δέῃ ὑπολογίζεσθαι οὔτ' εἰ ἀποθνήσκειν δεῖ παραμένοντας καὶ ἡσυχίαν
15 ἄγοντας οὔτ' ἄλλο ὁτιοῦν πάσχειν πρὸ τοῦ ἀδικεῖν.

ΚΡ. Καλῶς μέν μοι δοκεῖς λέγειν, ὦ Σώκρατες· ὅρα δὲ
τί δρῶμεν.

ΣΩ. Σκοπῶμεν, ὦ ἀγαθέ, κοινῇ, καὶ εἴ πῃ ἔχεις ἀντιλέγειν

---

4. τὰς σκέψεις: drawn into the construction of the relative clause, to which precedence has been given, instead of αὖται αἱ σκέψεις, ἃς λέγεις, σκέμματά εἰσιν κτλ.—The article is commonly not retained in such a case, e.g. οὓς ἡ πόλις νομίζει θεοὺς οὐ νομίζων. The corresponding demonstrative ταῦτα goes into the gender of the predicate.

5 f. μὴ . . . ᾖ: sc. ὅρα κτλ. *Look to it, Crito, lest all this, at bottom, may prove to be,* etc. A milder way of saying ταῦτα σκέμματα ὄντα φαίνεται, strengthened by ὡς ἀληθῶς. Cf. μὴ οὐ τοῦτ' ᾖ *Ap.* 39 a.

7. καὶ ἀναβιωσκομένων γ' ἄν: *and would bring them to life again too.* The ἄν forms with this participle the apodosis. Usually ἀναβιώσκεσθαι is intransitive, like ἀναβιῶναι.

8. ὁ λόγος οὕτως αἱρεῖ: *the argument requires this.*

11. καὶ αὐτοί: *we ourselves, too,* stands for Crito and Socrates. Crito is responsible, in the supposed case, not only for his expenditure of money (χρήματα τελοῦντες), but also for instigating the act of Socrates, or rather for persuading him to allow various things to be done for him. — **ἐξάγοντες** κτλ.: strictly Crito would be ὁ ἐξάγων, and Socrates ὁ ἐξαγόμενος.

13. ἄδικα: predicate.

15. οὔτε πάσχειν: sc. εἰ δεῖ, to be supplied from the preceding clause. — **πρὸ τοῦ ἀδικεῖν**: cf. *Ap.* 28 b d. "There must be no question about submitting to the uttermost (ὁτιοῦν πάσχειν) rather than committing unrighteousness." See also **54 b.**

49 a

ἐμοῦ λέγοντος, ἀντίλεγε, καί σοι πείσομαι· εἰ δὲ μή, παῦσαι e
20 ἤδη, ὦ μακάριε, πολλάκις μοι λέγων τὸν αὐτὸν λόγον, ὡς χρὴ
ἐνθένδε ἀκόντων Ἀθηναίων ἐμὲ ἀπιέναι· ὡς ἐγὼ περὶ πολλοῦ ποιοῦμαι πείσας σε ταῦτα πράττειν, ἀλλὰ μὴ ἄκοντος.
ὅρα δὲ δὴ τῆς σκέψεως τὴν ἀρχήν, ἐάν σοι ἱκανῶς λέγηται,
καὶ πειρῶ ἀποκρίνεσθαι τὸ ἐρωτώμενον ᾗ ἂν μάλιστα οἴῃ. 49
25 ΚΡ. Ἀλλὰ πειράσομαι.

Χ. ΣΩ. Οὐδενὶ τρόπῳ φαμὲν ἑκόντας ἀδικητέον εἶναι, ἢ
τινὶ μὲν ἀδικητέον τρόπῳ, τινὶ δ᾽ οὔ; ἢ οὐδαμῶς τό γ᾽ ἀδικεῖν οὔτ᾽ ἀγαθὸν οὔτε καλόν, ὡς πολλάκις ἡμῖν καὶ ἐν τῷ
ἔμπροσθεν χρόνῳ ὡμολογήθη; [ὅπερ καὶ ἄρτι ἐλέγετο·] ἢ
5 πᾶσαι ἡμῖν ἐκεῖναι αἱ πρόσθεν ὁμολογίαι ἐν ταῖσδε ταῖς ὀλί-

21. ὡς: inasmuch as, equivalent to
ἐπεί. Cf. Latin quippe.
22. ἀλλὰ μὴ ἄκοντος: not contrary
to your will, opposed distinctly to
πείσας σε, with your approval. Cf.
49 e fin. The vivid contrast of these
two clauses makes the omission of
σοῦ, the subject of ἄκοντος, the easier.
Indeed, cases are common where a
personal or a demonstrative pronoun or
some vague general notion of persons
or things is the subject implied.
23. ἐὰν λέγηται . . . : if haply the
statement may satisfy you. ἐάν does
not like εἰ (cf. 48 b) mean whether. —
The subject of the dependent sentence
is made by anticipation (prolepsis) the
object of ὅρα. Cf. Milton, Sonnet to
Sir Henry Vane (xiv),

Besides, to know
Both spiritual power and civil, what each
means,
What severs each, thou hast learned, which
few have done.

Cf. below (49 d). — Socrates is earnestly enforcing a principle.

24. ᾗ . . . οἴῃ: sc. κατὰ τὸ ἀληθὲς ἂν
ἀποκρίνεσθαι τὸ ἐρωτώμενον.
X. If to do wrong is never right,
then to return evil for evil is wrong, and
one must never render ill for ill. Agreement on this fundamental principle is
important. Few people hold it.
1. ἑκόντας: sc. ἡμᾶς. The infinitive
with a verbal often depends on an implied δεῖ, even when no δεῖ precedes.
Cf. 51 c. Here ἀδικητέον is equivalent
to δεῖ ἀδικεῖν. GMT. 923.
2. ἢ οὐδαμῶς κτλ.: here the first
member of the disjunctive question
is resumed, so that the questioner
gives notice to the questioned, as it
were, of his opinion. — "Is this a
relative or an absolute rule?"
3. ἡμῖν: equivalent to ὑφ᾽ ἡμῶν.
5. ἢ πᾶσαι κτλ.: here and in the
words ἢ παντὸς μᾶλλον κτλ. below, we
see that Crito does not assent readily.
After each double question (1) οὐδενὶ
. . . ὡμολογήθη; (2) ἢ πᾶσαι . . . παντὶ
τρόπῳ; Socrates has looked at Crito
for an answer. Finally he extorts the

49 a

γαις ἡμέραις ἐκκεχυμέναι εἰσίν, καὶ πάλαι, ὦ Κρίτων, ἆρα
τηλικοίδε [γέροντες] ἄνδρες πρὸς ἀλλήλους σπουδῇ διαλεγόμενοι ἐλάθομεν ἡμᾶς αὐτοὺς παίδων οὐδὲν διαφέροντες; b
ἢ παντὸς μᾶλλον οὕτως ἔχει ὥσπερ τότ' ἐλέγετο ἡμῖν, εἴτε
10 φασὶν οἱ πολλοὶ εἴτε μή, καὶ εἴτε δεῖ ἡμᾶς ἔτι τῶνδε χαλεπώτερα πάσχειν εἴτε καὶ πρᾳότερα, ὅμως τό γ' ἀδικεῖν τῷ ἀδικοῦντι καὶ κακὸν καὶ αἰσχρὸν τυγχάνει ὂν παντὶ τρόπῳ;
φαμὲν ἢ οὔ;

ΚΡ. Φαμέν.

15   ΣΩ. Οὐδαμῶς ἄρα δεῖ ἀδικεῖν.

ΚΡ. Οὐ δῆτα.

ΣΩ. Οὐδ' ἀδικούμενον ἄρα ἀνταδικεῖν, ὡς οἱ πολλοὶ οἴονται, ἐπειδή γ' οὐδαμῶς δεῖ ἀδικεῖν.

ΚΡ. Οὐ φαίνεται.   c

20   ΣΩ. Τί δὲ δή; κακουργεῖν δεῖ, ὦ Κρίτων, ἢ οὔ;

ΚΡ. Οὐ δεῖ δήπου, ὦ Σώκρατες.

ΣΩ. Τί δέ; ἀντικακουργεῖν κακῶς πάσχοντα, ὡς οἱ πολλοί φασι, δίκαιον ἢ οὐ δίκαιον;

---

briefest assent by the pointed φαμὲν
ἢ οὔ; in line 13 below.

6. ἐκκεχυμέναι κτλ.: *are thrown
away.* Cf. *Henry VIII* iii. 2, "Crom-
well, I charge thee, *fling away* ambi-
tion." Similar is the Latin e f f u n d e r e
gratiam, laborem. — **καὶ πάλαι**
κτλ.: διαφέροντες forms the predicative
complement of ἐλάθομεν (GMT. 887),
and διαλεγόμενοι indicates concession.
The present tense tells of what was
going on. GMT. 147. 2.

11. ὅμως . . . παντὶ τρόπῳ: a more
distinct reiteration of what ἢ παντὸς
μᾶλλον κτλ. has already stated.

19. οὐ φαίνεται: *plainly not.* As
οὔ φημι means *I deny.* rather than *I do*

not assert, so οὐ φαίνεται means not *it
does not appear,* but *it does appear not.*

20. κακουργεῖν: this, like κακῶς
ποιεῖν, covers more cases than ἀδικεῖν
— it includes ἀδικεῖν and also cases of
harm done where little or no question
of right and wrong is involved. Apparently, it was more commonly used
in every-day matters than ἀδικεῖν.

22. κακῶς κτλ. : *if one is wronged.*
— **ὡς οἱ πολλοί φασι:** the English idiom
puts this after δίκαιον. — That "doing harm to one's enemies" was part
and parcel of the popularly accepted
rule of life is plain from many passages. Compare the character of Cyrus
the younger : φανερὸς δ' ἦν, καὶ εἴ τίς τι

49 d

25

30

KP. Οὐδαμῶς.

ΣΩ. Τὸ γάρ που κακῶς ποιεῖν ἀνθρώπους τοῦ ἀδικεῖν
οὐδὲν διαφέρει.

KP. Ἀληθῆ λέγεις.

ΣΩ. Οὔτ᾽ ἄρα ἀνταδικεῖν δεῖ οὔτε κακῶς ποιεῖν οὐδένα ἀνθρώπων, οὐδ᾽ ἂν ὁτιοῦν πάσχῃ ὑπ᾽ αὐτῶν. καὶ ὅρα, ὦ Κρίτων, ταῦτα καθομολογῶν ὅπως μὴ παρὰ δόξαν ὁμολογῇς. d
οἶδα γὰρ ὅτι ὀλίγοις τισὶ ταῦτα καὶ δοκεῖ καὶ δόξει. οἷς
οὖν οὕτω δέδοκται καὶ οἷς μή, τούτοις οὐκ ἔστι κοινὴ βουλή,

ἀγαθὸν ἢ κακὸν ποιήσειεν αὐτόν, νικᾶν
πειρώμενος κτλ. Xen. An. i. 9. 11. Cf.
also Meno's definition of virtue, αὕτη
ἐστὶν ἀνδρὸς ἀρετή, ἱκανὸν εἶναι τὰ τῆς
πόλεως πράττειν, καὶ πράττοντα τοὺς μὲν
φίλους εὖ ποιεῖν, τοὺς δ᾽ ἐχθροὺς κακῶς
Meno 71 e. Plato eloquently defends
his more Christian view throughout
the first book of the *Republic*, in the
Gorgias, and elsewhere. That the
many assert vengeance to be right,
Socrates might say is proved by every-
day experience in dealing with men.
Many recognized authorities encouraged them in such a view. That the
historical (in contrast to the Platonic)
Socrates at least did not contradict
this maxim of popular morality is argued from one place in Xenophon's
Memorabilia (ii. 6. 35), where, apparently with the ready approval of Critobulus, Socrates says, ὅτι ἔγνωκας ἀνδρὸς
ἀρετὴν εἶναι νικᾶν τοὺς μὲν φίλους εὖ
ποιοῦντα, τοὺς δ᾽ ἐχθροὺς κακῶς. This,
however, does not make him responsible for the maxim, since he practically
quotes it from the mouth of the Many.
Indeed, the context has a playful
color which ought to warn us not to
take Socrates precisely at his word.

27. ἀληθῆ λέγεις: not every Athenian would have granted this, but
Crito was no Sophist, and had been
long under the influence of Socrates.
In the New Testament, ἀδικέω is sometimes used like κακουργέω, for *hurt,
harm.* Cf. ὁ νικῶν οὐ μὴ ἀδικηθῇ ἐκ τοῦ
θανάτου τοῦ δευτέρου Rev. ii. 11; καὶ τὸ
ἔλαιον καὶ τὸν οἶνον μὴ ἀδικήσῃς ib. vi. 6;
ib. vii. 2 ff.

28. οὔτ᾽ ἄρα κτλ: the completest
presentation of this precept must be
sought in the teaching of Christ. Cf.
ἀλλὰ ὑμῖν λέγω τοῖς ἀκούουσιν· ἀγαπᾶτε
τοὺς ἐχθροὺς ὑμῶν, καλῶς ποιεῖτε τοῖς
μισοῦσιν ὑμᾶς St. Luke vi. 27.

30. καθομολογῶν, ὁμολογῇς: see on
ἐργάζεσθαι 44 d.

31. ὀλίγοις: i.e. only to a few.

32. τούτοις οὐκ ἔστι κτλ.: this is
strongly set forth in the *Gorgias*,
where the Sophist and the true Philosopher represent respectively these
two clashing theories. They have no
common standing-ground. The one
thinks the other foolish, and the other
thinks the first immoral. Starting from
different premises they were not likely
to reach the same conclusion, and
their discussions were futile.

49 d
ἀλλ' ἀνάγκη τούτους ἀλλήλων καταφρονεῖν, ὁρῶντας τὰ ἀλλήλων βουλεύματα. σκόπει δὴ οὖν καὶ σὺ εὖ μάλα, πότερον
33 κοινωνεῖς καὶ συνδοκεῖ σοι καὶ ἀρχώμεθα ἐντεῦθεν βουλευό-
μενοι, ὡς οὐδέποτ' ὀρθῶς ἔχοντος οὔτε τοῦ ἀδικεῖν οὔτε τοῦ
ἀνταδικεῖν οὔτε κακῶς πάσχοντα ἀμύνεσθαι ἀντιδρῶντα κα-
κῶς· ἢ ἀφίστασαι καὶ οὐ κοινωνεῖς τῆς ἀρχῆς; ἐμοὶ μὲν
γὰρ καὶ πάλαι οὕτω καὶ νῦν ἔτι δοκεῖ· σοὶ δ' εἴ πῃ ἄλλῃ e
10 δέδοκται, λέγε καὶ δίδασκε. εἰ δ' ἐμμένεις τοῖς πρόσθε, τὸ
μετὰ τοῦτο ἄκουε.

ΚΡ. Ἀλλ' ἐμμένω τε καὶ συνδοκεῖ μοι· ἀλλὰ λέγε.

ΣΩ. Λέγω δὴ αὖ τὸ μετὰ τοῦτο, μᾶλλον δ' ἐρωτῶ· πότερον
ἃ ἄν τις ὁμολογήσῃ τῳ δίκαια ὄντα ποιητέον ἢ ἐξαπατητέον;
45 ΚΡ. Ποιητέον.

ΧΙ. ΣΩ. Ἐκ τούτων δὴ ἄθρει. ἀπιόντες ἐνθένδ' ἡμεῖς μὴ
πείσαντες τὴν πόλιν, πότερον κακῶς τινας ποιοῦμεν, καὶ 50
ταῦτα οὓς ἥκιστα δεῖ ἢ οὔ; καὶ ἐμμένομεν οἷς ὡμολογήσαμεν δικαίοις οὖσιν ἢ οὔ;

36. ὡς οὐδέποτε κτλ. : a statement
of what is involved in ἐντεῦθεν, which
is equivalent to ἐκ τούτου τοῦ λόγου
(setting out from this principle). ὡς
with the genitive absolute is used in
this same way also after λέγειν.

37. ἀνταδικεῖν: explained by the
following.

38. τῆς ἀρχῆς: cf. καὶ ἀρχώμεθα
ἐντεῦθεν, above. ἀρχή is the starting-
point of an investigation, — a principle, a conviction. Cf. **48 e**.

39. καὶ πάλαι κτλ.: Cf. οὐ μόνον
κτλ. **46 b**.

44. ἢ ἐξαπατητέον: Socrates says
this rather than ἢ οὐ ποιητέον because
of the preceding ἃ ἄν τις ὁμολογήσῃ τῳ.
Such an admission pledges a man to put
his principle in practice. ἐξαπατᾶν is

not only construed with an accusative
of the person, here easily supplied from
τῳ, but furthermore takes the accusative of the thing.

XI. If Socrates shall leave the prison
without the consent of the Athenians,
will he not overthrow the laws and the
whole city, so far as lies in his power?
And will he have any excuse to offer
except that the city has wronged him?

2. μὴ πείσαντες: cf. **51 b**, and note,
and πείθειν αὐτὴν ᾗ τὸ δίκαιον πέφυκε in
51 c. — τὴν πόλιν: i e. τοὺς Ἀθηναίους.

3. οὓς ἥκιστα κτλ. : sc. κακῶς ποιεῖν.
— οἷς οὖσιν : for τούτοις ἃ ὡμολογήσαμεν δίκαια ὄντα. ὡμολογήσαμεν would require the accusative as in **49 e**, above,
but the dative is assimilated regularly
to the omitted object of ἐμμένομεν.

50 b

5 ΚΡ. Οὐκ ἔχω, ὦ Σώκρατες, ἀποκρίνασθαι πρὸς ὃ ἐρωτᾷς· οὐ γὰρ ἐννοῶ.

ΣΩ. Ἀλλ' ὧδε σκόπει. εἰ μέλλουσιν ἡμῖν ἐνθένδε εἴτε ἀποδιδράσκειν, εἴθ' ὅπως δεῖ ὀνομάσαι τοῦτο, ἐλθόντες οἱ νόμοι καὶ τὸ κοινὸν τῆς πόλεως ἐπιστάντες ἔροιντο· " Εἰπέ 10 μοι, ὦ Σώκρατες, τί ἐν νῷ ἔχεις ποιεῖν; ἄλλο τι ἢ τούτῳ τῷ ἔργῳ ᾧ ἐπιχειρεῖς διανοεῖ τούς τε νόμους ἡμᾶς ἀπολέσαι καὶ b σύμπασαν τὴν πόλιν τὸ σὸν μέρος; ἢ δοκεῖ σοι οἷόν τ' ἔτι ἐκείνην τὴν πόλιν εἶναι καὶ μὴ ἀνατετράφθαι, ἐν ᾗ αἱ γενό- μεναι δίκαι μηδὲν ἰσχύουσιν, ἀλλ' ὑπ' ἰδιωτῶν ἄκυροί τε 15 γίγνονται καὶ διαφθείρονται;" τί ἐροῦμεν, ὦ Κρίτων, πρὸς ταῦτα καὶ ἄλλα τοιαῦτα; πολλὰ γὰρ ἄν τις ἔχοι, ἄλλως τε καὶ ῥήτωρ, εἰπεῖν ὑπὲρ τούτου τοῦ νόμου ἀπολλυμένου, ὃς τὰς δίκας τὰς δικασθείσας προστάττει κυρίας εἶναι. ἢ ἐροῦ-

---

5. οὐκ ἔχω κτλ.: Crito seems afraid of understanding what is meant; the consequences alarm him. This natural state of mind on his part gives reason for a reconsideration of the whole sub- ject from a new point of view.

8. εἴθ' ὅπως κτλ.: this softening phrase is used out of consideration for Crito, who had said ἐξιέναι. To use the word applied to runaway slaves might give him offense.

9. τὸ κοινὸν τῆς πόλεως: the com- monwealth. Cf. Σπαρτιητέων τῷ κοινῷ διαπεμπομένους Hdt. i. 67, sent by the commonwealth of Sparta. So Cicero says commune Siciliae. —The per- sonification of the state and the laws which here follows is greatly admired and has been abundantly imitated, e.g. by Cicero in his first Catilinarian Ora- tion (7. 18). — The somewhat abrupt transition from ἡμῖν above to ὦ Σώ- κρατες suggests the fact that in this

matter Socrates considered himself alone responsible to the Laws.

10. μοί: one of the Laws acts as spokesman.

13. εἶναι: the attention is drawn to εἶναι, exist, by the negative statement of this idea in μὴ ἀνατετράφθαι, not to be utterly overturned, which follows.

17. ῥήτωρ: "this would be a good theme for an eloquent speaker." — ὑπὲρ τούτου τοῦ νόμου κτλ.: on behalf of this law if its existence were in jeopardy. Cf. ἐπιχειρεῖς ἀπολλύναι d below. This notion of threatened suffering is often attached to the present and imperfect of this verb. The wording of this pas- sage recalls the Athenian usage which required that a law, if any one pro- posed to change or repeal it, should be defended by regularly appointed advo- cates (συνήγοροι), but the Laws here are thoroughly personified, as wronged per- sons.

50 c
μὲν πρὸς αὐτοὺς ὅτι "'Ηδίκει γὰρ ἡμᾶς ἡ πόλις καὶ οὐκ ὀρθῶς c
20 τὴν δίκην ἔκρινε"; ταῦτα ἢ τί ἐροῦμεν;
ΚΡ. Ταῦτα νὴ Δία, ὦ Σώκρατες.

XII. ΣΩ. Τί οὖν, ἂν εἴπωσιν οἱ νόμοι· "Ὦ Σώκρατες, ἢ
καὶ ταῦτα ὡμολόγητο ἡμῖν τε καὶ σοί, ἢ ἐμμένειν ταῖς δίκαις
αἷς ἂν ἡ πόλις δικάζῃ;" εἰ οὖν αὐτῶν θαυμάζοιμεν λεγόντων,
ἴσως ἂν εἴποιεν ὅτι "Ὦ Σώκρατες, μὴ θαύμαζε τὰ λεγόμενα,
5 ἀλλ' ἀποκρίνου, ἐπειδὴ καὶ εἴωθας χρῆσθαι τῷ ἐρωτᾶν τε καὶ
ἀποκρίνεσθαι. φέρε γάρ, τί ἐγκαλῶν ἡμῖν καὶ τῇ πόλει ἐπι- a
χειρεῖς ἡμᾶς ἀπολλύναι; οὐ πρῶτον μέν σε ἐγεννήσαμεν
ἡμεῖς καὶ δι' ἡμῶν ἐλάμβανεν τὴν μητέρα σου ὁ πατὴρ καὶ
ἐφύτευσέν σε; φράσον οὖν, τούτοις ἡμῶν, τοῖς νόμοις τοῖς
10 περὶ τοὺς γάμους, μέμφει τι ὡς οὐ καλῶς ἔχουσιν;" "Οὐ
μέμφομαι," φαίην ἄν. "'Αλλὰ τοῖς περὶ τὴν τοῦ γενομένου
τροφήν τε καὶ παιδείαν, ἐν ᾗ καὶ σὺ ἐπαιδεύθης; ἢ οὐ καλῶς
προσέταττον ἡμῶν οἱ ἐπὶ τούτοις τεταγμένοι νόμοι, παραγ-
γέλλοντες τῷ πατρὶ τῷ σῷ σε ἐν μουσικῇ καὶ γυμναστικῇ

XII. *Does not Socrates owe to the laws his lawful birth, and his training of mind and body? Can it be that while he would not think of returning a blow which his father might give him, he yet thinks it right to return a wrong which the city may have done him? Is not the city more honored and more holy than father or mother?*

2. καὶ ταῦτα: i.e. that in certain cases the sentence of the laws might be set at nought. — " Was *this* the agreement? " — **ἢ ἐμμένειν:** or (*was the agreement between us*) *that you would abide*, etc.

3. αἷς ἂν δικάζῃ: cf. 50 b and 51 e.

5. χρῆσθαι κτλ.: *you are accustomed to asking and answering.*

9 f. τοῖς περὶ τοὺς γάμους: Socrates

may have been thinking particularly of those laws regarding marriage which established the legitimacy (and thus the citizenship and rights of inheritance) of children (γνησιότης).

10. ἔχουσιν: dative of participle.

11. ἀλλά: instead of ἔπειτα δέ, which would have been written here to correspond to πρῶτον μέν, if Socrates's answer had not intervened. The English idiom might use *or*.

14. ἐν μουσικῇ καὶ γυμναστικῇ: these words cover the whole of education (παιδεία), as Plato says, ἔστι που ἡ μὲν ἐπὶ σώμασι γυναστική, ἡ δ' ἐπὶ ψυχῇ μουσική *Rep.* ii. 376 e. " The education of the average Greek gentleman, like that of the average English gentleman, comprised a certain amount of

51 a

15 παιδεύειν ;" "Καλῶς," φαίην ἄν. "Εἶεν. ἐπειδὴ δ' ἐγένου e
καὶ ἐξετράφης καὶ ἐπαιδεύθης, ἔχοις ἂν εἰπεῖν πρῶτον μὲν
ὡς οὐχὶ ἡμέτερος ἦσθα καὶ ἔκγονος καὶ δοῦλος, αὐτός τε καὶ
οἱ σοὶ πρόγονοι; καὶ εἰ τοῦθ' οὕτως ἔχει, ἆρ' ἐξ ἴσου οἴει εἶναι
σοὶ τὸ δίκαιον καὶ ἡμῖν, καὶ ἅττ' ἂν ἡμεῖς σὲ ἐπιχειρῶμεν
20 ποιεῖν, καὶ σοὶ ταῦτα ἀντιποιεῖν οἴει δίκαιον εἶναι ; ἢ πρὸς μὲν
ἄρα σοι τὸν πατέρα οὐκ ἐξ ἴσου ἦν τὸ δίκαιον καὶ πρὸς τὸν
δεσπότην, εἴ σοι ὢν ἐτύγχανεν, ὥστ' ἅπερ πάσχοις, ταῦτα
καὶ ἀντιποιεῖν, οὔτε κακῶς ἀκούοντα ἀντιλέγειν οὔτε τυπτό-
μενον ἀντιτύπτειν οὔτ' ἄλλα τοιαῦτα πολλά· πρὸς δὲ τὴν 51
25 πατρίδα ἄρα καὶ τοὺς νόμους ἔσται σοι, ὥστ' ἐὰν σὲ ἐπιχειρῶμεν ἡμεῖς ἀπολλύναι δίκαιον ἡγούμενοι εἶναι, καὶ σὺ

mental cultivation and a certain amount of athletic exercise. The former, besides reading, writing, and some elementary mathematics, consisted mainly in the reciting and learning by heart of poetry, along with the elements of music, and sometimes of drawing. Perhaps because so much of the poetry was originally sung or accompanied, the word 'music' was sometimes applied to the education in literature as well as in music proper, and it is in this wider sense that Plato habitually uses it. Under the term 'gymnastic' was understood the whole system of diet and exercise which, varying with the customs of different states, had for its common object the production of bodily health and strength, and the preparation for military service." *The Theory of Education in Plato's Republic*, by Nettleship, in *Hellenica*, p. 88. — The Muses in Greece had a much wider field than is assigned them now.

17. δοῦλος: opposed to δεσπότης.

— This high standard of obedience to the established law was familiar to the Athenians before Plato wrote. —αὐτός τε κτλ.: cf. *Ap.* 42 a.

20. ἢ πρὸς μὲν . . . πρὸς δὲ κτλ.: the first clause is logically subordinate. See on δεινὰ ἂν εἴην *Ap.* 28 d. — Notice the position of σοί, which is nevertheless not the emphatic word.

21. ἦν: opposed to the future (ἔσται).

22. δεσπότην: cf. δοῦλος in l. 17, above. — ἅπερ πάσχοις: *anything that was* (at any time) *done to you.*

23. κακῶς ἀκούοντα ἀντιλέγειν: equivalent to λοιδορούμενον ἀντιλοιδορεῖν.

24. οὔτε . . . πολλά: an explanation of ὥστε . . . ἀντιποιεῖν, in which the negative of οὐκ ἐξ ἴσου ἦν is repeated.

25. ἔσται: sc. ἐξ ἴσου τὸ δίκαιον.

25 f. ὥστε . . . καὶ σὺ δ' ἐπιχειρήσεις: *so that you in your own turn will,* etc. The dependent clause of result becomes independent. — σύ, when expressed in Attic, has emphatic position. καί indicates equality.

51 a

δ᾽ ἡμᾶς τοὺς νόμους καὶ τὴν πατρίδα καθ᾽ ὅσον δύνασαι
ἐπιχειρήσεις ἀνταπολλύναι, καὶ φήσεις ταῦτα ποιῶν δίκαια
πράττειν, ὁ τῇ ἀληθείᾳ τῆς ἀρετῆς ἐπιμελόμενος; ἢ οὕτως
30 εἶ σοφός, ὥστε λέληθέν σε ὅτι μητρός τε καὶ πατρὸς καὶ
τῶν ἄλλων προγόνων ἁπάντων τιμιώτερόν ἐστιν ἡ πατρὶς
καὶ σεμνότερον καὶ ἁγιώτερον καὶ ἐν μείζονι μοίρᾳ καὶ b
παρὰ θεοῖς καὶ παρ᾽ ἀνθρώποις τοῖς νοῦν ἔχουσι, καὶ σέβεσθαι δεῖ καὶ μᾶλλον ὑπείκειν καὶ θωπεύειν πατρίδα χαλε-
35 παίνουσαν ἢ πατέρα, καὶ ἢ πείθειν ἢ ποιεῖν ἃ ἂν κελεύῃ, καὶ
πάσχειν, ἐάν τι προστάττῃ παθεῖν, ἡσυχίαν ἄγοντα, ἐάν τε
τύπτεσθαι ἐάν τε δεῖσθαι, ἐάν τ᾽ εἰς πόλεμον ἄγῃ τρωθησόμε-

28. **ταῦτα ποιῶν** κτλ. : *in doing
these things you were acting rightly.*

29. **ὁ ἐπιμελόμενος** κτλ. : the irony
comes out in *οὕτως εἶ σοφός, ὥστε λέληθέν
σε.* ἢ conveys the covert reproof of
the question, *are you really ?*

30. **ὅτι** : all the rest of the quotation is subordinate. In English the
conjunction *that* would be repeated
before each principal division.

31. **ἡ πατρίς** : by the addition of
the article the definite fatherland of
each man is indicated. Cf. below, b,
and **54 c**. For the article, cf. *Henry V*
iv. 6, " He smiled me in *the* face." —
On the facts, cf. Cicero, *de Off.* i. 17. 57,
cari sunt parentes, cari liberi,
propinqui, familiares ; sed omnes omnium caritates patria
una complexa est, pro qua quis
bonus dubitet mortem oppe-
tere, si ei sit profuturus? Cf.
also Hector's *εἷς οἰωνὸς ἄριστος, ἀμύνεσθαι περὶ πάτρης,* Hom. M 243.

32. **ἐν μείζονι μοίρᾳ** : after the
analogy of Homeric expressions like
that used by Poseidon of Zeus, *μενέτω*

τριτάτῃ ἐνὶ μοίρῃ Hom. O 195, i.e. in the
one of the three parts of the world
allotted to him as one of the three sons
of Cronus.

33. **σέβεσθαι** κτλ. : the subject of
σέβεσθαι is an implied *τινά,* not *πατρίδα.*

34. **πατρίδα χαλεπαίνουσαν** : the
accusative follows *σέβεσθαι* (as a mortal
to a divinity), *ὑπείκειν* (as a younger person), and *θωπεύειν* (as a slave), though
ὑπείκειν should be followed by the
dative. See on *Ap.* 41 c.

35. **πείθειν** : used absolutely, as in
Ap. 35 c, *to change her mind, to con-
vert to your way of thinking.*

36. **ἡσυχίαν ἄγοντα** : i.e. without
gainsaying or reproaches. — **ἐάν τε,
ἐάν τε** : the first two *ἐάν τε* clauses (like
εἴτε ... εἴτε, sive ... sive), with *προστάττῃ* understood, are explanatory of
ἐάν τι προστάττῃ παθεῖν, while the third
takes a new verb with a new apodosis.
The two former are specifications under
πάσχειν, the third instances analogous
cases where unqualified obedience to
the state is necessary. The emergen-
cies of war are taken as typical of a

51 d

νον ἢ ἀποθανούμενον, ποιητέον ταῦτα, καὶ τὸ δίκαιον οὕτως
ἔχει, καὶ οὐχὶ ὑπεικτέον οὐδ᾽ ἀναχωρητέον οὐδὲ λειπτέον τὴν
40 τάξιν, ἀλλὰ καὶ ἐν πολέμῳ καὶ ἐν δικαστηρίῳ καὶ πανταχοῦ
ποιητέον ἃ ἂν κελεύῃ ἡ πόλις καὶ ἡ πατρίς, ἢ πείθειν αὐτὴν ⊂
ᾗ τὸ δίκαιον πέφυκε, βιάζεσθαι δ᾽ οὐχ ὅσιον οὔτε μητέρα οὔτε
πατέρα, πολὺ δὲ τούτων ἔτι ἧττον τὴν πατρίδα;" τί φήσομεν
πρὸς ταῦτα, ὦ Κρίτων; ἀληθῆ λέγειν τοὺς νόμους ἢ οὔ;
45 ΚΡ. Ἔμοιγε δοκεῖ.

XIII. ΣΩ. "Σκόπει τοίνυν, ὦ Σώκρατες," φαῖεν ἂν ἴσως
οἱ νόμοι, "εἰ ἡμεῖς ταῦτα ἀληθῆ λέγομεν, ὅτι οὐ δίκαια ἡμᾶς
ἐπιχειρεῖς δρᾶν ἃ νῦν ἐπιχειρεῖς. ἡμεῖς γάρ σε γεννήσαντες, ἐκθρέψαντες, παιδεύσαντες, μεταδόντες ἁπάντων ὧν οἷοί
5 τ᾽ ἦμεν καλῶν σοὶ καὶ τοῖς ἄλλοις πᾶσι πολίταις, ὅμως d
προαγορεύομεν τῷ ἐξουσίαν πεποιηκέναι Ἀθηναίων τῷ βουλομένῳ, ἐπειδὰν δοκιμασθῇ καὶ ἴδῃ τὰ ἐν τῇ πόλει πράγματα
καὶ ἡμᾶς τοὺς νόμους, ᾧ ἂν μὴ ἀρέσκωμεν ἡμεῖς, ἐξεῖναι
λαβόντα τὰ αὑτοῦ ἀπιέναι ὅποι ἂν βούληται. καὶ οὐδεὶς

host of others, and then with ἐν δικαστηρίῳ the argument is brought to a head.

39. λειπτέον κτλ.: cf. *Ap.* 29 a.

41. πείθειν: with δεῖ implied in the
verbal. Cf. **49 a.**

42. ᾗ πέφυκε: an explanation of
πείθειν, which implies διδάσκειν.

XIII. *The laws not only have cared
for Socrates's birth and education, and
given him a share in all the good things
of life, but also have allowed him to
take his family and property and seek
another home if he chose. Since he has
chosen to remain in Athens, he has
agreed to obey the laws.*

1. σκόπει τοίνυν κτλ.: an application of the universal truth to a particular instance.

2. ὅτι κτλ.: the relation of δίκαια to

ἃ κτλ. is the same in which ἀληθῆ of the
clause preceding stands to ταῦτα.—Supply an infinitive with ἃ as its object.

3. γεννήσαντες: cf. **50 d.**

4. οἷοί τε: sc. μεταδοῦναι.

6. τῷ πεποιηκέναι: dative of means.
— τῷ βουλομένῳ: construe with ἐξουσίαν. It is resumed in ᾧ ἂν μὴ ἀρέσκωμεν.

7. ἐπειδὰν δοκιμασθῇ: every youth's
claim to be declared an Athenian citizen
was strictly examined on the completion
of his eighteenth year. If he proved
of Athenian parentage, and otherwise
qualified, he was declared of age, and
enrolled on the register of his deme.

8. ἐξεῖναι: repeats ἐξουσίαν of l. 6.
The Spartan had no such liberty.

9. λαβόντα: the dative might be
used.

51 d

10 ἡμῶν τῶν νόμων ἐμποδών ἐστιν οὐδ' ἀπαγορεύει, ἐάν τέ τις
βούληται ὑμῶν εἰς ἀποικίαν ἰέναι, εἰ μὴ ἀρέσκοιμεν ἡμεῖς
τε καὶ ἡ πόλις, ἐάν τε μετοικεῖν ἄλλοσέ ποι ἐλθών, ἰέναι
ἐκεῖσ' ὅποι ἂν βούληται ἔχοντα τὰ αὑτοῦ. ὃς δ' ἂν ὑμῶν ε
παραμείνῃ, ὁρῶν ὃν τρόπον ἡμεῖς τάς τε δίκας δικάζομεν
15 καὶ τἆλλα τὴν πόλιν διοικοῦμεν, ἤδη φαμὲν τοῦτον ὡμολογηκέναι ἔργῳ ἡμῖν ἃ ἂν ἡμεῖς κελεύωμεν ποιήσειν ταῦτα,
καὶ τὸν μὴ πειθόμενον τριχῇ φαμὲν ἀδικεῖν, ὅτι τε γεννηταῖς
οὖσιν ἡμῖν οὐ πείθεται, καὶ ὅτι τροφεῦσι, καὶ ὅτ. ὁμολογήσας ἡμῖν πείσεσθαι οὔτε πείθεται οὔτε πείθει ἡμᾶς, εἰ μὴ
20 καλῶς τι ποιοῦμεν, — προτιθέντων ἡμῶν καὶ οὐκ ἀγρίως 52
ἐπιταττόντων ποιεῖν ἃ ἂν κελεύωμεν, ἀλλὰ ἐφιέντων δυοῖν
θάτερα, ἢ πείθειν ἡμᾶς ἢ ποιεῖν, τούτων οὐδέτερα ποιεῖ.

XIV. "ταύταις δή φαμεν καὶ σέ, Σώκρατες, ταῖς αἰτίαις
ἐνέξεσθαι, εἴ περ ποιήσεις ἃ ἐπινοεῖς, καὶ οὐχ ἥκιστα Ἀθηναίων σέ, ἀλλ' ἐν τοῖς μάλιστα." εἰ οὖν ἐγὼ εἴποιμι· "Διὰ τί
δή;" ἴσως ἄν μου δικαίως καθάπτοιντο λέγοντες, ὅτι ἐν τοῖς
5 μάλιστα Ἀθηναίων ἐγὼ αὐτοῖς ὡμολογηκὼς τυγχάνω ταύτην

---

11. εἰ μὴ ἀρέσκοιμεν κτλ. : repeats
ᾧ ἂν μὴ ἀρέσκωμεν.

16. ἔργῳ : by his act, — in remaining in the city, cf. 52 d.

20. προτιθέντων ἡμῶν : ἢ πείθεσθαι
ἢ πείθειν must be supplied from what
precedes. The same idea is then
expressed negatively, and once again
positively. αἴρεσιν προτιθέναι is also
used, meaning to leave a man free to
choose. Socrates cannot repeat too
often that the state is right, as against
those who seek to evade the authority
of its law. This fact accounts for the
clause which follows, τούτων οὐδέτερα
ποιεῖ, a mere repetition of οὔτε πείθεται
οὔτε πείθει ἡμᾶς.

22. θάτερα : the notion of plural-
ity has here practically disappeared,
as is often true also in the case of
ταῦτα.

XIV. Socrates, above the other Athenians, has chosen to remain in the city,
and thus has bound himself to live as
the laws direct. He has n t preferred
Lacedaemon, Crete, or any other city,
to Athens and her laws.

2. ἐνέξεσθαι : for the form, cf. θρέψονται καὶ παιδεύσονται 54 a, — survi-
vals of the ancient use of the future
middle for the future passive. — καί :
and what is more.

4. ἐν τοῖς μάλιστα : sc. ἐνεχομένοις.
Cf. 43 c.

52 c

τὴν ὁμολογίαν. φαῖεν γὰρ ἂν ὅτι "'Ω Σώκρατες, μεγάλα
ἡμῖν τούτων τεκμήριά ἐστιν, ὅτι σοι καὶ ἡμεῖς ἠρέσκομεν b
καὶ ἡ πόλις· οὐ γὰρ ἂν ποτε τῶν ἄλλων 'Αθηναίων ἁπάντων διαφερόντως ἐν αὐτῇ ἐπεδήμεις, εἰ μή σοι διαφερόντως
10 ἤρεσκε, καὶ οὔτ' ἐπὶ θεωρίαν πώποτ' ἐκ τῆς πόλεως ἐξῆλ-
θες, [ὅτι μὴ ἅπαξ εἰς 'Ισθμόν,] οὔτ' ἄλλοσε οὐδαμόσε, εἰ μή
ποι στρατευσόμενος, οὔτ' ἄλλην ἀποδημίαν ἐποιήσω πώποτε
ὥσπερ οἱ ἄλλοι ἄνθρωποι, οὐδ' ἐπιθυμία σε ἄλλης πόλεως
οὐδ' ἄλλων νόμων ἔλαβεν εἰδέναι, ἀλλ' ἡμεῖς σοι ἱκανοὶ ἦμεν
15 καὶ ἡ ἡμετέρα πόλις· οὕτω σφόδρα ἡμᾶς ᾑροῦ καὶ ὡμολό- c
γεις καθ' ἡμᾶς πολιτεύσεσθαι τά τ' ἄλλα καὶ παῖδας ἐν αὐτῇ
ἐποιήσω, ὡς ἀρεσκούσης σοι τῆς πόλεως. ἔτι τοίνυν ἐν
αὐτῇ τῇ δίκῃ ἐξῆν σοι φυγῆς τιμήσασθαι, εἰ ἐβούλου, καὶ
ὅπερ νῦν ἄκουσης τῆς πόλεως ἐπιχειρεῖς, τόθ' ἑκούσης ποι-
20 ῆσαι. σὺ δὲ τότε μὲν ἐκαλλωπίζου ὡς οὐκ ἀγανακτῶν εἰ δέοι
τεθνάναι σε, ἀλλ' ᾑροῦ, ὡς ἔφησθα, πρὸ τῆς φυγῆς θάνατον·

10. καὶ οὔτε . . . οὔτε: the prominence of the hypothetical expression
(οὐ γὰρ ἂν κτλ.) grows less here, and
completely disappears with οὐδέ, as
the contradictory ἀλλά plainly shows.
θεωρία means not only a state embassy
to games and festivals (cf. Phaedo
58 b), but also attendance at religious
festivals, particularly at the great
national games, on the part of private
individuals. Cf. ἐλάττω ἀπεδήμησας
53 a.
   12. εἰ μή ποι στρατευσόμενος: for
the campaigns of Socrates, see on Ap.
28 e.
   14. εἰδέναι: added for the sake of
clearness and precision. The result
is that the preceding genitive seems to
be a case of prolepsis. Cf. τόξων ἐν
εἰδότες ἴφι μάχεσθαι Hom. B 720. —

The subject or object of the infinitive
is often put by anticipation as the
object of its governing verb, noun,
or adjective.
   16. τά τ' ἄλλα καί: cf. ἄλλως τε
καί. — καὶ . . . ἐποιήσω: is freed from
its connection with ὡμολόγεις, to which,
however, τά τ' ἄλλα is still attached.
Cf. καὶ . . . γέγονε Ap. 36 a. This irregularity was hardly avoidable, since a participle would have been clumsy, and
the idea does not suit a clause with ὅτι.
Accordingly it was hardly possible to
subordinate it to πολιτεύεσθαι.
   17. ἔτι τοίνυν: transition to a new
point, which, however, remains closely
connected with the leading idea.
   18. φυγῆς τιμήσασθαι: cf. Ap.
37 c and τιμᾶται θανάτου Ap. 36 b.
   20. τότε μέν: cf. Ap. 37 c–38 a.

52 c

νῦν δ' οὔτ' ἐκείνους τοὺς λόγους αἰσχύνει, οὔθ' ἡμῶν τῶν
νόμων ἐντρέπει, ἐπιχειρῶν διαφθεῖραι, πράττεις τε ἅπερ ἂν d
δοῦλος φαυλότατος πράξειεν, ἀποδιδράσκειν ἐπιχειρῶν παρὰ
25 τὰς συνθήκας τε καὶ τὰς ὁμολογίας, καθ' ἃς ἡμῖν συνέθου
πολιτεύεσθαι. πρῶτον μὲν οὖν ἡμῖν τοῦτο αὐτὸ ἀπόκριναι,
εἰ ἀληθῆ λέγομεν φάσκοντές σε ὡμολογηκέναι πολιτεύεσθαι
καθ' ἡμᾶς ἔργῳ, ἀλλ' οὐ λόγῳ, ἢ οὐκ ἀληθῆ." τί φῶμεν
πρὸς ταῦτα, ὦ Κρίτων; ἄλλο τι ἢ ὁμολογῶμεν;
30   ΚΡ. Ἀνάγκη, ὦ Σώκρατες.

ΣΩ. "Ἄλλο τι οὖν" ἂν φαῖεν "ἢ συνθήκας τὰς πρὸς
ἡμᾶς αὐτοὺς καὶ ὁμολογίας παραβαίνεις, οὐχ ὑπὸ ἀνάγκης e
ὁμολογήσας οὐδ' ἀπατηθεὶς οὐδ' ἐν ὀλίγῳ χρόνῳ ἀναγκα-
σθεὶς βουλεύσασθαι, ἀλλ' ἐν ἔτεσιν ἑβδομήκοντα, ἐν οἷς
35 ἐξῆν σοι ἀπιέναι, εἰ μὴ ἠρέσκομεν ἡμεῖς μηδὲ δίκαιαι ἐφαί-
νοντό σοι αἱ ὁμολογίαι εἶναι; σὺ δ' οὔτε Λακεδαίμονα
προηροῦ οὔτε Κρήτην, ἃς δὴ ἑκάστοτε φὴς εὐνομεῖσθαι,
οὔτ' ἄλλην οὐδεμίαν τῶν Ἑλληνίδων πόλεων οὐδὲ τῶν βαρ-
βαρικῶν, ἀλλ' ἐλάττω ἐξ αὐτῆς ἀπεδήμησας ἢ οἱ χωλοί τε 53

---

22. ἐκείνους τοὺς λόγους αἰσχύνει:
not *ashamed of those words*, but,
ashamed to face those words. The
words are personified and confront
him with his inconsistency. Cf. **46 b**.

28. ἀλλ' οὐ λόγῳ: *not in mere
words*. That ὡμολογηκέναι is the verb
with which ἔργῳ is connected appears
from the context. Cf. **51 e**.

33. ὁμολογήσας: concessive. The
other participles of the sentence are
subordinate to this.

34. ἐν ἔτεσιν ἑβδομήκοντα: cf. *Ap.*
17 d. Strictly, the time would be only
the fifty or fifty-two years since he
came of age.

37. ἃς δὴ ἑκάστοτε κτλ.: Plato,

like many others, often praises these
states, whose similar institutions were
all of them based upon the common
character due to their Dorian origin.
In his *Memorabilia*, Xenophon, himself an ardent admirer of Sparta,
reports various conversations where
Socrates praises Dorian institutions.
See (*Mem.* iii. 5 and iv. 4) his com-
mendation of the strict obedience to
law at Sparta and of the education
which prepares men for it. The education of Spartan women was less
admired. — For ἑκάστοτε, cf. **46 d**.

39. ἐλάττω ἀπεδήμησας: cf. where
Phaedrus says to Socrates, as they are
taking a walk in the country. σὺ δέ

53 b
40 καὶ τυφλοὶ καὶ οἱ ἄλλοι ἀνάπηροι· οὕτω σοι διαφερόντως
τῶν ἄλλων Ἀθηναίων ἤρεσκεν ἡ πόλις τε καὶ ἡμεῖς οἱ νόμοι
— δῆλον ὅτι· τίνι γὰρ ἂν πόλις ἀρέσκοι ἄνευ νόμων; νῦν
δὲ δὴ οὐκ ἐμμένεις τοῖς ὡμολογημένοις; ἐὰν ἡμῖν γε πείθῃ,
ὦ Σώκρατες· καὶ οὐ καταγέλαστός γ' ἔσει ἐκ τῆς πόλεως
45 ἐξελθών.

XV. "σκόπει γὰρ δή, ταῦτα παραβὰς καὶ ἐξαμαρτάνων
τι τούτων, τί ἀγαθὸν ἐργάσει σαυτὸν ἢ τοὺς ἐπιτηδείους τοὺς
σαυτοῦ; ὅτι μὲν γὰρ κινδυνεύσουσί γέ σου οἱ ἐπιτήδειοι καὶ b
αὐτοὶ φεύγειν καὶ στερηθῆναι τῆς πόλεως ἢ τὴν οὐσίαν ἀπο-
5 λέσαι, σχεδόν τι δῆλον· αὐτὸς δὲ πρῶτον μὲν ἐὰν εἰς τῶν
ἐγγύτατά τινα πόλεων ἔλθῃς, ἢ Θήβαζε ἢ Μέγαράδε, — εὐνομοῦνται γὰρ ἀμφότεραι, — πολέμιος ἥξεις, ὦ Σώκρατες, τῇ

γε, ὦ θαυμάσιε, ἀτοπώτατός τις φαίνει.
ἀτεχνῶς γὰρ ξεναγουμένῳ (a stranger
come to see the sights in town) τινὶ καὶ
οὐκ ἐπιχωρίῳ ἔοικας· οὕτως ἐκ τοῦ ἄστεος
οὔτ' εἰς τὴν ὑπερορίαν (foreign parts)
ἀποδημεῖς, οὔτ' ἔξω τείχους ἔμοιγε δοκεῖς
τὸ παράπαν ἐξιέναι. Socrates answers,
συγγίγνωσκέ μοι, ὦ ἄριστε, φιλομαθὴς γάρ
εἰμι· τὰ μὲν οὖν χωρία καὶ τὰ δένδρα
οὐδέν μ' ἐθέλει διδάσκειν, οἱ δ' ἐν τῷ ἄστει
ἄνθρωποι, Phaedrus 230 c — ἐλάττω:
adverbial cognate accusative.

44. καταγέλαστος: with reference
to his preceding actions. Cf. σὺ δὲ τότε
μὲν κτλ. 52 c, above.

45. ἐξελθών: causal.

XV. If Socrates breaks his covenant with the Laws, all law-abiding men
will look upon him with suspicion. If
he goes to any well-ordered city, then, he
will not be received with favor. If he
goes to Thessaly, on the other hand, —
what can he talk about there? He certainly cannot say there, after his flight,
what he has been saying at Athens,

without making himself ridiculous.
The Thessalians might be amused by the
story of his escape from prison; but if
he offend any one there, he will hear
unpleasant truths. But why should he
go to Thessaly? If he takes his children with him, then these will be made
aliens to Athens. But if he does not
take his children with him, he might as
well be in Hades as in Thessaly, so far
as they are concerned.

1. σκόπει: prefixed to an independent sentence just as ὁρᾷς often is.
Cf. 47 a.—ταῦτα: i.e. τὰ ὡμολογημένα.—
παραβὰς καὶ ἐξαμαρτάνων: i.e. ἐὰν παρα-
βῇς καὶ ἐξαμαρτάνῃς. The present tense
marks the continuance of the action.

5. σχεδόν τι: cf. 46 b. The adverbial use of τι is common with πάνυ,
σχεδόν, πλέον, μᾶλλον and πολύ. — πρῶτον μέν: the corresponding clause follows below (d) in a different form. Cf.
ἀλλά, 50 d.

7. εὐνομοῦνται: in Thebes, before
and during the Peloponnesian War, a

τούτων πολιτεία, καὶ ὅσοιπερ κήδονται τῶν αὐτῶν πόλεων,
ὑποβλέψονταί σε διαφθορέα ἡγούμενοι τῶν νόμων, καὶ βε-
10 βαιώσεις τοῖς δικασταῖς τὴν δόξαν ὥστε δοκεῖν ὀρθῶς τὴν
δίκην δικάσαι· ὅστις γὰρ νόμων διαφθορεύς ἐστι, σφόδρα c
που δόξειεν ἂν νέων γε καὶ ἀνοήτων ἀνθρώπων διαφθορεὺς
εἶναι. πότερον οὖν φεύξει τάς τ' εὐνομουμένας πόλεις καὶ
τῶν ἀνδρῶν τοὺς κοσμιωτάτους; καὶ τοῦτο ποιοῦντι ἆρα
15 ἄξιόν σοι ζῆν ἔσται; ἢ πλησιάσεις τούτοις καὶ ἀναισχυν-
τήσεις διαλεγόμενος — τίνας λόγους, ὦ Σώκρατες; ἢ οὕσπερ
ἐνθάδ', ὡς ἡ ἀρετὴ καὶ ἡ δικαιοσύνη πλείστου ἄξιον τοῖς ἀνθρώποις, καὶ τὰ νόμιμα καὶ οἱ νόμοι; καὶ οὐκ οἴει ἄσχημον
ἂν φανεῖσθαι τὸ τοῦ Σωκράτους πρᾶγμα; οἴεσθαί γε χρή. d
20 ἀλλ' ἐκ μὲν τούτων τῶν τόπων ἀπαρεῖς, ἥξεις δ' εἰς Θετταλίαν παρὰ τοὺς ξένους τοὺς Κρίτωνος· ἐκεῖ γὰρ δὴ πλείστη
ἀταξία καὶ ἀκολασία, καὶ ἴσως ἂν ἡδέως σου ἀκούοιεν ὡς
γελοίως ἐκ τοῦ δεσμωτηρίου ἀπεδίδρασκες, σκευήν τέ τινα

moderate oligarchy ruled (ὀλιγαρχία
ἰσόνομος, different from the δυναστεία
ὀλίγων of the time of the Persian wars),
in political sympathy with Sparta.
Megara also had an oligarchical form
of government, and had been, since the
battle of Coroneia (447 B.C.), on the
Spartan side.

8. τούτων: referring either to the
cities (instead of ἐν τούτοις) or to their
inhabitants.

9. ὑποβλέψονται: the implication
of suspicion is conveyed by the ὑπό as
in ὑφορᾶν, ὑποψία, cf. οἱ δὲ Ἕλληνες
ὑφορῶντες τούτους αὐτοὶ ἐφ' ἑαυτῶν ἐχώ-
ρουν ἡγεμόνας ἔχοντες Xen. An. ii. 4. 10.
— καὶ βεβαιώσεις κτλ.: "iudicibus
opinionem confirmabis ut recte
videantur tulisse sententiam."
Wolf.

14. ποιοῦντι: if you do this.

17. ἄξιον: neuter predicate.

19. ἂν φανεῖσθαι: ἂν with the fut.
is very rare. — τὸ τοῦ Σωκράτους πρᾶγμα: little more than a periphrasis for
Σωκράτης. Cf. τὸ σὸν πρᾶγμα Ap. 20 c.
— οἴεσθαί γε χρή: a common way of answering one's own questions. Cf. 54 b.

20. μέν: repeats the μέν of l. 5.

21. τοὺς ξένους: sc. as suggested by
Crito, 45 c. — ἐκεῖ γὰρ δὴ κτλ.: Socrates speaks as if the fact were familiar
to Crito. The nobles of Thessaly were
rich and hospitable, and bore the reputation of being violent and licentious.
Some light is thrown upon the subject
by the character of Meno given by
Xenophon, An. ii. 6. 21 ff.

23. σκευήν τέ τινα κτλ.: to this
first clause the disjunctive ἢ διφθέραν ἢ
ἄλλα is subordinated. — The διφθέρα
was, according to the Schol. on Ar.

54 a

περιθέμενος, ἢ διφθέραν λαβὼν ἢ ἄλλα οἷα δὴ εἰώθασιν
25 ἐνσκευάζεσθαι οἱ ἀποδιδράσκοντες, καὶ τὸ σχῆμα τὸ σαυτοῦ μεταλλάξας· ὅτι δὲ γέρων ἀνήρ, σμικροῦ χρόνου τῷ
βίῳ λοιποῦ ὄντος ὡς τὸ εἰκός, ἐτόλμησας οὕτως αἰσχρῶς e
ἐπιθυμεῖν ζῆν, νόμους τοὺς μεγίστους παραβάς, οὐδεὶς ὃς
ἐρεῖ; ἴσως, ἂν μή τινα λυπῇς· εἰ δὲ μή, ἀκούσει, ὦ Σώκρα-
30 τες, πολλὰ καὶ ἀνάξια σαυτοῦ. ὑπερχόμενος δὴ βιώσει πάντας ἀνθρώπους καὶ δουλεύων· τί ποιῶν ἢ εὐωχούμενος ἐν
Θετταλίᾳ, ὥσπερ ἐπὶ δεῖπνον ἀποδεδημηκὼς εἰς Θετταλίαν;
λόγοι δ' ἐκεῖνοι οἱ περὶ δικαιοσύνης τε καὶ τῆς ἄλλης ἀρετῆς
ποῦ ἡμῖν ἔσονται; ἀλλὰ δὴ τῶν παίδων ἕνεκα βούλει ζῆν, 54
35 ἵνα αὐτοὺς ἐκθρέψῃς καὶ παιδεύσῃς; τί δέ; εἰς Θετταλίαν
αὐτοὺς ἀγαγὼν θρέψεις τε καὶ παιδεύσεις, ξένους ποιήσας,
ἵνα καὶ τοῦτο ἀπολαύσωσιν; ἢ τοῦτο μὲν οὔ, αὐτοῦ δὲ τρε-

Nub. 73, a ποιμενικὸν περιβόλαιον. σκευή
and ἐνσκευάζεσθαι refer to change of
costume, and are also used of the
costumes of actors. σχῆμα, on the
other hand, relates to the other dis-
guises of face and figure necessary to
complete the transformation.

27. ἐτόλμησας: see on τόλμης, *Ap.*
38 d.

28. οὐδεὶς ὅς: *will there be nobody to
say this?* Here, as in many common
idioms, the verb "to be" is omitted.

29. ἴσως: the English idiom uses
a negative, *perhaps not.* — ἀκούσει . . .
ἀνάξια: like ἀκούειν κακά (ὑπό τινος), the
passive of λέγειν κακά. Cf. **50 e.** The
καί between πολλά and ἀνάξια should
not be translated.

30. δή: *accordingly.* Socrates will
have to make up his mind to it, he has
no choice.

31. καὶ δουλεύων: better understood absolutely than with an implied
dative. Here we have a blunt state-

ment of the fact which Socrates had in
mind in saying ὑπερχόμενος. — τί ποιῶν
ἢ κτλ.: the participle goes with the verb
of the foregoing clause and has the chief
thought, — "what will you do?"

34. ἡμῖν: ethical dative. — ἀλλὰ
δή: a new objection raised and answered by the Laws themselves in respect to what Crito said, **45 c d.** —
ἀλλά: relates to the preceding thought,
— "of course these sayings are nowhere; but do you actually wish?"

37. ἵνα καὶ τοῦτο κτλ.: i.e. in addition to all other obligations. ἀπολαύειν often is, as here, used ironically.
How a Greek looked upon exile is
plain from passages in tragedy as well
as in Homer. Shakespeare shows the
same spirit in *Richard II* i. 3,

What is my sentence then but speechless
death,
Which robs my tongue from breathing native breath?

— αὐτοῦ: i.e. at Athens.

54 a

φόμενοι σοῦ ζῶντος βέλτιον θρέψονται καὶ παιδεύσονται,
μὴ συνόντος σοῦ αὐτοῖς; οἱ γὰρ ἐπιτήδειοι οἱ σοὶ ἐπιμε-
40 λήσονται αὐτῶν. πότερον ἐὰν εἰς Θετταλίαν ἀποδημήσῃς
ἐπιμελήσονται, ἐὰν δ᾽ εἰς Ἅιδου ἀποδημήσῃς οὐχὶ ἐπιμελήσονται; εἴ πέρ γέ τι ὄφελος αὐτῶν ἐστι τῶν σοι φασκόντων b
ἐπιτηδείων εἶναι, οἴεσθαί γε χρή.

XVI. "ἀλλ᾽, ὦ Σώκρατες, πειθόμενος ἡμῖν τοῖς σοῖς
τροφεῦσι, μήτε παῖδας περὶ πλείονος ποιοῦ μήτε τὸ ζῆν
μήτ᾽ ἄλλο μηδὲν πρὸ τοῦ δικαίου, ἵνα εἰς Ἅιδου ἐλθὼν
ἔχῃς πάντα ταῦτα ἀπολογήσασθαι τοῖς ἐκεῖ ἄρχουσιν· οὔτε
5 γὰρ ἐνθάδε σοι φαίνεται ταῦτα πράττοντι ἄμεινον εἶναι οὐδὲ
δικαιότερον οὐδ᾽ ὁσιώτερον, οὐδ᾽ ἄλλῳ τῶν σῶν οὐδενί,
οὔτ᾽ ἐκεῖσε ἀφικομένῳ ἄμεινον ἔσται. ἀλλὰ νῦν μὲν ἠδικη-
μένος ἄπει, ἐὰν ἀπίῃς, οὐχ ὑφ᾽ ἡμῶν τῶν νόμων ἀλλ᾽ ὑπ᾽ ἀν- c
θρώπων· ἐὰν δ᾽ ἐξέλθῃς οὕτως αἰσχρῶς ἀνταδικήσας τε καὶ
10 ἀντικακουργήσας, τὰς σαυτοῦ ὁμολογίας τε καὶ συνθήκας

38. θρέψονται καὶ παιδεύσονται:
see on ἐνέξεσθαι 52 a.

42. τῶν . . . εἶναι: explanation of
αὐτῶν. σοί is not to be construed with
φασκόντων.

43. οἴεσθαί γε χρή: cf. 53 d.

XVI. Socrates should take the advice
of the Laws, and give the greatest honor
to the right, — in order that he may
have a better account of his life to offer
to the rulers in Hades. He has been
wronged by men, not by the Laws. But
if he shall escape from prison, breaking
his covenants with them, the Laws will
be wroth with him while he lives, and
when he dies, their brethren, the Laws in
Hades, will not receive him with favor.

2. παῖδας: Xanthippe is not thought
to stand in such need of Socrates's
care.

3. πρό: after περὶ πλείονος, cf. πρὸ
τοῦ ἀδικεῖν 48 d.

4. ἀπολογήσασθαι: a future judgment on the deeds done in the body is
asserted by Socrates also at the close
of the Gorgias.

5. ταῦτα: i.e. that which Crito
urges.

6. οὐδ᾽ ἄλλῳ τῶν σῶν: for no one
of your friends either. The Laws add
this for Crito's benefit.

7. νῦν μέν: assuming that Socrates
has made up his mind not to take
Crito's advice.

8. ἄπει: sc. to Hades. — ὑπ᾽ ἀνθρώπων: referring to the fallible mortals
who act as guardians and representatives of the blameless laws. Cf. ἄνθρωπος, ὅστις πρῶτον καὶ αὐτὸ τοῦτο οἶδε,
τοὺς νόμους Ap. 24 e.

54 d

τὰς πρὸς ἡμᾶς παραβὰς, καὶ κακὰ ἐργασάμενος τούτους οὓς
ἥκιστα ἔδει, — σαυτόν τε καὶ φίλους καὶ πατρίδα καὶ ἡμᾶς,
— ἡμεῖς τέ σοι χαλεπανοῦμεν ζῶντι, καὶ ἐκεῖ οἱ ἡμέτεροι
ἀδελφοί, οἱ ἐν Ἅιδου νόμοι, οὐκ εὐμενῶς σε ὑποδέξονται,
15 εἰδότες ὅτι καὶ ἡμᾶς ἐπεχείρησας ἀπολέσαι, τὸ σὸν μέρος.
ἀλλὰ μή σε πείσῃ Κρίτων ποιεῖν ἃ λέγει μᾶλλον ἢ ἡμεῖς." d

XVII. Ταῦτα, ὦ φίλε ἑταῖρε Κρίτων, εὖ ἴσθι ὅτι ἐγὼ
δοκῶ ἀκούειν, ὥσπερ οἱ κορυβαντιῶντες τῶν αὐλῶν δοκοῦσιν ἀκούειν, καὶ ἐν ἐμοὶ αὕτη ἡ ἠχὴ τούτων τῶν λόγων βομ-
βεῖ καὶ ποιεῖ μὴ δύνασθαι τῶν ἄλλων ἀκούειν· ἀλλ' ἴσθι,
5 ὅσα γε τὰ νῦν ἐμοὶ δοκοῦντα, ἐὰν λέγῃς παρὰ ταῦτα, μάτην
ἐρεῖς. ὅμως μέντοι εἴ τι οἴει πλέον ποιήσειν, λέγε.

ΚΡ. Ἀλλ', ὦ Σώκρατες, οὐκ ἔχω λέγειν.

---

11. παραβάς, ἐργασάμενος: subordinated to the foregoing participles.

16. μή σε κτλ. : *do not be persuaded.*

XVII. *The words of the Laws ring
in Socrates's ears, so that he cannot
listen to any others ; but Crito may
speak, if he has anything to say on the
other side.*

1. ὦ φίλε ἑταῖρε Κρίτων : Socrates
speaks with tenderness in order to
make his refusal the less hard to bear.
The exceptional feature in this form
of address lies in the mention of Crito's
name at the end.

2. οἱ κορυβαντιῶντες : here a species
of madness seems to be indicated,
under the influence of which men
imagined that they heard the flutes
that were used in Corybantian revels.
Cf. ὥσπερ οἱ κορυβαντιῶντες οὐκ ἔμφρονες
ὄντες ὀρχοῦνται, οὕτω καὶ οἱ μελοποιοὶ οὐκ
ἔμφρονες ὄντες τὰ καλὰ μέλη ταῦτα ποιοῦσιν *Ion* **534 a,** and the song of the
bacchanals in Eur. *Bacch.* 123–127,

Corybantes, wearing helms three-rimmed,
  Stretched skins to make my drum's full
    round ;
Then they, in hollowed caves, lithe-limbed,
  With drums, and, with the flute's shrill
    sound
Full Phrygian, bacchic ditties hymned.

4. ποιεῖ : sc. ἐμέ. **—τῶν ἄλλων :** sc.
λόγων.

5. ὅσα γε κτλ. : a limitation added
to soften the assertion. Cf. ὅσα γε
τἀνθρώπεια **46 e.** No object is needed
with λέγῃς. λέγειν παρὰ κτλ. comes
very near the meaning of ἀντιλέγειν.
Cf. the omission of the object ἐμέ with
the preceding ποιεῖ μὴ δύνασθαι κτλ. —
Grote calls attention to the fact that
the argument of the Laws in the *Crito*
represents feelings common to all loyal
Athenians, not peculiar to Socrates, so
that, in a way, the *Crito* is Plato's answer to the adverse criticisms of the
many to whom Socrates's attitude in
the *Apology* had appeared defiance of
the laws.

54 e

ΣΩ. Ἔα τοίνυν, ὦ Κρίτων, καὶ πράττωμεν ταύτῃ, ἐπειδὴ e ταύτῃ ὁ θεὸς ὑφηγεῖται.

8. ἔα: used absolutely with a following subjunctive or imperative to dismiss a matter that has been under discussion. Cf. ἔα, ἦν δ᾽ ἐγώ· μὴ γάρ πω τὸ ἐμοὶ ϳοκοῦν σκοπῶμεν, ἀλλ᾽ ὃ σὺ λέγεις νῦν *Charm.* **163 e**; ἔα, ὦ Διονυσόδωρε, εὐφήμει καὶ μὴ χαλεπῶς με προδίδασκε *Euthyd.* **302 c.**

9. ταύτῃ: the repetition of the same word is effective. — θεός : cf. τῷ θεῷ, *Ap.* **19 a.** Socrates's belief in God's care is clear. — Here, as at the end of his defense proper, *Ap.* **35 d,** and at the end of his closing words in court, *Ap.* **42 a,** Socrates mentions ὁ θεός. Dante closes each one of the three parts of his great poem with a reference to *the stars.* This is no accident in either case, though Plato had a philosopher's reason which Dante could not give, except for the closing line of the Paradiso, which is ὁ θεός translated into the language of the poet, " L'Amor che muove il Sole e l'altre stelle," *The love which moves the sun and the other stars.*

ΠΛΑΤΩΝΟΣ ΦΑΙΔΩΝ

ΕΧΕΚΡΑΤΗΣ, ΦΑΙΔΩΝ

I. ΕΧΕΚΡΑΤΗΣ. Αὐτός, ὦ Φαίδων, παρεγένου Σωκράτει ϑ
ἐκείνῃ τῇ ἡμέρᾳ, ᾗ τὸ φάρμακον ἔπιεν ἐν τῷ δεσμωτηρίῳ,
ἢ ἄλλου του ἤκουσας;
ΦΑΙΔΩΝ. Αὐτός, ὦ Ἐχέκρατες.

ό   ΕΧ. Τί οὖν δή ἐστιν ἄττα εἶπεν ὁ ἀνὴρ πρὸ τοῦ θανάτου;
καὶ πῶς ἐτελεύτα; ἡδέως γὰρ ἂν ἐγὼ ἀκούσαιμι. καὶ γὰρ
οὔτε τῶν πολιτῶν Φλειασίων οὐδεὶς πάνυ τι ἐπιχωριάζει τὰ
νῦν Ἀθήναζε, οὔτε τις ξένος ἀφῖκται χρόνου συχνοῦ ἐκεῖθεν, b
ὅστις ἂν ἡμῖν σαφές τι ἀγγεῖλαι οἷός τ᾿ ἦν περὶ τούτων, πλήν
10 γε δὴ ὅτι φάρμακον πιὼν ἀποθάνοι· τῶν δ᾿ ἄλλων οὐδὲν εἶχεν
φράζειν.

I–VII. Prologue in two scenes:
I–III, Introductory. IV–VII, Conversation of Socrates with his friends,
gradually leading to the discussion of
the immortality of the soul.

I. *After the death of Socrates, in
the spring of 399 B.C., his young friend
Phaedo, returning to his home in Elis,
falls in with Echecrates at Phlius, in
Peloponnesus, a little southwest of
Corinth. Echecrates had learned about
Socrates's trial, and is eager to hear the
details of his death. In particular, why
had Socrates been kept in prison for a
month before he was put to death?
This, Phaedo tells him, was because of
a festival of Apollo at Delos: a boat*

*with a festal embassy had been sent to
Delos by the Athenians, and during its
absence the city was to be kept ceremonially pure.*

2. τὸ φάρμακον: cf. **117 a**.

4. αὐτός: sc. παρεγενόμην.

6. ἐτελεύτα: for the imperfect, see
SCG. 211. "Describe the closing
scenes, give the details."

8. ᾿Αθήναζε: Phlius had been on
the side of Sparta in the Peloponnesian
War, and its relations to Athens were
not close. — **χρόνου**: temporal genitive.
Cf. ἔτους l. 24.

9. ὅστις ἄν: for the construction cf.
Ap. **38 d**.

10. εἶχεν: sc. ὁ ξένος

58 a

ΦΑΙΔ. Οὐδὲ τὰ περὶ τῆς δίκης ἄρα ἐπύθεσθε ὃν τρόπον 58
ἐγένετο;

ΕΧ. Ναί, ταῦτα μὲν ἡμῖν ἤγγειλέ τις, καὶ ἐθαυμάζομέν
15 γ᾽ ὅτι πάλαι γενομένης αὐτῆς πολλῷ ὕστερον φαίνεται ἀπο-
θανών. τί οὖν ἦν τοῦτο, ὦ Φαίδων;

ΦΑΙΔ. Τύχη τις αὐτῷ, ὦ Ἐχέκρατες, συνέβη· ἔτυχε γὰρ
τῇ προτεραίᾳ τῆς δίκης ἡ πρύμνα ἐστεμμένη τοῦ πλοίου ὃ
εἰς Δῆλον Ἀθηναῖοι πέμπουσιν.

20 ΕΧ. Τοῦτο δὲ δὴ τί ἐστιν;

ΦΑΙΔ. Τοῦτ᾽ ἔστι τὸ πλοῖον, ὥς φασιν Ἀθηναῖοι, ἐν ᾧ
Θησεύς ποτ᾽ εἰς Κρήτην τοὺς "δὶς ἑπτὰ" ἐκείνους ᾤχετο
ἄγων καὶ ἔσωσέ τε καὶ αὐτὸς ἐσώθη. τῷ οὖν Ἀπόλλωνι ηὔ- b
ξαντο, ὡς λέγεται, τότε, εἰ σωθεῖεν, ἑκάστου ἔτους θεωρίαν
25 ἀπάξειν εἰς Δῆλον· ἣν δὴ ἀεὶ καὶ νῦν ἔτι ἐξ ἐκείνου κατ᾽ ἐνιαυτὸν τῷ θεῷ πέμπουσιν. ἐπειδὰν οὖν ἄρξωνται τῆς θεωρίας,
νόμος ἐστὶν αὐτοῖς ἐν τῷ χρόνῳ τούτῳ καθαρεύειν τὴν πόλιν καὶ δημοσίᾳ μηδένα ἀποκτεινύναι, πρὶν ἂν εἰς Δῆλόν
τ᾽ ἀφίκηται τὸ πλοῖον καὶ πάλιν δεῦρο· τοῦτο δ᾽ ἐνίοτ᾽ ἐν

---

17. ἔτυχε : resumes τύχη συνέβη.

18. ἐστεμμένη : sc. with laurel.

20. τοῦτο κτλ.: this question with its answers shows that Plato had in mind more than the Athenian reading public.

21. The ingenuity of the Athenians was puzzled by the question whether this was or was not the original boat. It had not been rebuilt at any time, yet the original timbers had gradually been replaced. This was the ancient form of the modern puzzle with regard to the boy's jack-knife, which was the same knife, but had a new handle and a new blade.

22. δὶς ἑπτά : according to the myth, the tribute of seven young men and seven maidens was required of

Athens by King Minos of Crete. The young prince Theseus volunteered to be part of the tribute, and, winning the love and aid of Ariadne, Minos's daughter, slew the Minotaur. A recently recovered dithyramb of Bacchylides (xvi) begins κυανόπρωρα (dark-prowed) μὲν ναῦς μενέκτυπον (steadfast-in-conflict) | Θησέα δὶς ἑπτά τ᾽ ἀγλαοὺς (splendid) ἄγουσα | κούρους Ἰαόνων | Κρητικὸν τάμνε πέλαγος.

24. σωθεῖεν : sc. Θησεὺς καὶ οἱ δὶς ἑπτά. — ἔτους : for the genitive, cf. Crito 44 a, 57 a.

29. δεῦρο : used as if the speaker ware still in Athens. Possibly it was the expression of the law.

58 e

30 πολλῷ χρόνῳ γίγνεται, ὅταν τύχωσιν ἄνεμοι ἀπολαβόντες
αὐτούς. ἀρχὴ δ' ἐστὶ τῆς θεωρίας, ἐπειδὰν ὁ ἱερεὺς τοῦ c
Ἀπόλλωνος στέψῃ τὴν πρύμναν τοῦ πλοίου· τοῦτο δ' ἔτυχεν,
ὥσπερ λέγω, τῇ προτεραίᾳ τῆς δίκης γεγονός. διὰ ταῦτα καὶ
πολὺς χρόνος ἐγένετο τῷ Σωκράτει ἐν τῷ δεσμωτηρίῳ, ὁ με-
35 ταξὺ τῆς δίκης τε καὶ τοῦ θανάτου.

II. ΕΧ. Τί δὲ δὴ τὰ περὶ αὐτὸν τὸν θάνατον, ὦ Φαίδων;
τί ἦν τὰ λεχθέντα καὶ πραχθέντα, καὶ τίνες οἱ παραγενόμενοι
τῶν ἐπιτηδείων τῷ ἀνδρί; ἢ οὐκ εἴων οἱ ἄρχοντες παρεῖναι,
ἀλλ' ἔρημος ἐτελεύτα φίλων;

5 ΦΑΙΔ. Οὐδαμῶς, ἀλλὰ παρῆσάν τινες, καὶ πολλοί γε.   d

ΕΧ. Ταῦτα δὴ πάντα προθυμήθητι ὡς σαφέστατα ἡμῖν
ἀπαγγεῖλαι, εἰ μή τίς σοι ἀσχολία τυγχάνει οὖσα.

ΦΑΙΔ. Ἀλλὰ σχολάζω γε καὶ πειράσομαι ὑμῖν διηγήσα-
σθαι· καὶ γὰρ τὸ μεμνῆσθαι Σωκράτους καὶ αὐτὸν λέγοντα
10 καὶ ἄλλου ἀκούοντα ἔμοιγ' ἀεὶ πάντων ἥδιστον.

ΕΧ. Ἀλλὰ μήν, ὦ Φαίδων, καὶ τοὺς ἀκουσομένους γε
τοιούτους ἑτέρους ἔχεις· ἀλλὰ πειρῶ ὡς ἂν δύνῃ ἀκριβέ-
στατα διεξελθεῖν πάντα.

ΦΑΙΔ. Καὶ μὴν ἔγωγε θαυμάσια ἔπαθον παραγενόμενος. e
15 οὔτε γὰρ ὡς θανάτῳ παρόντα με ἀνδρὸς ἐπιτηδείου ἔλεος

---

31. αὐτούς: implied in πλοῖον above.

34. πολὺς χρόνος : *a long time* is a relative expression. In general at Athens the execution of a criminal convicted on a capital charge seems to have taken place on the day after the condemnation. Hence a delay of thirty days seemed long.

II. " *But as to the death itself : who of his friends were present, and how did Socrates die ?*" *Phaedo had a strange experience. Neither sadness nor pleasure completely filled his mind.*

3. τῷ ἀνδρί : courteous. Cf. ἀνήρ, l. 16, and contrast **116 d, 117 e**.

4. φίλων: ablatival genitive with ἔρημος.

8. σχολάζω : replies to ἀσχολία. Cf. *Ap.* **23 b**.

12. τοιούτους : predicate, *of like mind.* — This, with ἡμῖν and ὑμῖν above, is the only indication of a group of listeners.

14. παραγενόμενος : coincident in time with ἔπαθον.

15. οὔτε : correl. with οὔτ' αἰ, l. 22.

58 e

εἰσῄει· εὐδαίμων γάρ μοι ἀνὴρ ἐφαίνετο, ὦ Ἐχέκρατες, καὶ
τοῦ τρόπου καὶ τῶν λόγων, ὡς ἀδεῶς καὶ γενναίως ἐτελεύτα,
ὥστε μοι ἐκεῖνον παρίστασθαι μηδ᾽ εἰς Ἅιδου ἰόντα ἄνευ
θείας μοίρας ἰέναι, ἀλλὰ καὶ ἐκεῖσε ἀφικόμενον εὖ πράξειν,
20 εἴ πέρ τις πώποτε καὶ ἄλλος. διὰ δὴ ταῦτα οὐδὲν πάνυ μοι 59
ἐλεινὸν εἰσῄει, ὡς εἰκὸς ἂν δόξειεν εἶναι παρόντι πένθει·
ϟῦτ᾽ αὖ ἡδονὴ ὡς ἐν φιλοσοφίᾳ ἡμῶν ὄντων, ὥσπερ εἰώθε-
μεν· καὶ γὰρ οἱ λόγοι τοιοῦτοί τινες ἦσαν· ἀλλ᾽ ἀτεχνῶς
ἄτοπόν τί μοι πάθος παρῆν καί τις ἀήθης κρᾶσις ἀπό τε τῆς
25 ἡδονῆς συγκεκραμένη ὁμοῦ καὶ ἀπὸ τῆς λύπης, ἐνθυμουμένῳ
ὅτι αὐτίκα ἐκεῖνος ἔμελλε τελευτᾶν. καὶ πάντες οἱ παρόντες
σχεδόν τι οὕτω διεκείμεθα, ὁτὲ μὲν γελῶντες, ἐνίοτε δὲ δα-
κρύοντες, εἷς δ᾽ ἡμῶν καὶ διαφερόντως, Ἀπολλόδωρος· οἶσθα
γάρ που τὸν ἄνδρα καὶ τὸν τρόπον αὐτοῦ.   b
30 ΕΧ. Πῶς γὰρ οὔ;
ΦΑΙΔ. Ἐκεῖνός τε τοίνυν παντάπασιν οὕτως εἶχεν, καὶ
αὐτὸς ἔγωγ᾽ ἐτεταράγμην καὶ οἱ ἄλλοι.
ΕΧ. Ἔτυχον δ᾽, ὦ Φαίδων, τίνες παραγενόμενοι;
ΦΑΙΔ. Οὗτός τε δὴ ὁ Ἀπολλόδωρος τῶν ἐπιχωρίων παρῆν
35 καὶ ὁ Κριτόβουλος καὶ ὁ πατὴρ αὐτοῦ καὶ ἔτι Ἑρμογένης καὶ
Ἐπιγένης καὶ Αἰσχίνης καὶ Ἀντισθένης· ἦν δὲ καὶ Κτήσιπ-

---

17. **τοῦ τρόπου**: for construction,
cf. *Crito* 43 b.

18. **παρίστασθαι**: ἐκεῖνον ... ἰέναι
s subject.

19. **θείας μοίρας**: cf. θεία μοίρα, *Ap.*
33 c.

20. **εἴ περ κτλ.**: The English idiom
does not use *and* or *other*, but throws
all the stress on *any one*.

21. **οὐδὲν ἐλεινόν**: repeats οὔτε ἔλεος.
— **πένθει**: dative with παρά in παρόντι,
which in turn agrees with μοι or τινί,
after εἰκός (εἴ τις παρείη πένθει).

22. **ἡδονή**: sc. εἰσῄει, i.e. Phaedo
did not find his usual pleasure in the
philosophical discussions.

29. **τὸν τρόπον**: cf. 117 d; in *Symp.*
173 d we hear that he was commonly
called ὁ μανικός.

33. **ἔτυχον κτλ.**: *who were present?*
The English idiom throws little stress
on this verb.

34. The personal friends and asso-
ciates of Socrates are mentioned first.
— Xenophon at this time was in Asia
Minor with Thibro.

59 d

πος ὁ Παιανιεὺς καὶ Μενέξενος καὶ ἄλλοι τινὲς τῶν ἐπιχωρίων· Πλάτων δ' οἶμαι ἠσθένει.

ΕΧ. Ξένοι δέ τινες παρῆσαν; c

40 ΦΑΙΔ. Ναί, Σιμμίας τέ γ' ὁ Θηβαῖος καὶ Κέβης καὶ Φαιδώνδης, καὶ Μεγαρόθεν Εὐκλείδης τε καὶ Τερψίων.

ΕΧ. Τί δέ; Ἀρίστιππος καὶ Κλεόμβροτος παρεγένοντο;

ΦΑΙΔ. Οὐ δῆτα· ἐν Αἰγίνῃ γὰρ ἐλέγοντο εἶναι.

ΕΧ. Ἄλλος δέ τις παρῆν;

45 ΦΑΙΔ. Σχεδόν τι οἶμαι τούτους παραγενέσθαι.

ΕΧ. Τί οὖν δή; τίνες φὴς ἦσαν οἱ λόγοι;

III. ΦΑΙΔ. Ἐγώ σοι ἐξ ἀρχῆς πάντα πειράσομαι διηγήσασθαι. ἀεὶ γὰρ δὴ καὶ τὰς πρόσθεν ἡμέρας εἰώθεμεν φοι- d τᾶν καὶ ἐγὼ καὶ οἱ ἄλλοι παρὰ τὸν Σωκράτη, συλλεγόμενοι ἕωθεν εἰς τὸ δικαστήριον, ἐν ᾧ καὶ ἡ δίκη ἐγένετο· πλησίον 5 γὰρ ἦν τοῦ δεσμωτηρίου. περιεμένομεν οὖν ἑκάστοτε, ἕως ἀνοιχθείη τὸ δεσμωτήριον, διατρίβοντες μετ' ἀλλήλων· ἀνεῴγετο γὰρ οὐ πρῴ· ἐπειδὴ δ' ἀνοιχθείη, εἰσῇμεν παρὰ τὸν Σωκράτη καὶ τὰ πολλὰ διημερεύομεν μετ' αὐτοῦ. καὶ δὴ καὶ τότε πρῳαίτερον συνελέγημεν. τῇ γὰρ προτεραίᾳ [ἡμέρᾳ] ἐπειδὴ

---

38. Πλάτων: Plato names himself only here and *Ap.* **34 a, 38 b**. His illness at this time, according to tradition, was due to his grief. By his explicit statement of his absence, he relieves himself from responsibility for the exactness of the report.

39. ξένοι: contrasted with ἐπιχωρίων.

42. Ἀρίστιππος κτλ. : this seems to be intended as a reproach. These might have been present.

46. λόγοι: this refers to **59 a.**

III. *On each day of Socrates's confinement in prison his companions had visited him, but this morning they met*

earlier than usual, since they had learned that the boat had arrived from Delos. As they enter his room, they find that he has just been released from fetters, and Xanthippe with their little boy is sitting beside him. Xanthippe is sent home. Socrates rubs his leg, where the fetter and pain have been, and remarks on the curious relation between pleasure and pain : either is wont to follow the other. If Aesop had observed this he would have made a fable of it.

2. καὶ τὰς κτλ. : cf. l. 9.

7. ἀνοιχθείη : the optative indicates the indefinite frequency of the past action.

59 e

10 ἐξήλθομεν ἐκ τοῦ δεσμωτηρίου ἑσπέρας, ἐπυθόμεθα ὅτι τὸ e
πλοῖον ἐκ Δήλου ἀφιγμένον εἴη. παρηγγείλαμεν οὖν ἀλλήλοις ἥκειν ὡς πρῳαίτατα εἰς τὸ εἰωθός. καὶ ἥκομεν καὶ ἡμῖν
ἐξελθὼν ὁ θυρωρός, ὅσπερ εἰώθει ὑπακούειν, εἶπεν περιμένειν
καὶ μὴ πρότερον παριέναι, ἕως ἂν αὐτὸς κελεύσῃ· "Λύουσι
15 γάρ," ἔφη, "οἱ Ἕνδεκα Σωκράτη καὶ παραγγέλλουσιν ὅπως
ἂν τῇδε τῇ ἡμέρᾳ τελευτήσῃ." οὐ πολὺν δ' οὖν χρόνον
ἐπισχὼν ἧκεν καὶ ἐκέλευεν ἡμᾶς εἰσιέναι. εἰσελθόντες οὖν
κατελαμβάνομεν τὸν μὲν Σωκράτη ἄρτι λελυμένον, τὴν δὲ 60
Ξανθίππην (γιγνώσκεις γάρ) ἔχουσάν τε τὸ παιδίον αὐτοῦ
20 καὶ παρακαθημένην. ὡς οὖν εἶδεν ἡμᾶς ἡ Ξανθίππη, ἀνηυ-
φήμησέ τε καὶ τοιαῦτ' ἄττα εἶπεν, οἷα δὴ εἰώθασιν αἱ γυναῖκες, ὅτι "Ὦ Σώκρατες, ὕστατον δή σε προσεροῦσι νῦν οἱ
ἐπιτήδειοι καὶ σὺ τούτους." καὶ ὁ Σωκράτης βλέψας εἰς τὸν
Κρίτωνα, "Ὦ Κρίτων," ἔφη, "ἀπαγέτω τις αὐτὴν οἴκαδε."
25 καὶ ἐκείνην μὲν ἀπῆγόν τινες τῶν τοῦ Κρίτωνος βοῶσάν τε
καὶ κοπτομένην· ὁ δὲ Σωκράτης ἀνακαθιζόμενος εἰς τὴν 1
κλίνην συνέκαμψέ τε τὸ σκέλος καὶ ἐξέτριψε τῇ χειρί, καὶ
τρίβων ἅμα, "Ὡς ἄτοπον," ἔφη, "ὦ ἄνδρες, ἔοικέ τι εἶναι
τοῦτο, ὃ καλοῦσιν οἱ ἄνθρωποι ἡδύ· ὡς θαυμασίως πέφυκε
30 πρὸς τὸ δοκοῦν ἐναντίον εἶναι, τὸ λυπηρόν, τὸ ἅμα μὲν αὐτὼ
μὴ 'θέλειν παραγίγνεσθαι τῷ ἀνθρώπῳ, ἐὰν δέ τις διώκῃ τὸ
ἕτερον καὶ λαμβάνῃ, σχεδόν τι ἀναγκάζεσθαι λαμβάνειν καὶ
τὸ ἕτερον, ὥσπερ ἐκ μιᾶς κορυφῆς συνημμένω δύ' ὄντε. καί
μοι δοκεῖ," ἔφη, "εἰ ἐνενόησεν αὐτὰ Αἴσωπος, μῦθον ἂν c
35 συνθεῖναι, ὡς ὁ θεὸς βουλόμενος αὐτὰ διαλλάξαι πολεμοῦντα,
ἐπειδὴ οὐκ ἐδύνατο, συνῆψεν εἰς ταὐτὸν αὐτοῖς τὰς κορυφάς,

---

10. ἑσπέρας: for the genitive, cf.
ἔτους 57 b.
13. ὑπακούειν: cf. *Crito* 43 a.
19. παιδίον: cf. 116 b and *Ap.* 34 d.
25. τινὲς τῶν κτλ. : *some of Crito's*

attendants. An Athenian gentleman
was accompanied by one or more
body-servants wherever he went.
30. τὸ μὴ 'θέλειν: accusative of specification, —*in that the two are unwilling.*

60 e

καὶ διὰ ταῦτα ᾧ ἂν τὸ ἕτερον παραγένηται ἐπακολουθεῖ
ὕστερον καὶ τὸ ἕτερον. ὥσπερ οὖν καὶ αὐτῷ μοι ἔοικεν,
ἐπειδὴ ὑπὸ τοῦ δεσμοῦ ἦν ἐν τῷ σκέλει τὸ ἀλγεινόν, ἥκειν
10 δὴ φαίνεται ἐπακολουθοῦν τὸ ἡδύ."

IV. ὁ οὖν Κέβης ὑπολαβὼν " Νὴ τὸν Δία, ὦ Σώκρατες,"
ἔφη, " εὖ γ' ἐποίησας ἀναμνήσας με. περὶ γάρ τοι τῶν ποιη- d
μάτων ὧν πεποίηκας, ἐντείνας τοὺς τοῦ Αἰσώπου λόγους καὶ
τὸ εἰς τὸν Ἀπόλλω προοίμιον, καὶ ἄλλοι τινές με ἤδη ἤροντο,
5 ἀτὰρ καὶ Εὔηνος πρῴην, ὅ τί ποτε διανοηθείς, ἐπειδὴ δεῦρο
ἦλθες, ἐποίησας αὐτά, πρότερον οὐδὲν πώποτε ποιήσας. εἰ
οὖν τί σοι μέλει τοῦ ἔχειν ἐμὲ Εὐήνῳ ἀποκρίνασθαι, ὅταν
με αὖθις ἐρωτᾷ (εὖ οἶδα γὰρ ὅτι ἐρήσεται), εἰπέ, τί χρὴ λέγειν." " Λέγε τοίνυν," ἔφη, " αὐτῷ, ὦ Κέβης, τἀληθῆ, ὅτι
10 οὐκ ἐκείνῳ βουλόμενος οὐδὲ τοῖς ποιήμασιν αὐτοῦ ἀντί-
τεχνος εἶναι ἐποίησα ταῦτα· ἤδη γὰρ ὡς οὐ ῥᾴδιον εἴη· e
ἀλλ' ἐνυπνίων τινῶν ἀποπειρώμενος τί λέγει, καὶ ἀφοσιούμε-
νος, εἰ πολλάκις ταύτην τὴν μουσικήν μοι ἐπιτάττοι ποιεῖν.
ἦν γὰρ δὴ ἄττα τοιάδε· πολλάκις μοι φοιτῶν τὸ αὐτὸ ἐνύ-
15 πνιον ἐν τῷ παρελθόντι βίῳ, ἄλλοτ' ἐν ἄλλῃ ὄψει φαινόμε-
νον, τὰ αὐτὰ δὲ λέγον, ' Ὦ Σώκρατες,' ἔφη, ' μουσικὴν ποίει

---

40. ἐπακολουθοῦν : participle.

IV–VII. Second half of the prologue.

IV. The mention of Aesop reminds
Cebes of Socrates's putting into verse,
during his stay in the prison, some of
Aesop's fables, and then of Euenus's
question, why Socrates had composed
these verses and a hymn to Apollo now,
though never before had he written
poetry.

2. ποιημάτων : the first verses of
the fable and the hymn have been
preserved by Diogenes Laërtius. The
hymn began Δῆλι' Ἀπολλον χαῖρε καὶ

Ἀρτεμι παῖδε κλεεινώ. The fable began
Αἴσωπός ποτ' ἔλεξε Κορίνθιον ἄστυ νέ-
μουσιν, | μὴ κρίνειν ἀρετὴν λαοδίκῳ σοφίῃ.
We have no reason to suppose that
Socrates was greater as a poet than as
a sculptor.

5. Εὔηνος : cf. Ap. 20 b, and the note
on l. 24. — ὅ τι διανοηθείς : cf. ὅ τι μαθών, Ap. 36 b.

7. ἐμέ : subject of ἔχειν.

12. ἐνυπνίων κτλ. : prolepsis, — try-
ing the meaning of certain dreams. —
For Socrates's relation to dreams, cf
Ap. 33 c, and Crito 44 a.

13. ἐπιτάττοι : sc. τὰ ἐνύπνια.

60 e

καὶ ἐργάζου.' καὶ ἐγὼ ἔν γε τῷ πρόσθεν χρόνῳ ὅπερ ἔπραττον τοῦτο ὑπελάμβανον αὐτό μοι παρακελεύεσθαί τε καὶ ἐπι- 6ĺ
κελεύειν, ὥσπερ οἱ τοῖς θέουσι διακελευόμενοι, καὶ ἐμοὶ οὕτω
20 τὸ ἐνύπνιον ὅπερ ἔπραττον τοῦτο ἐπικελεύειν, μουσικὴν ποιεῖν,
ὡς φιλοσοφίας μὲν οὔσης μεγίστης μουσικῆς, ἐμοῦ δὲ τοῦτο
πράττοντος· νῦν δ' ἐπειδὴ ἥ τε δίκη ἐγένετο καὶ ἡ τοῦ θεοῦ
ἑορτὴ διεκώλυέ με ἀποθνῄσκειν, ἔδοξε χρῆναι, εἰ ἄρα πολλάκις μοι προστάττοι τὸ ἐνύπνιον ταύτην τὴν δημώδη μουσικὴν
25 ποιεῖν, μὴ ἀπειθῆσαι αὐτῷ, ἀλλὰ ποιεῖν. ἀσφαλέστερον γὰρ
εἶναι μὴ ἀπιέναι πρὶν ἀφοσιώσασθαι ποιήσαντα ποιήματα, b
πιθόμενον τῷ ἐνυπνίῳ. οὕτω δὴ πρῶτον μὲν εἰς τὸν θεὸν
ἐποίησα, οὗ ἦν ἡ παροῦσα θυσία· μετὰ δὲ τὸν θεόν, ἐννοήσας ὅτι τὸν ποιητὴν δέοι, εἴ περ μέλλοι ποιητὴς εἶναι, ποιεῖν
30 μύθους, ἀλλ' οὐ λόγους, καὶ αὐτὸς οὐκ ἦ μυθολογικός, διὰ
ταῦτα δὴ οὓς προχείρους εἶχον μύθους καὶ ἠπιστάμην τοὺς
Αἰσώπου, τούτους ἐποίησα, οἷς πρώτοις ἐνέτυχον. V. ταῦτα
οὖν, ὦ Κέβης, Εὐήνῳ φράζε, καὶ ἐρρῶσθαι καί, ἂν σωφρονῇ,
ἐμὲ διώκειν ὡς τάχιστα. ἄπειμι δ', ὡς ἔοικε, τήμερον· κε- c
λεύουσι γὰρ Ἀθηναῖοι."
    καὶ ὁ Σιμμίας, "Οἷον παρακελεύει," ἔφη, "τοῦτο, ὦ Σώ-

---

19. θέουσι: men shout " Run, run!"
to the man who is running. Cf. Hom.
Ψ 766 ἴαχον δ' ἐπὶ πάντες Ἀχαιοὶ | νίκης
ἱεμένῳ, μάλα δὲ σπεύδοντι κέλευον.
    20. μουσικὴν ποιεῖν: in apposition
with τοῦτο.
    21. τοῦτο: i.e. φιλοσοφίαν.
    24. δημώδη: almost contemptuous
in contrast with ἡ μεγίστη μουσική.
    26. εἶναι: the construction with
ἔδοξε is continued.
    28. θυσία: equivalent to ἑορτή
above. —μετὰ τὸν θεόν: i.e. after com-
posing the hymn to Apollo.

32. τοὺς Αἰσώπου: in apposition
with οὕς. Cf. τὰς σκέψεις Crito 48 c.
    V. Socrates sends to Euenus the
preceding explanation of his verses,
with his greetings, and a bidding to
follow him. At the last part of the
message Cebes is surprised: Euenus is
not likely to care to follow Socrates.
But Socrates insists that a true lover of
wisdom will be glad to die, — though he
will not take his own life. Here the
reader sees the first step toward the
topic of philosophical discussion.
    4. οἷον: an exclamation, H. 1001 ᴀ.

61 e

5 κρατες, Εὐήνῳ! πολλὰ γὰρ ἤδη ἐντετύχηκα τῷ ἀνδρί· σχεδὸν οὖν ἐξ ὧν ἐγὼ ᾔσθημαι οὐδ' ὁπωστιοῦν σοι ἑκὼν εἶναι
πείσεται." "Τί δέ;" ἦ δ' ὅς· "οὐ φιλόσοφος Εὔηνος;"
"Ἔμοιγε δοκεῖ," ἔφη ὁ Σιμμίας. "Ἐθελήσει τοίνυν καὶ
Εὔηνος καὶ πᾶς ὅτῳ ἀξίως τούτου τοῦ πράγματος μέτεστιν.
10 οὐ μέντοι ἴσως βιάσεται αὐτόν· οὐ γάρ φασι θεμιτὸν εἶναι."
καὶ ἅμα λέγων ταῦτα καθῆκε τὰ σκέλη ἐπὶ τὴν γῆν, καὶ d
καθεζόμενος οὕτως ἤδη τὰ λοιπὰ διελέγετο. ἤρετο οὖν αὐτὸν
ὁ Κέβης· "Πῶς τοῦτο λέγεις, ὦ Σώκρατες, τὸ μὴ θεμιτὸν
εἶναι ἑαυτὸν βιάζεσθαι, ἐθέλειν δ' ἂν τῷ ἀποθνῄσκοντι τὸν
15 φιλόσοφον ἕπεσθαι;" "Τί δέ, ὦ Κέβης; οὐκ ἀκηκόατε σύ
τε καὶ Σιμμίας περὶ τῶν τοιούτων Φιλολάῳ συγγεγονότες;"
"Οὐδέν γε σαφῶς, ὦ Σώκρατες." "Ἀλλὰ μὴν καὶ ἐγὼ ἐξ
ἀκοῆς περὶ αὐτῶν λέγω· ἃ μὲν οὖν τυγχάνω ἀκηκοώς, φθόνος οὐδεὶς λέγειν. καὶ γὰρ ἴσως καὶ μάλιστα πρέπει μέλ-
20 λοντα ἐκεῖσε ἀποδημεῖν διασκοπεῖν τε καὶ μυθολογεῖν περὶ ε
τῆς ἀποδημίας [τῆς ἐκεῖ], ποίαν τινὰ αὐτὴν οἰόμεθα εἶναι·
τί γὰρ ἄν τις καὶ ποιοῖ ἄλλο ἐν τῷ μέχρι ἡλίου δυσμῶν
χρόνῳ;"

6. ἑκὼν εἶναι: cf. *Ap.* 37 a.
9. πράγματος: i.e. φιλοσοφίας.
11. καὶ ἅμα λέγων κτλ.: this remark
indicates the incidental way in which
the last clause was uttered. Socrates
has no thought that he is introducing
a philosophical discussion. In a similar
fashion in 60 b Socrates's casual move-
ment is mentioned and there gives rise
to the beginning of the conversation.
13. τὸ μὴ εἶναι: in apposition with
τοῦτο. For the articular infinitive as
representative of the indicative, see
SCG. 328.
16. Φιλολάῳ: a Pythagorean philosopher, who was a native of Croton

or Tarentum. He appears to have lived
at Thebes many years. The first publication of the Pythagorean doctrines
is attributed to him. — συγγεγονότες:
cf. συνουσίας, *Ap.* 20 a.
20. μυθολογεῖν: cf. *Ap.* 39 e where
Socrates is about to talk with his friends,
— those who voted for his acquittal.
21. ἀποδημίας: cf. *Ap.* 40 e.— ἐκεῖ:
cf. 117 c.
22. ἡλίου δυσμῶν: cf. 116 e. In
89 c Socrates will defend his point ἕως
ἔτι φῶς ἐστιν. The civil day began and
ended at sunset. The condemned man
was allowed to live until the very close
of the day.

61 e

VI. " Κατὰ τί δὴ οὖν ποτε οὔ φασι θεμιτὸν εἶναι αὐτὸν ἑαυτὸν ἀποκτεινύναι, ὦ Σώκρατες; ἤδη γὰρ ἔγωγε, ὅπερ νυνδὴ
σὺ ἤρου, καὶ Φιλολάου ἤκουσα, ὅτε παρ᾽ ἡμῖν διῃτᾶτο,
ἤδη δὲ καὶ ἄλλων τινῶν, ὡς οὐ δέοι τοῦτο ποιεῖν· σαφὲς
5 δὲ περὶ αὐτῶν οὐδενὸς πώποτε οὐδὲν ἀκήκοα." " Ἀλλὰ προ- 62
θυμεῖσθαι χρή," ἔφη· "τάχα γὰρ ἂν καὶ ἀκούσαις. ἴσως
μέντοι θαυμαστόν σοι φανεῖται, εἰ τοῦτο μόνον τῶν ἄλλων
ἁπάντων ἁπλοῦν ἐστιν καὶ οὐδέποτε τυγχάνει τῷ ἀνθρώπῳ,
ὥσπερ καὶ τἆλλα, ἔστιν ὅτε καὶ οἷς βέλτιον ὂν τεθνάναι ἢ
10 ζῆν· οἷς δὲ βέλτιον τεθνάναι, θαυμαστὸν ἴσως σοι φαίνεται,
εἰ τούτοις τοῖς ἀνθρώποις μὴ ὅσιον αὐτοὺς ἑαυτοὺς εὖ ποιεῖν,
ἀλλ᾽ ἄλλον δεῖ περιμένειν εὐεργέτην." καὶ ὁ Κέβης ἠρέμα
ἐπιγελάσας, " Ἴττω Ζεύς," ἔφη, τῇ αὑτοῦ φωνῇ εἰπών. " Καὶ
γὰρ ἂν δόξειεν," ἔφη ὁ Σωκράτης, " οὕτω γ᾽ εἶναι ἄλογον· b
15 οὐ μέντοι ἀλλ᾽ ἴσως γ᾽ ἔχει τινὰ λόγον. ὁ μὲν οὖν ἐν ἀπορρή-
τοις λεγόμενος περὶ αὐτῶν λόγος, ὡς ἔν τινι φρουρᾷ ἐσμὲν

VI. Apparent Digression on Sui-
cide. *If death is not a good, then the
philosopher will not care to die ; but if
it is a good, why is he not free to secure
it for himself ? Why does Socrates say
that a man should not take his own life ?
We belong to the gods, and are their
creatures. And just as we should be
angry if one of our slaves killed himself,
without consulting our wishes, so the
gods might be angry if we should take
our own lives, when they might have
some work for us to do, — and if we
should not wait for them to send death
to us.*

1. **αὐτὸν ἑαυτόν**: the two words
form a single reflexive. Cf. *αὐτοὺς
ἑαυτούς* 62 a, *αὐτὸ ἑαυτό* 62 c, *αὐτός γε
αὑτοῦ* 62 d.

2. **ὅπερ**: *as to that question of yours.*

7. " Few rules are absolute, and
very likely at some times (*ἔστιν ὅτε*) and
for some persons (*ἔστιν οἷς*) death may
be better than life."

8. **ἁπάντων**: partitive genitive with
μόνον.

13. **ἴττω Ζεύς**: Cebes was a Theban,
and the Boeotian dialect did not change
ϝίδ-τω to *ἴστω*, as in Attic, but to *ϝίττω*
or *ἴττω*. In strictness, as a Theban,
Cebes would have said *ἴττω Δεύς*, but
our Mss. make him mix dialects.

14. **γάρ**: *yes.* — **οὕτω γε**: *when
looked at in this way,* — contrasted
with *ταύτῃ* l. 26.

15. **ἔχει λόγον**: cf. *Ap.* 31 b.

16. **ὡς κτλ.**: explains *ὁ λεγόμενος
λόγος.* — **ἐν φρουρᾷ**: cf. piis omnibus
retinendus animus est in cus-
todia corporis nec iniussu eius

62 d

οἱ ἄνθρωποι καὶ οὐ δεῖ δὴ ἑαυτὸν ἐκ ταύτης λύειν οὐδ' ἀποδιδράσκειν, μέγας τέ τίς μοι φαίνεται καὶ οὐ ῥᾴδιος διιδεῖν·
οὐ μέντοι ἀλλὰ τόδε γέ μοι δοκεῖ, ὦ Κέβης, εὖ λέγεσθαι, τὸ
20 θεοὺς εἶναι ἡμῶν τοὺς ἐπιμελουμένους καὶ ἡμᾶς τοὺς ἀνθρώπους ἐν τῶν κτημάτων τοῖς θεοῖς εἶναι· ἢ σοὶ οὐ δοκεῖ
οὕτως;" "Ἔμοιγε," φησὶν ὁ Κέβης. "Οὐκοῦν," ἦ δ' ὅς,
" καὶ σὺ ἂν τῶν σαυτοῦ κτημάτων εἴ τι αὐτὸ ἑαυτὸ ἀποκτει- c
νύοι, μὴ σημήναντός σου ὅτι βούλει αὐτὸ τεθνάναι, χαλε-
25 παίνοις ἂν αὐτῷ, καὶ εἴ τινα ἔχοις τιμωρίαν, τιμωροῖο ἄν;"
" Πάνυ γ'," ἔφη. "Ἴσως τοίνυν ταύτῃ οὐκ ἄλογον, μὴ πρότερον αὐτὸν ἀποκτεινύναι δεῖν, πρὶν ἂν ἀνάγκην τινὰ θεὸς
ἐπιπέμψῃ, ὥσπερ καὶ τὴν νῦν ἡμῖν παροῦσαν."

VII. " Ἀλλ' εἰκός," ἔφη ὁ Κέβης, "τοῦτό γε φαίνεται.
ὃ μέντοι νυνδὴ ἔλεγες, τὸ τοὺς φιλοσόφους ῥᾳδίως ἂν ἐθέλειν ἀποθνῄσκειν, ἔοικεν τοῦτο, ὦ Σώκρατες, ἀτόπῳ, εἴ περ ὃ d
νυνδὴ ἐλέγομεν εὐλόγως ἔχει, τὸ θεόν τ' εἶναι τὸν ἐπιμελού-
5 μενον ἡμῶν καὶ ἡμᾶς ἐκείνου κτήματα εἶναι. τὸ γὰρ μὴ
ἀγανακτεῖν τοὺς φρονιμωτάτους ἐκ ταύτης τῆς θεραπείας
ἀπιόντας, ἐν ᾗ ἐπιστατοῦσιν αὐτῶν οἵπερ ἄριστοί εἰσιν τῶν
ὄντων ἐπιστάται θεοί, οὐκ ἔχει λόγον. οὐ γάρ που αὐτός
γ' αὐτοῦ οἴεται ἄμεινον ἐπιμελήσεσθαι ἐλεύθερος γενόμενος·

a quo ille est vobis datus ex
hominum vita migrandum est
Cicero, de Rep. vi. 8.

23. ἄν: repeated after χαλεπαίνοις.
Cf. Αp. 40 d.—κτημάτων: distinguished
from χρημάτων.

26. ταύτῃ: opposed to οὕτω l. 14.
— μὴ πρότερον κτλ. : i.e. should wait
until God should send for him.

VII. This seems reasonable, but
why should a lover of truth desire to die,
and not prefer to remain here in the care
of the gods, his good masters? And is

not Socrates unreasonable in his willing-
ness to leave this present life? Socrates
must defend himself against this charge.

2. τὸ... ἀποθνῄσκειν: in apposition
with the relative ὅ. Cf. the construction of τὸ θεὸν εἶναι two lines below.

3. ἔοικεν ἀτόπῳ: equivalent to ἔοικεν
ἄτοπον εἶναι. Cf. Αp. 31 b.

6. τὸ μὴ ἀγανακτεῖν: subject of ἔχει
λόγον.

8. θεοί: for construction, cf. τοὺς
Αἰσώπου 61 b.

9. οἴεται: sc. ὁ φρονιμώτατος, —

62 d

10 ἀλλ᾽ ἀνόητος μὲν ἄνθρωπος τάχ᾽ ἂν οἰηθείη ταῦτα, [φευκτέον
εἶναι ἀπὸ τοῦ δεσπότου,] καὶ οὐκ ἂν λογίζοιτο ὅτι οὐ δεῖ ἀπό
γε τοῦ ἀγαθοῦ φεύγειν, ἀλλ᾽ ὅ τι μάλιστα παραμένειν, διὸ
ἀλογίστως ἂν φεύγοι, ὁ δὲ νοῦν ἔχων ἐπιθυμοῖ που ἂν ἀεὶ
εἶναι παρὰ τῷ αὑτοῦ βελτίονι. καίτοι οὕτως, ὦ Σώκρατες,
15 τοὐναντίον εἶναι εἰκὸς ἢ ὃ νυνδὴ ἐλέγετο· τοὺς μὲν γὰρ φρο-
νίμους ἀγανακτεῖν ἀποθνήσκοντας πρέπει, τοὺς δ᾽ ἄφρονας
χαίρειν." ἀκούσας οὖν ὁ Σωκράτης ἡσθῆναί τέ μοι ἔδοξε τῇ
τοῦ Κέβητος πραγματείᾳ, καὶ ἐπιβλέψας εἰς ἡμᾶς " Ἀεί τοι,"   63
ἔφη, " ὁ Κέβης λόγους τινὰς ἀνερευνᾷ, καὶ οὐ πάνυ εὐθέως
20 ἐθέλει πείθεσθαι ὅ τι ἄν τις εἴπῃ." Καὶ ὁ Σιμμίας " Ἀλλὰ
μήν," ἔφη, " ὦ Σώκρατες, νῦν γέ μοι δοκεῖ τι καὶ αὐτῷ λέγειν Κέβης· τί γὰρ ἂν βουλόμενοι ἄνδρες σοφοὶ ὡς ἀληθῶς
δεσπότας ἀμείνους αὑτῶν φεύγοιεν καὶ ῥᾳδίως ἀπαλλάττοιντο
αὐτῶν; καί μοι δοκεῖ Κέβης εἰς σὲ τείνειν τὸν λόγον, ὅτι οὕτω
25 ῥᾳδίως φέρεις καὶ ἡμᾶς ἀπολείπων καὶ ἄρχοντας ἀγαθούς,
ὡς αὐτὸς ὁμολογεῖς, θεούς." " Δίκαια," ἔφη, " λέγετε. οἶμαι b
γὰρ ὑμᾶς λέγειν ὅτι χρή με πρὸς ταῦτα ἀπολογήσασθαι
ὥσπερ ἐν δικαστηρίῳ." " Πάνυ μὲν οὖν," ἔφη ὁ Σιμμίας.

VIII. " Φέρε δή," ἦ δ᾽ ὅς, " πειραθῶ πιθανώτερον πρὸς

change from indefinite plural to the
singular.

10. φευκτέον εἶναι : explains ταῦτα.

14. οὕτως : cf. οὗτω 62 b.

15. ἤ : than, after the comparative
idea in τοὐναντίον.

21. τἰ λέγειν : cf. οὐδὲν λέγει, Ἀρ. 30 b.

22. ὡς ἀληθῶς : construe with σοφοί.

23. ῥᾳδίως : cf. l. 2.

24. εἰς σέ : i.e. Cebes not only makes
his point, but makes it against Socrates.

26. θεούς : in apposition with ἄρχοντας. — **δίκαια** : predicate.

Here closes the prologue, which
serves simply as a background for the
scene of the dialogue, a setting for the

argument. The companions of Socrates have gathered simply as friends,
and for no philosophical discussion,
but by degrees they have come to the
consideration of the relation of the
true lover of truth to death.

VIII. Introductory to the first
topic, — why a philosopher should meet
death with joy. *Socrates has strong
hopes that the dead have existence, and
that the good have a happy existence. He
expects to come to a company of good men,
and certainly to come to good gods.*

1. πιθανώτερον : a humorous allusion to Socrates's failure to convince
the court.

114 d

ὑμᾶς ἀπολογήσασθαι· ἢ πρὸς τοὺς δικαστάς. ἐγὼ γάρ,"
ἔφη, " ὦ Σιμμία τε καὶ Κέβης, εἰ μὲν μὴ ᾤμην ἥξειν πρῶτον μὲν παρὰ θεοὺς ἄλλους σοφούς τε καὶ ἀγαθούς, ἔπειτα
5 καὶ παρ' ἀνθρώπους τετελευτηκότας ἀμείνους τῶν ἐνθάδε,
ἠδίκουν ἂν οὐκ ἀγανακτῶν τῷ θανάτῳ· νῦν δ' εὖ ἴστε ὅτι
παρ' ἄνδρας τ' ἐλπίζω ἀφίξεσθαι ἀγαθούς· καὶ τοῦτο μὲν c
οὐκ ἂν πάνυ διισχυρισαίμην. ὅτι μέντοι παρὰ θεοὺς δεσπότας πάνυ ἀγαθοὺς [ἥξειν], εὖ ἴστε ὅτι, εἴ πέρ τι ἄλλο τῶν
10 τοιούτων, διισχυρισαίμην ἂν καὶ τοῦτο. ὥστε διὰ ταῦτα
οὐχ ὁμοίως ἀγανακτῶ, ἀλλ' εὐελπίς εἰμι εἶναί τι τοῖς τετε-
λευτηκόσι καί, ὥσπερ γε καὶ πάλαι λέγεται, πολὺ ἄμεινον
τοῖς ἀγαθοῖς ἢ τοῖς κακοῖς."

· · · · · · · · ·

114

LXIII. "Τὸ μὲν οὖν ταῦτα διισχυρίσασθαι οὕτως ἔχειν, d
ὡς ἐγὼ διελήλυθα, οὐ πρέπει νοῦν ἔχοντι ἀνδρί· ὅτι μέντοι
ἢ ταῦτ' ἐστὶν ἢ τοιαῦτ' ἄττα περὶ τὰς ψυχὰς ἡμῶν καὶ τὰς
οἰκήσεις, ἐπείπερ ἀθάνατόν γ' ἡ ψυχὴ φαίνεται οὖσα, τοῦτο

3. πρῶτον μέν: as often, the form
of the sentence is changed later.
6. ἠδίκουν ἄν: I should be wrong.
SCG. 429. — ἀγανακτῶν: cf. Crito 43 c.
— νῦν δ'.: contrasted with εἰ μέν in l. 3
above.
7. παρ' ἄνδρας: cf. Ap. 41 a. — τοῦτο μέν: i.e. ἀφίξεσθαι κτλ. To this, μέντοι is adversative.
9. εἴ περ κτλ. : cf. 59 a.
11. ὁμοίως: sc. as I otherwise should.
In the first division of the argument, Socrates shows that pure, absolute truth cannot be attained while the
soul is hampered by the body. The
lover of truth, then, is ever eager to
free his soul from the fetters of the
body. But this argument assumes the
immortality of the soul, and the latter

must be proved. — After his argument,
Socrates gives briefly his view of the
universe, — including Inferno, Purga-
torio, and Paradiso.

LXIII. Socrates would not insist
on the exactness of the lines of his picture of the life of the soul after death,
but believes that something like it is true.
The immortality of the soul has been
shown, and a good man may be of good
cheer as regards the future. Here Socrates reverts to the situation at 63 b.

1. ταῦτα: subject of οὕτως ἔχειν. —
τὸ διισχυρίσασθαι: subject of πρέπει.
Cf. 63 c.
2. ὅτι κτλ. : this clause is resumed
by τοῦτο.
4. ἀθάνατον: neuter predicate, in
spite of the gender of the subject.

114 d

5 καὶ πρέπειν μοι δοκεῖ καὶ ἄξιον κινδυνεῦσαι οἰομένῳ οὕτως
ἔχειν· καλὸς γὰρ ὁ κίνδυνος· καὶ χρὴ τὰ τοιαῦτα ὥσπερ
ἐπᾴδειν ἑαυτῷ, διὸ δὴ ἔγωγε καὶ πάλαι μηκύνω τὸν μῦθον.
ἀλλὰ τούτων δὴ ἕνεκα θαρρεῖν χρὴ περὶ τῇ ἑαυτοῦ ψυχῇ
ἄνδρα ὅστις ἐν τῷ βίῳ τὰς μὲν ἄλλας ἡδονὰς τὰς περὶ τὸ e
10 σῶμα καὶ τοὺς κόσμους εἴασε χαίρειν, ὡς ἀλλοτρίους τ᾽ ὄντας
καὶ πλέον θάτερον ἡγησάμενος ἀπεργάζεσθαι, τὰς δὲ περὶ τὸ
μανθάνειν ἐσπούδασέ τε καὶ κοσμήσας τὴν ψυχὴν οὐκ ἀλλο-
τρίῳ ἀλλὰ τῷ αὑτῆς κόσμῳ, σωφροσύνῃ τε καὶ δικαιοσύνῃ
καὶ ἀνδρείᾳ καὶ ἐλευθερίᾳ καὶ ἀληθείᾳ, οὕτω περιμένει τὴν 115
15 εἰς Ἅιδου πορείαν, ὡς πορευσόμενος ὅταν ἡ εἱμαρμένη καλῇ.
ὑμεῖς μὲν οὖν," ἔφη, " ὦ Σιμμία τε καὶ Κέβης καὶ οἱ ἄλλοι,
εἰς αὖθις. ἔν τινι χρόνῳ ἕκαστος πορεύσεσθε· ἐμὲ δὲ νῦν ἤδη
καλεῖ, φαίη ἂν ἀνὴρ τραγικός, ἡ εἱμαρμένη, καὶ σχεδόν τί
μοι ὥρα τραπέσθαι πρὸς τὸ λουτρόν· δοκεῖ γὰρ δὴ βέλτιον
20 εἶναι λουσάμενον πιεῖν τὸ φάρμακον καὶ μὴ πράγματα ταῖς
γυναιξὶ παρέχειν νεκρὸν λούειν."

LXIV. ταῦτα δὴ εἰπόντος αὐτοῦ, ὁ Κρίτων, " Εἶεν," ἔφη, b
" ὦ Σώκρατες· τί δὲ τούτοις ἢ ἐμοὶ ἐπιστέλλεις ἢ περὶ τῶν

5. οἰομένῳ: has the main idea, —
"it is worth while to believe, even at
some risk."

7. ἐπᾴδειν: sc. to charm away the
childish fear of death which remains
in the soul.

9. περὶ τὸ σῶμα: equivalent to τοῦ
σώματος. Cf. περὶ τὸ μανθάνειν, below.

10. τοὺς κόσμους: sc. τοῦ σώματος.

11. θάτερον: euphemistic for κακόν.

14. ἀληθείᾳ: This corresponds to
what became the fourth cardinal virtue,
— σοφία. The four, as they were generally accepted later, seem to have been
enunciated first in Plato's Republic,

Book iv: σοφία, ἀνδρεία, δικαιοσύνη,
σωφροσύνη. — οὕτω: refers to κοσμήσας,
above.

15. ὡς πορευσόμενος: ready to go.

18. τραγικός: Socrates is still in a
playful mood.

20. λουσάμενον: the chief matter is
expressed by the participle, "to bathe
before I drink the drug."

21. λούειν: explanatory infinitive;
cf. Crito 45 c.

LXIV. What last instructions will
Socrates give to his friends? What can
they do to please him? Nothing new.
Just what he is always saying, — that if
they care for themselves, they will please

115 d

παίδων ἢ περὶ ἄλλου του, ὅ τι ἂν σοι ποιοῦντες ἡμεῖς ἐν
χάριτι μάλιστα ποιοῖμεν;" "Ἅπερ ἀεὶ λέγω," ἔφη, "ὦ Κρί-
5 των· οὐδὲν καινότερον· ὅτι ὑμῶν αὐτῶν ἐπιμελούμενοι ὑμεῖς,
καὶ ἐμοὶ καὶ τοῖς ἐμοῖς καὶ ὑμῖν αὐτοῖς ἐν χάριτι ποιήσετε
ἅττ' ἂν ποιῆτε, κἂν μὴ νῦν ὁμολογήσητε· ἐὰν δ' ὑμῶν μὲν
αὐτῶν ἀμελῆτε, καὶ μὴ 'θέλητε, ὥσπερ κατ' ἴχνη κατὰ τὰ
νῦν τ' εἰρημένα καὶ τὰ ἐν τῷ ἔμπροσθεν χρόνῳ ζῆν, οὐδ' ἐὰν
10 πολλὰ ὁμολογήσητε ἐν τῷ παρόντι καὶ σφόδρα, οὐδὲν πλέον c
ποιήσετε." "Ταῦτα μὲν τοίνυν προθυμηθησόμεθα," ἔφη,
"οὕτω ποιεῖν· θάπτωμεν δέ σε τίνα τρόπον;" "Ὅπως ἄν,"
ἔφη," βούλησθε, ἐάν πέρ γε λάβητέ με καὶ μὴ ἐκφύγω ὑμᾶς."
γελάσας δ' ἅμα ἡσυχῇ καὶ πρὸς ἡμᾶς ἀποβλέψας εἶπεν, "Οὐ
15 πείθω, ὦ ἄνδρες, Κρίτωνα, ὡς ἐγώ εἰμι οὗτος ὁ Σωκράτης, ὁ
νυνὶ διαλεγόμενος, καὶ διατάττων ἕκαστον τῶν λεγομένων,
ἀλλ' οἴεταί με ἐκεῖνον εἶναι, ὃν ὄψεται ὀλίγον ὕστερον νεκρόν,
καὶ ἐρωτᾷ δή, πῶς με θάπτῃ. ὅτι δ' ἐγὼ πάλαι πολὺν λόγον d
πεποίημαι, ὡς, ἐπειδὰν πίω τὸ φάρμακον, οὐκέτι ὑμῖν παρα-
20 μενῶ, ἀλλ' οἰχήσομαι ἀπιὼν εἰς μακάρων δή τινας εὐδαιμο-

him even if they make no promises now.
— How shall they bury Socrates? They
cannot bury Socrates, and they may do
what they like with his body.

5. ὑμῶν κτλ.: cf. Ap. 29 e, 36 c.

6. ἐμοῖς: masculine, cf. περὶ παίδων,
above.

11. ταῦτα μὲν κτλ.: simply marks
the transition. Cf. Crito 44 d.—προθυμηθησόμεθα: cf. 62 a.

12. θάπτωμεν: deliberative subjunctive. Crito means to ask Socrates's
preference for cremation or inhuma-
tion. Cf. Cum enim de immortali-
tate animorum disputavisset et
iam moriendi tempus urgeret,
rogatus a Critone quem ad mo-

dum sepeliri vellet, "Multam
vero" inquit "operam, amici,
frustra consumpsi. Critoni
enim nostro non persuasi me
hinc avolaturum neque mei
quicquam relicturum. Verum
tamen, Crito, si me adsequi po-
tueris aut sicubi nanctus eris,
ut tibi videbitur, sepelito.
Sed, mihi crede, nemo me ves-
trum, cum hinc excessero, con-
sequetur." Cicero, Tusc. i. 103.

15. οὗτος: contrasted with ἐκεῖνον,
below.

18. θάπτῃ: the mood of direct
quotation is retained. — ὅτι κτλ.: resumed by ταῦτα.

115 d

νίας, ταῦτα [μοι] δοκῶ αὐτῷ ἄλλως λέγειν, παραμυθούμενος
ἅμα μὲν ὑμᾶς, ἅμα δ᾽ ἐμαυτόν. ἐγγυήσασθε οὖν με πρὸς
Κρίτωνα," ἔφη, " τὴν ἐναντίαν ἐγγύην ἢ ἣν οὗτος πρὸς τοὺς
δικαστὰς ἠγγυᾶτο. οὗτος μὲν γὰρ ἦ μὴν παραμενεῖν· ὑμεῖς
25 δ᾽ ἦ μὴν μὴ παραμενεῖν ἐγγυήσασθε, ἐπειδὰν ἀποθάνω,
ἀλλὰ οἰχήσεσθαι ἀπιόντα, ἵνα Κρίτων ῥᾷον φέρῃ, καὶ μὴ ε
ὁρῶν μου τὸ σῶμα ἢ καόμενον ἢ κατορυττόμενον ἀγανακτῇ
ὑπὲρ ἐμοῦ ὡς δεινὰ πάσχοντος, μηδὲ λέγῃ ἐν τῇ ταφῇ ὡς
ἢ προτίθεται Σωκράτη ἢ ἐκφέρει ἢ κατορύττει. εὖ γὰρ
30 ἴσθι," ἦ δ᾽ ὅς, " ὦ ἄριστε Κρίτων, τὸ μὴ καλῶς λέγειν οὐ
μόνον εἰς αὐτὸ τοῦτο πλημμελές, ἀλλὰ καὶ κακόν τι ἐμποιεῖ
ταῖς ψυχαῖς. ἀλλὰ θαρρεῖν τε χρὴ καὶ φάναι τοὐμὸν σῶμα
θάπτειν, καὶ θάπτειν οὕτως ὅπως ἄν σοι φίλον ᾖ καὶ μάλιστα 116
ἡγῇ νόμιμον εἶναι."

LXV. ταῦτ᾽ εἰπὼν ἐκεῖνος μὲν ἀνίστατο εἰς οἴκημά τι ὡς
λουσόμενος, καὶ ὁ Κρίτων εἵπετο αὐτῷ, ἡμᾶς δ᾽ ἐκέλευε περιμένειν. περιεμένομεν οὖν πρὸς ἡμᾶς αὐτοὺς διαλεγόμενοι
περὶ τῶν εἰρημένων καὶ ἀνασκοποῦντες, τοτὲ δ᾽ αὖ περὶ τῆς

21. ταῦτα: i.e. all the preceding
argument.

24. ἠγγυᾶτο: the tense implies that
the offer was not accepted. This cannot refer to the offer of surety for the
payment of a fine (cf. παραμενεῖν), but
suggests that Crito may have desired
to relieve Socrates from the month's
imprisonment, by giving bonds for his
appearance to meet his sentence.

27. τὸ σῶμα: in strong contrast
with ἐμοῦ.

31. εἰς αὐτὸ τοῦτο: i.e. as being
false. — πλημμελές: predicate.

34. νόμιμον: here, again, an indication of Socrates's care to obey both
written and unwritten laws.

LXV. Socrates leaves his friends in
order to bathe, and then to converse
with his family. When he returns to
his friends, the day is far spent, and he
says little more. The attendant of the
Eleven comes to bid him farewell, sure
that Socrates will not be angry with
him for bringing the word of death.
Socrates tells Crito to have the drug
brought. Others may have delayed
drinking the hemlock as long as a
gleam of day lasted, but he has nothing to gain by drinking the drug a little
later.

2. ὡς λουσόμενος: saying that he
was going to bathe. — περιμένειν: cf.
59 d.

116 d

5 συμφορᾶς διεξιόντες, ὅση ἡμῖν γεγονυῖα εἴη, ἀτεχνῶς ἡγούμενοι ὥσπερ πατρὸς στερηθέντες διάξειν ὀρφανοὶ τὸν ἔπειτα
βίον. ἐπειδὴ δ' ἐλούσατο καὶ ἠνέχθη παρ' αὐτὸν τὰ παιδία, b
— δύο γὰρ αὐτῷ ὑεῖς σμικροὶ ἦσαν, εἷς δὲ μέγας, — καὶ αἱ
οἰκεῖαι γυναῖκες ἀφίκοντο, ἐναντίον τοῦ Κρίτωνος διαλεχθείς
10 τε καὶ ἐπιστείλας ἄττα ἐβούλετο, τὰς μὲν γυναῖκας καὶ τὰ
παιδία ἀπιέναι ἐκέλευσεν, αὐτὸς δ' ἧκε παρ' ἡμᾶς. καὶ ἦν
ἤδη ἐγγὺς ἡλίου δυσμῶν· χρόνον γὰρ πολὺν διέτριψεν ἔνδον.
ἐλθὼν δ' ἐκαθέζετο λελουμένος, καὶ οὐ πολλὰ μετὰ ταῦτα διε-
λέχθη, καὶ ἧκεν ὁ τῶν ἕνδεκα ὑπηρέτης καὶ στὰς παρ' αὐτόν,
15 "Ὦ Σώκρατες," ἔφη, "οὐ καταγνώσομαι σοῦ ὅπερ ἄλλων c
καταγιγνώσκω, ὅτι μοι χαλεπαίνουσι καὶ καταρῶνται, ἐπειδὰν αὐτοῖς παραγγέλλω πίνειν τὸ φάρμακον ἀναγκαζόντων
τῶν ἀρχόντων. σὲ δ' ἐγὼ καὶ ἄλλως ἔγνωκα ἐν τούτῳ τῷ
χρόνῳ γενναιότατον καὶ πρᾳότατον καὶ ἄριστον ἄνδρα ὄντα
20 τῶν πώποτε δεῦρο ἀφικομένων, καὶ δὴ καὶ νῦν εὖ οἶδ' ὅτι
οὐκ ἐμοὶ χαλεπαίνεις, γιγνώσκεις γὰρ τοὺς αἰτίους, ἀλλὰ
ἐκείνοις. νῦν, οἶσθα γὰρ ἃ ἦλθον ἀγγέλλων, χαῖρέ τε καὶ
πειρῶ ὡς ῥᾷστα φέρειν τὰ ἀναγκαῖα." καὶ ἅμα δακρύσας d
μεταστρεφόμενος ἀπῄει. καὶ ὁ Σωκράτης ἀναβλέψας πρὸς
25 αὐτόν, "Καὶ σύ," ἔφη, "χαῖρε, καὶ ἡμεῖς ταῦτα ποιήσομεν."
καὶ ἅμα πρὸς ἡμᾶς, "Ὡς ἀστεῖος," ἔφη, "ὁ ἄνθρωπος· καὶ
παρὰ πάντα μοι τὸν χρόνον προσῄει καὶ διελέγετο ἐνίοτε

6. ὀρφανοί: predicate. The subject of the infinitive is subject also of
περιεμένομεν.

7. παιδία: cf. Ap. 34 d.

9. γυναῖκες: among these, of course,
Xanthippe is included. She returns to
the prison in the afternoon, though
she was conducted home in the morning (60 a). — Of Socrates's other living
kin, nothing is known.

15. καταγνώσομαι: cf. Ap. 25 a.

18. ἀρχόντων: i.e. the Eleven. Cf.
Ap. 39 e, and 44 a. — ἐν τούτῳ κτλ.:
i.e. while Socrates was in prison.

20. τῶν ἀφικομένων: partitive genitive, — "of all whom I ever knew."

22. ἐκείνοις: the jailer assumes that
Socrates will be angry with some one,
but believes that he will hold the right
persons responsible for his death. —
ἀγγέλλων: expresses purpose. Cf. πείθων Ap. 30 a.

116 d

καὶ ἦν ἀνδρῶν λῷστος, καὶ νῦν ὡς γενναίως με ἀποδακρύει.
ἀλλ᾽ ἄγε δή, ὦ Κρίτων, πειθώμεθα αὐτῷ, καὶ ἐνεγκάτω τις τὸ
30 φάρμακον, εἰ τέτριπται· εἰ δὲ μή, τριψάτω ὁ ἄνθρωπος." καὶ
ὁ Κρίτων, " Ἀλλ᾽ οἶμαι," ἔφη, " ἔγωγε, ὦ Σώκρατες, ἔτι ἥλιον e
εἶναι ἐπὶ τοῖς ὄρεσιν καὶ οὔπω δεδυκέναι. καὶ ἅμα ἐγὼ οἶδα
καὶ ἄλλους πάνυ ὀψὲ πίνοντας, ἐπειδὰν παραγγελθῇ αὐτοῖς,
δειπνήσαντάς τε καὶ πιόντας εὖ μάλα, καὶ συγγενομένους
35 γ᾽ ἐνίους ὧν ἂν τύχωσιν ἐπιθυμοῦντες. ἀλλὰ μηδὲν ἐπείγου·
ἔτι γὰρ ἐγχωρεῖ." καὶ ὁ Σωκράτης, " Εἰκότως γε," ἔφη, " ὦ
Κρίτων, ἐκεῖνοί τε ταῦτα ποιοῦσιν, οὓς σὺ λέγεις, οἴονται γὰρ
κερδανεῖν ταῦτα ποιήσαντες, καὶ ἔγωγε ταῦτα [εἰκότως] οὐ
ποιήσω· οὐδὲν γὰρ οἶμαι κερδανεῖν ὀλίγον ὕστερον πιὼν 117
40 ἄλλο γε ἢ γέλωτα ὀφλήσειν παρ᾽ ἐμαυτῷ, γλιχόμενος τοῦ
ζῆν καὶ φειδόμενος οὐδενὸς ἔτι ἐνόντος. ἀλλ᾽ ἴθι," ἔφη, " πιθοῦ
καὶ μὴ ἄλλως ποίει."

LXVI. Καὶ ὁ Κρίτων ἀκούσας ἔνευσε τῷ παιδὶ πλησίον
ἑστῶτι, καὶ ὁ παῖς ἐξελθὼν καὶ συχνὸν χρόνον διατρίψας
ἧκεν ἄγων τὸν μέλλοντα διδόναι τὸ φάρμακον, ἐν κύλικι

31. ἥλιον: the day was not gone,
while the sun's light could be seen.
Cf. 61 e.
38. ταῦτα ποιήσαντες: by doing this.
40. παρ᾽ ἐμαυτῷ: in my own judgment. Cf. the proverb μὴ ἴσθι φρόνιμος
παρὰ σεαυτῷ, Prov. iii. 7, cf. Rom.
xii. 16.
41. φειδόμενος κτλ. : seems to be
an allusion to Hesiod's advice to use
the wine freely both when the jar was
first opened, and when it was nearly
exhausted, but to be sparing of it the
rest of the time. — πιθοῦ: cf. Crito
44 b. SCG. 403.
LXVI. The drug is brought. Socrates asks if he may pour a libation to
a god, but learns that only so much has

been prepared as it is well for him to
drink. He prays, however, that his departure may be for his happiness. His
friends cannot restrain their tears when
he drinks the drug, but he rebukes their
lamentations, and expresses his desire
to die in peace.
1. τῷ παιδί: doubtless Crito's personal attendant. Cf. 60 a.
3. τὸν μέλλοντα κτλ. : i.e. a spe-
cialist, who had charge of the execution. — τὸ φάρμακον : this is nowhere
specified by Plato, but was κώνειον,
or the seeds of the poison hemlock,
which, as is seen, were prepared by
grinding or pounding in a druggist's
mortar. As a means of execution of
a sentence of death, this seems to have

117 d

φέροντα τετριμμένον· ἰδὼν δὲ ὁ Σωκράτης τὸν ἄνθρωπον,
5 "Εἶεν," ἔφη, "ὦ βέλτιστε, σὺ γὰρ τούτων ἐπιστήμων, τί
χρὴ ποιεῖν;" "Οὐδὲν ἄλλο," ἔφη, "ἢ πιόντα περιιέναι, ἕως
ἄν σου βάρος ἐν τοῖς σκέλεσι γένηται, ἔπειτα κατακεῖσθαι· b
καὶ οὕτως αὐτὸ ποιήσει." καὶ ἅμα ὤρεξε τὴν κύλικα τῷ
Σωκράτει· καὶ ὃς λαβὼν καὶ μάλα ἵλεως, ὦ Ἐχέκρατες,
10 οὐδὲν τρέσας οὐδὲ διαφθείρας οὔτε τοῦ χρώματος οὔτε τοῦ
προσώπου, ἀλλ' ὥσπερ εἰώθει ταυρηδὸν ὑποβλέψας πρὸς τὸν
ἄνθρωπον, "Τί λέγεις," ἔφη, "περὶ τοῦδε τοῦ πώματος πρὸς
τὸ ἀποσπεῖσαί τινι; ἔξεστιν, ἢ οὔ;" "Τοσοῦτον," ἔφη,
"ὦ Σώκρατες, τρίβομεν, ὅσον οἰόμεθα μέτριον εἶναι πιεῖν."
15 "Μανθάνω," ἦ δ' ὅς· "ἀλλ' εὔχεσθαί γέ που τοῖς θεοῖς ἔξεστί c
τε καὶ χρή, τὴν μετοίκησιν τὴν ἐνθένδε ἐκεῖσε εὐτυχῆ γενέ-
σθαι· ἃ δὴ καὶ ἐγὼ εὔχομαί τε καὶ γένοιτο ταύτῃ." καὶ
ἅμ' εἰπὼν ταῦτα ἐπισχόμενος καὶ μάλα εὐχερῶς καὶ εὐκόλως
ἐξέπιεν. καὶ ἡμῶν οἱ πολλοὶ τέως μὲν ἐπιεικῶς οἷοί τε ἦσαν
20 κατέχειν τὸ μὴ δακρύειν, ὡς δὲ εἴδομεν πίνοντά τε καὶ πεπω-
κότα, οὐκέτι, ἀλλ' ἐμοῦ γε βίᾳ καὶ αὐτοῦ ἀστακτὶ ἐχώρει τὰ
δάκρυα, ὥστε ἐγκαλυψάμενος ἀπέκλαον ἐμαυτόν· οὐ γὰρ δὴ
ἐκεῖνόν γε, ἀλλὰ τὴν ἐμαυτοῦ τύχην, οἷον ἀνδρὸς ἑταίρου d
ἐστερημένος εἴην. ὁ δὲ Κρίτων ἔτι πρότερος ἐμοῦ, ἐπειδὴ

been used at Athens first in the time of the Thirty. According to Lysias xii. 17, πίνειν κώνειον was the ordinary παράγγελμα under their rule. Plato once (*Lysis* 219 e) mentions this as a poison for which wine was an anti-dote. According to modern authori-ties, the effects of this poison are much more violent than would seem from Plato's story.

7. σου: construe with σκέλεσι. — κατακεῖσθαι: construe with χρή.

8. αὐτό: nominative, *itself*.

10. χρώματος: genitive with οὐδέν only as obj. of διαφθείρας, not as obj. of τρέσας.

13. τοσοῦτον: i.e. *only* so much.

17. γένοιτο ταύτῃ: *so may it be.*

20. τὸ μὴ δακρύειν: the negative repeats that contained in κατέχειν.

21. ἐμοῦ γε καὶ αὐτοῦ: genitive with βίᾳ.

22. ἐγκαλυψάμενος: sc. with a fold of his mantle. Cf. l. 43.

23. οἷον: an idea of thinking is implied. H. 100J.

117 d
25 οὐχ οἷός τ᾽ ἦν κατέχειν τὰ δάκρυα, ἐξανέστη. ᾽Απολλόδωρος
δὲ καὶ ἐν τῷ ἔμπροσθεν χρόνῳ οὐδὲν ἐπαύετο δακρύων, καὶ
δὴ καὶ τότε ἀναβρυχησάμενος [κλάων καὶ] ἀγανακτῶν οὐδένα
ὅντινα οὐ κατέκλασε τῶν παρόντων, πλήν γε αὐτοῦ Σωκράτους. ἐκεῖνος δέ, "Οἶα," ἔφη, " ποιεῖτε, ὦ θαυμάσιοι! ἐγὼ
30 μέντοι οὐχ ἥκιστα τούτου ἕνεκα τὰς γυναῖκας ἀπέπεμψα, ἵνα
μὴ τοιαῦτα πλημμελοῖεν· καὶ γὰρ ἀκήκοα, ὅτι ἐν εὐφημίᾳ
χρὴ τελευτᾶν. ἀλλ᾽ ἡσυχίαν τε ἄγετε καὶ καρτερεῖτε." καὶ e
ἡμεῖς ἀκούσαντες ᾐσχύνθημέν τε καὶ ἐπέσχομεν τοῦ δακρύειν.
ὁ δὲ περιελθών, ἐπειδή οἱ βαρύνεσθαι ἔφη τὰ σκέλη, κατε-
35 κλίνη ὕπτιος· οὕτω γὰρ ἐκέλευεν ὁ ἄνθρωπος· καὶ ἅμα
ἐφαπτόμενος αὐτοῦ [οὗτος ὁ δοὺς τὸ φάρμακον] διαλιπὼν
χρόνον ἐπεσκόπει τοὺς πόδας καὶ τὰ σκέλη, κᾆπειτα σφόδρα
πιέσας αὐτοῦ τὸν πόδα ἤρετο, εἰ αἰσθάνοιτο· ὁ δ᾽ οὐκ ἔφη·
καὶ μετὰ τοῦτο αὖθις τὰς κνήμας· καὶ ἐπανιὼν οὕτως ἡμῖν 118
40 ἐπεδείκνυτο, ὅτι ψύχοιτό τε καὶ πηγνῦτο. καὶ αὐτὸς ἥπτετο
καὶ εἶπεν ὅτι, ἐπειδὰν πρὸς τῇ καρδίᾳ γένηται αὐτῷ, τότε
οἰχήσεται. ἤδη οὖν σχεδόν τι αὐτοῦ ἦν τὰ περὶ τὸ ἦτρον
ψυχόμενα, καὶ ἐκκαλυψάμενος, ἐνεκεκάλυπτο γάρ, εἶπεν, ὃ
δὴ τελευταῖον ἐφθέγξατο, "῏Ω Κρίτων," ἔφη, "τῷ ᾽Ασκλη-
45 πιῷ ὀφείλομεν ἀλεκτρυόνα· ἀλλὰ ἀπόδοτε καὶ μὴ ἀμελή-
σητε." "᾽Αλλὰ ταῦτα," ἔφη, "ἔσται," ὁ Κρίτων· "ἀλλ᾽ ὅρα,

28. τῶν παρόντων: partitive with οὐδένα.

29. οἶα: cf. οἶον 61 c.

30. τούτου ἕνεκα: explained by the ἵνα clause.

31. εὐφημίᾳ κτλ.: a Pythagorean doctrine.

33. τοῦ δακρύειν: ablative genitive.

35. ὕπτιος: predicate. To this, οὕτω refers.

40. πηγνῦτο: optative. The mode-sign ι is absorbed by the υ.

41. γένηται: the subject is implied in ψύχοιτο κτλ.

43. ὅ κτλ.: and this was the last etc.

44. ᾽Ασκληπιῷ: a cock was an offering of thanksgiving to the god of health, for recovery from illness. This expression is no clinging to an old superstition in Socrates's last moments, but is his figurative way of saying that now he is freed from all the ills of the body.

118 a

εἴ τι ἄλλο λέγεις." ταῦτα ἐρομένου αὐτοῦ οὐδὲν ἔτι ἀπεκρί-
νατο, ἀλλ' ὀλίγον χρόνον διαλιπὼν ἐκινήθη τε καὶ ὁ ἄνθρωπος ἐξεκάλυψεν αὐτόν, καὶ ὃς τὰ ὄμματα ἔστησεν· ἰδὼν δὲ
50 ὁ Κρίτων συνέλαβε τὸ στόμα καὶ τοὺς ὀφθαλμούς.

LXVII. Ἥδε ἡ τελευτή, ὦ Ἐχέκρατες, τοῦ ἑταίρου ἡμῖν
ἐγένετο, ἀνδρός, ὡς ἡμεῖς φαῖμεν ἄν, τῶν τότε ὧν ἐπειράθη
μεν ἀρίστου καὶ [ἄλλως] φρονιμωτάτου καὶ δικαιοτάτου.

47. **εἴ τι ἄλλο λέγεις**: *whether you
have anything else to say.*

LXVII. 2. **τῶν τότε**: *of his time.*
The expression is suited to the time
of composition of the dialogue. Cf.
δεῦρο **58 b.**

3. **ἄλλως**: *in general.* — In this
praise, the narrator gives the impression of studied moderation. This is
consistent with Plato's practice of presenting his portrait of Socrates without
comment or criticism.

ΠΛΑΤΩΝΟΣ ΣΥΜΠΟΣΙΟΝ

(ALCIBIADES PRAISES SOCRATES)

XXXII. "Σωκράτη δ' ἐγὼ ἐπαινεῖν, ὦ ἄνδρες, οὕτως ἐπιχειρήσω, δι' εἰκόνων. οὗτος μὲν οὖν ἴσως οἰήσεται ἐπὶ τὰ
γελοιότερα, ἔσται δ' ἡ εἰκὼν τοῦ ἀληθοῦς ἕνεκα, οὐ τοῦ
γελοίου. φημὶ γὰρ δὴ ὁμοιότατον αὐτὸν εἶναι τοῖς σιληνοῖς
5 τούτοις τοῖς ἐν τοῖς ἑρμογλυφείοις καθημένοις, οὕστινας b
ἐργάζονται οἱ δημιουργοὶ σύριγγας ἢ αὐλοὺς ἔχοντας, οἳ
διχάδε διοιχθέντες φαίνονται ἔνδοθεν ἀγάλματα ἔχοντες
θεῶν. καὶ φημὶ αὖ ἐοικέναι αὐτὸν τῷ σατύρῳ τῷ Μαρσύᾳ.
ὅτι μὲν οὖν τό γ' εἶδος ὅμοιος εἶ τούτοις, ὦ Σώκρατες,
10 οὐδ' αὐτὸς ἄν που ἀμφισβητήσαις· ὡς δὲ καὶ τἆλλα ἔοικας,
μετὰ τοῦτο ἄκουε. ὑβριστὴς εἶ· ἢ οὔ; ἐὰν γὰρ μὴ ὁμολο-

At a feast held at the house of
Agatho, the tragic poet, to celebrate
the victory which he had just won in
the Lenaean festival of 416 B.C., several
have spoken in praise of Love, and then
Alcibiades, who is now in his greatest
glory, just before the Sicilian Expedition, praises Socrates.

XXXII. *Socrates is like one of the
ugly images of a seated satyr, which,
when opened, proves to contain a beautiful shrine and the figure of a god.*

1. οὗτως: explained by δι' εἰκόνων.

5. τούτοις: indicates the familiarity
of such images. — **καθημένοις:** these
figures generally represented Silenus
in a sitting posture, playing the pipe.

6. αὐλούς: object of ἔχοντας.

7. διοιχθέντες: sc. as by the two
wings of a double door. Cf. **222 a.**

9. εἶδος: in the *Symposium* of
Xenophon, Socrates is represented as
humorously urging the advantages of
his broad, turned-up nose, his project-
ing eyes, and his thick lips, and finally
as saying: ἐκεῖνο δ' οὐδὲν τεκμήριον
λογίζει ὡς ἐγώ σου καλλίων εἰμί, ὅτι καὶ
Ναΐδες θεαὶ οὖσαι τοὺς Σιληνοὺς ἐμοὶ
ὁμοιοτέρους τίκτουσιν ἢ σοί; (*Symp.*
v. 7), —*the Naiad nymphs, goddesses,
bear Silens, and these are more like to
Socrates than to Critobulus.*

11. ὑβριστής: a reference to his
teasing irony. — **ἢ οὔ:** *are you not?*

215 e

γῆς, μάρτυρας· παρέξομαι. ἀλλ' οὐκ αὐλητής; πολύ γε
θαυμασιώτερος ἐκείνου· ὁ μέν γε δι' ὀργάνων ἐκήλει τοὺς c
ἀνθρώπους τῇ ἀπὸ τοῦ στόματος δυνάμει, καὶ ἔτι νυνὶ ὃς ἂν
15 τὰ ἐκείνου αὐλῇ (ἃ γὰρ Ὄλυμπος ηὔλει, Μαρσύου λέγω, τοῦ
διδάξαντος), — τὰ οὖν ἐκείνου ἐάν τ' ἀγαθὸς αὐλητὴς αὐλῇ
ἐάν τε φαύλη αὐλητρίς, μόνα κατέχεσθαι ποιεῖ καὶ δηλοῖ
τοὺς τῶν θεῶν τε καὶ τελετῶν δεομένους, διὰ τὸ θεῖα εἶναι.
σὺ δ' ἐκείνου τοσοῦτον· μόνον διαφέρεις, ὅτι ἄνευ ὀργάνων
20 ψιλοῖς λόγοις ταὐτὸν τοῦτο ποιεῖς. ἡμεῖς γοῦν ὅταν μέν του
ἄλλου ἀκούωμεν ὶ ἐγοντος καὶ πάνυ ἀγαθοῦ ῥήτορος ἄλλους d
λόγους, οὐδὲν μέλει, ὡς ἔπος εἰπεῖν, οὐδενί· ἐπειδὰν δὲ σοῦ
τις ἀκούῃ ἢ τῶν σῶν λόγων ἄλλου λέγοντος, κἂν πάνυ φαῦλος ᾖ ὁ λέγων, ἐάν τε γυνὴ ἀκούῃ ἐάν τ' ἀνὴρ ἐάν τε μει-
25 ράκιον, ἐκπεπληγμένοι ἐσμὲν καὶ κατεχόμεθα.

" ἐγὼ γοῦν, ὦ ἄνδρες, εἰ μὴ ἔμελλον κομιδῇ δόξειν μεθύειν,
εἶπον ὀμόσας ἂν ὑμῖν, οἷα δὴ πέπονθα αὐτὸς ὑπὸ τῶν τούτου
λόγων καὶ πάσχω ἔτι καὶ νυνί. ὅταν γὰρ ἀκούω, πολύ μοι e
μᾶλλον ἢ τῶν κορυβαντιώντων ἥ τε καρδία πηδᾷ καὶ δάκρυα
30 ἐκχεῖται ὑπὸ τῶν λόγων τῶν τούτου. ὁρῶ δὲ καὶ ἄλλους
παμπόλλους ταὐτὰ πάσχοντας. Περικλέους δ' ἀκούων καὶ
ἄλλων ἀγαθῶν ῥητόρων εὖ μὲν ἡγούμην λέγειν, τοιοῦτον

12. **μάρτυρας παρέξομαι** : technical
language, as if Alcibiades were con-
ducting a case in court. Cf. *Ap.* 31 c.
—**ἀλλά** : or ; cf. *Ap* 37 c.

13. **ἐκείνου** : i.e. Marsyas, who had
vied with Apollo (Xen. *An.* i. 2. 8).

14. **τῇ ἀπὸ** κτλ. : i.e. just like Socrates.

15. **τὰ ἐκείνου** : sc. μέλη or αὐλήματα.

16. **οὖν** : resumptive.

20. **ψιλοῖς λόγοις** : repeats ἄνευ
ὀργάνων. — **ταὐτὸν τοῦτο** : i.e. κατέχεσθαι
κτλ

22. **λόγους** : object of λέγοντος.

23. **ἄλλου λέγοντος** : sc. αὐτούς
When another repeats them.

26. **κομιδῇ** : Alcibiades does not
claim to be quite sober at this moment,
but elsewhere ascribes his present frank-
ness to the wine which he has drunk.

27. **εἶπον** κτλ. : "I would take my
oath." — πέποιθα : cf. *Ap.* 17 a.

29. **κορυβαντιώντων** : limits ἡ καρδία
unexpressed. Cf. *Crito* 54 d.

32. **εὖ λέγειν** : supply αὐτόν or αὐτούς
as subject.

215 e

δ' οὐδὲν ἔπασχον, οὐδ' ἐτεθορύβητό μου ἡ ψυχὴ οὐδ' ἠγα-
νάκτει ὡς ἀνδραποδωδῶς διακειμένου· ἀλλ' ὑπὸ τουτουΐ τοῦ
35 Μαρσύου πολλάκις δὴ οὕτω διετέθην, ὥστε μοι δόξαι μὴ 216
βιωτὸν εἶναι ἔχοντι ὡς ἔχω. καὶ ταῦτα, ὦ Σώκρατες, οὐκ ἐρεῖς
ὡς οὐκ ἀληθῆ. καὶ ἔτι γε νῦν σύνοιδ' ἐμαυτῷ, ὅτι εἰ ἐθέλοιμι
παρέχειν τὰ ὦτα, οὐκ ἂν καρτερήσαιμι, ἀλλὰ ταὐτὰ ἂν πά-
σχοιμι. ἀναγκάζει γάρ με ὁμολογεῖν, ὅτι πολλοῦ ἐνδεὴς ὢν
40 αὐτὸς ἔτι ἐμαυτοῦ μὲν ἀμελῶ, τὰ δ' Ἀθηναίων πράττω. βίᾳ
οὖν ὥσπερ ἀπὸ τῶν Σειρήνων ἐπισχόμενος τὰ ὦτα οἴχομαι
φεύγων, ἵνα μὴ αὐτοῦ καθήμενος παρὰ τούτῳ καταγηράσω.
πέπονθα δὲ πρὸς τοῦτον μόνον ἀνθρώπων, ὃ οὐκ ἄν τις οἴοιτο b
ἐν ἐμοὶ ἐνεῖναι, — τὸ αἰσχύνεσθαι ὁντινοῦν· ἐγὼ δὲ τοῦτον
45 μόνον αἰσχύνομαι. σύνοιδα γὰρ ἐμαυτῷ ἀντιλέγειν μὲν οὐ
δυναμένῳ, ὡς οὐ δεῖ ποιεῖν ἃ οὗτος κελεύει, ἐπειδὰν δ' ἀπέλθω,
ἡττημένῳ τῆς τιμῆς τῆς ὑπὸ τῶν πολλῶν. δραπετεύω οὖν
αὐτὸν καὶ φεύγω, καὶ ὅταν ἴδω, αἰσχύνομαι τὰ ὡμολογημένα. c
καὶ πολλάκις μὲν ἡδέως ἂν ἴδοιμι αὐτὸν μὴ ὄντα ἐν ἀνθρώ-
50 ποις· εἰ δ' αὖ τοῦτο γένοιτο, εὖ οἶδα ὅτι πολὺ μεῖζον ἂν
ἀχθοίμην, ὥστε οὐκ ἔχω ὅ τι χρήσωμαι τούτῳ τῷ ἀνθρώπῳ.
XXXIII. "καὶ ὑπὸ μὲν δὴ τῶν αὐλημάτων καὶ ἐγὼ καὶ
ἄλλοι πολλοὶ τοιαῦτα πεπόνθασιν ὑπὸ τοῦδε τοῦ σατύρου·
ἄλλα δ' ἐμοῦ ἀκούσατε ὡς ὅμοιός τ' ἐστὶν οἷς ἐγὼ ᾔκασα

---

36. βιωτόν: cf. *Crito* 47 e.—ἔχοντι:
equivalent to διακειμένου, above. Cf.
Ap. 22 e.

37. ἔτι γε νῦν: i.e. though Alcibiades was no longer young, but perhaps
the most influential man in Athens.

40. ἐμαυτοῦ ἀμελῶ: cf. *Ap.* 29 d e.

44. τὸ αἰσχύνεσθαι: in apposition
with ὅ.

46. δυναμένῳ: supplementary participle. Cf. *Ap.* 34 b.

47. ὑπό: because of the verbal
idea in τιμῆς, which is equivalent to
τιμᾶσθαι. Cf. τὴν δόσιν ὑμῖν *Ap.* 30 d.

48. τὰ ὡμολογημένα: for the construction, cf. *Ap.* 34 b. — Alcibiades is
obliged to confess himself convinced
that he ought to lead a very different
life from that which he leads.

XXXIII. *Socrates cares nothing for
beauty nor for wealth.*

3. ἐμοῦ ἀκούσατε: *let* ME *tell you.*

220 a

αὐτὸν, καὶ τὴν δύναμιν ὡς θαυμασίαν ἔχει. εὖ γὰρ ἴστε ὅτι
5 οὐδεὶς ὑμῶν τοῦτον γιγνώσκει· ἀλλὰ ἐγὼ δηλώσω, ἐπείπερ d
ἠρξάμην. ὁρᾶτε γὰρ ὅτι Σωκράτης ἐρωτικῶς διάκειται τῶν
καλῶν καὶ ἀεὶ περὶ τούτους ἐστὶν καὶ ἐκπέπληκται, ὡς τὸ
σχῆμα αὐτοῦ. τοῦτο οὐ σιληνῶδες; σφόδρα γε. τοῦτο γὰρ
οὗτος ἔξωθεν περιβέβληται, ὥσπερ ὁ γεγλυμμένος σιληνός·
10 ἔνδοθεν δὲ ἀνοιχθεὶς πόσης οἴεσθε γέμει, ὦ ἄνδρες συμπόται,
σωφροσύνης; ἴστε ὅτι οὔτ᾽ εἴ τις καλός ἐστι μέλει αὐτῷ
οὐδέν, ἀλλὰ καταφρονεῖ τοσοῦτον ὅσον οὐδ᾽ ἂν εἷς οἰηθείη,
οὔτ᾽ εἴ τις πλούσιος, οὔτ᾽ εἰ ἄλλην τινὰ τιμὴν ἔχων τῶν ὑπὸ e
πλήθους μακαριζομένων· ἡγεῖται δὲ πάντα ταῦτα τὰ κτή-
15 ματα οὐδενὸς ἄξια καὶ ἡμᾶς οὐδὲν εἶναι, ἵνα λέγω ὑμῖν, εἰρωνευόμενος δὲ καὶ παίζων πάντα τὸν βίον πρὸς τοὺς ἀνθρώπους
διατελεῖ. σπουδάσαντος δὲ αὐτοῦ καὶ ἀνοιχθέντος οὐκ οἶδα
εἴ τις ἑώρακεν τὰ ἐντὸς ἀγάλματα· ἀλλ᾽ ἐγὼ ἤδη ποτ᾽ εἶδον,
κἀμοὶ ἔδοξεν οὕτω θεῖα καὶ χρυσᾶ εἶναι καὶ πάγκαλα καὶ θαυ- 217
20 μαστά, ὥστε ποιητέον εἶναι ἔμβραχυ ὅ τι κελεύοι Σωκράτης."

. . . .
219
XXXV. "καὶ μετὰ ταῦτα στρατεία ἡμῖν εἰς Ποτείδαιαν e
ἐγένετο κοινὴ καὶ συνεσιτοῦμεν ἐκεῖ. πρῶτον μὲν οὖν ἐν
τοῖς πόνοις οὐ μόνον ἐμοῦ περιῆν, ἀλλὰ καὶ τῶν ἄλλων
ἁπάντων. ὁπότ᾽ ἀναγκασθεῖμεν ἀποληφθέντες που, οἷα δὴ 220

4. δύναμιν: proleptic. — **θαυμασί-**
αν: predicate.
6. καλῶν: construed with ἐρωτικῶς.
7. ὡς τὸ σχῆμα: to judge by his
bearing.
12. καταφρονεῖ: τῶν καλῶν, i.e. τοῦ
κάλλους.
15. οὐδέν: cf. 220 a, Ap. 30 b. —
ἵνα λέγω ὑμῖν: parenthetical.
16. εἰρωνευόμενος: mainly by pretense of ignorance in order to mislead
the interlocutor. Cf. Ap. 38 a. For

the contrast with σπουδάσαντος, cf. Ap.
24 c.
17. σπουδάσαντος: inceptive.
XXXV. Alcibiades tells of Socrates's endurance and self-control when
on service in the army in Thrace.
2. συνεσιτοῦμεν: the two were not of
the same deme or phyle, so the messes
must have been formed unofficially.
4. ἀποληφθέντες: cf. Phaedo 58 c.
— **οἷα δή**: sc. γίγνεται, as is wont to
happen.

5 ἐπὶ στρατείας, ἀσιτεῖν, οὐδὲν ἦσαν οἱ ἄλλοι πρὸς τὸ καρτε-
ρεῖν· ἔν τ' αὖ ταῖς εὐωχίαις μόνος ἀπολαύειν οἷός τ' ἦν τά
τ' ἄλλα, καὶ πίνειν οὐκ ἐθέλων, ὁπότε ἀναγκασθείη, πάντας
ἐκράτει, καὶ ὃ πάντων θαυμαστότατον, Σωκράτη μεθύοντα
οὐδεὶς πώποτε ἑώρακεν ἀνθρώπων. τούτου μὲν οὖν μοι δοκεῖ
10 καὶ αὐτίκα ὁ ἔλεγχος ἔσεσθαι· πρὸς δ' αὖ τὰς τοῦ χειμῶνος
καρτερήσεις, — δεινοὶ γὰρ αὐτόθι χειμῶνες, — θαυμάσια
εἰργάζετο τά τ' ἄλλα, καί ποτ' ὄντος πάγου οἵου δεινοτάτου, b
καὶ πάντων ἢ οὐκ ἐξιόντων ἔνδοθεν, ἢ εἴ τις ἐξίοι, ἠμφιεσμέ-
νων τε θαυμαστὰ δὴ ὅσα καὶ ὑποδεδεμένων καὶ ἐνειλιγμένων
15 τοὺς πόδας εἰς πίλους καὶ ἀρνακίδας, οὗτος δ' ἐν τούτοις
ἐξῄει ἔχων ἱμάτιον μὲν τοιοῦτον οἷόνπερ καὶ πρότερον εἰώθει
φορεῖν, ἀνυπόδητος δὲ διὰ τοῦ κρυστάλλου ῥᾷον ἐπορεύετο
ἢ οἱ ἄλλοι ὑποδεδεμένοι. οἱ δὲ στρατιῶται ὑπέβλεπον αὐτὸν
ὡς καταφρονοῦντα σφῶν.

5. οὐδέν: predicate. Cf. 216 e.

7. τά τ' ἄλλα καί: *and in particular.* — **πίνειν** κτλ. : i.e., though Socrates did not care for wine, he could
drink more than any one else, without
being affected by it.

9. τούτου: i.e. of Socrates's clear
head, untroubled by wine. Alcibiades
foresaw that much wine was likely to
be drunk this night. — At the close of
this Symposium, at daybreak, most
of the rest are asleep, or go home to
bed, but Socrates goes to the Lyceum
(gymnasium), and spends the day according to his wont.

11. καρτερήσεις: plural with reference to repeated instances. — **δεινοὶ
χειμῶνες**: according to Thucydides
(ii. 70), the Athenian generals at last
gave favorable terms of capitulation,
in part, because of their men's suffering from the winter.

12. οἷου κτλ. : equivalent to τοιούτου οἷος δεινότατος. Cf. θαυμαστὰ ὅσα,
below, equivalent to θαυμαστόν ἐστιν
ὅσα, and the use of ὡς with a superlative.

15. οὗτος δέ: as if ἄλλοι μέν had
preceded.

17. ἀνυπόδητος: cf. Xen. *Mem.*
i. 6. 2.

18. ὑποδεδεμένοι: *who had shoes.*

19. καταφρονοῦντα: Socrates's indifference to cold seemed a reflection
on his comrades' effeminacy.

XXXVI. *Of Socrates's power of
concentration of thought, and his
bravery in battle as shown at Potidaea
and in the retreat from Delium. Such
a man had never been before. Brasidas might be compared with Achilles,
and Pericles with Nestor and Antenor.
But no such comparison could be found
for Socrates.*

220 e

XXXVI. "καὶ ταῦτα μὲν δὴ ταῦτα· c

'οἷον δ' αὖ τόδ' ἔρεξε καὶ ἔτλη καρτερὸς ἀνὴρ'

ἐκεῖ ποτε ἐπὶ στρατιᾶς, ἄξιον ἀκοῦσαι. συννοήσας γὰρ
αὐτόθι ἕωθέν τι εἱστήκει σκοπῶν, καὶ ἐπειδὴ οὐ προύχώρει
5 αὐτῷ, οὐκ ἀνίει ἀλλὰ εἱστήκει ζητῶν. καὶ ἤδη ἦν μεσημβρία, καὶ ἄνθρωποι ᾐσθάνοντο, καὶ θαυμάζοντες ἄλλος ἄλλῳ
ἔλεγον ὅτι 'Σωκράτης ἐξ ἑωθινοῦ φροντίζων τι ἕστηκεν.'
τελευτῶντες δέ τινες τῶν νέων, ἐπειδὴ ἑσπέρα ἦν, δειπνήσαν-
τες, καὶ γὰρ θέρος τότε γ' ἦν, χαμεύνια ἐξενεγκάμενοι ἅμα d
10 μὲν ἐν τῷ ψύχει καθηῦδον, ἅμα δ' ἐφύλαττον αὐτὸν εἰ καὶ
τὴν νύκτα ἑστήξοι. ὁ δ' εἱστήκει μέχρι ἕως ἐγένετο καὶ ἥλιος
ἀνέσχεν· ἔπειτα ᾤχετ' ἀπιὼν προσευξάμενος τῷ ἡλίῳ.

"εἰ δὲ βούλεσθε ἐν ταῖς μάχαις· τοῦτο γὰρ δὴ δίκαιόν
γ' αὐτῷ ἀποδοῦναι· ὅτε γὰρ ἡ μάχη ἦν, ἐξ ἧς ἐμοὶ καὶ
15 τἀριστεῖα ἔδοσαν οἱ στρατηγοί, οὐδεὶς ἄλλος ἐμὲ ἔσωσεν
ἀνθρώπων ἢ οὗτος, τετρωμένον οὐκ ἐθέλων ἀπολιπεῖν, ἀλλὰ e
συνδιέσωσε καὶ τὰ ὅπλα καὶ αὐτὸν ἐμέ. καὶ ἐγὼ μέν, ὦ Σώκρατες, καὶ τότ' ἐκέλευον σοὶ διδόναι τἀριστεῖα τοὺς στρατη-
γούς, καὶ τοῦτό γέ μοι οὔτε μέμψει οὔτ' ἐρεῖς ὅτι ψεύδομαι·

---

1. **ταῦτα κτλ.** : formula of transition. Cf. *Crito* 44 d, *Phaedo* 115 c.
2. Quoted with slight change from
Homer, δ 271, where Menelaus at
Sparta caps Helen's story of Odysseus.
—**οἷον . . . ἔτλη** : "the doings and suf-
ferings." Cf. *Phaedo* 117 d.
4. **προύχώρει** : sc. τὸ σκοπεῖν.
7. **φροντίζων** : cf. φροντιστὴς Ap.18 b.
8. **τελευτῶντες** : cf. τελευτῶν Ap.
22 c.
12. **τῷ ἡλίῳ** : cf. *Ap.* 26 d, where
Meletus charges Socrates with lack of
respect for the sun. Socrates was punc-

tilious in his observance of the ordinary
forms of worship and reverence.
13. **εἰ δὲ βούλεσθε** : the sentence is
not completed. The speaker has in
mind something like οἷος ἦν ἐν ταῖς
μάχαις ἐρῶ.
14. **ἀποδοῦναι** : Alcibiades would
give Socrates his due. — **ἡ μάχη** : sc.
at Potidaea, 432 b.c. See on *Ap.* 28 e.
17. **ἐγὼ μέν** : opposed to ἀλλὰ . . .
αὐτός.
19. **τοῦτό γε** : Socrates might blame
Alcibiades for much else, but not for
this.

220 e

20 ἀλλὰ γὰρ τῶν στρατηγῶν πρὸς τὸ ἐμὸν ἀξίωμα ἀποβλεπόν-
των καὶ βουλομένων ἐμοὶ διδόναι τἀριστεῖα, αὐτὸς προθυ-
μότερος ἐγένου τῶν στρατηγῶν ἐμὲ λαβεῖν ἢ σαυτόν. ἔτι
τοίνυν, ὦ ἄνδρες, ἄξιον ἦν θεάσασθαι Σωκράτη, ὅτ᾽ ἀπὸ 221
Δηλίου φυγῇ ἀνεχώρει τὸ στρατόπεδον· ἔτυχον γὰρ παρα-
25 γενόμενος ἵππον ἔχων, οὗτος δ᾽ ὅπλα. ἀνεχώρει οὖν ἐσκεδα-
σμένων ἤδη τῶν ἀνθρώπων οὗτός τ᾽ ἅμα καὶ Λάχης· καὶ
ἐγὼ περιτυγχάνω, καὶ ἰδὼν εὐθὺς παρακελεύομαί τ᾽ αὐτοῖν
θαρρεῖν, καὶ ἔλεγον ὅτι οὐκ ἀπολείψω αὐτώ. ἐνταῦθα δὴ
καὶ κάλλιον ἐθεασάμην Σωκράτη ἢ ἐν Ποτειδαίᾳ· αὐτὸς·γὰρ
30 ἧττον ἐν φόβῳ ἢ διὰ τὸ ἐφ᾽ ἵππου εἶναι· πρῶτον μὲν ὅσον
περιῆν Λάχητος τῷ ἔμφρων εἶναι· ἔπειτα ἔμοιγ᾽ ἐδόκει, ὦ b
Ἀριστόφανες, τὸ σὸν δὴ τοῦτο, καὶ ἐκεῖ διαπορεύεσθαι
ὥσπερ καὶ ἐνθάδε, ῾βρενθυόμενος καὶ τὠφθαλμὼ παραβάλλων,᾽ ἠρέμα παρασκοπῶν καὶ τοὺς φιλίους καὶ τοὺς πολε-
35 μίους, δῆλος ὢν παντὶ καὶ πάνυ πόρρωθεν, ὅτι εἴ τις ἅψεται
τούτου τοῦ ἀνδρός, μάλα ἐρρωμένως ἀμυνεῖται. διὸ καὶ
ἀσφαλῶς ἀπῄει καὶ οὗτος καὶ ὁ ἑταῖρος· σχεδὸν γάρ τι τῶν

---

22. ἢ σαυτόν: rather than your-
self. αὐτός might have been used, but
the accusative points the contrast.

24. ἀπὸ Δηλίου: sc. in 424 B.C.
Plato refers to this event in Laches
181 b, and to the battle of Potidaea at
the beginning of his Charmides.

25. ἵππον ἔχων: at Potidaea, Alcibiades was a hoplite; cf. ὅπλα above.
—ἀνεχώρει: the singular shows that
Laches is mentioned as an after-
thought. Cf. ἀπῄει l. 37, below.

27. περιτυγχάνω: historical present.

30. ἐφ᾽ ἵππου: obviously a mounted
man was more secure on a retreat.

31. τῷ ἔμφρων εἶναι: dative of re-

spect. The case of ἔμφρων makes clear
the subject of εἶναι.

32. τὸ σὸν δὴ τοῦτο: cf. Ap.
34 d.

33. βρενθυόμενος κτλ.: reference to
ὅτι βρενθύει τ᾽ ἐν ταῖσιν ὁδοῖς, καὶ τὠ-
φθαλμὼ παραβάλλεις, | κἀνυπόδητος κτλ.
Clouds 362, where Aristophanes describes Socrates's manner on the
streets of Athens. His bearing was
the same in the midst of danger. The
allusion to Aristophanes is not at all
in the tone of one who believed that
the comedy of the Clouds really had
much influence in causing prejudice
against Socrates. **— παραβάλλων:** explained by παρασκοπῶν.

221 e

οὕτω διακειμένων ἐν τῷ πολέμῳ οὐδ' ἅπτονται, ἀλλὰ τοὺς προτροπάδην φεύγοντας διώκουσιν.   c

40 "πολλὰ μὲν οὖν ἄν τις καὶ ἄλλα ἔχοι Σωκράτη ἐπαινέσαι καὶ θαυμάσια· ἀλλὰ τῶν μὲν ἄλλων ἐπιτηδευμάτων τάχ' ἄν τις καὶ περὶ ἄλλου τοιαῦτα εἴποι, τὸ δὲ μηδενὶ ἀνθρώπων ὅμοιον εἶναι, μήτε τῶν παλαιῶν μήτε τῶν νῦν ὄντων, τοῦτο ἄξιον παντὸς θαύματος. οἷος γὰρ Ἀχιλλεὺς ἐγένετο, ἀπει-
45 κάσειεν ἄν τις καὶ Βρασίδαν καὶ ἄλλους, καὶ οἷος αὖ Περι-κλῆς, καὶ Νέστορα καὶ Ἀντήνορα, εἰσὶ δὲ καὶ ἕτεροι· καὶ d τοὺς ἄλλους κατὰ ταῦτ' ἄν τις ἀπεικάζοι· οἷος δ' οὑτοσὶ γέγονεν τὴν ἀτοπίαν ἄνθρωπος, καὶ αὐτὸς καὶ οἱ λόγοι αὐτοῦ, οὐδ' ἐγγὺς ἂν εὕροι τις ζητῶν, οὔτε τῶν νῦν οὔτε τῶν
50 παλαιῶν, εἰ μὴ ἄρα εἰ οἷς ἐγὼ λέγω ἀπεικάζοι τις αὐτόν, ἀνθρώπων μὲν μηδενί, τοῖς δὲ σιληνοῖς καὶ σατύροις, αὐτὸν καὶ τοὺς λόγους.

XXXVII. "καὶ γὰρ οὖν καὶ τοῦτο ἐν τοῖς πρώτοις παρέ-λιπον, ὅτι καὶ οἱ λόγοι αὐτοῦ ὁμοιότατοί εἰσι τοῖς σιληνοῖς τοῖς διοιγομένοις. εἰ γὰρ ἐθέλοι τις τῶν Σωκράτους ἀκούειν e λόγων, φανεῖεν ἂν γελοῖοι τὸ πρῶτον· τοιαῦτα καὶ ὀνόματα
5 καὶ ῥήματα ἔξωθεν περιαμπέχονται, σατύρου τινὰ ὑβριστοῦ δοράν. ὄνους γὰρ κανθηλίους λέγει καὶ χαλκέας τινὰς καὶ σκυτοτόμους καὶ βυρσοδέψας, καὶ ἀεὶ διὰ τῶν αὐτῶν τὰ αὐτὰ

---

43. τὸ ... εἶναι: resumed in τοῦτο, subject of ἄξιόν ἐστι. — ὅμοιον: masculine.

45. ἀπεικάσειεν κτλ. : by a slight shift, instead of τοιοῦτος ἦν κτλ. Similarly, below, after οὑτοσί.

46. καὶ ἕτεροι: sc. who might be compared with Pericles.

47. ἀπεικάζοι: sc. ἄλλοις.

XXXVII. Socrates's sayings themselves, too, are like these figures of satyrs. They are in unusual form, and an in-

considerate man might laugh at them. But of all sayings these are most divine, and contain the most images of virtue, and reach to all springs of human action.

1. τοῦτο: refers to the following clause.

3. διοιγομένοις: that come open.

4. ὀνόματα κτλ.: cf. Ap. 17 b.

5. περιαμπέχονται: the λόγοι are personified, — like the νόμοι in the Crito, 51 c. Cf. 216 d.

221 e

φαίνεται λέγειν, ὥστ᾽ ἄπειρος καὶ ἀνόητος ἄνθρωπος πᾶς ἂν
τῶν λόγων καταγελάσειεν. διοιγομένους δ᾽ ἰδὼν δή τις καὶ 222
10 ἐντὸς αὐτῶν γιγνόμενος πρῶτον μὲν νοῦν ἔχοντας ἔνδον
μόνους εὑρήσει τῶν λόγων, ἔπειτα θειοτάτους καὶ πλεῖστα
ἀγάλματ᾽ ἀρετῆς ἐν αὑτοῖς ἔχοντας καὶ ἐπὶ πλεῖστον τείνον-
τας, μᾶλλον δ᾽ ἐπὶ πᾶν ὅσον προσήκει σκοπεῖν τῷ μέλλοντι
καλῷ κἀγαθῷ ἔσεσθαι.
15   " ταῦτ᾽ ἐστίν, ὦ ἄνδρες, ἃ ἐγὼ Σωκράτη ἐπαινῶ."

10. νοῦν ἔχοντας : predicate.
11. θειοτάτους : in the *Clitophon*,
407 a, Socrates with his admonitions
for virtue is compared to ἐπὶ μηχανῆς
τραγικῆς θεός.

12. ἐπὶ πλεῖστον: i.e. the real bearing of Socrates's discussions was not
limited to ὄνοι and χαλκεῖς. Cf. *Mem.* i.
1. 16, *Laches* 187 e, Introd. §§ 9 and 25.
15. ἐπαινῶ : refers to 215 a.

ΞΕΝΟΦΩΝΤΟΣ
ΑΠΟΜΝΗΜΟΝΕΥΜΑΤΑ

I. 1. 3

Πολλάκις ἐθαύμασα τίσι ποτὲ λόγοις ᾿Αθηναίους ἔπεισαν 1
οἱ γραψάμενοι Σωκράτην ὡς ἄξιος εἴη θανάτου τῇ πόλει. ἡ
μὲν γὰρ γραφὴ κατ᾿ αὐτοῦ τοιάδε τις ἦν· "᾿Αδικεῖ Σωκράτης οὓς μὲν ἡ πόλις νομίζει θεοὺς οὐ νομίζων, ἕτερα δὲ καινὰ
5 δαιμόνια εἰσφέρων· ἀδικεῖ δὲ καὶ τοὺς νέους διαφθείρων."

Πρῶτον μὲν οὖν, ὡς οὐκ ἐνόμιζεν οὓς ἡ πόλις νομίζει 2
θεούς, ποίῳ ποτ᾿ ἐχρήσαντο τεκμηρίῳ; θύων τε γὰρ φανερὸς ἦν πολλάκις μὲν οἴκοι, πολλάκις δ᾿ ἐπὶ τῶν κοινῶν τῆς
πόλεως βωμῶν, καὶ μαντικῇ χρώμενος οὐκ ἀφανὴς ἦν·
10 διετεθρύλητο γὰρ ὡς φαίη Σωκράτης τὸ δαιμόνιον ἑαυτῷ
σημαίνειν· — ὅθεν δὴ καὶ μάλιστά μοι δοκοῦσιν αὐτὸν
αἰτιάσασθαι καινὰ δαιμόνια εἰσφέρειν. ὁ δ᾿ οὐδὲν καινότε- 3
ρον εἰσέφερε τῶν ἄλλων, ὅσοι μαντικὴν νομίζοντες οἰωνοῖς

I. 1. *How could the court have been
persuaded that Socrates was deserving
of death?* He worshiped the gods of
Athens, and introduced no new divinities. All his actions were pious and
reverent. (Xenophon, himself, of course,
was in Asia Minor at the time of Socrates's trial, and did not hear the
arguments.)

1. ᾿Αθηναίους: equivalent to δικασταί. Cf. *Ap.* 17 c.

2. τῇ πόλει: dative of interest.

3. ἡ μὲν γραφή: contrasted with

the arguments in its support. — Cf.
Ap. 24 b.

6. πρῶτον μέν: correlative to the
charge of corrupting the youth, in the
second chapter.

7. θύων: supplementary participle
with φανερὸς ἦν.

8. οἴκοι: every house was expected
to have a family altar in the court.

10. ὡς κτλ.: subject of διετεθρύλητο.
— δαιμόνιον: cf. *Ap.* 31 d.

13. τῶν ἄλλων: *than the others*, i.e.
than the rest do.

I. 1. 3

τε χρῶνται καὶ φήμαις καὶ συμβόλοις καὶ θυσίαις· οὗτοί τε
15 γὰρ ὑπολαμβάνουσιν οὐ τοὺς ὄρνιθας οὐδὲ τοὺς ἀπαντῶντας
εἰδέναι τὰ συμφέροντα τοῖς μαντευομένοις, ἀλλὰ τοὺς θεοὺς
διὰ τούτων αὐτὰ σημαίνειν, κἀκεῖνος δ᾿ οὕτως ἐνόμιζεν.
ἀλλ᾿ οἱ μὲν πλεῖστοί φασιν ὑπό τε τῶν ὀρνίθων καὶ τῶν 4
ἀπαντώντων ἀποτρέπεσθαί τε καὶ προτρέπεσθαι· Σωκράτης
20 δ᾿ ὥσπερ ἐγίγνωσκεν, οὕτως ἔλεγε· τὸ δαιμόνιον γὰρ ἔφη
σημαίνειν. καὶ πολλοῖς τῶν συνόντων προηγόρευε τὰ μὲν
ποιεῖν, τὰ δὲ μὴ ποιεῖν, ὡς τοῦ δαιμονίου προσημαίνοντος·
καὶ τοῖς μὲν πειθομένοις αὐτῷ συνέφερε, τοῖς δὲ μὴ πειθομένοις μετέμελε. καίτοι τίς οὐκ ἂν ὁμολογήσειεν αὐτὸν 5
25 βούλεσθαι μήτ᾿ ἠλίθιον μήτ᾿ ἀλαζόνα φαίνεσθαι τοῖς συνοῦσιν; ἐδόκει δ᾿ ἂν ἀμφότερα ταῦτα, εἰ προαγορεύων ὡς ὑπὸ θεοῦ
φαινόμενα ψευδόμενος ἐφαίνετο. δῆλον οὖν ὅτι οὐκ ἂν προ-
έλεγεν, εἰ μὴ ἐπίστευεν ἀληθεύσειν. ταῦτα δὲ τίς ἂν ἄλλῳ
πιστεύσειεν ἢ θεῷ; πιστεύων δὲ θεοῖς πῶς οὐκ εἶναι θεοὺς
30 ἐνόμιζεν; ἀλλὰ μὴν ἐποίει καὶ τάδε πρὸς τοὺς ἐπιτηδείους· 6
τὰ μὲν γὰρ ἀναγκαῖα συνεβούλευε καὶ πράττειν ὡς νομίζοιεν
ἄριστ᾿ ἂν πραχθῆναι, περὶ δὲ τῶν ἀδήλων ὅπως ἀποβήσοιτο
μαντευσομένους πέμπειν εἰ ποιητέα. καὶ τοὺς μέλλοντας 7
οἴκους τε καὶ πόλεις καλῶς οἰκήσειν μαντικῆς ἔφη προσδεῖ-
35 σθαι· τεκτονικὸν μὲν γὰρ ἢ χαλκευτικὸν ἢ γεωργικὸν [ἢ
ἀνθρώπων ἀρχικὸν] ἢ τῶν τοιούτων ἔργων ἐξεταστικὸν
ἢ λογιστικὸν ἢ οἰκονομικὸν ἢ στρατηγικὸν γενέσθαι, πάντα
τὰ τοιαῦτα μαθήματα καὶ ἀνθρώπου γνώμῃ αἱρετὰ ἐνόμιζεν

18. φασιν: contrasted with ὑπολαμβάνουσιν.
26. ἐδόκει ἄν: contrary to fact in
past time. — ἀμφότερα ταῦτα: i.e. ἠλίθιος and ἀλαζών. For the gender, cf.
Symp. 220 d.
28. ἀληθεύσειν: should prove to
speak the truth. — ταῦτα: accusative

of specification, in these matters.
31. γάρ: need not be translated.
32. ἀδήλων κτλ.: uncertain as to
their issue.
33. μαντευσομένους: e.g. so Socrates sent Xenophon to Delphi; Xen.
An. iii. 1. 5. — εἰ ποιητέα: whether
they should be done.

I. 1. 10

εἶναι· τὰ δὲ μέγιστα τῶν ἐν τούτοις ἔφη τοὺς θεοὺς ἑαυτοῖς ἱ
40 καταλείπεσθαι, ὧν οὐδὲν δῆλον εἶναι τοῖς ἀνθρώποις. οὔτε
γὰρ τῷ καλῶς ἀγρὸν φυτευσαμένῳ δῆλον ὅστις καρπώσεται,
οὔτε τῷ καλῶς οἰκίαν οἰκοδομησαμένῳ δῆλον ὅστις ἐνοική-
σει, οὔτε τῷ στρατηγικῷ δῆλον εἰ συμφέρει στρατηγεῖν,
οὔτε τῷ πολιτικῷ δῆλον εἰ συμφέρει τῆς πόλεως προστα-
45 τεῖν, οὔτε τῷ καλὴν γήμαντι, ἵν' εὐφραίνηται, δῆλον εἰ διὰ
ταύτην ἀνιάσεται, οὔτε τῷ δυνατοὺς ἐν τῇ πόλει κηδεστὰς
λαβόντι δῆλον εἰ διὰ τούτους στερήσεται τῆς πόλεως. τοὺς ξ
δὲ μηδὲν τῶν τοιούτων οἰομένους εἶναι δαιμόνιον, ἀλλὰ πάντα
τῆς ἀνθρωπίνης γνώμης, δαιμονᾶν ἔφη· δαιμονᾶν δὲ καὶ
50 τοὺς μαντευομένους ἃ τοῖς ἀνθρώποις ἔδωκαν οἱ θεοὶ μαθοῦσι
διακρίνειν, — οἷον εἴ τις ἐπερωτῴη πότερον ἐπιστάμενον ἡνιο-
χεῖν ἐπὶ ζεῦγος λαβεῖν κρεῖττον ἢ μὴ ἐπιστάμενον, ἢ πότερον ἐπιστάμενον κυβερνᾶν ἐπὶ τὴν ναῦν κρεῖττον λαβεῖν ἢ
μὴ ἐπιστάμενον, — ἢ ἃ ἔξεστιν ἀριθμήσαντας ἢ μετρήσαν-
55 τας ἢ στήσαντας εἰδέναι· τοὺς τὰ τοιαῦτα παρὰ·τῶν θεῶν
πυνθανομένους ἀθέμιστα ποιεῖν ἡγεῖτο· ἔφη δὲ δεῖν, ἃ μὲν
μαθόντας ποιεῖν ἔδωκαν οἱ θεοί, μανθάνειν, ἃ δὲ μὴ δῆλα
τοῖς ἀνθρώποις ἐστί, πειρᾶσθαι διὰ μαντικῆς παρὰ τῶν θεῶν
πυνθάνεσθαι· τοὺς θεοὺς γὰρ οἷς ἂν ὦσιν ἵλεῳ σημαίνειν.

60 Ἀλλὰ μὴν ἐκεῖνός γε ἀεὶ μὲν ἦν ἐν τῷ φανερῷ· πρωΐ τε 1
γὰρ εἰς τοὺς περιπάτους καὶ τὰ γυμνάσια ᾔει καὶ πληθούσης
ἀγορᾶς ἐκεῖ φανερὸς ἦν, καὶ τὸ λοιπὸν ἀεὶ τῆς ἡμέρας ἦν
ὅπου πλείστοις μέλλοι συνέσεσθαι· καὶ ἔλεγε μὲν ὡς τὸ

40. δῆλον εἶναι: infinitive of indirect discourse, in a subordinate
clause.

46. εἰ ἀνιάσεται: the English idiom
introduces a negative, *whether or not*.
Cf. *Ap.* 29 a.

47. στερήσεται: for the future
middle as passive, cf. *Crito* **54** a.

49. γνώμης: predicate genitive of
possession. — δαιμονᾶν: Socrates did
not disdain to play upon words.

50. μαθοῦσι: *by learning.* Cf. ἀριθμήσαντας, *by counting,* below.

60. ἀεὶ μὲν κτλ.: i.e. he was always
in the public eye, yet no one ever, etc.
(l. 65).

πολύ, τοῖς δὲ βουλομένοις ἐξῆν ἀκούειν. οὐδεὶς δὲ πώποτε 11
65 Σωκράτους οὐδὲν ἀσεβὲς οὐδὲ ἀνόσιον οὔτε πράττοντος εἶδεν
οὔτε λέγοντος ἤκουσεν. οὐδὲ γὰρ περὶ τῆς τῶν πάντων φύσεως
ᾗπερ τῶν ἄλλων οἱ πλεῖστοι διελέγετο, σκοπῶν ὅπως ὁ καλού-
μενος ὑπὸ τῶν σοφιστῶν κόσμος ἔφυ καὶ τίσιν ἀνάγκαις
ἕκαστα γίγνεται τῶν οὐρανίων, ἀλλὰ καὶ τοὺς φροντίζοντας
70 τὰ τοιαῦτα μωραίνοντας ἀπεδείκνυεν. καὶ πρῶτον μὲν αὐτῶν 12
ἐσκόπει πότερά ποτε νομίσαντες ἱκανῶς ἤδη τἀνθρώπινα εἰδέναι ἔρχονται ἐπὶ τὸ περὶ τῶν τοιούτων φροντίζειν, ἢ τὰ μὲν
ἀνθρώπεια παρέντες, τὰ δαιμόνια δὲ σκοποῦντες, ἡγοῦνται
τὰ προσήκοντα πράττειν. ἐθαύμαζε δ' εἰ μὴ φανερὸν αὐτοῖς 13
75 ἐστιν ὅτι ταῦτα οὐ δυνατόν ἐστιν ἀνθρώποις εὑρεῖν. ἐπεὶ
καὶ τοὺς μέγιστον φρονοῦντας ἐπὶ τῷ περὶ τούτων λέγειν οὐ
ταὐτὰ δοξάζειν ἀλλήλοις, ἀλλὰ τοῖς μαινομένοις ὁμοίως δια-
κεῖσθαι πρὸς ἀλλήλους. τῶν τε γὰρ μαινομένων τοὺς μὲν 14
οὐδὲ τὰ δεινὰ δεδιέναι, τοὺς δὲ καὶ τὰ μὴ φοβερὰ φοβεῖσθαι·
80 καὶ τοῖς μὲν οὐδ' ἐν ὄχλῳ δοκεῖν αἰσχρὸν εἶναι λέγειν ἢ
ποιεῖν ὁτιοῦν, τοῖς δὲ οὐδ' ἐξιτητέον εἰς ἀνθρώπους εἶναι
δοκεῖν· καὶ τοὺς μὲν οὔθ' ἱερὸν οὔτε βωμὸν οὔτ' ἄλλο τῶν
θείων οὐδὲν τιμᾶν, τοὺς δὲ καὶ λίθους καὶ ξύλα τὰ τυχόντα καὶ
θηρία σέβεσθαι· τῶν τε περὶ τῆς τῶν πάντων φύσεως μερι-
85 μνώντων τοῖς μὲν δοκεῖν ἓν μόνον τὸ ὂν εἶναι, τοῖς δ' ἄπειρα
τὸ πλῆθος· καὶ τοῖς μὲν ἀεὶ πάντα κινεῖσθαι, τοῖς δ' οὐδὲν ἄν

---

66. τῶν πάντων: the universe.

68. σοφιστῶν: without unpleasant
connotation.

69. φροντίζοντας: cf. Ap. 18 b.

70. πρῶτον μέν: cf. l. 89. —αὐτῶν: cf.
Ap. 17 a. It refers to τοὺς φροντίζοντας κτλ.

74. εἰ: with ἐθαύμαζε, instead of
ὅτι. Cf. l. 105, iv. 8. 6.

78. τῶν μαινομένων: partitive genitive. Parallel to τῶν μεριμνώντων l. 84.

83. ξύλα τὰ τυχόντα: i.e. probably
fetiches, of which the worship in
Greece was more common than would
be inferred from the higher literature.

85. ἓν μόνον: the doctrine of the
Eleatics (Monists). —τὸ ὄν: that which
is, the universe. — ἄπειρα: the doctrine
of the Atomists.

86. οὐδὲν κτλ.: the doctrine of
Zeno.

I. 1. 18

ποτε κινηθῆναι· καὶ τοῖς μὲν πάντα γίγνεσθαί τε καὶ ἀπόλλυσθαι, τοῖς δ' οὔτ' ἂν γενέσθαι ποτὲ οὐδὲν οὔτ' ἀπολεῖσθαι.
ἐσκόπει δὲ περὶ αὐτῶν καὶ τάδε· "Ἆρ', ὥσπερ οἱ τὰ ἀνθρώ- 15
90 πεια μανθάνοντες ἡγοῦνται τοῦθ', ὅ τι ἂν μάθωσιν, ἑαυτοῖς
τε καὶ τῶν ἄλλων ὅτῳ ἂν βούλωνται ποιήσειν, οὕτω καὶ οἱ
τὰ θεῖα ζητοῦντες νομίζουσιν, ἐπειδὰν γνῶσιν αἷς ἀνάγκαις
ἕκαστα γίγνεται, ποιήσειν, ὅταν βούλωνται, καὶ ἀνέμους καὶ
ὕδατα καὶ ὥρας καὶ ὅτου ἂν ἄλλου δέωνται τῶν τοιούτων, ἢ
95 τοιοῦτο μὲν οὐδὲν οὐδ' ἐλπίζουσιν, ἀρκεῖ δ' αὐτοῖς γνῶναι
μόνον ᾗ τῶν τοιούτων ἕκαστα γίγνεται;" περὶ μὲν οὖν τῶν 16
ταῦτα πραγματευομένων τοιαῦτα ἔλεγεν· αὐτὸς δὲ περὶ τῶν
ἀνθρωπείων ἀεὶ διελέγετο, σκοπῶν τί εὐσεβές, τί ἀσεβές, τί
καλόν, τί αἰσχρόν, τί δίκαιον, τί ἄδικον, τί σωφροσύνη,
100 τί μανία, τί ἀνδρεία, τί δειλία, τί πόλις, τί πολιτικός, τί
ἀρχὴ ἀνθρώπων, τί ἀρχικὸς ἀνθρώπων, καὶ περὶ τῶν
ἄλλων, ἃ τοὺς μὲν εἰδότας ἡγεῖτο καλοὺς κἀγαθοὺς εἶναι,
τοὺς δ' ἀγνοοῦντας ἀνδραποδώδεις ἂν δικαίως κεκλῆσθαι.

Ὅσα μὲν οὖν μὴ φανερὸς ἦν ὅπως ἐγίγνωσκεν, οὐδὲν 17
105 θαυμαστὸν ὑπὲρ τούτων περὶ αὐτοῦ παραγνῶναι τοὺς δικα-
στάς· ὅσα δὲ πάντες ᾔδεσαν, οὐ θαυμαστὸν εἰ μὴ τούτων
ἐνεθυμήθησαν; βουλεύσας γάρ ποτε καὶ τὸν βουλευτικὸν 18
ὅρκον ὀμόσας, ἐν ᾧ ἦν κατὰ τοὺς νόμους βουλεύσειν, ἐπιστάτης ἐν τῷ δήμῳ γενόμενος, ἐπιθυμήσαντος τοῦ δήμου
110 παρὰ τοὺς νόμους [ἐννέα στρατηγοὺς] μιᾷ ψήφῳ τοὺς ἀμφὶ
Θράσυλλον καὶ Ἐρασινίδην ἀποκτεῖναι πάντας, οὐκ ἠθέλη-
σεν ἐπιψηφίσαι, ὀργιζομένου μὲν αὐτῷ τοῦ δήμου, πολλῶν
δὲ καὶ δυνατῶν ἀπειλούντων· ἀλλὰ περὶ πλείονος ἐποιήσατο
εὐορκεῖν ἢ χαρίσασθαι τῷ δήμῳ παρὰ τὸ δίκαιον καὶ φυλά-

87. πάντα κτλ.: the doctrine of
Heraclitus.

96. περὶ μὲν κτλ.: transitional.

102. ἅ: object of εἰδότας.

105. ὑπέρ: differs little from περί.

107. βουλεύσας: cf. Ap. 32 ff.

108. ὅρκον: cognate accusative.

— ἐν ᾧ: cf. Ap. 17 a.

115 ξασθαι τοὺς ἀπειλοῦντας. καὶ γὰρ ἐπιμελεῖσθαι θεοὺς ἐνό- 19
μιζεν ἀνθρώπων, οὐχ ὃν τρόπον οἱ πολλοὶ νομίζουσιν· οὗτοι
μὲν γὰρ οἴονται τοὺς θεοὺς τὰ μὲν εἰδέναι, τὰ δ᾿ οὐκ εἰδέναι·
Σωκράτης δ᾿ ἡγεῖτο πάντα μὲν θεοὺς εἰδέναι, τά τε λεγόμενα
καὶ πραττόμενα καὶ τὰ σιγῇ βουλευόμενα, πανταχοῦ δὲ
120 παρεῖναι καὶ σημαίνειν τοῖς ἀνθρώποις περὶ τῶν ἀνθρωπείων
πάντων.

Θαυμάζω οὖν ὅπως ποτὲ ἐπείσθησαν Ἀθηναῖοι Σωκράτην 20
περὶ θεοὺς μὴ σωφρονεῖν, τὸν ἀσεβὲς μὲν οὐδέν ποτε περὶ
τοὺς θεοὺς οὔτ᾿ εἰπόντα οὔτε πράξαντα, τοιαῦτα δὲ καὶ
125 λέγοντα καὶ πράττοντα [περὶ θεῶν], οἷά τις ἂν καὶ λέγων
καὶ πράττων εἴη τε καὶ νομίζοιτο εὐσεβέστατος.

. . . .

"Ἀλλ᾿," ἔφη γε ὁ κατήγορος, "Σωκράτει ὁμιλητὰ γενο- 2̲12
μένω Κριτίας τε καὶ Ἀλκιβιάδης πλεῖστα κακὰ τὴν πόλιν
ἐποιησάτην. Κριτίας μὲν γὰρ τῶν ἐν τῇ ὀλιγαρχίᾳ πάντων
κλεπτίστατός τε καὶ βιαιότατος καὶ φονικώτατος ἐγένετο,
5 Ἀλκιβιάδης δὲ αὖ τῶν ἐν τῇ δημοκρατίᾳ πάντων ἀκρατέ-
στατός τε καὶ ὑβριστότατος καὶ βιαιότατος." ἐγὼ δ᾿, εἰ μέν 13
τι κακὸν ἐκείνω τὴν πόλιν ἐποιησάτην, οὐκ ἀπολογήσομαι·
τὴν δὲ πρὸς Σωκράτην συνουσίαν αὐτοῖν ὡς ἐγένετο διηγήσομαι. ἐγενέσθην μὲν γὰρ δὴ τὼ ἄνδρε τούτω φύσει φιλο- 14
τιμοτάτω πάντων Ἀθηναίων, βουλομένω τε πάντα δι᾿ ἑαυτῶν

119. Cf. Psalm cxxxix.
122. At the conclusion of the passage, the author returns to his first
thought.
I. 2. 12–18. *Critias and Alcibiades
were companions of Socrates, it is true.
These, however, came to him not because they really desired to live as he
lived, but because they thought that he
would make them able to speak and to
ιct. By his words and example, he*

*kept them temperate while they re-
mained with him, but after they had
left him they forgot his lessons of life.*
2. τὴν πόλιν: object of κακὰ ἐποιησάτην.
3. ὀλιγαρχίᾳ, 5. δημοκρατίᾳ: cf.
the like contrast in *Ap.* 32 c.
7. εἰ ἐποιησάτην: a logical condition.
9. ἐγενέσθην μέν: correlative with
ᾔδεσαν δέ, below.

I. 2. 18

πράττεσθαι καὶ πάντων ὀνομαστοτάτω γενέσθαι· ᾔδεσαν δὲ
Σωκράτην ἀπ' ἐλαχίστων μὲν χρημάτων αὐταρκέστατα ζῶντα,
τῶν ἡδονῶν δὲ πασῶν ἐγκρατέστατον ὄντα, τοῖς δὲ διαλεγο-
μένοις αὐτῷ πᾶσι χρώμενον ἐν τοῖς λόγοις ὅπως βούλοιτο.

15 ταῦτα δ' ὁρῶντε καὶ ὄντε οἵω προείρησθον, πότερόν τις αὐτὼ 15
φῇ τοῦ βίου τοῦ Σωκράτους ἐπιθυμήσαντε καὶ τῆς σωφροσύνης ἣν ἐκεῖνος εἶχεν, ὀρέξασθαι τῆς ὁμιλίας αὐτοῦ, ἢ νομί-
σαντε, εἰ ὁμιλησαίτην ἐκείνῳ, γενέσθαι ἂν ἱκανωτάτω λέγειν
τε καὶ πράττειν; ἐγὼ μὲν γὰρ ἡγοῦμαι, θεοῦ διδόντος αὐτοῖν 16
20 ἢ ζῆν ὅλον τὸν βίον ὥσπερ ζῶντα Σωκράτην ἑώρων, ἢ τεθνάναι, ἑλέσθαι ἂν μᾶλλον αὐτὼ τεθνάναι. δῆλω δ' ἐγενέσθην
ἐξ ὧν ἐπραξάτην· ὡς γὰρ τάχιστα κρείττονε τῶν συγγιγνο-
μένων ἡγησάσθην εἶναι, εὐθὺς ἀποπηδήσαντε Σωκράτους
ἐπραττέτην τὰ πολιτικά, ὧνπερ ἕνεκα Σωκράτους ὠρεχθήτην.

25 Ἴσως οὖν εἴποι τις ἂν πρὸς ταῦτα, ὅτι ἐχρῆν τὸν Σωκρά- 17
την μὴ πρότερον τὰ πολιτικὰ διδάσκειν τοὺς συνόντας ἢ
σωφρονεῖν· ἐγὼ δὲ πρὸς τοῦτο μὲν οὐκ ἀντιλέγω· πάντας
δὲ τοὺς διδάσκοντας ὁρῶ αὐτοὺς δεικνύντας τε τοῖς μανθάνουσιν, ᾗπερ αὐτοὶ ποιοῦσιν ἃ διδάσκουσι, καὶ τῷ λόγῳ προ-
30 βιβάζοντας. οἶδα δὲ καὶ Σωκράτην δεικνύντα τοῖς συνοῦσιν
ἑαυτὸν καλὸν κἀγαθὸν ὄντα καὶ διαλεγόμενον κάλλιστα περὶ
ἀρετῆς καὶ τῶν ἄλλων ἀνθρωπίνων. οἶδα δὲ κἀκείνω σωφρο- 18
νοῦντε ἔστε Σωκράτει συνήστην, οὐ φοβουμένω μὴ ζημιοῖντο
ἢ παίοιντο ὑπὸ Σωκράτους, ἀλλ' οἰομένω τότε κράτιστον εἶναι
35 τοῦτο πράττειν.

* * * * * * *

12. ἐλαχίστων: see Introd. § 17,
Ap. 31 c.
13. ἡδονῶν: equivalent to ἐπιθυμιῶν.
16. φῇ: deliberative subjunctive.
— ἐπιθυμήσαντε: causal.
19. διδόντος: conditional.

21. ἄν: construe with ἑλέσθαι.
30. καὶ Σωκράτην: Socrates, too,
— as well as other good teachers.
32. κἀκείνω: they too, — as well as
other scholars, — obey their teachers.
33. φοβουμένω: causal.

I. 6. 1

Ἄξιον δ᾽ αὐτοῦ καὶ ἃ πρὸς Ἀντιφῶντα τὸν σοφιστὴν διε- 6
λέχθη μὴ παραλιπεῖν. ὁ γὰρ Ἀντιφῶν ποτε βουλόμενος
τοὺς συνουσιαστὰς αὐτοῦ παρελέσθαι προσελθὼν τῷ Σωκράτει παρόντων αὐτῶν, ἔλεξε τάδε· "Ὦ Σώκρατες, ἐγὼ μὲν 2
5 ᾤμην τοὺς φιλοσοφοῦντας εὐδαιμονεστέρους χρῆναι γίγνε-
σθαι· σὺ δέ μοι δοκεῖς τἀναντία τῆς φιλοσοφίας ἀπολελαυ-
κέναι· ζῇς γοῦν οὕτως ὡς οὐδ᾽ ἂν εἷς δοῦλος ὑπὸ δεσπότῃ
διαιτώμενος μείνειε· σῖτά τε σιτῇ καὶ ποτὰ πίνεις τὰ φαυλό-
τατα, καὶ ἱμάτιον ἠμφίεσαι οὐ μόνον φαῦλον ἀλλὰ τὸ αὐτὸ
10 θέρους τε καὶ χειμῶνος, ἀνυπόδητός τε καὶ ἀχίτων διατελεῖς.
καὶ μὴν χρήματά γε οὐ λαμβάνεις, ἃ καὶ κτωμένους εὐφραί- 3
νει καὶ κεκτημένους ἐλευθεριώτερόν τε καὶ ἥδιον ποιεῖ ζῆν. εἰ
οὖν, ὥσπερ καὶ τῶν ἄλλων ἔργων οἱ διδάσκαλοι τοὺς μαθητὰς
μιμητὰς ἑαυτῶν ἀποδεικνύουσιν, οὕτω καὶ σὺ τοὺς συνόντας
15 διαθήσεις, νόμιζε κακοδαιμονίας διδάσκαλος εἶναι." καὶ 4
ὁ Σωκράτης πρὸς ταῦτα εἶπε· "Δοκεῖς μοι, ὦ Ἀντιφῶν,
ὑπειληφέναι με οὕτως ἀνιαρῶς ζῆν ὥστε πέπεισμαι σὲ μᾶλλον
ἀποθανεῖν ἂν ἑλέσθαι ἢ ζῆν ὥσπερ ἐγώ. ἴθι οὖν ἐπισκεψώ-
μεθα τί χαλεπὸν ᾔσθησαι τοῦ ἐμοῦ βίου. πότερον, ὅτι τοῖς 5
20 μὲν λαμβάνουσιν ἀργύριον ἀναγκαῖόν ἐστιν ἀπεργάζεσθαι
τοῦτο ἐφ᾽ ᾧ ἂν μισθὸν λάβωσιν, ἐμοὶ δὲ μὴ λαμβάνοντι
οὐκ ἀνάγκη διαλέγεσθαι ᾧ ἂν μὴ βούλωμαι; ἢ τὴν δίαιτάν

I. 6. 1–10. *Philosophers ought to
be happier than other men, but Antiphon thinks that Socrates is one of the
most miserable of men. So Socrates
shows that his wants are supplied. To
need nothing is to be like the gods; to
need as little as possible is to be near
them.*
1. αὐτοῦ: cf. *Ap.* 17 a.
3. συνουσιαστάς: cf. *Ap.* 20 a.
7. ἀπολελαυκέναι: ironical. — ὡς:
construe with διαιτώμενος.

10. ἀνυπόδητος: cf. *Symp.* 220 b.
— διατελεῖς: ὤν might have been
added.
13 f. καὶ τῶν ἄλλων, καὶ σύ: cf. καὶ
πράττειν i. 1. 6.
15. κακοδαιμονίας: contrast with
l. 5.
18. Cf. i. 2. 16.
19. βίου: cf. αὐτῶν i. 1. 12. — ὅτι:
because.
20. τοῖς μὲν κτλ.: the μέν-clause is
subordinate. Cf. *Ap.* 28 e.

I. 6. 9

μου φαυλίζεις, ὡς ἧττον μὲν ὑγιεινὰ ἐσθίοντος ἐμοῦ ἢ σοῦ,
ἧττον δ' ἰσχὺν παρέχοντα; ἢ ὡς χαλεπώτερα πορίσασθαι
25 τὰ ἐμὰ διαιτήματα τῶν σῶν διὰ τὸ σπανιώτερά τε καὶ πολυ-
τελέστερα εἶναι; ἢ ὡς ἡδίω σοὶ ἃ σὺ παρασκευάζῃ ὄντα ἢ
ἐμοὶ ἃ ἐγώ; οὐκ οἶσθ' ὅτι ὁ μὲν ἥδιστα ἐσθίων ἥκιστα ὄψου
δεῖται, ὁ δὲ ἥδιστα πίνων ἥκιστα τοῦ μὴ παρόντος ἐπιθυμεῖ
ποτοῦ; τά γε μὴν ἱμάτια οἶσθ' ὅτι οἱ μεταβαλλόμενοι ψύχους 6
30 καὶ θάλπους ἕνεκα μεταβάλλονται, καὶ ὑποδήματα ὑποδοῦν-
ται ὅπως μὴ διὰ τὰ λυποῦντα τοὺς πόδας κωλύωνται πορεύ-
εσθαι· ἤδη οὖν ποτε ᾔσθου ἐμὲ ἢ διὰ ψῦχος μᾶλλόν του
ἔνδον μένοντα, ἢ διὰ θάλπος μαχόμενόν τῳ περὶ σκιᾶς, ἢ
διὰ τὸ ἀλγεῖν τοὺς πόδας οὐ βαδίζοντα ὅπου ἂν βούλωμαι;
35 οὐκ οἶσθ' ὅτι οἱ φύσει ἀσθενέστατοι τῷ σώματι μελετήσαντες 7
τῶν ἰσχυροτάτων ἀμελησάντων κρείττους τε γίγνονται πρὸς
ἃ ἂν μελετήσωσι καὶ ῥᾷον αὐτὰ φέρουσιν; ἐμὲ δὲ ἄρα
οὐκ οἴει, τῷ σώματι ἀεὶ τὰ συντυγχάνοντα μελετῶντα καρτε-
ρεῖν, πάντα ῥᾷον φέρειν σοῦ μὴ μελετῶντος; τοῦ δὲ μὴ δου- 8
40 λεύειν γαστρὶ μηδ' ὕπνῳ καὶ λαγνείᾳ οἴει τι ἄλλο αἰτιώτερον
εἶναι ἢ τὸ ἕτερα ἔχειν τούτων ἡδίω, ἃ οὐ μόνον ἐν χρείᾳ ὄντα
εὐφραίνει, ἀλλὰ καὶ ἐλπίδας παρέχοντα ὠφελήσειν ἀεί; καὶ
μὴν τοῦτό γ' οἶσθα, ὅτι οἱ μὲν οἰόμενοι μηδὲν εὖ πράττειν
οὐκ εὐφραίνονται, οἱ δ' ἡγούμενοι καλῶς προχωρεῖν ἑαυτοῖς ἢ
45 γεωργίαν ἢ ναυκληρίαν ἢ ἄλλ' ὅ τι ἂν τυγχάνωσιν ἐργαζόμενοι ὡς εὖ πράττοντες εὐφραίνονται. οἴει οὖν ἀπὸ πάντων τού- 9
των τοσαύτην ἡδονὴν εἶναι ὅσην ἀπὸ τοῦ ἑαυτόν θ' ἡγεῖσθαι
βελτίω γίγνεσθαι καὶ φίλους ἀμείνους κτᾶσθαι; ἐγὼ τοίνυν

23. ὡς: on the ground that.
24. χαλεπώτερα: predicate. ὄντα
is in mind.
32 ff. As in Symp. 220 b.
34. πόδας: accusative of specification.

35. τῷ σώματι: in body. — μελετήσαντες: by practice.
42. παρέχοντα: causal.
48. ἀμείνους: predicate,— not only
is Socrates himself becoming better,
but his friends also are improving.

I. 6. 9

διατελῶ ταῦτα νομίζων. ἐὰν δὲ δὴ φίλους ἢ πόλιν ὠφε-
50 λεῖν δέῃ, ποτέρῳ ἡ πλείων σχολὴ τούτων ἐπιμελεῖσθαι, τῷ
ὡς ἐγὼ νῦν, ἢ τῷ ὡς σὺ μακαρίζεις, διαιτωμένῳ; στρα-
τεύοιτο δὲ πότερος ἂν ῥᾷον, ὁ μὴ δυνάμενος ἄνευ πολυτε-
λοῦς διαίτης ζῆν, ἢ ᾧ τὸ παρὸν ἀρκοίη; ἐκπολιορκηθείη δὲ
πότερος ἂν θᾶττον, ὁ τῶν χαλεπωτάτων εὑρεῖν δεόμενος, ἢ ὁ
55 τοῖς ῥᾴστοις ἐντυγχάνειν ἀρκούντως χρώμενος; ἔοικας, ὦ 10
Ἀντιφῶν, τὴν εὐδαιμονίαν οἰομένῳ τρυφὴν καὶ πολυτέλειαν
εἶναι· ἐγὼ δὲ νομίζω τὸ μὲν μηδενὸς δεῖσθαι θεῖον εἶναι, τὸ
δ' ὡς ἐλαχίστων ἐγγυτάτω τοῦ θείου, καὶ τὸ μὲν θεῖον κράτιστον, τὸ δ' ἐγγυτάτω τοῦ θείου ἐγγυτάτω τοῦ κρατίστου."

. . . . Lib. 4

8

λέξω δὲ καὶ ἃ Ἑρμογένους τοῦ Ἱππονίκου ἤκουσα περὶ 4
αὐτοῦ. ἔφη γάρ, ἤδη Μελήτου γεγραμμένου αὐτὸν τὴν
γραφήν, αὐτὸς ἀκούων αὐτοῦ πάντα μᾶλλον ἢ περὶ τῆς
δίκης διαλεγομένου λέγειν αὐτῷ ὡς χρὴ σκοπεῖν ὅ τι ἀπο-
5 λογήσεται, τὸν δὲ τὸ μὲν πρῶτον εἰπεῖν· "Οὐ γὰρ δοκῶ σοι
τοῦτο μελετῶν διαβεβιωκέναι;" ἐπεὶ δὲ αὐτὸν ἤρετο ὅπως,
εἰπεῖν αὐτὸν ὅτι οὐδὲν ἄλλο ποιῶν διαγεγένηται ἢ διασκοπῶν μὲν τά τε δίκαια καὶ τὰ ἄδικα, πράττων δὲ τὰ δίκαια καὶ
τῶν ἀδίκων ἀπεχόμενος, ἥνπερ νομίζοι καλλίστην μελέτην
10 ἀπολογίας εἶναι. αὐτὸς δὲ πάλιν εἰπεῖν· "Οὐχ ὁρᾷς, ὦ Σώ- 5
κρατες, ὅτι οἱ Ἀθήνησι δικασταὶ πολλοὺς μὲν ἤδη μηδὲν

---

55. ῥᾴστοις κτλ. : easiest to obtain.
58. τοῦ θείου : genitive with adverb
of place.

IV. 8. 4–9. Not long before Socrates's trial, Hermogenes asks him why he
is not preparing his defense. Socrates
replies, in the first place, he has been preparing his defense, his whole life long,
by a just life, and in the second place
his inward monitor has checked him

when he has begun the preparation of a
formal defense. Doubtless it is better
for him to die before he loses his powers
of thought and his memory.

3. γραφήν : cognate accusative. —
αὐτός : construe with the subject of
λέγειν, which is the same as the subject
of ἔφη.

9. πράττων . . . **ἀπεχόμενος** : observe the 'chiasmus.'

ἀδικοῦντας λόγῳ παραχθέντες ἀπέκτειναν, πολλοὺς δὲ ἀδικοῦντας ἀπέλυσαν;" "Ἀλλὰ νὴ τὸν Δία," φάναι αὐτόν, "ὦ
Ἑρμόγενες, ἤδη μου ἐπιχειροῦντος φροντίσαι τῆς πρὸς τοὺς
15 δικαστὰς ἀπολογίας ἠναντιώθη τὸ δαιμόνιον." καὶ αὐτὸς 6
εἰπεῖν· "Θαυμαστὰ λέγεις·" τὸν δέ, "Θαυμάζεις," φάναι,
" εἰ τῷ θεῷ δοκεῖ βέλτιον εἶναι ἐμὲ τελευτᾶν τὸν βίον
ἤδη; οὐκ οἶσθ᾽ ὅτι μέχρι μὲν τοῦδε τοῦ χρόνου ἐγὼ οὐδενὶ
ἀνθρώπων ὑφείμην ἂν οὔτε βέλτιον οὔθ᾽ ἥδιον ἐμοῦ βεβιωκέ-
20 ναι; ἄριστα μὲν γὰρ οἶμαι ζῆν τοὺς ἄριστα ἐπιμελομένους τοῦ
ὡς βελτίστους γίγνεσθαι, ἥδιστα δὲ τοὺς μάλιστα αἰσθανομέ-
νους ὅτι βελτίους γίγνονται. ἃ ἐγὼ μέχρι τοῦδε τοῦ χρόνου 7
ᾐσθανόμην ἐμαυτῷ συμβαίνοντα, καὶ τοῖς ἄλλοις ἀνθρώποις ἐντυγχάνων καὶ πρὸς τοὺς ἄλλους παραθεωρῶν ἐμαυ-
25 τὸν οὕτω διατετέλεκα περὶ ἐμαυτοῦ γιγνώσκων· καὶ οὐ μόνον
ἐγώ, ἀλλὰ καὶ οἱ ἐμοὶ φίλοι οὕτως ἔχοντες περὶ ἐμοῦ διατε-
λοῦσιν, οὐ διὰ τὸ φιλεῖν ἐμέ, καὶ γὰρ οἱ [τοὺς] ἄλλους
φιλοῦντες οὕτως ἂν εἶχον πρὸς τοὺς ἑαυτῶν φίλους, ἀλλὰ
διόπερ καὶ αὐτοὶ ἂν οἴονται ἐμοὶ συνόντες βέλτιστοι γίγνε-
30 σθαι. εἰ δὲ βιώσομαι πλείω χρόνον, ἴσως ἀναγκαῖον ἔσται 8
τὰ τοῦ γήρως ἐπιτελεῖσθαι, καὶ ὁρᾶν τε καὶ ἀκούειν ἧττον,
καὶ διανοεῖσθαι χεῖρον, καὶ δυσμαθέστερον ἀπ‹›βαίνειν καὶ
ἐπιλησμονέστερον, καὶ ὧν πρότερον βελτίων ἦν, τούτων
χείρω γίγνεσθαι· ἀλλὰ μὴν ταῦτά γε μὴ αἰσθανομένῳ μὲν
35 ἀβίωτος ἂν εἴη ὁ βίος, αἰσθανόμενον δὲ πῶς οὐκ ἀνάγκη
χεῖρόν τε καὶ ἀηδέστερον ζῆν; ἀλλὰ μὴν εἰ γ᾽ ἀδίκως ἀπο- 9
θανοῦμαι, τοῖς μὲν ἀδίκως ἐμὲ ἀποκτείνασιν αἰσχρὸν ἂν εἴη
τοῦτο· ἐμοὶ δὲ τί αἰσχρὸν τὸ ἑτέρους μὴ δύνασθαι περὶ ἐμοῦ
τὰ δίκαια μήτε γνῶναι μήτε ποιῆσαι;"

15. ἠναντιώθη: cf. *Ap.* 31 d, 40 a.

22. ἅ: equivalent to καὶ ταῦτα.

31. τὰ τοῦ γήρως: explained by
the following infinitives.

33. ὧν: masculine.

34. μὴ αἰσθανομένῳ: i.e. if he were
so dull as not to perceive this.

38. τοῦτο: i.e. Socrates's death.

APPENDIX

MANUSCRIPTS

ALL the extant Mss. that contain any considerable portion of Plato's works follow an arrangement of them into nine successive tetralogies or groups of four members each. Since this arrangement seems to be original with Thrasyllus (or if not original with him adopted by him from a scholar only slightly earlier, perhaps Tyrannio, Cicero's friend), and since Thrasyllus was instructor to the emperor Tiberius, it follows that the archetype of no Ms. now known to exist (except the papyri) can much antedate the Christian era. The following table exhibits Thrasyllus's tetralogies, and also names the best Ms. in which each tetralogy is preserved:

I	Euthyphro	Apology	Crito	Phaedo	Clarkianus (B)	
II	Cratylus	Theaetetus	Sophist	Statesman	"	"
III	Parmenides	Philebus	Symposium	Phaedrus	"	"
IV	Alcibiades I	Alcibiades II	Hipparchus	Anterastae	"	"
V	Theages	Charmides	Laches	Lysis	"	"
VI	Euthydemus	Protagoras	Gorgias	Meno	"	"
VII	Hippias maior	Hippias minor	Io	Menexenus	Venetus	T
VIII	Clitophon	Republic	Timaeus	Critias	Parisinus	A
IX	Minos	Laws	Epinomis	Letters	"	"

Schanz constructs the pedigree of the existing Mss. of Plato, and traces them all to an archetype or parent Ms. which consisted of two volumes: Vol. I contained the first seven tetralogies; Vol. II contained the last two tetralogies, together with a number of works attributed with more or less confidence to Plato. The copies made of Vol. I were of two kinds, (1) incomplete, omitting the seventh tetralogy, and (2) complete. The codex Clarkianus, the capital authority for the first six tetralogies, represents an *incomplete* copy of Vol. I of the archetype. The complete copy of

Vol. I is represented by the less trustworthy codex Venetus T, the best authority for the seventh tetralogy.

I. CODEX CLARKIANUS, referred to by the single letter B because the Ms. is called also *Bodleianus*. It is now in the Bodleian Library at Oxford, and is "the fairest specimen of Grecian calligraphy which has descended to modern times." It was beautifully written on parchment, in the year 895 A.D., by a skillful scribe, one Joannes, for the use of Arethas, who afterwards became archbishop of Caesarea. Edward Daniel Clarke found this Ms. in October, 1801, in the library of a monastery on the island of Patmos. See M. Schanz, *Novae Commentationes Platonicae*, pp. 105–118; and Clarke, *Travels in Various Countries of Europe, Asia, and Africa*, ii. 2. 348 ff. An admirable facsimile of this Ms. was published in two volumes at Leyden by Sijthoff, in 1898, 1899.

II. CODEX VENETUS T, Bekker's †. This Ms. is now in St. Mark's Library in Venice, and is chiefly valuable where the Clarkianus fails, i.e. for the seventh tetralogy. For a detailed account of it, see Schanz, *Ueber den Platocodex der Marcus-Bibliothek in Venedig*, 1877, and the preface to Vol. IX of the same scholar's critical edition of Plato's works. The date of the significant parts of this Ms. falls in the twelfth century.

III. PARISINUS A, No. 1807 (formerly 94 and 2087). This Ms. is now in the National Library at Paris; it was probably written early in the tenth century after Christ. It comprises the eighth and ninth tetralogies of Thrasyllus, together with seven spurious dialogues. The *Clitophon*, with which it begins, is numbered twenty-nine. See Schanz, *Studien zur Geschichte des Platonischen Textes*, and the general introduction to his critical edition of Plato's works.

IMPORTANT EDITIONS OF PLATO'S COMPLETE WORKS

The first printed edition of Plato's works was published by Aldus at Venice, in 1513, with the aid of Marcus Musurus, formerly of Crete, perhaps the most scholarly of the Greeks of his age, and one of the most valuable associates of Aldus in the Aldine Academy.

An edition of Plato's works, with the commentary of Proclus, was published at Basle in 1534, by Valder, with the aid of Simon Grynaeus.

In 1578, Henricus Stephanus (Henri Estienne, or Henry Stephens), aided by Joannes Serranus (Jean de Serre), published at Paris a magnificent edition in three folio volumes, dedicated respectively to Queen Elizabeth, King James VI of Scotland, and the Consuls of the republic of Berne.

The pages were subdivided in five parts by letters ([a], b, c, d, e), and the paging and lettering of this edition are used in the margins of most modern editions, as the most convenient and definite basis of reference. The first real advance upon the text of Stephanus was in

PLATONIS DIALOGI *ex recensione Imm. Bekker.* Berolini, 1816–1823. (10 vols.) This edition was based on the collation of many Mss.

The most important complete edition with commentary is

PLATONIS OPERA OMNIA *recensuit, prolegomenis et commentariis illustravit Stallbaum.* 10 vols. (Gothae) Lipsiae, 1827 +. The commentary appears in a greatly improved form in the later editions of several of the volumes.

A convenient text edition is

PLATONIS DIALOGI *secundum Thrasylli tetralogias dispositi, ex recognitione C. F. Hermann.* 6 vols. Lipsiae, 1851 +.

The most important (but still incomplete) critical edition is

PLATONIS OPERA *quae feruntur omnia ad codices denuo collatos edidit M. Schanz.* Lipsiae, 1875 +.

The latest complete edition of the text, with brief critical apparatus, is

PLATONIS OPERA *recognovit, brevique adnotatione critica instruxit Ioannes Burnet.* 5 vols. Oxonii, 1899 +.

IMPORTANT EDITIONS OF THE APOLOGY AND CRITO

The APOLOGY OF PLATO, *with a revised text and English notes, and a digest of Platonic idioms.* By *James Riddell.* Oxford, 1867.

PLATONIS APOLOGIA SOCRATIS ET CRITO ET PHAEDO, *editio quinta aliquanto auctior et emendatior quam curavit Wohlrab.* Lipsiae, (1827,) 1877. (This is Vol. I, Sect. I, II, of Stallbaum's complete Plato, mentioned above, now published by Teubner.)

PLATONS VERTEIDIGUNGSREDE DES SOCRATES UND KRITON, *erklärt von Christian Cron.* Achte Auflage. Leipzig, 1882. (This edition was the basis of Professor Dyer's, and is the first part of an edition of the selected works of Plato, edited for the use of German gymnasia by Cron and Deuschle.)

CHANGES FROM PROFESSOR DYER'S TEXT

Partly on the authority of inscriptions, and partly as the result of further study of the Mss. and of the ancient grammarians, the spelling of the text has been revised. In the following list the first form of each pair has replaced the other: ἀθρόος, ἀθρόος, — ἀποκτείνυμι, ἀποκτίννυμι, — ἀποτεῖσαι, ἀποτῖσαι, — ἐάν περ, ἐάνπερ, — εἴ περ, εἴπερ, — εἰς αὖθις, εἰσαῦθις, — εἰώθεμεν, εἰώθειμεν, — ἐκτείσω, ἐκτίσω, — ἐκτείσειν, ἐκτίσειν, — ἐκτεῖσαι, ἐκτῖσαι. — ἐλεινόν, ἐλεεινόν, — ἐξῄει, ἐξῄειν, — ηὐδαιμόνισα, εὐδαιμόνισα, — καόμενον, καιόμενον, — κλάω and compounds, κλαίω, — κωμῳδοποιός, κωμῳδιοποιός, — νυνδή, νῦν δή, — ὅμοιος, ὁμοῖος, — ὅ τι, ὅτι, — Παράλιος, Πάραλος, — Ποτείδαια, Ποτίδαια, — πρῳαίτατα, πρωϊαίτατα, — σύν, and its compounds, for ξύν, as συνῄδη for ξυνῄδειν, — ὑεῖ, υἱέε, — υός etc., υἱός, — ὧδε, ᾧδε.

The final ε of a conjunction has often been elided. In a critical edition perhaps elision should be carried much farther, and crasis might be marked more systematically. We do not suppose that Plato sometimes said ὁ ἀνήρ and a few lines later ἁνήρ,— and wrote τὰ αὐτά and ταὐτά in neighboring sentences.

The reviser hopes that the use of quotation marks will prove a reasonable convenience to the learner. In a few passages the punctuation has been changed, in order to make the grammatical construction more distinct, in accordance with English and American rules of punctuation. Several paragraphs have been divided, for the sake of making the rhetorical divisions clearer.

The text of the present edition differs from that of Professor Dyer's edition also in the following readings : **17 b** οὖν for γοῦν. **17 d** πλείω omitted. **18 b** οὐδὲν ἀληθές inserted. **22 b** αὖ inserted. **23 e** συντεταμένως for ξυντεταγμένως. **27 e** [οὐ] omitted. **30 b** ποιήσαντος for ποιήσοντος. **32 a** ἂν inserted. **35 b** ἡμᾶς for ὑμᾶς. **37 d** ὅποι inserted. **46 b** νῦν πρῶτον for μόνον νῦν. **48 b** [τῷ] omitted.

In addition to the foregoing, note the following

DEVIATIONS FROM THE TEXT OF GERMAN EDITORS

In general : ἀνηυφήμησα, ἀνευφήμησα, — ηὐξάμην, εὐξάμην, — πρῳαίτερον, πρωϊαίτερον, — Φαιδώνδης, Φαιδωνίδης.

APOLOGY AND CRITO — Cron-Uhle (1895)

17 b line 12 ἔγωγ' οὐ κατὰ τούτους εἶναι: ἔγωγε — οὐ κατὰ τούτους — εἶναι. —**19 c** 13 Μελήτου: Μελήτων. — **20 e** 18 μηδ' ἐὰν: μηδὲ ἂν. — **22 b** 21 ἔγνων οὖν αὖ: ἔγνων οὖν. — **22 d** 9 ὥστε με: ὥστ' ἐμέ. — **22 e** 11 οὕτω: οὕτως. — **23 a** 9 τοῦτο λέγειν: τοῦτ' σὺ λέγειν. — **23 e** 18 καὶ πάλαι καὶ νῦν: καὶ πάλαι καὶ. — **23 e** 21 καὶ τῶν πολιτικῶν: [καὶ τῶν πολιτικῶν]. — **24 e** 10 οὗτοι, ὦ Σώκρατες, — οἱ δικασταί: οὗτοι, ὦ Σώκρατες, οἱ δικασταί. — **26 a** 23 ὅ: οὐ. — **26 e** 30 ἐμοὶ μὲν γὰρ: ἐμοὶ γάρ. — **27 e** 31 [ταῦτα]: ταῦτα. — **30 b** 62 ποιήσαντος: ποιήσοντος. — **30 e** 19 [ὑπὸ τοῦ θεοῦ]: ὑπὸ τοῦ θεοῦ. — **31 b** 36 μέντοι τι: μέν τι. —

31 d 6 [φωνή] : om. — 31 d 12 [πάλαι] : πάλαι. — 32 a 4 ἄμ' ἂν : ἅμα κἂν. — 32 b 8 Ἀντιοχὶς : [Ἀντιοχὶς]. — 32 c 12 [καὶ ἐναντία ἐψηφισάμην] : καὶ ἐναντία ἐψηφισάμην. — 33 a 11 ἐπιθυμεῖ : ἐπιθυμοῖ. — 33 d 17 [καὶ τιμωρεῖσθαι] : καὶ τιμωρεῖσθαι. — 36 c 10 [ἰὼν] : ἰών. — 37 b 12 ἐμαυτῷ. τί : ἐμαυτῷ, τί. — 38 b 14 νῦν δὲ — οὐ : νῦν δὲ οὐ. — 39 c 7 οἰόμενοι : οἰόμενοι μὲν. — 40 a 9 ἡ τοῦ δαιμονίου : [ἡ τοῦ δαιμονίου]. — 40 c 5 τοῦ τόπου τοῦ : [τοῦ τόπου τοῦ]. — 41 b 35 τίς αὐτῶν : τίς δὴ αὐτῶν. — 41 b 36 δ' ἄν : δἄν. — 41 c 43 ἀληθῆ : ἀληθῆ ἐστιν. — 42 a 22 πλὴν ἢ : πλὴν εἰ. 44 b 15 Ἄτοπον : ὡς ἄτοπον. — 45 b 18 οὗτοι : αὖ τοι. — 45 b 19 Σιμμίας : Σιμίας. — 46 a 26 εἰ δέ τι : εἰ δ' ἔτι. — 46 b 4 οὐ νῦν πρῶτον : οὐ μόνον νῦν. — 47 a 31 τὰς δ' οὔ ; τί φῇς : τὰς δ' οὔ; [οὐδὲ πάντων, ἀλλὰ τῶν μέν, τῶν δ' οὔ;] τί φῇς. — 49 a 7 [γέροντες] : γέροντες. — 51 a 25 ἔσται : ἐξέσται. — 51 e 19 πείσεσθαι : πείθεσθαι. — 52 b 11 [ὅτι μὴ ἅπαξ εἰς Ἰσθμόν] : ὅ τι μὴ ἅπαξ εἰς Ἰσθμόν. — 53 e 27 οὕτως αἰσχρῶς : οὕτω γλίσχρως.

PHAEDO — Wohlrab (1895)

57 a 7 Φλειασίων : Φλιασίων. — 59 c 40 τέ γ' ὁ : γε ὁ. — 59 d 9 [ἡμέρᾳ] : ἡμέρᾳ. — 59 e 17 ἐκέλευεν : ἐκέλευσεν. — 60 b 31 μὴ 'θέλειν : μὴ ἐθέλειν. — 60 d 5 ὅ τί ποτε : ὅτι ποτέ. — 60 e 13 εἰ πολλάκις : εἰ ἄρα πολλάκις. — 61 b 26 ποιήματα, πιθόμενον : ποιήματα καὶ πειθόμενον. — 61 c 7 τί δέ : τ'. δαί. — 61 d 17 σαφῶς : σαφές. — 61 e 21 [τῆς ἐκεῖ] : τῆς ἐκεῖ. — 61 e 1 δὴ οὖν : οὖν δή. — 62 c 27 πρὶν ἂν : πρίν. — 62 d 10 [φευκτέον . . . δεσπότου] : φευκτέον . . . δεσπότου. — 63 a 21 γέ μοι : γ' ἐμοί. — 63 c 9 [ἥξειν] : ἥξειν. — 115 c 15 οὗτος ὁ : οὗτος. — 115 d 21 ταῦτα [μοι] δοκῶ : ταῦτά μοι δοκῶ. — 116 b 9 ἐναντίον : ἐκείναις ἐναντίον. — 116 e 38 [εἰκότως] : εἰκότως. — 117 a 41 πιθοῦ : πείθου. — 117 d 27 [κλάων καὶ] : κλαίων καί. — 117 e 34 κατεκλίνη : κατεκλίθη. — 117 e 36 [οὗτος . . . φάρμακον] : οὗτος . . . φάρμακον. — 118 a 3 [ἄλλως] : ἄλλως.

SYMPOSIUM — Hug (1884)

215 e 30 ὑπὸ τῶν λόγων τῶν τούτου : [ὑπὸ τῶν λόγων τούτου]. — 216 a 36 ὦ Σώκρατες : Σώκρατες. — 216 d 7 ἐκπέπληκται, ὡς : ἐκπέπληκται, [καὶ αὖ ἀγνοεῖ πάντα καὶ οὐδὲν οἶδεν,] ὡς. — 216 e 15 ἵνα λέγω ὑμῖν : λέγω ὑμῖν. — 219 e 2 ἐν : ⟨ἐν⟩. — 220 a 4 ἀναγκασθεῖμεν : ἀναγκασθείημεν. — 220 c 3 στρατιᾶς : στρατείας. — 221 b 37 ἑταῖρος : ἕτερος. — 222 a 9 δή : αὖ.

MEMORABILIA — Breitenbach-Mücke (1889)

1. 6. 10 δεῖσθαι : δέεσθαι. — 4. 8. 9 τοῦτο · ἐμοί : τοῦτο · [εἰ γὰρ τὸ ἀδικεῖν αἰσχρόν ἐστι, πῶς οὐκ αἰσχρὸν καὶ τὸ ἀδίκως ὁτιοῦν ποιεῖν ;] ἐμοί.

VOCABULARY

ἀ-βίωτος adj. (βίος): not to be lived, not worth living

ἀβρΰνομαι: plume myself

ἀγαθός adj.: good

ἄγαλμα, -ατος n.: (delight), image

ἀγανακτέω, fut. ἀγανακτήσω, aor. ἠγανάκτησα: am vexed, am irritated, am troubled, am angry, grieve

ἀγαπάω, fut. ἀγαπήσω: love, welcome

ἀγγελίᾱ f.: message, tidings

ἀγγέλλω, aor. ἤγγειλα: report, announce

ἄγγελος m.: messenger, reporter

ἀγιώτερος comp. adj.: more holy

ἀ-γνοέω (γιγνώσκω): am ignorant, do not know

ἀγορᾱ́ f. (ἀγείρω): (place of assembly), market-place

ἀγρίως adv.: (wildly), harshly, roughly

ἀγροικότερος comp. adj. (ἀγρός): (of the field), too boorish, too rude

ἀγρός m. (acre): field

ἀγρ-υπνίᾱ f. (ὕπνος): wakefulness

ἄγω, aor. ἤγαγον: lead, bring, fetch. ἄγε, as interjection, come! SCG. 411; GMT. 251

ἀγών, -ῶνος m. (agony): contest, trial, suit, court

ἀγωνίζομαι: contend, contest, struggle

Ἀδείμαντος m.: Adimantus, brother of Plato. 34 a

ἀδελφός m.: brother

ἀ-δεῶς adv. (δέος): fearlessly

ἄ δηλος adj.: hidden, obscure, concealed, dark

ἀ-διά-φθαρτος adj. (φθείρω): uncorrupted, not ruined

ἀ-δικέω, fut. ἀδικήσω, pf. pass. ἠδίκημαι, verbal ἀδικητέον (δίκη): am unjust (ἄδικός εἰμι), am guilty, am wrong, do evil, act unjustly

ἀ-δίκημα, -ατος n.: unjust act, wrong deed

ἀ-δικίᾱ f.: injustice, wrong

ἄ-δικος adj.: unjust, unrighteous

ἀ-δίκως adv.: unjustly, unfairly

ἀ-δύνατος adj.: impossible

ἀεί adv.: always, ever, in every case, at each time, at any time, for the time being (25 c)

ἀερο-βατέω (ἀήρ, βαίνω): walk the air, tread the air

ἀ-ηδέστερον comp. adv.: with less pleasure

ἀ-ηδής, -ές adj. (ἡδύς): unpleasant, uninteresting

ἀ-ήθης, -ες adj. (ἦθος): unwonted, unusual

ἀ-θάνατος adj.: immortal, undying, would never die

ἀ-θέμιστος (Themis): what is not allowed by the gods, Latin nefas

ἄ-θεος adj. (atheist): god-less, without gods

Ἀθήνᾱζε adv.: to Athens

Ἀθηναῖος adj.: Athenian, man of Athens

Ἀθήνησι adv.: at Athens

ἀθρέω: look, observe, regard

ἀθρόος adj.: together, all at once

Αἰακός m.: Aeacus, king of Aegina, and grandfather of Achilles and

197

Telamonian Ajax. He was made a judge in Hades after his death. 41 a; *Gorgias* 523 e

Ἀιαντό-δωρος *m.*: Aeantodōrus. 34 a

Ἀίᾱς, -αντος *m.*: Ajax, the mightiest of the Achaean warriors before Troy, after Achilles; but by an unjust judgment the arms of Achilles, on the latter's death, were given to Odysseus. In his disappointment, Ajax went mad and killed himself. 41 b

Αἰγίνη *f.*: Aegina, a large island, a dozen miles from the port of Athens. 59 c

Ἅιδης, -ου *m.*: Hades. ἐν Ἅιδου, in (the realm of) Hades. 29 b

αἴνιγμα, -ατος *n.* (enigma): what is darkly indicated, a riddle

αἰνίττομαι: hint at, utter in a riddle

αἱρετός *verbal adj.* (αἱρέω): to be gained

αἱρέω, *fut.* αἱρήσω, *aor. mid.* εἱλόμην, *pf.* ἥρηκεν, *verbal* αἱρετός: take, secure (my) conviction, overcome, compel; *mid.* choose, elect

αἰσθάνομαι, *aor.* ᾐσθόμην, *pf.* ᾔσθημαι: perceive, feel

αἴσθησις, -εως *f.* (an-aesthesia, aesthetic): perception, sensation

Αἰσχίνης, -ου *m.*: Aeschines, a young companion of Socrates. 33 e, 59 b. (Not the orator, the rival and antagonist of Demosthenes.)

αἰσχίων, -ονος *comp. adj.*: more shameful

αἰσχρός *adj.*: disgraceful, shameful

αἰσχρῶς *adv.*: shamefully

αἰσχύνομαι, *aor. pass.* ᾐσχύνθην (αἰσχύνη): am ashamed; *with acc.* am abashed before, respect

Αἴσωπος *m.*: Aesop, the writer of fables, a Lydian contemporary of Croesus. 60 c

αἰτέω, *aor.* ᾔτησα: ask, claim, demand

αἰτίᾱ *f.*: responsibility, blame, charge

αἰτιάομαι, *aor. inf.* αἰτιάσασθαι: accuse, charge

αἴτιον *n.*: cause

αἴτιος *adj.*: responsible, to blame

αἰτιώτερος *comp. adj.*: rather the cause

ἀκοή *f.* (ἀκούω): hearing, hearsay. ἐξ ἀκοῆς, what (I) have heard

ἀ-κολασίᾱ *f.*: wantonness, license

ἀ-κόλαστος *adj.* (κολάζω): wanton

ἀκολουθέω, *fut.* ἀκολουθήσω: follow

ἀκούσιος *adj.* (ἄκων): unwilling, involuntary

ἀκούω, *fut.* ἀκούσομαι, *aor.* ἤκουσα, *pf.* ἀκήκοα (acoustics): hear, listen, am told. κακῶς ἀκούω, hear ill, *i.e.* am reproached, *as passive of* κακῶς λέγω

ἀ-κρατέστατος *sup. adj.* (κράτος): most unrestrained

ἀκρῑβέστατα *sup. adv.*: most exactly, most accurately

ἀκροάομαι, *fut.* ἀκροάσομαι: hear, listen

ἀκροᾱτής, -οῦ *m.*: hearer, listener. οἱ ἀκροαταί, the audience

ἄ-κῡρος *adj.*: of no effect, null and void

ἄκων, -οντος *adj.* (ἑκών): unwilling, unwillingly

ἀλαζών, -όνος *m.*: braggart, boaster

ἀλγεινός *adj.*: painful, grievous

ἀλγέω: suffer pain, ache

ἀλεκτρυών, -όνος *m.*: cock. 118 a

ἀλήθεια *f.*: truth. τῇ ἀληθείᾳ, in truth

ἀληθεύω, *fut.* ἀληθεύσω: speak the truth

ἀληθής, -ές *adj.*: true. τὸ ἀληθές, the truth

ἀληθῶς *adv.*: truly. ὡς ἀληθῶς, in truth

ἁλίσκομαι, *aor.* ἑάλων, *pf.* ἑάλωκα: am taken, am caught, am convicted

Ἀλκιβιάδης, -ου *m.*: Alcibiades, son of Clinias, born about 450 B.C., — the most brilliant of the young men of

Athens in Socrates's time; but an unprincipled leader. *Symp.* **215** ; Xen. *Mem.* i. 2. 12

ἀλλά *conj.* : but. *After a condition, sometimes it may be translated at any rate, at least.* ἀλλ' ἤ, except, **20 d**, *after a negative, seems to be due to a combination of* οὐδὲν ἀλλά *and* οὐδὲν ἄλλο ἤ.

ἀλλήλων, ἀλλήλοις, ἀλλήλους *recip. pron.* (ἄλλος): each other

ἄλλο τι ἤ: *originally*, is anything else true than; *it became a mere sign of a question implying the answer* "*yes*," *like the Latin* nonne, — doubtless; You do, do you not?

ἄλλο-θι *adv.*: elsewhere

ἀλλοῖος *adj.*: of a different kind, different. Cf. οἷος, τοιοῦτος. *Having a comparative idea, it may be followed by* ἤ.

ἀλλοιότερος *comp. adj.*: rather of a different kind

ἄλλος, -η, -ον *indef. pron.* (alius): other (cf. ἕτερος)

ἄλλοσε *adv.*: elsewhither, elsewhere

ἀλλότριος *adj.*: of another, alien, foreign to (my) nature

ἄλλως *adv.*: otherwise; otherwise than well, foolishly, vainly. ἄλλως τε καί, (both otherwise and), especially

ἀ-λόγιστος *adj.*: inconsiderate, unreasoning

ἀ-λογίστως *adv.*: inconsiderately

ἄ-λογος *adj.*: unreasonable

ἀ-λογώτατος *sup. adj.*: most unreasonable

ἅμα *adv.*: at the same time. τρίβων ἅμα, as he rubbed (it)

ἀ-μαθέστερος *comp. adj.*: more ignorant, less learned

ἀ-μαθής, -ές *adj.* (μανθάνω): ignorant, unlearned

ἀ-μαθίᾱ *f.*: ignorance, folly

ἁμάρτημα, -ατος *n.*: mistake, error, fault

ἀμείβομαι: change

ἀμείνων, -ονος *comp. adj.*: better. Cf. ἀγαθός.

ἀ-μέλεια *f.*: lack of care, neglect

ἀ-μελέω, *aor.* ἠμέλησα, *pf.* ἠμέληκα: neglect, am careless, do not practice

ἀ-μήχανον *n.* (μηχανή): immeasurable degree, infinity

ἀμύνομαι, *fut.* ἀμυνοῦμαι: avenge (my-)self, defend (my)self

ἀμφί *prep.*: about, around. οἱ ἀμφί "Ἄνυτον, Anytus and his associates

ἀμφι-γνοέω (know): am in doubt

ἀμφι-έννῡμι, *pf. pass.* ἠμφίεσμαι: clothe; *pf. pass.* am clad

Ἀμφίπολις, -εως *f.*: Amphipolis, an Athenian colony in Macedonia, on the Strymon. The Athenians under Cleon sought vainly to recover it from the Spartan Brasidas in 422 b.c. **28 e**

ἀμφισ-βητέω, *aor.* ἠμφεσβήτησα: dispute

ἀμφότερος *adj.* (ambo, ἀμφί): both. κατ' ἀμφότερα, in either case

ἄν: *for* ἐάν, εἰ ἄν, if, *with subjunctive*

ἄν *modal adv.*: *with potential optative; in the conclusion of a condition contrary to fact; and with a past tense of the indicative, marking repetition of the action, as* **22 b**

ἀνα-βαίνω, *aor.* ἀνέβην, *pf.* ἀναβέβηκα: come up (upon the tribune)

ἀνα-βιβάζω *aor. mid.* ἀνεβιβασάμην (βαίνω): bring up, cause to come up

ἀνα-βιώσκομαι (βίος): bring to life again

ἀνα-βλέπω, *aor.* ἀνέβλεψα: look up

ἀνα-βρῡχάομαι, *aor.* ἀνεβρῡχησάμην: howl, bawl, cry out

ἀνα-γιγνώσκω, *aor.* ἀνέγνων: read

ἀναγκάζω, aor. pass. ἠναγκάσθην: compel, require, constrain

ἀναγκαῖος adj.: necessary, inevitable

ἀνάγκη f.: necessity, necessary, binding law

ἀνα-ζητέω, pf. ἀνεζήτηκα: search out

ἀν-αιρέω, aor. ἀνεῖλον: (take up), declare (of an oracle); mid. take up (for burial)

ἀν-αισχυντέω: have the shamelessness

ἀν-αισχυντία f.: shamelessness, effrontery

ἀν-αισχυντότατος (αἰσχύνη) sup. adj.: most shameless, most impudent

ἀν-αισχύντως adv.: shamelessly

ἀνα-καθίζομαι: sit up

ἀνα-λαμβάνω, aor. ἀνέλαβον: take up

ἀν-ᾱλίσκω: expend

ἀν-ᾱλωσις, -εως f.: spending

ἀνα-μιμνῄσκω, aor. ἀνέμνησα, pass. ἀνεμνήσθην: recall, remind, mid. remember

ἀν-ανδρία f. (ἀνήρ): unmanliness

'Αναξαγόρᾱς, -ου m.: Anaxagoras, a philosopher born at Clazomenae, near Smyrna, about 500 B.C.; died at Lampsacus about 428 B.C. Introd. § 5

ἀν-άξιος adj.: unworthy

ἀνα-πείθω: persuade

ἀνά-πηρος adj.: maimed, crippled, helpless

ἀνα-πίμπλημι, aor. ἀνέπλησα: infect, implicate

ἀνα-σκοπέω: consider anew

ἀνα-τρέπω, pf. pass. ἀνατέτραμμαι: overturn, subvert, ruin

ἀνα-φέρω, fut. ἀνοίσω: refer

ἀνα-χωρέω, verbal ἀναχωρητέον: draw back, withdraw, retreat

ἀνδραποδώδης, -ες (εἶδος) adj.: slavish

ἀνδραποδωδῶς adv.: like a slave, slavishly

ἀνδρείᾱ f. (ἀνήρ): manliness, bravery

ἀνδρεῖος adj.: manly

ἀν-έλεγκτος adj. (ἐλέγχω): unrefuted, irrefutable

ἀν-ελεύθερος adj.: illiberal, unworthy of a free man

ἀν-έλπιστος adj. (ἐλπίς): unlooked-for, unexpected

ἄνεμος m.: wind

ἀν-εξ-έταστος adj.: without examination, without inquiry

ἀν-ερευνάω: search out, seek

ἀν-έρομαι: question, ask, inquire

ἀν-ερωτάω: question, ask again

ἄνευ improper prep.: without

ἀν-ευφημέω, aor. ἀνηυφήμησα: break the silence, cry aloud

ἀν-έχω, aor. ἀνέσχον: hold up, mid. suffer, endure, with gen. and suppl. participle. ἥλιος ἀνέσχεν, the sun rose

ἀνήρ, gen. ἀνδρός, m.: man (Latin vir)

ἀνήρ: by crasis for ὁ ἀνήρ

ἀνθρώπειος adj.: belonging to men. ὅσα τἀνθρώπεια, humanly speaking

ἀνθρώπινος adj.: human, of a man, attainable by man

ἄνθρωπος m. or f.: man (Latin homo)

ἀνιάομαι, fut. ἀνιάσομαι: grieve, have grief

ἀνιαρῶς adv.: miserably

ἀν-ίημι: give up, relax (one's efforts)

ἀν-ίσταμαι: rise, stand up

ἀ-νόητος adj.: thoughtless, witless

ἀν-οίγνῡμι, impf. ἀνεῳγόμην, aor. pass. ἀνεῴχθην: open

ἀν-όσιος adj.: unholy

ἀντ-αδικέω, aor. ἀντηδίκησα: do an unjust act in return, retaliate

ἀντ-απόλλῡμι: destroy in return

ἀντ-εῖπον aor.: replied, answered

'Αντήνωρ, -ορος m.: Antenor, the wisest counselor of the Trojans. 221 c ἀντί prep. with gen.: instead of, in place of

ἀντι-βόλησις, -εως f.: entreaty

ἀντι-γραφή f.: written charge, indictment

ἀντι-δράω: do in return, retaliate

ἀντι-κακουργέω, aor. ἀντεκακούργησα: do harm in return

ἀντι-λέγω: reply, speak back, say in return, gainsay

'Αντιοχίς, -ίδος f.: Antiochis, the Athenian "tribe" of which Socrates was a member. 32 b

ἀντι-παρα-βάλλω: place over against, compare

ἀντι-παρα-τίθημι, aor. partic. ἀντιπαραθείς: place alongside, compare with

ἀντι-ποιέω: do in return

'Αντισθένης, -ους m.: Antisthenes, founder of the school of Cynics. 59 b

ἀντί-τεχνος m. (τέχνη): competitor, rival

ἀντι-τῑμάομαι, fut. ἀντιτῑμήσομαι: propose as penalty on (my) -part, — with gen.

ἀντι-τύπτω: strike back, beat in turn

'Αντιφῶν, -ῶντος m.: Antiphon, a sophist. 33 e; Xen. Mem. i. 6. (Not to be confounded with the orator of the same name.)

ἀντ-ωμοσίᾱ f. (ὄμνυμι): charge under oath, affidavit

ἀν-υπό-δητος adj. (δέω): unshod, without shoes, barefoot

"Ανυτος, -ου m.: Anytus, one of the accusers of Socrates. 18 b. Introd. § 36

ἀξίᾱ f. (sc. τίμη): worth, deserts. κατὰ τὴν ἀξίαν, according to (my) deserts

ἄξιος adj.: worthy of, deserving of, deserved, fitting, worth while. ἄξιον λόγου, worth mentioning. ἄξιον

ἀκοῦσαι, worth hearing. ἄξιός εἰμι,] deserve

ἀξιό-χρεως, -ων, nom. pl. ἀξιόχρεῳ, adj.: responsible, worthy of credit, trustworthy

ἀξιόω, aor. ἠξίωσα (ἄξιος): think fair, consider reasonable, count worthy of, suppose true, claim, ask as reasonable

ἀξίωμα, -ατος n.: dignity, distinction

ἀξίως adv.: worthily, in a manner worthy

ἀπ-αγγέλλω, aor. ἀπήγγειλα: report

ἀπ-αγορεύω: forbid, warn off

ἀπ-άγω: lead off (to prison, by summary process), take away, conduct. — ἀπαγωγή was allowed only when a man was taken in the act of crime.

ἀπ-αίρω, fut. ἀπαρῶ: remove from, depart from

ἀπ-αλλαγή f.: relief, way of escape

ἀπ-αλλάττω, fut. pass. ἀπαλλάξομαι, pf. ἀπήλλαγμαι, aor. ἀπηλλάγην: free from, release from; mid. take my leave, depart

ἀπ-αν-αισχυντέω, aor. ἀπανῃσχύντησα: have the shamelessness for

ἀπ-αντάω (ἄντα): meet

ἅπαξ adv.: once

ἅπᾱς, ἅπᾱσα, ἅπᾱν adj. (πᾶς): all

ἀπατάω, aor. pass. ἠπατήθην (ἀπάτη): deceive, trick

ἀπ-αυθᾱδίζομαι: am self-willed

ἀ-πειθέω, aor. ἠπείθησα: am disobedient, do not obey

ἀπ-εικάζω, aor. ἀπῄκασα: liken, compare

ἀπειλέω: threaten

ἄπ-ειμι: go away, will go away, depart

ἄ-πειρος adj. (πέρας): boundless, unlimited

ἄ-πειρος adj. (πεῖρα): inexperienced, unacquainted with, ignorant. ἄπειρος γραμμάτων, unlettered

ἀπ-ελαύνω : drive off, drive away

ἀπ-εργάζομαι (ἔργον): work, effect, accomplish

ἀπ-έρχομαι, aor. ἀπῆλθον: go away, depart

ἀπ-εχθάνομαι : am hated, make myself hated

ἀπ-έχθεια f.: enmity, hatred

ἀπ-έχθομαι (ἔχθος): am hated

ἀπ-έχομαι : abstain from

ἀπ-ηλλάχθαι : pf. pass. inf. of ἀπαλλάττω

ἀ-πιστέω, aor. ἠπίστησα: disobey, do not believe

ἄ-πιστος adj.: incredible, not to be believed

ἁ-πλοῦς adj.: simple, invariable, absolute

ἀπό prep. with gen. (ab): from

ἀπο-βαίνω, fut. ἀποβήσομαι: come off, become, result, prove

ἀπο-βάλλω, aor. ἀπέβαλον: cast away, lose

ἀπο-βλέπω, aor. ἀπέβλεψα : look off, glance off, regard

ἀπο-δακρύω : weep, grieve for

ἀπο-δείκνῦμι and ἀπο-δεικνύω, aor. ἀπέδειξα: demonstrate, prove, show, make

ἀπο-δημέω, aor. ἀπεδήμησα, pf. ἀποδεδήμηκα: am absent, am abroad; depart, journey

ἀπο-δημίᾱ f.: departure, absence (from Athens)

ἀπο-διδράσκω : run away, flee

ἀπο-δίδωμι, aor. imv. ἀπόδοτε: pay, render

ἀπο-θνῄσκω, fut. ἀποθανοῦμαι, aor. ἀπέθανον: die, am put to death

ἀπ-οικίᾱ f.: colony, settlement

ἀπο-κάμνω, aor. ἀπέκαμον: am weary, hesitate

ἀπο-κλάω (κλάω): bewail

ἀπο-κρίνομαι, aor. ἀπεκρῑνάμην : answer, reply

ἀπο-κρύπτω, aor. mid. ἀπεκρυψάμην (apocrypha): conceal, hide, put in the shade

ἀπο-κτείνω and ἀπο-κτείνῦμι, fut. ἀποκτενῶ, aor. ἀπέκτεινα, pf. ἀπέκτονα: slay, kill, put to death

ἀπο-λαμβάνω, aor. ἀπέλαβον, aor. pass. ἀπελήφθην: take off, cut off, shut off, carry away

ἀπο-λαύω, pf. ἀπολέλαυκα: enjoy, receive good from

ἀπο-λείπω, fut. ἀπολείψω, aor. ἀπέλιπον: leave at one side, abandon, forsake

Ἀπολλό-δωρος m.: Apollodōrus, of Phalerum, an enthusiastic follower of Socrates. 34 a, 59 a, 117 d

ἀπ-όλλῦμι, fut. mid. ἀπολοῦμαι, aor. ἀπώλεσα, mid. ἀπωλόμην, pf. ἀπόλωλα: destroy, lose; mid. go out of existence; aor. mid. perished; pf. have perished, am ruined

Ἀπόλλων, -ωνος m.: Apollo. 60 d

ἀπο-λογέομαι, fut. ἀπολογήσομαι, aor. ἀπελογησάμην, verbal ἀπολογητέον: make (my) defense, defend (my)self, reply

ἀπολογίᾱ (λέγω): defense, reply. (Never used in the sense of the English apology, which acknowledges an act, and regrets it. ἀπολογία denies the charge.)

ἀπο-λύω : release ; mid. loose from (my)self, free (my)self from

ἀπο-πειράομαι : test, try, make experiment

ἀπο-πέμπω, aor. ἀπέπεμψα : send away, dismiss

ἀπο-πηδάω, aor. ἀπεπήδησα : leap away, hurry off

ἀ-πορέω : am at a loss, do not know, doubt

ἀ-πορίᾱ f.: lack, want

ἀπό-ρρητος adj. (εἴρηκα) : not to be spoken, secret, — perhaps referring to esoteric Orphic doctrines

ἀ-πορώτατος sup. adj.: most difficult to meet (or to manage), most perplexing

ἀπο-σπένδω, aor. ἀπέσπεισα: pour a libation (σπονδή)

ἀπο-τίνω, aor. ἀπέτεισα: pay

ἀπο-τρέπω, aor. ἀπέτρεψα: turn away from, dissuade from

ἀπο-φαίνω, fut. ἀποφανῶ: show, make clear

ἀπο-φεύγω, fut. ἀποφεύξομαι, aor. ἀπέφυγον, pf. ἀποπέφευγα : escape, am acquitted, — with direct object

ἀπο-ψηφίζομαι, aor. ἀπεψηφισάμην (ψῆφος): vote free, acquit, vote for (my) acquittal

ἅπτω, fut. ἅψομαι, pf. pass. ἧμμαι: fasten ; mid. feel of, touch, lay hold of

ἄρα inferential conj.: so, then, accordingly, as it seems, perchance

ἆρα : introduces a question. Cf. ἦ.

ἀργύριον n.: silver, money

ἀρέσκω : please, gratify

ἀρετή f.: virtue, excellence, first duty

ἀριθμέω, aor. ἠρίθμησα : count

ἀριθμός m.: number

ἀριστεῖον n. (ἄριστος): prize of bravery

Ἀρίστιππος m.: Aristippus, founder of the Cyrenaic school of philosophy, born about 435 B.C. 59 c

ἄριστος sup. adj. : best. Cf. ἀγαθός, βέλτιστος.

Ἀριστοφάνης, -ους m.: Aristophanes, the chief comic poet of Greece; born about 444 B.C., and died about 385 B.C. Socrates and his teaching weie ridiculed in the Clouds of Aristophanes, presented in 423 B.C.

Ἀρίστων, -ωνος m.: Aristo, Plato's father. 34 a

ἀρκεῖ impers.: it is sufficient

ἀρκούντως adv.: contentedly

ἀρνακίς, -ίδος f. (ἄρνες): lamb-skin

ἄρουρα, Homeric gen. ἀρούρης: plowed land, land, earth

ἄρτι adv.: just now, just

ἀρχή f.: beginning, principle, premise. τὴν ἀρχήν, at all. ἐξ ἀρχῆς, from the beginning

ἀρχή f.: office, government, rule, authority

ἀρχικός adj.: skilled in ruling

ἄρχομαι, aor. ἠρξάμην: begin. ἀρχόμενος, at the beginning ; cf. τελευτῶν

ἄρχω, aor. ἦρξα: lead, command, rule, hold office. ὁ ἄρχων, the commander; οἱ ἄρχοντες, the rulers, magistrates

ἀ-σέβεια f.: impiety

ἀ-σεβής, -ές adj.: impious

ἀ-σθενέστατος sup. adj.: weakest

ἀ-σθενέω (σθένος): am weak, am ill

ἀ-σῑτέω (σῖτος): am without food, fas.

Ἀσκληπιός m. : Asclepius (Aesculapius), the god of healing. 118 a

ἀσπάζομαι: salute, have affection, esteem

ἀ-στακτί adv.: not in drops, in streams

ἀστεῖος adj. (ἄστυ) : civil, courteous, polite

ἀστός m. (ἄστυ): man of the city, townsman, citizen

ἀ-σφάλεια f. (σφάλλω): safety, security

ἀ-σφαλέστερος comp. adj.: safer

ἀ-σφαλῶς adv.: safely

ἀ-σχήμων, -ονος adj.: unseemly

ἀ-σχολία f. (σχολή): lack of leisure, occupation. ἀσχολίαν ἄγω, am busy, am occupied

ἀ-ταξίᾱ f. (τάξις): disorder, misrule

ἄτε adjunct of a causal participle: since. ἅτε φιλότιμοι ὄντες, since they are ambitious

ἀτεχνῶς adv.: absolutely, completely, downright. ἀτεχνῶς ξένως ἔχω, am an entire stranger. (To be clearly distinguished from ἀτέχνως, "unscientifically.")

ἀ-τῑμάζω (τίμη): slight, treat without honor, dishonor, have lack of respect

ἀ-τῑμόω, aor. ἠτίμωσα: deprive of civil rights

ἀ-τοπίᾱ f.: strangeness, absurdity

ἄ-τοπος adj. (τόπος): (out of place), eccentric, extraordinary, singular

ἄττα: = τινά, n. pl. of τὶς, some one

ἅττα: = ἅτινα, n. pl. of ὅστις

αὖ adv.: again, in turn, on the other hand

αὐθᾱδέστερον comp. adv.: more self-willed

αὐθᾱδίζομαι (αὐθός, ἀνδάνω): am self-willed. αὐθαδιζόμενος, out of self-will

αὖθις adv.: again, later, hereafter. εἰς αὖθις, at a later time

αὐλέω: play on the flute

αὔλημα, -ατος n.: flute-playing

αὐλητής, -οῦ m.: flute-player

αὐλητικός adj.: belonging to flute-players

αὐλητρίς, -ίδος f.: female flute-player, flute-girl

αὐλός m.: flute

αὔριον adv.: to-morrow. εἰς αὔριον, on the morrow; cf. εἰς αὖθις

αὐτ-αρκέστατα sup. adv. (αὐτός, ἀρκεῖ): most independently, most contentedly

αὐτίκα adv.: straightway, forthwith, at once

αὐτόθι adv.: there

αὐτοῖς: for ἑαυτοῖς, reflexive pron., themselves

αὐτό-ματος adj. (automaton): of (his) own motion, of (his) own impulse, by chance

αὐτός, -ή, -ό: self, himself. In the oblique cases, when standing by itself, as a personal pronoun, him, her. ὁ αὐτός, ταὐτόν, the same

αὐτο-σχεδιάζω (σχεδία): form (my) own idea, judge off-hand, judge hastily

αὐτοῦ adv.: here

αὐτό-φωρος adj. (Latin fur): (as a very thief), caught in the act. ἐπ᾽ αὐτοφώρῳ, in the very act, manifestly

ἀφ-αίρεσις, -εως f.: taking away, confiscation

ἀ-φανής, -ές adj. (φαίνω): unseen

ἀ-φθονίᾱ f. (φθόνος): plenty, abundance

ἀφ-ίημι, fut. ἀφήσω, aor. partic. ἀφείς: let go, dismiss, abandon, throw away

ἀφ-ικνέομαι, fut. ἀφίξομαι, aor. ἀφῑκόμην, pf. ἀφῖγμαι: come, arrive

ἀφ-ίσταμαι: stand aloof, stand off, keep away

ἀφ-οσιόομαι, aor. ἀφωσιωσάμην (ὅσιος): clear (my)self of a scruple

ἄ-φρων, -ον adj.: senseless, foolish

ἄχθομαι (ἄχθος): am burdened, grieve, am angry, am offended

ἄχθος, -εος n.: burden

Ἀχιλλεύς, -έως m.: Achilles. 221 c; cf. 28 c

ἀ-χίτων, -ον adj. (cotton): without tunic

βαδίζω (βαίνω): walk, go

βαθύς, -εῖα, -ύ adj.: deep. ὄρθρος βαθύς, early dawn

βαρβαρικός adj. (barbaric): outside of Greece

βάρος, -εος n.: heaviness

βαρύνομαι: am heavy, am a burden

βαρύς, -εῖα, -ύ adj. (gravis): heavy, grievous

βαρύτατος sup. adj.: most grievous, most weighty

βαρύτερος comp. adj.: too heavy, too burdensome

βασιλεύς, -έως *m.*: king

βεβαιόω, *fut.* βεβαιώσω: confirm, establish

βέλτιστος *sup. adj.*: best

βελτίων, -ονος (*comp. of* ἀγαθός,—cf. βούλομαι): better

βίᾳ *adv.*: by force, in spite of

βιάζομαι (βία): use force (to), constrain, overpower

βιαιότατος *sup. adj.*: most violent

βιβλίον *n.* (Bible): book

βίος *m.*: life

βιόω, *fut.* βιώσομαι, *pf.* βεβίωκα: live

βιωτός *verbal adj.* (βίος): to be lived, (life) worth living

βλαβερός *adj.*: harmful, injurious

βλάπτω, *fut.* βλάψω, *aor.* ἔβλαψα, *aor. pass.* ἐβλάβην: injure, harm, hurt

βλέπω, *aor.* ἔβλεψα: look, see

βοάω, *fut.* βοήσομαι: cry aloud, shout, raise a shout

βοηθέω: aid, come to the defense of, defend, — *with dat.*

βομβέω: ring, hum, buzz

βούλευμα, -ατος *n.*: consideration, argument, decision

βουλευτής, -οῦ *m.* (βουλή): member of the senate, senator

βουλευτικός *adj.*: senatorial

βουλεύω, *aor.* ἐβούλευσα, *pf. mid.* βεβούλευμαι: am senator, act as senator; *aor.* was chosen to the senate; *mid.* deliberate, plan; *aor. mid.* decide

βουλή *f.*: deliberation, consideration, argument

βούλομαι: wish, desire, choose. ὁ βουλόμενος, whoever desires

βραδύς, -εῖα, -ύ *adj.*: slow

βραδύτερος *comp. adj.*: slower

Βρᾱσίδᾱς, -ου *m.*: Brasidas, the chief Spartan general in the first part of the Peloponnesian War; he fell in

the defense of Amphipolis, in 422 B.C. **221 c**

βραχύς, -εῖα, -ύ *adj.* (brevis): brief. ἐν βραχεῖ, in short

βρενθύομαι: have proud mien, hold (my) head high

βυρσο-δέψης, -ου *m.*: tanner

βωμός *m.* (βαίνω): altar

γαμέω, *aor.* ἔγημα: marry

γάμος *m.*: marriage

γάρ *causal part.* (γὲ, ἄρα): for. *Not always to be translated at the beginning of a narrative. It may indicate surprise, and be equivalent to* why !

γαστήρ, *gen.* γαστρός *f.* (gastric): belly, appetite

γελάω, *aor.* ἐγέλασα: laugh

γέλοιος, *adj.* (γέλως): laughable, ridiculous

γελοιότερος *comp. adj.*: more laughable, too ridiculous

γελοίως *adv.*: laughably

γέμω: am filled, teem

γενναῖος *adj.* (γένος): noble, well-bred, splendid

γενναιότατος *sup. adj.*: noblest

γενναίως *adv.*: nobly, generously, bravely

γεννάω, *aor.* ἐγέννησα: beget, give birth, bear, give life

γεννητής, -οῦ *m.*: parent, father

γένος, -εος *n.* (genus): race, stock, blood

γέρων, -οντος *m.*: old man; *as adj.* old

γεωργίᾱ *f.* (γῆ, ἔργον, George): farming

γεωργικός *adj. as n.* (Georgic): skilled in farming, farmer

γῆ *f.*: earth

γῆρας, *gen.* γήρως, *n.*: old age

γίγνομαι, *aor.* ἐγενόμην, *pf.* γέγονα (γένος): am born, become, come, am established, am formed, am made, take place, turn out; *pf.* am, have arisen

γιγνώσκω, *fut.* γνώσομαι, *aor.* ἔγνων, *pf.* ἔγνωκα (know): know, judge; *fut.*, *aor.*, *and pf.* come to know, learn, find out

γλίχομαι : stick, cling, long for

γλύφω, *pf. pass.* γέγλυμμαι : carve

γνησίως *adv.* (γένος): genuinely, nobly, honestly

γνώμη *f.* : judgment

Γοργίᾱς, -ου *m.* : Gorgias, a noted rhetorician from Leontini in Sicily; born about 490 B.C. and died about 380 B.C. The founder of the school of epideictic oratory. 19 e. Introd. § 12.

γοῦν (γὲ-οῦν) : now, at least, at any rate

γράμμα, -ατος *n.* (γράφω): letter; *pl.* letters, literature

γραφή : writing, formal charge, indictment

γράφω, *aor. mid.* ἐγραψάμην, *pf. mid.* γέγραμμαι : write ; *mid.* present in writing, present, indict

γυμνάζομαι, *verbal* γυμναστέον (γυμνός): engage in gymnastic exercises, practice

γυμνάσιον *n.* : gymnasium

γυμναστική *f.* : gymnastics, bodily exercises, in body

γυνή, *gen.* γυναικός *f.* (queen): woman

δαιμονάω : am insane, mad

δαιμόνιον *as n.* : divine influence, divinity

δαιμόνιος *adj.* (δαίμων): belonging to the gods, under the influence of the divinity, divine, superhuman, most excellent. δαιμόνιε, my dear sir

δαίμων, -ονος *m.* (demon): divine being, divinity, god. Already this seems to

be generally used of a lower order of divinities

δάκρυ, -υος *n.* (lacrima): tear

δακρύω, *aor.* ἐδάκρυσα : weep

δέδια *pf. as pres.*: fear

δεῖ : *impersonal of* δέω, need, lack

δείδω, *aor.* ἔδεισα (δέος): fear

δείκνῡμι : show, make clear

δειλίᾱ *f.* (δέος): cowardice

δεινός *adj.* (δέος): terrible, to be feared, dreadful, shameful, clever. δεινὸς λέγειν, a clever speaker, a skilled orator. οὐδὲν δεινόν, no fear

δεινότατος *sup. adj.*: most dreadful

δεινότερος *comp. adj.*: more to be feared

δειπνέω, *aor.* ἐδείπνησα : dine, sup

δεῖπνον *n.*: dinner

δέκα *numeral* (decem): ten

Δελφοί *m. pl.*: Delphi, the seat of the Pythian oracle. 20 e

δέομαι, *fut.* δεήσομαι, *aor.* ἐδεήθην (δεῖ): want, need, desire, ask, beg, implore

δεσμός *m.* (δέω, bind): fetter, bonds, imprisonment

δεσμωτήριον *n.*: prison

δεσπότης, -ου *m.* (despot): master, lord

δεῦρο *adv.*: hither ; *used in familiar tone as an imv.* come here !

δέχομαι, *aor.* ἐδεξάμην : receive, accept, take, choose

δέω (δεῖ): need, lack. πολλοῦ δέω, I am far from. πολλοῦ δεῖ, far from it. μὴ δεῖν, he ought not

δέω, *pf. pass.* δέδεμαι : bind, put in prison ; *pf. pass.* am in prison

δή *part.*: so, now, apparently, manifestly, really

Δήλιον *n.*: Delium, sanctuary of Delian Apollo, on the Attic coast, near the Boeotian frontier. Scene of a battle in 424 B.C., in which the Athenians were defeated by the Boeotians. 28 a

Δῆλος f.: Delos, birthplace of Apollo. 43 c, 58 b

δῆλος adj.: clear, open, manifest. δῆλον ὅτι, evidently

δηλόω, fut. δηλώσω: show, make clear

δημ-ηγορία f.: addressing the people, public speech

δημιουργός m. (δῆμος, ἔργον): worker for the people, craftsman

Δημό-δοκος m.: Demodocus. 33 e

δημο-κρατέομαι: am ruled by the people, am under a democracy

δημο-κρατία f. (κράτος): democracy

δῆμος m.: people, Assembly

δημοσίᾳ adv.: in public, by public process

δημοσιεύω: work as a public servant, am in public life

δημόσιος adj. (δῆμος): of the people. τὰ δημόσια, the work of the state

δημότης, -ου m.: fellow-demesman, of the same deme

δημώδης, -ες adj. (δῆμος): popular, in the ordinary sense

δή-που: doubtless, methinks, I am sure, of course

δῆτα part.: certainly, of course. τί δῆτα expresses surprise, what is this?

διά prep.: with gen. through, across; by means of, using. διὰ τοῦ βίου, through (my) life. διὰ ταχέων, quickly. With acc. because of, on account of, thanks to

δια-βάλλω, pf. pass. διαβέβλημαι: accuse (informally), create prejudice. Cf. διάβολος.

δια-βιόω, pf. διαβεβίωκα: pass (my) life, live (my) whole life

διαβολή f. (διαβάλλω): hurt, prejudice, slander. ἡ διαβολὴ ἡ ἐμή, the prejudice against me

δια-γίγνομαι, aor. διεγενόμην: come through, live through

δι-άγω, fut. διάξω: spend (my) time, lead (my life)

δια-θρῡλέω, plpf. pass. διετεθρύλητο: noise abroad, report commonly

δίαιτα f. (diet): manner of life

διαιτάομαι, impf. διῃτᾶτο: sojourn, live

διαίτημα, -ατος n.: food

διά-κειμαι: am disposed, am affected. (Perfect passive of διατίθημι.)

δια-κελεύομαι: shout encouragement

δια-κινδυνεύω: meet the danger, am in danger

δια-κρίνω: discern, determine

δια-κωλύω: prevent, hinder

δια-λέγομαι, pf. διείλεγμαι, aor. διελέχθην: converse, talk

δια-λείπω, aor. διέλιπον: leave a gap. διαλιπὼν χρόνον, after an interval of time

δι-αλλάττω, aor. διήλλαξα: reconcile

[διά-λογος m.: dialogue]

δια-μῡθο-λογέω, aor. διεμῡθολόγησα: talk familiarly, chat, converse

δια-νοέομαι, aor. διενοήθην (νοῦς): reason, think, consider, plan

διάνοια f.: thought, plan, intent

δια-πειράομαι: test, make trial, prove

δια-πορεύομαι: go on (my) way, march along

δια-σκοπέω: consider carefully, examine

δια-τάττω: arrange in order, guide

δια-τελέω, pf. διατετέλεκα (τέλος): continue (to the end)

δια-τίθημι, fut. διαθήσω, aor. pass. διετέθην: dispose. Cf. διάκειμαι.

διατριβή f.: pastime, pursuit

δια-τρίβω, aor. διέτριψα: pass (my) time, spend, converse

δια-φερόντως adv.: differing from, more than, particularly, specially

δια-φέρω: differ from, surpass, excel, am superior

δια-φεύγω, *fut.* διαφεύξομαι, *pf.* διαπέφευγα: flee, escape, am acquitted

δια-φθείρω, *fut.* διαφθερῶ, *aor.* διέφθειρα, *pf.* διέφθαρκα, *pass.* διέφθαρμαι, *fut.* διαφθαρήσομαι: corrupt, destroy, ruin; change

δια-φθορεύς, -έως *m.*: corrupter, destroyer

διδάσκαλος *m.*: teacher, master

διδάσκω, *fut.* διδάξω, *aor.* ἐδίδαξα: teach, instruct

δίδωμι, *fut.* δώσω, *aor. pl.* ἔδοσαν, *pf. pass.* δέδομαι (do): offer, give, present

δι-εῖδον, *inf.* διιδεῖν, *aor.*: saw through

δί-ειμι: go through

δι-έξ-ειμι, *aor.* διεξῆλθον: go through in detail, set forth, narrate, recount

δι-έρχομαι, *pf.* διελήλυθα: go through, set forth in detail, discuss

δι-ερωτάω: question in detail

δι-ηγέομαι, *fut.* διηγήσομαι, *aor.* διηγησάμην: narrate, tell (the) story

δι-ημερεύω (ἡμέρα): pass the day

διθύραμβος *m.*: dithyramb, a kind of choral lyric poem

δι-ισχῡρίζομαι, *aor.* διισχῡρισάμην (ἰσχυρός): insist, affirm confidently

δικάζω, *fut.* δικάσω, *aor.* ἐδίκασα, *aor. pass.* ἐδικάσθην: judge, decide

δίκαιος, -α, -ον (δίκη): just, right, righteous, fair, reasonable. δίκαιός εἰμι, it is just that I, I ought (cf. the Hibernian idiom, "You had a right to do it"). τὸ δίκαιον, justice

δικαιοσύνη *f.*: justice

δικαιότατος *sup. adj.*: most just

δικαιότερος *comp. adj.*: more just

δικαίως *adv.*: justly, with good reason

δικᾱνικός *adj.*: (pertaining to the courts), such as one hears in courts, wearisome

δικαστήριον *n.*: court of justice

δικαστής, -οῦ *m.* (δικάζω): judge

δίκη *f.*: suit at law, case, charge, judgment, justice

διό *conj.* (δι' ὅ): wherefore

δι-οίγω, *aor. pass. partic.* διοιχθέντες: open

δι-οικέω (οἶκος): administer, manage

δι-όλλῡμι, *aor.* διώλεσα: ruin, utterly destroy

δι-όμνῡμι, *aor.* διωμοσάμην: assert under oath, swear to

δι-ό-περ *conj.*: just because

δίς *adv.*: twice

διττός *adj.* (δύο): twofold, of two kinds, of two classes

διφθέρᾱ *f.* (diphtheria): hide, animal's skin, leather cloak (such as peasants wore)

διχά-δε *adv.*: in two parts, asunder

διώκω: pursue, follow

δοκέω, *fut.* δόξω, *aor.* ἔδοξα, *pf. pass.* δέδογμαι (δόξα, dogma): think, think good; seem, seem true, am thought, am reputed. ἔδοξέ μοι, I came to think. δεδογμένον, agreed, generally believed

δοκιμάζω, *aor. pass.* ἐδοκιμάσθην: prove, examine; receive to citizenship

δόξα *f.* (doxology, orthodox): reputation, glory, honor, opinion. παρὰ δόξαν (paradox), contrary to (my) real opinion

δοξάζω: opine, hold (an opinion)

δορά *f.* (δείρω, flay): skin, hide

δόσις, -εως *f.* (dose): gift

δουλεύω: am a slave, serve

δοῦλος *m.*: slave

δρᾶμα, -ατος *n.*: drama, theatrical play, spectacle

δραπετεύω: run away from (as a slave might)

δραχμή *f.*: drachma. An Athenian silver coin, worth about seventeen cents δράω (drama): do

δρῦς, gen. δρυός, f.: oak

δύναμαι: am able, can

δύναμις, -εως f.: power, might, strength

δυνατός adj.: strong, powerful, effectual, effective

δύο, gen. δυοῖν, numeral (duo): two

δυσ-μαθέστερος comp. adj. (μανθάνω): slower to learn

δύσμαι pl. f.: settings, setting

δυσ-τυχία f. (τύχη): misfortune

δυσ-χερής, -ές adj.: disagreeable, troublesome, hindrance

δύω, pf. δέδῦκα: sink, set (of the sun)

ἔα imv. of ἐάω as interjection: ah!, let it pass

ἑάλων aor. of ἁλίσκομαι: was captured, was overtaken

ἐάν = εἰ ἄν: if, with subjunctive

ἐάν τε . . . ἐάν τε: whether . . . or

ἑαυτοῦ, ἑαυτῷ, ἑαυτόν reflex. pron.: himself

ἑαυτῶν, ἑαυτοῖς reflex. pron.: themselves

ἐάω, fut. ἐάσω, aor. εἴᾱσα: permit, allow, disregard, dismiss. οὐκ ἐάω, forbid

ἑβδομήκοντα (ἑπτά): seventy

ἐγγυάομαι, aor. ἠγγυᾱσάμην: am surety, offer bonds

ἐγγύη f.: surety, bail

ἐγγυητής, -οῦ m.: surety, bondsman

ἐγγύς adv.: near, with genitive

ἐγγύτατα or ἐγγυτάτω sup. adv.: nearest, next

ἐγγυτέρω comp. adv.: nearer

ἐγείρω, aor. ἤγειρα: rouse, wake

ἐγ-καλέω: blame, censure, find fault, complain, accuse

ἐγ-καλύπτω, aor. mid. ἐνεκαλυψάμην, pf. ἐγκεκάλυμμαι: cover up, conceal; mid. cover my face

ἔγ-κλημα, -ατος n.: charge, accusation, complaint

ἐγ-κρατέστατος sup. adj.: with greatest self-control in

ἐγ-χωρεῖ impers.: it is possible, sc. to delay; there is still time

ἐγῷμαι: by crasis for ἐγὼ οἶμαι

ἐδεστέον: verbal adj. of ἐσθίω, eat

ἐθέλω, aor. ἠθέλησα: wish, desire, am willing, consent, am ready

ἐθίζω, pf. pass. εἴθισμαι (ἔθος): accustom, use

εἰ: if. εἰ δὲ μή, if not, otherwise. εἴ πέρ γε, at least if. εἴ τε . . . εἴ τε cond. part., whether . . . or. εἰ γάρ may introduce a wish

εἶδος, -εος n.: form, shape, appearance

εἶεν interj.: very well

εἰκάζω, aor. ᾔκασα: liken, compare

εἰκῇ adv.: at random, in chance order

εἰκός, -ότος n.: probable, reasonable. ὡς τὸ εἰκός, in all probability

εἰκότως adv.: with good reason, naturally

εἰκών, -όνος f. (icon): image, illustration, comparison, semblance

εἱμαρμένη f. pf. partic. (Μοῖρα): fated, Fate

εἰμί, impf. ἦ, inf. εἶναι, fut. ἔσομαι: am, exist. τῷ ὄντι, in truth. ἔστι ταῦτα, this is true. οὐκ ἔστιν ὅπως οὔ, it is not possible that not, surely

εἶμι, imv. ἴθι, inf. ἰέναι, partic. ἰών: go, come, will go. ἴθι is used as an interjection, Come!

εἶπον aor.: said, spoke

εἴρηκα pf. of φημί: have said, have spoken

εἰρημένα pf. partic. of φημί: said

εἰρωνεύομαι (irony): jest, dissemble

εἰς: into, as regards. εἰς ὑμᾶς, into your court, before you

εἷς, μία, ἕν numeral: one

εἰσ-άγω: lead in, introduce, bring in (to court), bring to trial εἴσ-ειμι: come in, enter

εἰσ-ηγέομαι: introduce, propose

εἰσ-ῆλθον: came in, was brought into court. (Used as passive of εἰσάγω.)

εἴσ-οδος f.: entrance, bringing in

εἰστήκει plpf. of ἵστημι: stood

εἰσ-φέρω: bring in, introduce

εἶτα adv.: then, and then

εἴωθα pf., plpf. εἰώθη (ἔθος): am wont, accustomed. εἰωθώς, accustomed

ἐκ, ἐξ, prep.: out of, from, as a result of. ἐκ παίδων, from childhood, while children ; ἐκ νέου, from youth up. ἐκ τούτων, from this, in the light of this

ἕκαστος adj.: each, every one

ἑκάστοτε adv.: at each time, on each occasion

ἑκάτερος adj.: each of two

ἐκ-βάλλω, aor. ἐξέβαλον: cast out, reject, throw overboard

ἔκ-γονος m.: offspring, child

ἐκεῖ adv.: there, yonder

ἐκεῖθεν adv.: thence, from there

ἐκεῖνος, -η, -ο pron.: that, yon

ἐκείνως adv.: in that way

ἐκεῖσε adv.: thither, there

ἐκ-καλύπτω, aor. ἐξεκάλυψα: uncover; mid. uncover (my) face

ἐκ-κλέπτω, aor. ἐξέκλεψα: steal away, steal out

ἐκκλησία f.: ecclesia, popular Assembly (of Athens)

ἐκκλησιαστής, -οῦ m.: ecclesiast, member of the Assembly

ἐκ-λέγω, aor. mid. ἐξελεξάμην: select, pick out

ἐκ-παιδεύω, aor. ἐξεπαίδευσα: educate, train up

ἐκ-πίνω, aor. ἐξέπιον: drink off, quaff

ἐκ-πλήττω, aor. ἐξέπληξα, pf. pass. ἐκπέπληγμαι: amaze, dismay, distract by fear; pass. am beside (my)self, am dazed

ἐκ-πολιορκέω, aor. pass. ἐξεπολιορκήθην: take by siege

ἐκ-τίνω, fut. ἐκτείσω, aor. ἐξέτεισα: pay (the fine) in full

ἐκτός adv.: outside, out

ἐκ-τρέφω, aor. ἐξέθρεψα, pass. ἐξετράφην: bring up, rear

ἐκ-τρίβω, aor. ἐξέτριψα: rub

Ἕκτωρ, -ορος m.: Hector, the mightiest defender of Troy. 28 c

ἐκ-φέρω, aor. mid. ἐξηνεγκάμην: carry out, carry forth

ἐκ-φεύγω, aor. ἐξέφυγον: escape, flee

ἐκ-χέω, pf. pass. ἐκκέχυμαι: pour out, cast out

ἑκών, -όντος adj.: willing, willingly, intentionally. With this, εἶναι is used loosely, so that ἑκὼν εἶναι does not differ materially from ἑκών. GMT. 780

ἐλάττων, -ον comp. adj.: less, of less consequence

ἐλάχιστος sup. adj.: least

ἔλεγχος m.: proof, test, account

ἐλέγχω, fut. ἐλέγξω, aor. ἤλεγξα: test, examine, prove, refute

ἐλεέω, aor. pass. ἐλεήθην (Kyrie eleison): pity, have mercy

ἐλεινός adj.: pitiful, of pity

ἔλεος m.: pity

ἐλευθερία f.: liberty, freedom

ἐλευθεριώτερον comp. adv.: more freely

ἐλεύθερος adj.: free

Ἑλληνίς, -ίδος f. adj.: of Greece, Hellenic

ἐλπίζω: hope

ἐλπίς, -ίδος f.: hope

ἐμαυτοῦ, ἐμαυτῷ, ἐμαυτόν reflexive pron.: myself

ἔμ-βραχυ adv. (brief): in short

ἐμμελῶς adv.: (in tune), suitably, reasonably. Nearly synonymous with ὀρθῶς. Its opposite is πλημμελῶς.

ἐμ-μένω, *fut.* ἐμμενῶ, *aor.* ἐνέμεινα: remain in, abide by

ἐμός, -ή, -όν *possess. pron.* (meus): my, mine, of me. ἡ ἐμὴ διαβολή, the prejudice against me

ἐμ-πίμπλημι, *pf.* ἐμπεπλήκᾱσιν: fill

ἐμ-πνέω: breathe, have breath, live

ἐμ-ποδών *adv.* (πούς): in the way, a hindrance

ἐμ-ποιέω: work in, do in, cause

ἔμ-προσθεν *adv.*: before, former. ἐν τοῖς ἔμπροσθεν, in the former part of my speech

ἔμ-φρων, -ον *adj.* (φρήν): possessed of his senses, with presence of mind, intelligent

ἐν *prep. with dative*: in, among, in the midst of. ἐν τοῖς (among these) *may strengthen a superlative, as* ἐν τοῖς βαρύτατα, with greatest sadness. 43 c. Cf. δόκιμος ὅμοια τῷ μάλιστα Hdt. vii. 118.

ἐν-αντία *and* ἐν-αντίον *adv.*: against, opposite, contrary, in the presence of. τοὐναντίον, just the opposite. ἐναντία λέγειν, contradict

ἐν-αντίος *adj.*: opposite, contrary

ἐναντιόω, *aor. pass. as mid.* ἠναντιώθην, *pf.* ἠναντίωμαι: oppose

ἐν-αργής, -ές *adj.*: clear, distinct, plain

ἐν-δεής, -ές (δέω): needy, in lack, deficient

ἐν-δείκνῡμι, *aor.* ἐνεδειξάμην: point out, indicate, show; indict, impeach. — ἔνδειξις was a form of indictment, usually laying information against one who discharged functions or exercised rights for which he was legally disqualified.

ἕνδεκα *numeral*: eleven. οἱ Ἕνδεκα, "the Eleven," had charge of the prisons of Athens, and the punishment of criminals. — Introd. § 57.

ἔνδο-θεν *adv.*: from within, within

ἔνδον *adv.*: within, in the inner room, at home

ἔν-ειμι: am in

ἕνεκα *improper prep.*: on account of, because

ἐν-ελίττω, *pf. pass.* ἐνείλιγμαι: wrap, roll up in

ἐν-έχομαι, *fut.* ἐνέξομαι: am held in, am liable to

ἐνθά-δε *adv.*: here

ἐνθέν-δε *adv.*: hence, from this

ἐνθουσιάζω (ἐν, θεός — enthusiasm): am possessed by the divinity, am inspired

ἐν-θῡμέομαι, *aor.* ἐνεθῡμήθην (θῡμός): ponder, reflect, consider in soul

ἐνιαυτός *m.*: year. κατ᾽ ἐνιαυτόν, yearly

ἔνι-οι (ἔστιν οἵ, *cf.* sunt qui) *adj.*: some

ἐνί-οτε *adv.*: sometimes, at times

ἐν-νοέω, *aor.* ἐνενόησα (νοῦς): notice, observe, consider

ἐν-οικέω, *fut.* ἐνοικήσω· dwell in, inhabit

ἐν-σκευάζομαι (σκευή): dress up in, array (my)self in

ἐνταῦθα *adv.*: there, here, at this point

ἐνταυθοῖ *adv.*: here, hither

ἐν-τείνω, *aor.* ἐν-έτεινα: stretch in, put into verse

ἐντεῦθεν *adv.*: thence, from this, as a result of this

ἐντός *adv.*: inside, within

ἐν-τρέπομαι: regard, respect, am abashed before, — *with gen.*

ἐν-τυγχάνω, *aor.* ἐνέτυχον, *pf.* ἐντετύχηκα: happen upon, fall in with, meet

ἐν-ύπνιον (ὕπνος) *n.*: dream

ἐξ *prep.*: out of. See ἐκ.

ἐξ-άγω, *fut.* ἐξάξω, *aor.* ἐξήγαγον: lead forth, take out

ἐξ-αιρέω, *aor. mid.* ἐξειλόμην: take out of, remove

ἐξ-αμαρτάνω, aor. ἐξήμαρτον: err, make a mistake

ἐξ-αν-ίστημι, aor. ἐξανέστην: cause to rise; aor. arose and went out

ἐξ-απατάω, fut. ἐξαπατήσω, aor. pass. ἐξηπατήθην, verbal ἐξαπατητέον (ἀπάτη): deceive, beguile

ἔξ-ειμι, verbal ἐξιτητέον: come out, go out

ἔξ-ειμι: see ἔξεστι.

ἐξ-ελαύνω, fut. ἐξελῶ, aor. ἐξήλασα: drive out (of the city), banish

ἐξ-ελέγχω, aor. ἐξήλεγξα, fut. pass. ἐξελεγχθήσομαι (ἔλεγχος): show up, refute, convict

ἐξ-εργάζομαι (ἔργον): work out, accomplish, perform

ἐξ-έρχομαι, aor. ἐξῆλθον: come out, go forth. ἐξελθών, in exile

ἔξ-εστι, partic. ἐξόν, impers.: it is permitted, it is granted, it is possible. οἷς ἔξεστι, who may. ἐξόν, though it was possible

ἐξ-ετάζω, fut. ἐξετάσω, aor. ἐξήτασα: examine, probe, scrutinize

ἐξέτασις, -εως f.: examination, investigation

ἐξεταστικός: skilled in examining

ἐξ-ευρίσκω, aor. ἐξηῦρον: find out, discover

ἐξ-ιτητέον: verbal of ἔξειμι

ἐξ-όν: acc. abs., it being permitted. Cf. ἔξεστι.

ἐξ-ουσία f. (ἔξεστι): liberty, permission

ἔξω-θεν adv.: without, outside

ἔοικα pf.: seem, am like, am likely

ἑορτή f.: festival, feast

ἐπ-ᾴδω (ἀείδω, ode): repeat as a charm

ἐπ-αινέω, aor. ἐπῄνεσα: praise, commend

ἔπ-αινος m.: praise, approval

ἐπ-αΐω: understand

ἐπ-ακολουθέω: follow, accompany

ἐπ-άν-ειμι: come up, move up

ἐπ-εγείρω, aor. ἐπήγειρα: rouse, waken

ἐπεί or ἐπειδή conj.: since, because; when

ἐπείγομαι: hasten, am in haste

ἐπειδάν = ἐπειδὴ ἄν: when

ἐπειδή conj.: since; when

ἔπ-ειμι: come (on), approach. ὁ ἐπιών, the next

ἔπ-ειτα conj.: then, next, secondly. ὁ ἔπειτα βίος, the rest of (my) life

ἐπ-ερωτάω: ask, inquire

ἐπ-έχω, fut. ἐπισχήσω, aor. ἐπέσχον: check, cease from, restrain, wait; mid. hold to (one's lips), stop (one's ears)

ἐπί prep.: (1) with gen., at. ἐπὶ τῶν τραπεζῶν, at the money-changers' tables. ἐπὶ στρατείας, on a campaign. ἐφ' ἵππου, on horseback. (2) With acc., to, for, before, against. ἐπὶ δικαστήριον, before a court of justice. ἐπ' αὐτὸ τοῦτο, for this very purpose. ἐπὶ τὰ γελοιότερα, to raise a laugh. (3) With dat., at, over, after. ἐπὶ Δηλίῳ, at Delium. ἐπὶ τούτοις, after these things, on these terms. ἐπὶ πόσῳ, at what price? ἐπὶ τούτῳ, on this condition, for this purpose, over this. τὸ ἐπὶ τούτῳ, the thing after this, i.e. the next question. Of end, ἐπὶ διαβολῇ τῇ ἐμῇ, to create a prejudice against me

ἐπι-βλέπω, aor. ἐπέβλεψα: glance at, look at

ἐπι-γελάω, aor. ἐπεγέλασα: laugh at

Ἐπιγένης, -ους m.: Epigenes. 33 e, 59 b. Son of Antiphon of Cephisia

ἐπι-δείκνῡμι, aor. ἐπέδειξα: display, set forth, make clear

ἐπι-δημέω (δῆμος): am in town, stay at home

ἐπι-εικέστατος sup. adj.: most reasonable, best

ἐπι-εικέστερος *comp.* ‚'*j.*: more reasonable, too good

ἐπι-εικής, -ές *adj.*: reasonable

ἐπι-εικῶς *adv.*: reasonably, considerably

ἐπι-θῡμέω, *aor.* ἐπεθύμησα: desire

ἐπι-θῡμίᾱ *f.*: desire, longing

ἐπι-κελεύω: urge on, incite

ἐπί-κωμῳδέω (comedy): ridicule, make fun of

ἐπι-λανθάνομαι, *aor.* ἐπελαθόμην (λήθη): forget

ἐπι-λησμονέστερος *comp. adj.* (λήθη): more forgetful

ἐπι-λύομαι: free, release, save

ἐπι-μελέομαι *and* ἐπι-μέλομαι, *fut.* ἐπιμελήσομαι, *aor.* ἐπεμελήθην: care for

ἐπι-νοέω: think of, have in mind

ἐπι-ορκέω: commit perjury, forswear (my)self, break (my) oath

ἐπι-πέμπω, *aor.* ἐπέπεμψα: send to

ἐπι-σκοπέω, *aor.* ἐπεσκεψάμην: examine, consider

ἐπίσταμαι, *impf.* ἠπιστάμην: know, understand, have skill in, am familiar with

ἐπι-στατέω: stand over, am master

ἐπιστάτης *m.* (ἵστημι): overseer, master; presiding officer (of the Assembly)

ἐπι-στέλλω, *aor.* ἐπέστειλα (epistle): direct, charge

ἐπιστήμη *f.*: knowledge, science

ἐπιστήμων, -ονος *adj.*: acquainted with, skilled in, *with gen.*

ἐπι-σχόμενος: *aor. partic. of* ἐπέχω

ἐπι-τάττω: enjoin, command, order

ἐπι-τελέομαι (τέλος): perform

ἐπιτήδειος *m.*: connection, friend

ἐπιτηδές *adv.*: expressly, on purpose

ἐπιτήδευμα, -ατος *n.*: pursuit, occupation

ἐπιτηδεύω, *aor. partic.* ἐπιτηδεύσας: pursue, follow, practice

ἐπι-τίθημι, *aor.* ἐπέθην, *mid.* ἐπεθέμην: place upon, put upon ; *mid.* set upon

ἐπι-τρέπω: permit, allow, commit

ἐπι-τυγχάνω, *aor.* ἐπέτυχον (τύχη): chance upon, occur to

ἐπι-φθονώτερος *comp. adj.*: arousing too much envy

ἐπι-χειρέω, *fut.* ἐπιχειρήσω, *aor.* ἐπεχείρησα, *verbal* ἐπιχειρητέον (χείρ): attempt, undertake, endeavor, try

ἐπι-χωριάζω (χώρα): visit, go to

ἐπι-χώριος *adj.*: of the place. οἱ ἐπιχώριοι, the townspeople

ἐπι-ψηφίζω, *aor.* ἐπεψήφισα: put the question to vote

ἕπομαι (sequor): follow

ἐπ-ονείδιστος *adj. of two endings* (ὄνειδος): reproached, shameful, disgraceful

ἔπος, -εος *n.*: word. ὡς ἔπος εἰπεῖν, so to speak, as one may say ; almost, — *qualifying a strong statement*

ἑπτά *numeral* (septem): seven

ἐργάζομαι, *fut.* ἐργάσομαι, *aor.* εἰργασάμην, *pf.* εἴργασμαι (ἔργον): work, do, make

ἔργον (work): work, deed, act, fact

ἔρδω, *Epic aor.* ἔρεξε: do

ἐρευνάω: search out, inquire after

ἔρημος *adj.*: deserted, desolate, separated from. δίκη ἐρήμη, a suit which goes by default, undefended

ἐρί-βωλος *adj.*: fertile

Ἑρμογένης *m.*: Hermogenes. 59 b; Xen. *Mem.* iv. 8. 4. Son of Hipponicus, and brother of the rich Callias

ἑρμο-γλυφεῖον *n.* (Ἑρμῆς): statuary's shop, where images of Hermes and other gods were made and sold

ἔρομαι, *impf.* ἠρόμην, *fut.* ἐρήσομαι: ask, inquire

ἐρρωμένως *adv.*: stoutly, vigorously

ἐρρῶσθαι *pf. pass. inf. of* ῥώννυμι: to be strong, "take care of (him)self." A familiar word (ἔρρωσο) on parting

ἔρχομαι, *aor.* ἦλθον: come, go

ἐρῶ *fut.*: I will say, — *followed by two accs., one of the person, the other of the thing said*

ἐρωτάω: ask, inquire of

ἐρωτικῶς *adv.*: amorously

ἐσθίω, *verbal* ἐδεστέον (edo): eat

ἐσκεδασμένα: scattered, *pf. pass. of* σκεδάννυμι

ἑσπέρᾱ *f.* (vesper): evening

ἔστε *rel. adv.*: as long as

ἐστεμμένη: *pf. pass. of* στέφω, crown

ἐστήξοι: would stand, *fut. pf. of* ἵστημι

ἔστιν ὅτε: (at) some times. 62 a

ἔσχατος *adj.*: extreme, the last

ἑταῖρος *m.*: companion, comrade, partisan

ἕτερος *adj.*: one or other of two, other, different, second. ἕτερος μέν, . . . ἕτερος δέ, one, . . . another

ἔτι *adv.*: besides, still, further, in addition, again

ἕτοιμος *adj.* (*with Homeric accent,* ἑτοῖμος): ready, prepared, in readiness

ἔτος, -εος *n.* (vetus): year

εὖ *adv.*: well. εὖ λέγεις, you say what I am glad to hear; good news! εὖ ποιεῖν, benefit

εὐ-αρίθμητος *adj.* (ἀριθμός): easily numbered, few in number

εὐ-δαιμονέστερος *comp. adj.*: happier, more fortunate

εὐ-δαιμονίᾱ *f.*: happiness, good fortune, joy

εὐ-δαιμονίζω, *aor.* ηὐδαιμόνισα: esteem happy. Cf. μακαρίζω.

εὐ-δαίμων, -ονος *adj.*: of happy divinity, happy, fortunate

εὐ-δοκιμέω: am held in high esteem, am honored

εὐ-δοκιμώτατος *sup. adj.*: most renowned

εὐ-ειδής, -ές *adj.*: fine-looking, comely

εὐ-έλεγκτος: easy to be tested, easily proved

εὔ-ελπις, -ιδος *adj.*: filled with good hope, hopeful

εὐ-εργεσίᾱ *f.*: benefit, good deed

εὐ-εργετέω, *pf. pass.* εὐεργέτημαι benefit. εὐεργέτηταί τι, he has received something (from me), I have done something for him

εὐ-εργέτης, -ου *m.* (ἔργον): benefactor, well-doer

Εὔηνος, -ου: Euenus (of Paros). 20 D, 60 d. A sophist and poet of no great distinction

εὐθέως *or* εὐθύς *adv.*: straightway, at once

Εὐκλείδης, -ου *m.*: Euclid (of Megara). 59 c. (Not the great mathematician.)

εὐ-κόλως *adv.*: with good temper, blithely

εὐ-λαβέομαι (λαμβάνω): am on my guard, am cautious

εὐ-λόγως *adv.*: reasonably. εὐλόγως ἔχει, it is reasonable

εὐ-μενῶς *adv.*: graciously, kindly

εὐ-νομέομαι (νόμος): have good laws

εὐ-ορκέω: keep (my) oath

εὑρίσκω, *fut.* εὑρήσω, *aor.* ηὗρον (eureka!): find

εὐ-σεβέστατος *sup. adj.*: most pious

εὐ-σεβέω: act piously

εὐ-σεβής, -ές *adj.*: pious

εὐ-τελής, -ές *adj.*: cheap, easily bought

εὐ-τυχής, -ές *adj.*: fortunate, happy

εὐ-φημίᾱ *f.*: silence, peace

εὐ-φραίνω (φρήν): cheer

εὐ-χερῶς *adv.*: easily

εὔχομαι, *aor.* ηὐξάμην: pray, vow

εὐ-ωχέομαι · feast

εὐ-ωχίᾱ *f.*: feast

ἐφ-άπτομαι : touch, feel of

ἐφ-εξῆς adv.: in order, one after another

ἐφ-ίημι : permit, allow

ἐφ-ίστημι, aor. ἐπέστην : set before ; aor. took (my) stand before

ἐφ' ᾧτε (ὅs) as conj.: on condition that

ἐχθρός m.: (personal) enemy

ἐχρῆν (χρὴ ἦν, χρῆν, with an inorganic augment prefixed): it were fitting

ἔχω, fut. ἕξω, aor. ἔσχον, pf. ἔσχηκα: have, possess, hold, am able. ἔχει with adv. = εἰμί with pred. adj.; as ἔχει οὕτως, so it is, is in this position. ὥσπερ ἔχω ἔχειν, to be as I am. Inceptive (aor.) ἔσχε, received, and (pf.) ἔσχηκα, have received. οὐκ ἔχω, do not know

ἔωθεν adv.: at dawn, early in the morning, from the dawn

ἑωθινός m. adj.: early morning

ἕως, ἕω f.: dawn, morning

ἕως conj.: until, as long as

ζάω, inf. ζῆν: live

ζεῦγος, -εος n.: (span), four-horse chariot

ζημιάω : punish

ζητέω, aor. ἐζήτησα : seek into, investigate, search out

ζήτησις, -εως f.: search, inquiry, investigation

ζῷον n. (zoölogy): living creature, animal

ἤ : either, or. Or sometimes introduces a question, as **26 b**, **36 b**

ἤ : than, after a comparative

ἦ : mere sign of a question, at its head

ἦ : impf. of εἰμί, am, or of ἠμί, say

ἦ μήν particles: in very truth, indeed

ᾗ rel. adv. (ᾗς): in what way

ᾖα : impf. of εἶμι, go

ἡβάω, aor. ἥβησα (Hebe): am in young manhood, aor. came to young manhood

ἡγέομαι, fut. ἡγήσομαι, aor. ἡγησάμην : consider, believe, think

ἡδέως adv. (ἡδύς): sweetly, gladly, pleasantly. ἡδέως ἂν διαλεχθείην, I should like to talk

ἤδη adv.: already, before now, now, at once

ἤδη plpf. as impf. (οἶδα): knew

ἥδιστος sup. adj.: sweetest, most delightful, with greatest pleasure

ἡδίων, -ον comp. adj.: pleasanter

ἥδομαι, aor. ἥσθην: am pleased

ἡδονή f.: pleasure, enjoyment

ἡδύς, -εῖα, -ύ adj.: pleasant

ἥκιστα adv.: least of all

ἥκω, fut. ἥξω: have come, am come, come, return

Ἠλεῖος adj.: Elean, of Elis (in western Peloponnesus)

ἠλίθιος adj.: simple, silly

ἡλικίᾱ f.: age, time of life

ἡλικιώτης, -ου m.: contemporary, of the same age

ἥλιος m.: sun

ἦμαρ, -ατος n. (ἡμέρα): day. Homeric word. **44 b**

ἡμέρᾱ f.: day

ἡμέτερος adj. (ἡμεῖς): our

ἠμί, impf. ἦν (cf. ait): say

ἡμί-θεος m.: demigod

ἡμί-ονος m.: (half-ass), mule

ἠμφι-εσμένος : clad. See ἀμφιέννυμι.

ἠνέχθην : aor. pass. of φέρω, bring

ἡνίκα rel. adv.: when, at what time

ἡνι-οχέω (ἔχω): (hold the reins), drive

Ἥρᾱ f.: Hera (Juno)

ἠρέμα adv.: quietly

ἥρως, -ωος m. (hero): demigod

Ἡσίοδος m.: Hesiod, author of the Theogony and Works and Days. **41 a**

ἡσυχῇ adv.: quietly
ἡσυχίᾱ f.: peace, quiet. ἡσυχίαν ἄγω, keep quiet
ἤ-τοι . . . ἤ: either . . . or
ἤτρον n.: abdomen, groin
ἡττάομαι, pf. ἥττημαι: am inferior to, am overcome by
ἧττον comp. adv.: less, to a smaller degree
ἥττων,-ον comp. adj.: weaker, worse, less
ἠχή f. (echo): sound, noise

θάλπος, -εος n.: warmth
θάνατος m.: death. περὶ θανάτου, in a case of life or death
θάπτω: bury
θαρραλέος adj.(θάρσος, dare): confident, in good cheer, cheerful
θαρρέω (dare): am of good cheer, have no fear
θάτερα or θάτερον (τὸ ἕτερον) n.: one or other, either; the other (than well), i.e. harm
θᾶττον comp. adv.: more swiftly, sooner
θάττων, -ονος adj. comp. of ταχύς: swift, quick
θαῦμα, -ατος n.: wonder, admiration
θαυμάζω, aor. ἐθαύμασα (θαῦμα, θέα): wonder, marvel, am surprised
θαυμάσιος adj.: wonderful, strange
θαυμασίως adv.: strangely
θαυμασιώτερος adj.: more wonderful
θαυμαστός adj.: strange, admirable, marvelous good
θαυμαστότατος sup. adj.: strangest
Θεάγης, -ους m.: Theages. 33 e
θεάομαι, aor. ἐθεασάμην: observe, see
θεῖος adj. (θεός): of the gods, divine
θειότατος sup. adj.: most divine
θέμις, -ιτος f.: divine right, according to divine law, Latin fas
θεμιτός adj.: according to divine will, holy

Θεό-δοτος m.: Theodotus. 33 e
Θεοζοτίδης, -ου m.: Theozotides. 33 e
θεό-μαντις, -εως m.: seer, inspired prophet
θεός m. or f.: god, goddess, divinity
θεραπείᾱ f.: care
θέρος, -ους n. (thermometer): summer
Θέτις, -ιδος f.: Thetis, goddess of the sea; wife of Peleus and mother of Achilles. 28 c
Θετταλίᾱ f.: Thessaly. 45 c
θέω: run
θεωρίᾱ f. (θεάομαι): sacred embassy. ἐπὶ θεωρίᾳ, to a festival
Θήβαζε adv.: to Thebes
Θηβαῖος adj.: Theban, of Thebes
θηρίον: wild beast
Θησεύς, -έως m.: Theseus, mythical king of Athens. 58 a
(θνήσκω), pf. τέθναα and τέθνηκα: die; pf. am dead, inf. death, being dead. ὁ τεθνεώς, the dead man
θόλος f.: Rotunda, the seat of government of the Thirty Tyrants at Athens
θορυβέω, aor. ἐθορύβησα, pf. pass. τεθορύβημαι (θόρυβος): make a turmoil, clamor, raise a disturbance; pass. am thrown into confusion
θρέψομαι: fut. mid. of τρέφω, bring up
θρηνέω: sing a dirge, wail
θυρ-ωρός m.: door-keeper, porter
θυσίᾱ f.: sacrifice
θύω: sacrifice
θωπεύω: fawn upon (as a slave), cajole, flatter

ἰᾱτρός m.: physician
ἰδίᾳ fem. dat. as adv.: in private, privately
ἰδιωτεύω: work as a private man
ἰδιώτης, -ου (idiot): private man, ordinary man
ἱερόν n.: temple, sanctuary

ἱκανός adj.: sufficient, adequate

ἱκανῶς adv.: sufficiently, fully, satisfactorily

ἱκανώτατος sup. adj.: most able

ἱκετεία f. (ἱκέτης): supplication, entreaty

ἱκνέομαι, aor. ἱκόμην: come to, reach

ἵλεως, nom. pl. ἵλεῳ adj.: gracious(ly), cheerful(ly)

ἱμάτιον n.: garment, cloak, pl. raiment

ἵνα adv.: where

ἵνα final conj.: in order that. ἵνα τί (sc. γένηται), why, wherefore? GMT. 331

Ἱππίᾱς, -ου: Hippias, a noted Sophist of Elis. 19 e. Introd. § 12

ἱππικός adj. as n. (ἵππος): belonging to horses, horse man

Ἱππό-νῑκος, -ου: Hipponīcus, a rich Athenian. 20 a

ἵππος m.: horse

ἴσᾱσιν: 3 pl. of οἶδα, know

Ἰσθμός f.: Isthmus, sc. of Corinth, where the Isthmian Games were held. 52 b

ἴσος adj.: equal. ἐξ ἴσου, on an equality, on equal terms

ἵστημι, 1 aor. ἔστησα, 2 aor. ἔστην, pf. ἔστηκα, fut. pf. ἑστήξω (stο): set, stand; weigh; 2 aor. and pf. system intrans. stand, stop. ὃς τὰ ὄμματα ἔστησεν, his eyes were set

ἰσχῡρός adj.: strong, powerful

ἰσχῡρότατος sup. adj.: strongest

ἰσχύς, -ύος f.: strength, power

ἰσχύω: am strong, have force

ἴσως adv.: (equally), possibly, perhaps, very likely

ἰτέον: verbal adj. of εἶμι, go

ἴττω: Boeotian form of ἴστω, imv. of οἶδα, know, am witness

ἴτω: imv. of εἶμι, go

ἴχνος, -εος n.: step, trace, pl. track, path

κἀγώ: by crasis for καὶ ἐγώ

καθ-άπτομαι: lay hold of, reproach

καθαρεύω: am pure, am clean

καθ-έζομαι: sit down

καθ-εύδω: sleep, slumber

καθ-ῆμαι: sit, sit idle; am established, am appointed

καθ-ίημι, aor. καθῆκα: let down

καθ-ίστημι: establish, set, appoint, bring

καθ-ομο-λογέω: grant, concede, allow

καί conj.: and, even, also, too. καὶ δή καί, and in particular, and what is more. καί . . . καί, both . . . and. After a word of likeness, καί may be translated as: ὅμοιος καί, such as

καινός adj.: new, strange

καινότερος comp. adj.: very new

καί-περ conj.: even. Esp. with concessive participles, — καίπερ ὄντες καὶ οὗτοι, although these too are

καιρός m.: favorable time, fit time, season. ἐν καιρῷ, opportunely

καί-τοι part.: and yet

κακίᾱ f.: evil, wickedness, vice, cowardice

κακο-δαιμονίᾱ f.: ill-fortune

κακός adj.: bad, evil, wicked; coward

κακουργέω (ἔργον): harm, injure

καλέω, aor. ἐκάλεσα, pf. pass. κέκλημαι: call

Καλλίᾱς, -ου: Callias, a rich Athenian. 20 a

καλλι-επέω, pf. pass. κεκαλλιέπημαι (κάλλος, ἔπος): express beautifully, adorn artistically

κάλλιον comp. adv.: better

κάλλιστος sup. adj.: most honorable

καλλόνομαι (κάλλος): pride myself

καλλ-ωπίζομαι (ὤψ): put on airs, act proudly

καλός adj.: beautiful, excellent, honorable, noble. καλόν, a fine thing καλῶς *adv.*: well, excellently. καλῶς λέγεις, quite right!

κανθήλιος *adj.*: pack (asses), sumpter. 221 e

καρδίᾱ *f.* (cor): heart

καρπόομαι, *fut.* καρπώσομαι (καρπός, harvest): reap

καρτερέω, *aor.* ἐκαρτέρησα: am strong, endure

καρτέρησις, -εως *f.*: endurance

καρτερός *adj.*: strong, mighty

κατάprep.: withgen., against. κατ' ἐμαυτοῦ, against myself. With acc., according to. κατὰ τούτους, after their pattern. κατὰ τὸν θεόν, according to the oracle of the god. κατ' ἀρχάς, at the beginning. κατὰ Θετταλίαν, through Thessaly, in Thessaly. καθ' ὅσον, as far as

κατα-γέλαστος *adj.*: laughed at, a laughing-stock, ridiculous

κατα-γελάω, *aor.* κατεγέλασα (γέλως): laugh at, deride

κατά-γελως, -ωτος *m.*: mockery, crowning absurdity

κατα-γηράσκω, *aor.* κατεγήρᾱσα: grow old, go down to old age

κατα-γιγνώσκω, *fut.* καταγνώσομαι: condemn, think to (one's) disadvantage

κατα-δαρθάνω, *aor.* κατέδαρθον: sleep

κατα-δέομαι, *aor.* κατεδεήθην: beg, beseech, supplicate, overpersuade

κατά-δηλος *adj.*: manifest, evident

κατά-κειμαι: lie down, recline

κατα-κλάω, *aor.* κατέκλασα: break down

κατα-κλίνω, *aor. pass.* κατεκλίνην: recline, lie down

κατα-λαμβάνω, *fut.* καταλήψομαι: take, come upon, seize, find

κατα-λείπω, *aor.* κατέλιπον: leave behind; *mid.* reserve

κατα-λύω, *aor. pass.* κατελύθην: (loose), overthrow

κατα-νοέω, *aor.* κατενόησα: observe, perceive

κατ-αράομαι: curse

κατα-σκεδάννῡμι, *aor.* κατεσκέδασα: scatter abroad, spread

κατα-φρονέω: despise, contemn

κατα-χαρίζομαι: give as a favor

κατα-ψηφίζομαι, *fut.* καταψηφιοῦμαι, *aor.* κατεψηφισάμην: vote against, vote for (my) condemnation

κατ-έρχομαι, *aor.* κατῆλθον: come down, return from exile

κατ-έχω: hold down, check, restrain, possess

κατηγορέω, *fut.* κατηγορήσω, *aor.* κατηγόρησα, *pf.* κατηγόρηκα, *pass.* κατηγόρημαι (κατήγορος): accuse, make charges, with genitive. ἃ κατηγόρουν, the charges which they brought

κατηγορίᾱ *f.*: accusation, charge

κατήγορος (ἀγορά): accuser

κατ-ορύττω: sink in the earth, bury

κάω (καίω, caustic): burn

Κέβης, -ητος *m.*: Cebes (of Thebes). 45 b, 59 c

Κεῖος *adj.*: Cean, of (the island) Ceos. 19 e

κελεύω, *aor.* ἐκέλευσα: bid, order, command

κέν (enclitic): epic modal adv. equiv. to Attic ἄν

κερδαίνω, *fut.* κερδανῶ: gain

κέρδος, -εος *n.*: gain, profit, advantage

κηδεστής, -οῦ *m.*: connection by marriage

κήδομαι: care for

κηλέω: charm, bewitch, beguile

Κηφῑσιεύς, -έως *m.*: Cephisian, of the deme Cephisia (at the head-waters of the river Cephisus). 33 e

κινδῡνεύω, *fut.* κινδῡνεύσω, *aor.* ἐκινδύνευσα: am in danger, meet danger, run a risk; may, very likely am

κίνδῡνος m.: danger,risk,chance,hazard
κῑνέω, aor. pass. as mid. ἐκῑνήθην: move, stir
Κλαζομένιος adj.: of Clazomenae (in Asia Minor, not far from Smyrna). 26 d
κλάω: wail, mourn, lament
Κλεόμβροτος m.: Cleombrotus. 59 c
κλεπτίστατος sup. adj. (κλέπτης): most thievish
κλίνη f.: couch, bed
κνήμη f.: lower leg
κοινῇ fem. dat. as adv.: in common with, together
κοινός adj.: common, public. τὸ κοινόν, the community
κοινωνέω: am a partner (κοινωνός), am in agreement, agree
κόλασις, -εως f.: chastisement, punishment
κολοόω: lop off, trim off, cut off, suppress
κομιδῇ fem. dat. as adv.: very, absolutely, exactly
κομίζω, pf. κεκόμικα: bring, provide
κόπτομαι: beat (my)self, beat (my) breast, mourn
κορυβαντιάω (Corybantes): am possessed, have the spirit of a Corybant. The Corybantes were priests of Phrygian Cybele, whose orgiastic rites were accompanied by dances and deafening music.
κορυφή f.: crest, head
κορωνίς, -ίδος f. adj.: curved, beaked
κοσμέω, aor. ἐκόσμησα, pf. pass. κεκόσμημαι (κόσμος): order, arrange carefully, adorn
κοσμιώτατος sup. adj.: most orderly, most law-abiding
κόσμος m.: (order), array, ornament; cosmos, universe, world
κρᾶσις, -εως f. (κεράννυμι): mixing, combination, union

κρατέω (κράτος): am strong, surpass, outdo
κράτιστος sup. adj. (κράτος): best
κρείττων, -ον comp. adj. (κράτος): stronger, better
Κρήτη f.: Crete. 52 e
κρίνω, aor. ἔκρῑνα: judge, try, decide
κρίσις, -εως f. (crisis): decision, judgment
Κριτίᾱς, -ου m.: Critias, son of Callaeschrus, of an old and prominent Athenian family, — chief leader of the Thirty. He fell in battle against the democracy in 404 B.C. Xen. Mem. i. 2. 12
Κριτό-βουλος: Critobūlus. 33 e, 59 b
Κρίτων, -ωνος: Crito, an old friend of Socrates. 33 d
κρούω, aor. ἔκρουσα: strike, smite, slap
κρύσταλλος m. (crystal): ice
κτάομαι, pf. κέκτημαι: acquire, pf. possess
κτῆμα, -ατος n.: possession
Κτήσιππος m.: Ctesippus. 59 b
κτῆσις, -εως f.: acquisition, possession
κυβερνάω (guberno): steer, command a ship
κύλιξ, -ικος f.: cup, drinking-cup
κύριος adj.: authoritative, supreme, enforced. οἱ κύριοι, those who have charge
κυών, gen. κυνός, m. (canis): dog
κωλύω: prevent, hinder
κωμῳδία f. (ᾠδή): comedy
κωμῳδοποιός adj. as noun: comic poet

λαγνείᾱ f.: wantonness, lust
Λακεδαίμων, -ονος f.: Lacedaemon. 52 e
λαμβάνω, aor. ἔλαβον: take, receive, attain, secure, catch
λανθάνω, aor. ἐλάθομεν, pf. λέληθα: escape (my) notice, elude

λατρείᾱ f. (idolatry): service

Λάχης, -ητος m.: Laches, one of the commanders of the first expedition sent by Athens to Sicily, 427 B.C. 221 a

λέγω, aor. εἶπον or ἔλεξε, pf. εἴρηκα (verbum), aor. pass. ἐλέχθην: say, speak, tell, mean. μέγα λέγω, utter a proud word. οὐδὲν λέγω, talk nonsense

λείπω, aor. ἔλιπον, verbal λειπτέον: leave, forsake, abandon

λέξις, -εως f. (λέγω): speaking, manner of speech

Λεοντῖνος adj.: Leontine, of Leontini (in Sicily, on the east coast, north of Syracuse)

λευκός adj.: white

Λέων, -ωντος m.: Leon (of Salamis), an upright and well-known citizen, put to death by the Thirty Tyrants. 32 c

λίᾱν adv.: exceedingly, very

λίθος, -ου m. (lithography): stone

λογίζομαι: calculate, reckon, consider

λογιστικός: skilled in calculation

λόγος m. (λέγω): word, statement, discussion, argument, talk, saying, story, speech, matter; doctrine, principle, cause, reason. λόγους ποιεῖσθαι, speak, talk

λοιδορέω: revile, abuse, rail at

λοιπός adj. (λείπω): remaining, rest of

λουτρόν n.: bath

λούω, fut. mid. λούσομαι, aor. ἐλουσάμην, pf. λέλουμαι: wash, bathe

Λύκων, -ωνος m.: Lyco, one of the accusers of Socrates. 23 e; Introd. § 36

λῡπέω: pain, grieve, trouble

λύπη f.: pain, grief

λῡπηρός adj.: painful

Λῡσανίᾱς, -ου m.: Lysanias. 33 e

λῦσι-τελεῖ impers.: it is well, it is of advantage, it is profitable

λύω, pf. pass. λέλυμαι: loose, release

λωβάομαι, fut. λωβήσομαι: ruin

λῷστος adj.: best

μά asseverative particle, with acc., implying a negation: (no) by. μὰ Δία, no, by Zeus

μάθημα, -ατος n.: instruction, teaching, lesson, matter of learning

μάθησις, -εως f. (μανθάνω): learning, teaching

μαθητής, -οῦ m.: pupil, scholar

μαίνομαι (mania): am mad

μάκαρ, -ος adj.: blessed, happy

μακαρίζω, aor. ἐμακάρισα (μάκαρ): esteem blessed, count happy

μακάριος adj.: blessed, happy

μάλα adv.: very

μάλιστα superl. adv.: especially, most of all, certainly. μάλιστα μέν, if possible. πηνίκα μάλιστα; about what time?

μᾶλλον comp. adv.: rather. παντὸς μᾶλλον, by all means, absolutely, above all

μανθάνω, aor. ἔμαθον: learn, am taught, get an idea, understand

μανίᾱ f. (mania): madness

μαντείᾱ f.: oracle, response of the god

μαντεῖον n.: oracle, oracular response

μαντεύομαι, fut. μαντεύσομαι, aor. ἐμαντευσάμην (μάντις): consult the oracle, inquire of the oracle, predict, deliver an oracle

μαντική f. (strictly, adj. sc. φωνή or τέχνη): prophetic power, prophecy, divination

Μαρσύᾱς m.: Marsyas. A Phrygian follower of Bacchus, who with his flute vied with Apollo's lyre, and was flayed by him. 215 b. Cf. Xen. An. i. 2. 8

μαρτυρέω, fut. μαρτυρήσω: am witness, testify

μάρτυς, -υρος m. (martyr): witness

μάτην adv.: in vain, idly

μάχη f.: fight, battle

μάχομαι, fut. μαχοῦμαι: fight, contend, battle

Μέγαρά-δε adv.: to Megara, a town on the coast, about half way between Athens and Corinth (strictly, Μέγαρα is here acc., with the suffix δε, towards)

Μεγαρό-θεν adv.: from Megara

μέγας, μεγάλη, μέγα (much): great, much, deep. μέγα λέγειν, utter a proud word

μέγεθος, -εος n.: greatness, size, bulk

μέγιστος superl. adj.: greatest

μεθύω (mead, a-methyst): am drunk

μείζων, -ον comp. adj.: greater

μειράκιον n.: lad, youth, boy, stripling

μέλει, partic. μέλον, aor. ἐμέλησεν, pf. μεμέληκεν, impers.: it is a care, with gen. ὧν οὐδὲν τούτῳ ἐμέλησεν, for which he had no care. μέλον γέ σοι, you being interested in the matter

μελετάω, aor. ἐμελέτησα: practice, exercise

μελέτη f.: practice, study

Μέλητος m.: Meletus, the chief accuser of Socrates. 19 c; Introd. § 36

μέλλω: am about to, will, shall, — used in forming a periphrastic future

μέλος, -εος n. (melody): tune

μέμνημαι, pf. of μιμνήσκω: remember

μέμφομαι, fut. μέμψομαι: blame, find fault

Μενέξενος m.: Menexenus. 59 b

μεντἄν: for μέντοι ἄν

μέν-τοι adversative adv.: however, but, in truth

μένω, aor. ἔμεινα: remain, am unchanged

μεριμνάω: have anxious thought

μέρος, -εος n.: part, portion. τὸ σὸν μέρος, so far as you are concerned

μεσημβρία f. (ἡμέρα): mid-day, noon

μετά prep.: with gen., with, together with. μετ' ὀργῆς, in anger. With acc., after. μεθ' Ἕκτορα, after Hector, i.e. after slaying Hector. τὸ μετὰ τοῦτο, the next thing, next (cf. τὸ ἐπὶ τούτῳ)

μετα-βάλλω: change

μετα-βολή f.: change

μετα-δίδωμι, aor. partic. μεταδόντες: give a share

μετα-λαμβάνω, aor. μετέλαβον: partake, receive

μετ-αλλάττω, aor. μετήλλαξα: change, alter

μετα-μέλει impers.: like Latin poenitet. μοι μεταμέλει, I regret

μεταξύ adv.: in the midst, between. λέγοντα μεταξύ, while speaking. GMT. 858

μετα-πέμπομαι, aor. μετεπεμψάμην: send for, summon

μετα-πίπτω: (change in falling), fall differently, am cast in the other (urn)

μετα-στρέφομαι: turn about

μέτ-ειμι: am among. Impers. μέτεστί μοι, I have a part

μετέωρος (μετά, ἀήρ, meteor) adj.: in mid air, above the earth

μετ-οικέω: change (my) home, remove, reside in a foreign city

μετ-οίκησις, -εως f. (οἶκος): change of habitation, transmigration

μετρέω, aor. ἐμέτρησα: measure

μέτριος adj.: moderate, well, fair

μετρίως adv. (μέτρον): reasonably, fairly. μετρίως ἔχει, it is fair and right

μετριώτατα sup. adv.: most reasonably

μέχρι prep.: until, up to

μή negative particle: not. In a question this implies a negative answer (Latin num). μὴ ὅτι, not to speak of, not to say μηδ-αμῶς *adv.*: in no way, by no means

μη-δέ *conj.*: but not, neither, nor, not even

μηδ-είς, μηδεμία, μηδέν *num. adj.*: no one

μηκέτι *adv.*: no longer

μηκύνω: lengthen, lengthen out, prolong

μηνύω, *aor.* ἐμήνῡσα: inform, lodge information. (A technical legal term.)

μήτηρ, -τρός *f.* (mater): mother

μηχανάομαι: contrive, devise

μηχανή *f.* (machine, mechanic): device, contrivance, way

μιαρώτατος *sup. adj.*: (defiled with blood), most vile, abominable

μῑκρός *adj.*: small, little

μῑμέω (mime): imitate

μῑμητής, -οῦ *m.*: imitator

μιμνῄσκω, *pf.* μέμνημαι: recall, *pf.* remember

Μίνως, -ωος *m.*: Minos, son of Zeus and Europa, king of Crete; judge in Hades after his death. *Ap.* **41 a**; λ 568; *Gorgias,* **523 e**

μισθόομαι, *aor.* ἐμισθωσάμην: hire

μισθός *m.*: pay, wages

μνᾶ, *gen.* μνᾶς: mina (100 drachmae, about $17)

μόγις *adv.*: with difficulty, after a struggle, reluctantly, barely

μοῖρα *f.*: fate, portion. ἐν μείζονι μοίρᾳ εἰμί, have larger place, am in higher esteem. θεία μοῖρα, divine will; blessing of the gods

μόνος *adj.* (monotone): only, alone

μορμο-λύττομαι: frighten with hobgoblins, scare

μόσχος *m.*: calf

Μουσαῖος *m.*: Musaeus, a mythical Greek bard. **41 a**

μουσική *f.* (*sc.* τέχνη) (Μοῦσα): music, mental discipline, in mind

μοχθηρίᾱ *f.*: wickedness

μοχθηρός *adj.*: evil, bad, base

μῡθο-λογέω: talk familiarly, talk

μῡθο-λογικός *adj.*: gifted in story-telling

μῦθος *m.*: myth, story, fable, tale

μῡ́ριος *adj.* (myriad): countless, untold, boundless

μύωψ, -ωπος *m.*: gadfly, spur

μωραίνω (sophomore?): am foolish

ναυ-κληρίᾱ *f.*: shipping

ναυ-μαχίᾱ *f.*: naval battle, sea-fight

ναῦς, *gen.* νεώς, *Homeric dat. pl.* νηυσι (navis): ship

νεκρός *m.*: dead body, corpse

νέος *adj.* (novus): new, young. οἱ νέοι, the youths, young men. ἐκ νέου, from youth

νεότης, -ητος *f.*: youth, youthful bravado

Νέστωρ, -ορος *m.*: Nestor, the oldest, wisest, and most eloquent of the Greeks before Troy. **221 c**

νεύω, *aor.* ἔνευσα: nod

νεώτερος *comp. adj.*: younger

νή: *particle of asseveration, with the accusative,* by

νῑκάω, *pf.* νενίκηκεν: conquer, win a victory

Νῑκό-στρατος *m.*: Nicostratus. **33 e**

νοέω: mean, think, indicate. τί νοεῖ, what is the meaning

νόθος *adj.*: illegitimate, of unequal parentage

νομίζω, *aor.* ἐνόμισα (νόμος): consider, think, believe in

νόμιμος *adj.*: lawful, established

νόμος *m.*: law

νοσώδης, -ες *adj.* (νόσος): diseased, unwholesome

νου-θετέω (τίθημι): admonish, warn

νοῦς, *gen.* νοῦ, *dat.* νῷ, *m.*: mind, thought, reason

νύμφη *f.*: nymph

νῦν, νῦνδή, or νῦνί: now. τὰ νῦν, nowadays. *Sometimes opposed to a hypothetical case rather than to time past or future*

νύξ, *gen.* νυκτός, *f.* (nox): night

νυστάζω: am sleepy

νωθέστερος *comp. adj.*: rather lazy, too sluggish

Ξανθίππη *f.*: Xanthippe, wife of Socrates. 60 a; Introd. § 16

ξένος *m.*: stranger, foreigner, alien, from out of town, guest-friend, friend

ξένως *adv.*: as a stranger

ξύλον *n.*: wood

ξύν: *see* σύν

ὁ, ἡ, τό *article*: the. τὸ δέ, but on the other hand, but the truth is. τὰ μέν . . . τὰ δέ, some things . . . others

ὅδε, ἥδε, τόδε *dem. pron.*: this, this here. *As an adv. of place*, Πλάτων ὅδε, Plato here. τῇδε, in this way

ὀδύρομαι: mourn, moan, grieve

Ὀδυσσεύς, -έως *m.*: Odysseus (Ulysses). 41 c

ὅ-θεν *rel. adv.*: whence. Cf. πόθεν.

οἷ *rel. adv.*: whither

οἷα: as, *adv. acc. of* οἷος

οἶδα, *imv.* ἴστε, *inf.* εἰδέναι, *plpf. as impf.* ᾔδη (wit): know

οἴκα-δε (οἶκος): homeward, to (my) home, home

οἰκεῖος *adj.* (οἶκος): of (my) house, of (my) family, (my) own. οἱ οἰκεῖοι, (my) relations, kinsfolk

οἰκέω (οἶκος): live, dwell; administer

οἴκημα *n.*: room, chamber

οἴκησις, -εως *f.*: dwelling

οἰκία *f.*: house

οἰκο-δομέομαι, *aor.* ᾠκοδομησάμην (timber): build a house

οἴκο-θεν *adv.* (οἶκος): from (my) house, from home

οἴκοι *loc. adv.*: at home

οἰκο-νομία *f.* (economy): management of (my) household affairs

οἰκο-νομικός *adj.*: skilled in managing a house

οἶκτος *m.*: lamentation, grief

οἴομαι (or οἶμαι), *fut.* οἰήσομαι, *aor.* ᾠήθην: think, suppose

οἷος *rel. pron.*: of what sort (= qualis), *correlative to* τοῖος such. οἷόν ἐστιν, its nature. οἷός τε, able; οἷόν τε, possible. οἷον δή, as for example. οἷα δή, as may happen. *In an exclamation*, οἷα ποιεῖτε, what are you doing!

οἴχομαι, *fut.* οἰχήσομαι: go off, go, depart. οἴχομαι φεύγων, flee away

οἰωνός *m.*: bird, bird of omen

ὀλιγ-αρχία *f.* (ἀρχή): oligarchy

ὀλίγος, -η, -ον: small, little. ὀλίγου (*sc.* δεῖ) almost. ἐν ὀλίγῳ (*sc.* χρόνῳ), in a little time, soon

ὀλιγ-ωρέω, *aor.* ὠλιγώρησα: make light of, think little of

ὅλος *adj.*: whole, entire. τὴν ἡμέραν ὅλην, all day long

Ὀλυμπίασιν (*adv.*, old locative pl.): at Olympia, in the Olympian games

Ὄλυμπος *m.*: Olympus, the most noted flute-player of antiquity. Very ancient melodies were ascribed to him. 215 c

Ὅμηρος *m.*: Homer. 41 a

ὁμιλέω, *aor.* ὡμίλησα (homily): associate with

ὁμιλητής, -οῦ *m.*: associate

ὁμιλία *f.* (homily): society, association

ὄμνυμι, *aor.* ὤμοσα, *pf.* ὀμώμοκα: swear, take an oath

ὅμοιος *adj.*: of like kind, alike

ὁμοιότατος *sup. adj.*: most like

ὁμοίως *adv.*: in like manner, just as

ὁμο-λογέω, *aor.* ὡμολόγησα, *pf.* ὡμολό-γηκα, *pass.* ὡμολόγημαι, *aor. pass.* ὡμολογήθην (λόγος): agree to, promise, acknowledge, confess. τὰ ὁμολογούμενα, the premises

ὁμο-λογίᾱ *f.*: agreement, compact

ὁμοῦ *adv.*: together

ὅμως *conj.*: yet, however, nevertheless

ὄναρ *n.*: dream

ὀνειδίζω, *fut.* ὀνειδιῶ: rebuke, reproach

ὀνίνημι, *fut.* ὀνήσομαι, *aor.* ὤνησα: benefit, oblige. ὥς ὤνησας, how you obliged me ! Thank you

ὄνομα, -ατος *n.* (nomen): name, word

ὀνομάζω: name, call

ὀνομαστότατος *sup. adj.*: most renowned

ὄνος *m.*: ass. 27 e

ὀξύς, -εῖα, -ύ *adj.* (oxide): keen

ὅπῃ *rel. adv.*: where, in what way, as

ὅπλα *n. pl.*: arms, *esp.* shield; heavy arms

ὁπόθεν *rel. adv.*: from which

ὅποι *rel. adv.*: whither, to what place

ὁπότε *rel. adv.*: when

ὁπότερος *rel. adj.*: which of (us) two

ὅπου *rel. adv.*: where

ὅπως *rel. adv.*: how, in what way, in order that. οὐκ ἔσθ' ὅπως οὐ, it is not possible that it would not, *i.e.* surely

ὁπωσ-τι-οῦν: (how-so-ever), in any way soever, in the least, at all. G. 432. 1; H. 285

ὁράω, *impf.* ἑώρων, *fut.* ὄψομαι, *aor.* εἶδον, *pf.* ἑώρακα: see, behold

ὄργανον *n.* (ἔργον, organ): instrument

ὀργή *f.*: anger, wrath, spirit

ὀργίζομαι, *aor.* ὠργίσθην (ὀργή): am angry

ὀρέγω, *aor.* ὤρεξα, *aor. pass. as mid.* ὠρέχθην: extend, offer; *mid.* reach after, desire

ὀρθός *adj.*: straight, right

ὀρθότης, -ητος *f.*: rightness, right

ὄρθρος *m.* (ὄρνυμι): dawn

ὀρθῶς *adv.*: rightly

ὅρκος *m.*: oath

ὁρμάω, *aor.* ὥρμησα: set out for, undertake

ὄρνις, -ῑθος *m.*: bird

ὄρος, -εος *n.*: mountain

ὀρφανίᾱ *f.*: orphanhood

ὀρφανός *m.* (orbus): orphan

Ὀρφεύς, -έως *m.*: Orpheus, the most famous mythical bard of antiquity, who was able by his song to charm wild beasts and trees. 41 a

ὀρχήστρᾱ *f.* (orchestra): dancing-place. 26 d

ὅς, ἥ, ὅ *rel. pron.*: who, which, what. In ἦ δ' ὅς, said he, *and in* καὶ ὅς, and he, ὅς *has its early demonstrative force.* — ὅπερ ἔλεγον, what I said, *i.e.* as I said

ὅσιος *adj.*: holy

ὁσιώτερος *comp. adj.*: more holy

ὅσος *rel. pron.*: as much as (= quantus), *pl.* as many as, all who. ὅσῳ, by as much as. ὅσον, how far, how much

ὁσ-περ, ἥ-περ, ὅ-περ: *see* ὅς and πέρ

ὅστε *rel. pron.*: in ἐφ' ᾧτε, on condition that, *with the infinitive.* 29 c

ὅσ-τις, ἥ τις, ὅ τι, *gen.* ὅτου, *indef. rel.*: whoever, whatever, who, what

ὁσ-τισ-οῦν κτλ. *indef. rel. as indef. pron.*: any one soever

ὅτε *rel. adv.*: when

ὁτέ *indef. adv.*: at some time. ὁτὲ μέν, at one time

ὅτι *conj.*: that, because. *Sometimes this is used to introduce a direct quotation, when it simply serves as quotation-marks* (as 23 b). ὅτι μή = εἰ μή, 52 b. ὅτι μάλιστα (quam maxime), as much as possible. Cf. ὡς.

ὅτι-οὖν *indef. rel. as indef. pron.*: anything whatsoever. Cf. ὁπωστιοῦν.

ὅτου, ὅτῳ: *gen. and dat. of* ὅστις, whoever

οὗ *adv.*: where

οὑγώ: *for* ὁ ἐγώ

οὐδ-αμόσε *adv.*: to no place

οὐδ-αμοῦ *adv.*: nowhere

οὐδ-αμῶς *adv.*: in no way, by no means, under no circumstances

οὐ-δέ *conj.*: but not, neither, nor, not even

οὐδ-είς, οὐδεμία, οὐδέν *num. adj.*: no one, nothing. οὐδεὶς ὅστις οὐ, *equiv. to* πᾶς, every one

οὐδέ-ποτε *adv.*: never

οὐδε-πώ-ποτε *adv.*: never in the world

οὐδ-έτερος *adj.*: neither of two

οὖν *conj.*: so, now, then, therefore, at any rate. δ᾽ οὖν, however that may be

οὐράνιος *adj.* (οὐρανός): belonging to the heavens, heavenly

οὖς, *gen.* ὠτός, *n.* (otology): ear

οὐσία *f.* (ὤν): (existence), property

οὗτος, αὕτη, τοῦτο *dem. pron.*: this, that. ταῦτα (23 b) *may be used adverbially as in Homer*, therefore. ταύτῃ, in this respect. καὶ ταῦτα *and* καὶ τοῦτο, and that too (*Latin* idque). *The Greek sometimes uses the demonstrative pron. as an adv., as* ἄλλοι οὗτοι, *others are here. This is the general demonstrative, which may be used either of what is near or of what is remote, if this is only thought of as at hand.*

οὕτω(ς) (*or* οὑτωσί, *deictic*) *dem. adv.*: thus, so. ἔχει οὑτωσί, the case is like this

ὀφείλω, *aor.* ὤφελον: owe. ὤφελον, they ought (implying "I wish they ..could")

ὄφελος *n.*: advantage, aid, use, good. ὅτου τι ὄφελος, who is worth anything

ὀφθαλμός *m.*: eye

ὀφλισκάνω, *fut.* -ὀφλήσω, *aor.* ὦφλον, *pf.* ὤφληκα: lose a fine, am fined, am mulcted, am sentenced to, incur

ὄχλος *m.*: throng, crowd

ὀψέ *adv.*: late

ὄψις, -εως *f.* (ὄψομαι): vision, appearance, form

ὄψον *n.*: sauce, relish

πάγ-καλος *adj.*: all-beautiful

παγ-κάλως *adv.*: altogether well

πάγος *m.*: frost, freezing

πάθος, -εος *n.*: suffering, affection, experience

Παιανιεύς, -έως *m.*: Paeanian. The deme of Paeania (that of the orator Demosthenes) lay on the eastern slope of Mt. Hymettus. 59 b

παιδείᾱ *f.*: education, training

παιδεύω, *fut.* παιδεύσω, *aor.* ἐπαίδευσα, *pass.* ἐπαιδεύθην, *fut. pass.* παιδεύσομαι (παῖς): teach, educate, train

παιδιά *f.*: child's play, play

παιδίον *n.* (παῖς): child, little child

παιδο-τρίβης, -ου *m.*: (rubber), gymnastic trainer

παίζω (παῖς): play, jest

παῖς, *gen.* παιδός, *m. or f.*: child, offspring; servant. ἐκ παίδων *or* ἐκ παιδός, from childhood, from boyhood. Cf. ἐκ νέου.

παίω: strike, flog

πάλαι *adv.* (palae-ontology): formerly, long ago. πάλαι θαυμάζω, I long have wondered

παλαιός *adj.*: ancient, old, man of old

Παλαμήδης, -εος *m.*: Palamedes. Mythical inventor of the alphabet, arithmetic, and many other devices. Unjustly slain by the Achaeans before Troy. 41 b πάλιν adv.: again

πάμ-πολυς, pl. πάμπολλοι, adj.: pl. very many

παντά-πᾶσι adv. (πᾶς): absolutely

πανταχοῦ adv.: everywhere

πάντως adv. (πᾶς): by all means, surely, certainly, in fact

πάνυ adv. (πᾶν): entirely, completely, very, earnestly, greatly, certainly. οὐ πάνυ, not very

παρά prep.: with gen., from, by the side of, by. With dat., with, in the judgment of. παρ' ἡμῖν, in our town. With acc., along, during; by the side of, to the side of, in comparison with, contrary to. παρὰ τοὺς νόμους, contrary to the laws. παρὰ τὸ δίκαιον, contrary to justice. παρὰ τοὺς ξένους, to the home of the friends. παρὰ τὸν χρόνον, during the time. παρ' ὀλίγον, by a small majority

παρα-βαίνω: transgress, break

παρα-βάλλω: cast to one side. τώφθαλμὼ παραβάλλων, glancing one side

παρ-αγγέλλω, aor. παρήγγειλα, aor. pass. παρηγγέλθην: pass the word along (as in a line of soldiers), give the word, direct

παρα-γίγνομαι, aor. παρεγενόμην: come along, am present

παρα-γιγνώσκω: judge wrongly

παρ-άγω, aor. pass. παρήχθην: lead aside, lead astray

παρά-δειγμα, -ατος n. (paradigm): example

παρα-θεωρέω (theory): observe in comparison

παρ-αιρέω, aor. παρειλόμην: mid. draw away (to one's self)

παρ-αιτέω, aor. mid. παρῃτησάμην: beg, entreat

παρα-κάθ-ημαι: sit by, sit beside

παρα-κελεύομαι: urge, exhort

παρα-κέλευσις, -εως f.: exhortation. ἐπὶ τῇ ὑμετέρᾳ παρακελεύσει, that I may urge you (to your duty)

παρα-κρούω: strike one side (a figure from the palestra), turn aside, deceive

παρα-λαμβάνω: receive, take in charge

παρα-λείπω, aor. παρέλιπον: pass by, pass over

Παρ-άλιος m.: Paralius. (He was treasurer of temple funds in 390 B.C., according to an inscription.) 33 e

παρα-μένω, fut. παραμενῶ, aor. παρέμεινα: remain by (my) side, remain (with)

παρα-μυθέομαι: comfort, encourage

παρά-νομος adj.: lawless, unlawful

παρα-νόμως adv.: contrary to the law

παρά-παν adv. (πᾶς): absolutely, entirely. With τό, like τὸ νῦν, τὸ πρῶτον

παρα-πλησίως adv.: in like manner, in much the same way

παρα-σκευάζω: prepare

παρα-σκοπέω: observe

παρα-χωρέω: make way, yield the floor

πάρ-ειμι: am present. οἱ παρόντες, the bystanders, those who (are) present. ἐν τῷ παρόντι, at present, now

πάρ-ειμι, aor. παρῆλθον: pass along, enter. παρελθὼν βίος, past life

παρ-έχω, fut. παρέξομαι, aor. mid. παρεσχόμην: present, furnish, produce, offer, cause

παρ-ίεμαι: entreat, request earnestly. Equiv. to παραιτέομαι

παρ-ίημι, aor. partic. παρείς: allow to pass, neglect

Πάριος adj.: Parian, from (the island) Paros. 20 a

παρ-ίστημι, pf. partic. παρεστώς: set beside, present; pf. intrans. stand beside, am present πᾶς, πᾶσα, πᾶν adj.: all, every, the whole

πάσχω, fut. πείσομαι, aor. ἔπαθον, pf. πέπονθα (πάθος): suffer, am affected, have experience, experience

πατήρ, -τρός m. (pater): father

πατρίς, -ίδος f. (patria): fatherland

Πάτροκλος m.: Patroclus, friend of Achilles, slain by Hector. 28 c

παύω, fut. παύσω, aor. mid. ἐπαυσάμην: stop, cease

πείθω, aor. ἔπεισα, mid. ἐπιθόμην, pf. pass. πέπεισμαι, fut. πείσομαι, aor. ἐπείσθην, verbal πειστέον: persuade, convince; mid. and pass. am persuaded, obey, believe, take (my) advice. πείσας, with (your) consent or approval

πειράομαι, fut. πειράσομαι, aor. ἐπειράθην: attempt, try, endeavor; have experience of, know

πέμπτος adj. (πέντε): fifth. πέμπτος αὐτός, with four others

πέμπω: send

πένης, -ητος m.: poor man

πένθος, -εος n. (πάθος): sorrow, mourning

πενίᾱ f. (penuria): poverty, need

πέντε (quinque): five

πέρ (πέρι): enclitic strengthening suffix. εἴ περ expresses a doubt

περί prep.: with gen., about, around, concerning, in regard to. With dat., in regard to. With acc., in regard to. τὸ περὶ σέ, nearly equiv. to τὸ σοῦ. περὶ τοὺς νέους, for the youth. When it follows its noun or pronoun, it has the accent upon the first syllable. περὶ πλείστου, of highest importance. περὶ πολλοῦ, of great importance

περι-αμπ-έχομαι: clothe, throw about (as a garment)

περι-άπτω: wrap about, cloak

περι-βάλλω, pf. pass. περιβέβλημαι: clothe; pass. am clad, cloaked

περι-γίγνομαι, pf. περιγέγονα: surpass, excel, am superior

περί-ειμι (εἰμί): surpass, excel

περί-ειμι, partic. περιιών (εἶμι): go around, go about, walk around

περι-εργάζομαι (ἔργον): am a busybody, meddle with what does not concern (me)

περι-έρχομαι, aor. περιῆλθον: go around, walk about

Περικλῆς, -έους m.: Pericles, the greatest statesman of Athens, who appeared in public life first (so far as is known) as the choregus for the Persians of Aeschylus in 472 b.c., and died in 429 b.c. 215 e

περι-μένω, fut. περιμενῶ, aor. περιέμεινα: wait, tarry, wait about, await

περί-πατος m. (Peripatetic): (walk-about), colonnade

περι-τίθημι, aor. partic. περιθέμενος: put about, wrap around

περιττότερος comp. adj. (περί): more than, unusual

περι-τυγχάνω: fall in with, happen to meet

περι-φέρω: bear about, carry about

πέτρᾱ, Homeric gen. πέτρης, f. (Peter): rock, stone

πή enclitic: in any way

πήγνυμαι: grow stiff

πηδάω: leap, bound

πηνίκα adv.: when, at what time? (Cf. πότε.)

πιέζω, aor. ἐπίεσα: press

πιθανός adj. (πείθω): persuasive, plausible

πιθανῶς adv.: persuasively, plausibly

πιθανώτερον comp. adv.: more persuasively

πῖλος m.: felt

πίνω, aor. ἔπιον, pf. πέπωκα, verbal ποτέον (potio): drink

πιστεύω (πείθω), aor. ἐπίστευσα: believe, trust, have confidence, rely on; aor. put confidence

πλάνη f. (planet): wandering, going to and fro

πλάττω (plastic): mold, make up

Πλάτων, -ωνος m.: Plato. 34 a, 38 b, 59 b. Introd. §§ 28 f.

πλεῖστος sup. of πολύς: most, greatest

πλείων (or πλέων), -ονος, nom. pl. πλείους (comp. of πολύς): more, more numerous. πλέον ποιεῖν, accomplish something, gain anything

πλῆθος, -εος n. (plēbs): multitude, mass, people, populace, democracy

πλήθω: am full

πλημμέλεια f. (μέλος): false note, mistake

πλημμελέω: strike a false note, err

πλημμελής, -ές adj.: mistaken, unreasonable. πλημμελές, a false note, mistake, error

πλήν conj. and prep.: except, but. πλὴν εἰ, equiv. to εἰ μή, unless

πλησιάω, fut. πλησιάσω: approach

πλησίον adv.: near, with gen.

πλοῖον n. (πλέω): boat, ship

πλούσιος adj.: rich, wealthy

πλουσιώτατος sup. adj.: richest, most wealthy

ποδαπός adj.: of what land?

πόθεν adv.: whence, from what source?

ποῖ adv.: whither, to what?

ποί encl. adv.: somewhither, somewhere

ποιέω, fut. ποιήσω, aor. ἐποίησα, pf. πεποίηκα, verbal ποιητέος: make, act, do, compose. ποιέω κακῶς, injure. πλέον τι ποιῆσαι, accomplish something, gain anything. περὶ πλείστου ποιεῖσθαι, count of highest impor-

tance. ἃ πεποιήκασι, the poems which they have composed. ποιοῦμαι τοὺς λόγους, make my talk, speak. ποιοῦμαι παῖδας, beget children, have a family. εὖ ἐποίησας, you did well, I am glad that you. εὖ ποιεῖν, benefit

ποίημα, -ατος n. (ποιέω): poem

ποίησις, -εως f. (poesy): poetry

ποιητέος: verbal adj. of ποιέω, do

ποιητής, -οῦ m. (ποιέω): (maker), poet

ποῖος adj.: of what kind?

πολεμέω: am at war, contend

πολέμιος adj.: public enemy, enemy

πόλεμος m.: war, battle

πόλις, -εως f.: city, state

πολῑτείᾱ f.: state, constitution

πολῑτεύομαι, fut. πολῑτεύσομαι: live as citizen

πολίτης, -ου (πόλις): man of the city, citizen, fellow-citizen

πολῑτικός adj. (πολίτης): political, of a citizen. As noun, statesman, public man. τὰ πολιτικά, the work of the city, affairs of state

πολλά adv.: often. τὰ πολλά, for the most part

πολλάκις adv.: often, frequently, again and again, at many times; perchance, possibly

πολλαχοῦ adv.: in many places, often

πολύ adv.: far, by far

πολυ-πραγμονέω: am a busybody, interfere, meddle

πολύς, πολλή, πολύ adj.: much, abundant, great, large, long, many. οἱ πολλοί, the many, the most, the masses. πολλῷ, (by) much. τὰ πολλά or ὡς τὸ πολύ, for the most part, generally

πολυ-τέλεια f.: expense

πολυ-τελέστερος comp. adj.: more expensive

πολυ-τελής, -ές adj. (τέλος): expensive

πονέω : labor, toil

πονηρίᾱ f.: evil, wickedness, sin

πονηρός adj.: bad, evil

πονηρότερος comp. adj.: worse

πόνος m.: labor, toil, task

πορείᾱ f. (πόρος): journey, going

πορεύομαι, fut. πορεύσομαι: journey, go, walk

πορίζω, aor. mid. ἐπορισάμην: provide, procure

πόρρω adv.: advanced, far on

πόρρω-θεν adv.: at a distance, from afar

πόσος interrog. adj.: how much, how great? pl. how many? Cf. ὅσος, τοσοῦτος. πόσου, for how much?

ποτέ encl. adv.: at one time, once. τί ποτε, whatever, what in the world?

Ποτείδαια f.: Potidaea, on the isthmus of Pallene, on the shore of Thrace. 28 e, 219 e

πότερα and πότερον adv.: whether? (Not always does it need to be translated.)

πότερος adj.: which of (the) two?

πότμος m.: fate, destiny, death

ποτόν n. (potio, πίνω): drink

ποῦ adv.: where?

πού encl. adv.: somewhere, anywhere, somehow, I presume

πούς, gen. ποδός m. (pes): foot

πρᾶγμα, -ατος n. (πράττω): doing, affair, interest, work, business, thing, trouble, case

πρᾱγματείᾱ f.: activity, insistence

πρᾱγματεύομαι, pf. pass. πεπρᾱγμάτευμαι: occupy (my)self, busy (my)self about, labor ; pf. pass. perfected, polished

πρᾶξις, -εως f.: action, matter, affair

πρᾱ́ότατος sup. adj.: most gentle, meekest

πρᾱ́ότερος comp. adj.: more gentle

πράττω, fut. πράξω, aor. ἔπραξα, pf. pass. πέπραγμαι, aor. ἐπράχθην, verbal πρακτέον: act, do, make, attend to, fare ; mid. exact. χρήματα πράττομαι, charge for services. εὖ πράττω, fare well, am happy. τὰ 'Αθηναίων πράττω, do the work of the Athenians, am in public life

πρᾱ́ως adv.: meekly, mildly

πρέπω : fit, suit. πρέπει impers., it is fitting

πρεσβεύω : rank first, revere

πρεσβύτερος comp. adj.: older, elder

πρεσβύτης, -ου m. (priscus): old man

πρίαμαι : buy, purchase

πρίν adv.: before

πρό prep. with gen.: before, in preference to

προ-αγορεύω : declare beforehand, give notice

προ-αιρέομαι : choose deliberately, prefer

προ-βιβάζω (βαίνω): lead forward

πρό-γονος m.: ancestor, forbear, forefather

προ-δίδωμι, aor. inf. προδοῦναι: give up, abandon, desert

Πρόδικος m.: Prodicus, a noted rhetorician and sophist from Ceos. 19 e. Introd. § 12

προ-θῡμέομαι, fut. προθῡμήσομαι: am eager, am pleased, strive

προ-θῡμίᾱ f.: zeal, good will, eagerness·

προ-θῡμότερος comp. adj.: more eager, more zealous

προῖκα adv.: freely, without charge, without expense

προ-κρίνω : judge superior, prefer

προ-λέγω, pf. pass. προείρημαι: say beforehand, foretell

προ-μηθέομαι : have forethought for, have regard for, with gen.

προ-οίμιον n.: (procemium), hymn
πρός prep.: with gen., before. πρὸς τῶν
θεῶν, in the name of the gods. πρὸς
Διός, in the name of Zeus. With dat.,
in addition to. πρὸς τούτοις, in addition to this. With acc., to, towards,
before, with reference to, as regards,
in view of, in relation to, in comparison with
προσ-δέομαι: need in addition
προσ-δοκάω, aor. προσεδόκησα (δόξα):
expect, await
προσ-ειμι: come to, go to
προσ-έρχομαι, aor. προσῆλθον: come to,
approach, meet
προσ-ερῶ fut.: will address
προσ-εύχομαι, aor. προσηυξάμην: pray
to, worship
προσ-έχω: hold towards, direct
προσ-ήκω: come to. Impers. προσήκει,
it is fitting. προσήκων, fitting, appropriate. οἱ προσήκοντες, the kinsmen,
relatives
προ-σημαίνω: show beforehand
πρόσθε(ν) adv.: before, former
προσ-καθ-ίζω: sit by, settle down upon
πρόσ-κειμαι: lie next, am attached (as
pf. pass. of προστίθημι, place upon,
attach, give to)
πρόσ-οιδα, inf. προσειδέναι: know in
addition. χάριν προσειδέναι, give
thanks in addition
προσ-ποιέομαι: claim, pretend
προ-στατέω (ἵστημι): am leader, lead
προσ-τάττω, aor. προσέταξα, pf. pass.
προστέταγμαι: enjoin upon, direct
προσ-τίθημι, pf. προστέθεικα: place upon, give
πρόσ-φημι, fut. προσερῶ: address
προσ-χράομαι, pf. προσκέχρημαι: use in
addition, use
πρόσ-ωπον n.: countenance, feature;
(theatrical mask), person

προτεραίος adj.: on the day before
πρότερον comp. adv.: sooner, formerly
πρότερος comp. adj.: before
προ-τίθημι: lay before, propose; mid.
lay out, of the πρόθεσις of the dead
body before burial. 115 e
προ-τρέπω: turn forward, urge on
προ-τροπά-δην adv. (τρέπω): headlong
πρό-χειρος adj. (χείρ): ready, at hand
προ-χωρέω: advance, go forward. προύχώρει αὐτῷ, he succeeded
πρύμνα f.: stern
πρυτανεῖον n.: prytanēum, the hall at
Athens in which guests of the city
dined. 36 d
πρυτανεύω: have the prytany. 32 b
πρύτανις, -εως m.: prytanis
πρῴ or πρωΐ adv. (πρό): early in the
morning
πρῴαίτατα sup. adv.: earliest
πρῴαίτερον comp. adv.: earlier
πρῴην adv.: the other day, day before
yesterday
πρῶτον sup. adv.: for the first time, firstly
πρῶτος sup. adj. (προ-ατος ?): first,
earliest
Πῡθία f.: Pythian priestess. 21 a
πυκνός adj.: close, frequent, constant
πυνθάνομαι, aor. ἐπυθόμην: inquire,
learn by inquiry, learn
πῶλος m. (foal): colt
πῶμα, -ατος n. (potio): draught
πώ-ποτε adv.: ever yet
πῶς adv.: in what way, how? How is
it that, why? πῶς γὰρ οὔ, certainly,
of course
πώς encl. adv.: in any way, in some
way, substantially

Ῥαδάμανθυς, -υος m.: Rhadamanthys,
brother of king Minos of Crete, and
one of the judges in the lower world.
41 a; cf. Ξ 322; Gorgias 523 d

ῥᾴδιος *adj.*: easy

ῥᾳδίως *adv.*: easily, readily, lightly, without good reason

ῥᾳ-θῡμότατος *sup. adj.* (θυμός): easiest, laziest

ῥᾷον *comp. adv.*: more easily

ῥᾷστος *sup. adj.*: easiest

ῥῆμα, -ατος *n.* (εἴρηκα): phrase, expression

ῥητέον *verbal of* φημί: it must be said

ῥήτωρ, -ορος (εἴρηκα): speaker, rhetorician, orator. οἱ ῥήτορες, the public men

ῥώννῡμι, *pf. pass.* ἔρρωμαι: make strong, strengthen. ἐρρῶσθαι. to be strong, "to take care of himself,"—*in greeting, like the Latin* valeo

Σαλαμίνιος *adj.*: Salaminian, of Salamis

Σαλαμίς, -ῖνος *f.*: Salamis, an island near the harbor of Athens. 32 c

σάτυρος *m.*: Satyrus, satyr. 215 b

σαυτῷ, σαυτόν *reflex. pron.*: thyself

σαφέστατα *sup. adv.* (σαφής): most clearly

σαφέστερον *comp. adv.*. more clearly

σαφής, -ές *adj.*: clear, distinct, definite

σαφῶς *adv.*: clearly, distinctly, openly

σέβομαι: revere, worship

Σειρῆνες *f. pl.*: Sirens, who beguiled mariners to their destruction. 216 a; cf. Homer μ 167 ff.

σελήνη *f.*: moon

σεμνότερος *comp. adj.* (σέβομαι): more august, more reverend

σημαίνω, *aor.* ἐσήμηνα (σῆμα): show, indicate

σημεῖον *n.*: sign, token

σῑγάω: am silent, am still

σῑγή *f.*: silence. σιγῇ, in silence

Σιληνός *m.*: Silēnus, foster-father and companion of Dionysus. 215 a, 216 d

Σιληνώδης, -ες *adj.*: Silen-like

Σιμμίᾱς, -ου *m.*: Simmias. 45 b, 59 c

Σίσυφος *m.*: Sisyphus. 41 c; cf. Homer Z 153; λ 593

σῑτέομαι (σῖτος): am fed, eat

σίτησις, -εως: feeding, dining

σῖτον *n.*: food

σκεδάννῡμι, *pf. pass.* ἐσκέδασμαι: scatter

σκέλος, -εος *n.* (iso-sceles): leg

σκέμμα, -ατος *n.*: consideration, speculation

σκεπτέον: *verbal of* σκοπέω

σκευή *f.*: costume, attire, contrived apparel

σκέψις, -εως *f.*: consideration, question

σκιά *f.*: shade

σκιᾱ-μαχέω: fight with shadows, "fight in the dark," "beat the air"

σκοπέω, *aor.* ἐσκεψάμην, *pf.* ἔσκεμμαι, *verbal* σκεπτέον: consider, examine, look at

σκῡτο-τόμος *m.* (τέμνω): shoemaker

σμῑκρός *adj.* (μικρός): small, little

σός, σή, σόν *possessive pron.* (tuus): thine

Σούνιον *n.*: Sunium, the southern promontory of Attica. 43 d

σοφίᾱ *f.*: wisdom

σοφιστής, -οῦ *m.* (σοφός): sophist, philosopher, rhetorician

σοφός *adj.*: wise

σοφώτατος *sup. adj.*: wisest

σοφώτερος *comp. adj.*: wiser

σπανιώτερος *comp. adj.*: more rare

σπεύδω, *aor.* ἔσπευσα (studium): hasten, strive for

σπουδάζω, *aor.* ἐσπούδασα: am in earnest, am serious, am eager for

σπουδῇ *adv.*: in earnest, seriously, in a serious matter

στάσις, -εως *f.* (ἵστημι): faction, party

στέρομαι, *pf. pass.* ἐστέρημαι, *fut.* στερήσομαι, *aor.* ἐστερήθην: am deprived, lose

στέφω, aor. ἔστεψα, pf. pass. ἔστεμμαι: crown

στόμα, -ατος n.: mouth, lips

στρατείᾱ f.: military expedition, campaign

στρατεύομαι, fut. στρατεύσομαι: serve in the army

στρατ-ηγέω: am general

στρατ-ηγίᾱ f. (strategy): generalship, command of an army

στρατ-ηγικός adj. (strategic): skilled in generalship

στρατ-ηγός m : general, commander

στρατιᾱ́ f.: army, expedition

στρατιώτης, -ου m.: soldier

στρατό-πεδον n.: camp, army

συγ-γίγνομαι, aor. συνεγενόμην, pf. συγγέγονα: come to be with, associate with, have intercourse with

συγ-γιγνώσκω: have sympathy with, am indulgent to

συγ-κάμπτω, aor. συνέκαμψα: bend

συγ-κεράννῦμι, pf. συγκέκρᾱμαι: mix, combine, unite

συγ-χωρέω, aor. συνεχώρησα: concede, yield

σῦκο-φάντης, -ου m.: (sycophant), malicious accuser. (Never used like modern "sycophant.")

συλ-λαμβάνω, aor. συνέλαβον: take together, close

συλ-λέγω, aor. pass. συνελέγην: collect

συμ-βαίνω, pf. συμβέβηκα: befall, happen. τὰ ἐμοὶ συμβεβηκότα, my experience

συμ-βάλλομαι: bring together, contribute

σύμ-βολον n. (βάλλω, symbol): (chance) meeting

συμ-βουλεύω, aor. συνεβούλευσα: give advice, counsel, advise

σύμ-πᾶς, σύμπᾱσα, σύμπᾱν: all together

συμ-πότης, -ου m. (πίνω): fellow banqueter

συμ-φέρω: (bring together), am of advantage

συμ-φεύγω, aor. συνέφυγον: flee with, go into exile with, am banished with

συμ-φορᾱ́ f.: misfortune

συν-άπτω, aor. συνῆψα, pf. pass. συνῆμμαι: fasten together

συν-δια-σῴζω, aor. συνδιέσωσε: aid in saving

συν-δια-ταλαιπωρέω: continue the toil with (the rest of parents)

συν-δοκεῖ impers.: it seems good to (you) too

σύν-ειμι, fut. συνέσομαι: am with, associate with, have to do with. οἱ συνόντες, (my) associates

συν-επι-σκοπέω, aor. συνεπεσκεψάμην: consider with (me), examine with (me)

συν-ήθης, -ες adj.: accustomed, familiar

συν-θήκη f. (τίθημι): covenant, agreement, contract

συν-νοέω, aor. συνενόησα: have a thought, aor. partic. taking up a thought

σύν-οιδα pf. as pres.; plpf. as impf., συνῄδη: am conscious, know very well, — with dat. after συν-

συν-ουσίᾱ f. (σύνειμι): association

συν-ουσιαστής, -οῦ m.: associate

συν-τεταγμένως adv. (τάττω): in array, with definite agreement

συν-τεταμένως adv. (τείνω): vehemently

συν-τίθημι, aor. inf. συνθεῖναι, aor. mid. συνεθέμην: put together, compose; mid. covenant, agree together

συν-τυγχάνω: happen

συν-ωμοσίᾱ f. (ὄμνυμι): conspiracy, club

συν-ωρίς, -ίδος f.: pair of horses

σῦριγξ, -γος f. (syrinx): shepherd's pipe

συσ-σῑτέω: eat together, am messmate

συχνός adj.: much. συχνοῦ χρόνου, in a long time

Σφήττιος adj.: Sphettian, of the deme Sphettos (of the tribe Acamantis). **33 e**

σφόδρα adv.: earnestly, seriously, exceedingly

σφοδρός adj.: earnest, enthusiastic, impetuous

σφοδρῶς adv.: violently, vehemently

σφῶν gen. of refl. pron.: themselves

σχεδόν adv. (ἔχω): nearly, almost, about

σχῆμα, -ατος (ἔχω, scheme) n.: appearance, bearing. (Cf. habitus.)

σχολάζω: am at leisure

σχολή f. (school): leisure. σχολὴν ἄγω, have leisure. Cf. ἡσυχίαν ἄγω.

σῴζω, aor. ἔσωσα, fut. pass. σωθήσομαι, aor. ἐσώθην: save, keep in safety; aor. pass. returned in safety

Σωκράτης, -ους m.: Socrates. (The best Mss. of Xenophon treat this as of the first declension.) Introd. §§ 13 f.

σῶμα, -ατος n.: body

σω-φρονέω (σώφρων, — σῶς, φρήν): am of sound mind, am sensible

σω-φροσύνη f.: temperance, self-control

τἀληθῆ: for τὰ ἀληθῆ

τἆλλα: for τὰ ἄλλα

τἄν: for τοι ἄν. **29 a**

τάν in ὦ τάν (ἔτης?): my friend, my good man

τάξις, -εως f. (τάττω): post, station

ταράττω, pf. pass. τετάραγμαι: trouble, confuse, disturb

τἀριστεῖα: for τὰ ἀριστεῖα, the meed of bravery

τάττω, aor. ἔταξα, pf. pass. τέταγμαι, aor. ἐτάχθην (tactics): station, place, set, appoint

ταυρηδόν adv.: like a bull

ταύτῃ adv. (οὗτος): in this respect, thus, so, in this point

ταὐτόν: for τὸ αὐτό, the same

ταφή f.: burial, funeral

τάχα adv.: perhaps, possibly

τάχιστα sup. adv.: most quickly

ταχύς, ταχεῖα, ταχύ adj.: swift. διὰ ταχέων, quickly

τείνω: tend, extend, direct

τεκμαίρω: infer, gather

τεκμήριον n.: sign, indication, bit of circumstantial evidence

τεκτονικός adj. (τέκτων): skilled in carpentry

Τελαμών, -ῶνος m.: Telamon. **41 b**

τελετή f.: initiation, mystic rite

τελευταῖος adj.: last

τελευτάω, aor. ἐτελεύτησα, pf. τετελεύτηκα: end, die. τελευτῶν, at last

τελευτή f. (τέλος): end, completion, death

τελέω, pf. τετέλεκα (τέλος): pay

Τερψίων, -ωνος m.: Terpsio. **59 c**

τέτταρες num. (quattuor): four

τέχνη f. (technical): art

τέως adv.: till then. Cf. ἕως.

τῇδε adv. of ὅδε: thus, in the following way

τηλικόσδε adj.: at (your) age

τηλικοῦτος adj.: at (my) age

τήμερον adv. (ἡμέρα): to-day

τηνικάδε: at this hour

τίθημι, aor. mid. ἐθέμην: place, set, count; cast (of a vote)

τῑμάω, aor. ἐτίμησα, fut. mid. τῑμήσομαι, aor. ἐτῑμησάμην (τιμή): honor, esteem, fix a penalty; mid. propose as a penalty, with gen. of price

τῑμή f.: honor

τίμημα, -ατος n.: assessment, award, judgment

τῑμιώτερος comp. adj. (τιμή): more precious

τῑμωρέω, *fut.* τῑμωρήσω, *aor. mid.* ἐτῑμωρησάμην: avenge, gain satisfaction; punish

τῑμωρίᾱ *f.*: punishment, vengeance

τὶς, *gen.* τινός *or* τού, *dat.* τῷ, *n. pl. acc.* ἅττα, (*encl.*) *indef. pron.*: some one, a certain, one, many a one, some. ἤ τι ἤ οὐδέν, little or nothing

τίς, τί, *gen.* τίνος, *interrog. pron.*: who? what?

τιτρώσκω, *pf. pass.* τέτρωμαι, *fut. pass.* τρωθήσομαι: wound

(τλάω), *aor.* ἔτλην (τόλμη): dare

τοί: = σοί, *in a Homeric quotation.* **28 c.** *Generally a weak ethical dative,* you know, doubtless, you see

τοί-νυν *inferential particle*: well then, well, *often used in a transition*

τοιόσδε *dem. pron.*: such as this, like this

τοιοῦτος, τοιαύτη, τοιοῦτο *dem. pron.* (τοῖος): such, of this kind. *It may refer to what follows (as* **47 a**).

τολμάω, *aor.* ἐτόλμησα: dare, have the heart

τόλμη *f.*: daring, assurance, effrontery

τόπος *m.* (topography): place, region

τοσόσδε, τοσήδε, τοσόνδε: so much, so great; *pl.* so many

τοσοῦτος, τοσαύτη, τοσοῦτο (τόσος): so great, so heavy, so much; *pl.* so many. εἰς τοσοῦτον, to such a pitch

τότε *adv.*: then

τοτέ *adv.*: at one time. τοτὲ δ᾽ αὖ, but again

τού *encl.*: *gen. of* τὶς

τοὐναντίον: *for* τὸ ἐναντίον, the opposite

τοὔνομα: *for* τὸ ὄνομα, the name

τραγικός *adj.*: tragic

τραγῳδίᾱ (τράγος, ᾠδή) *f.*: tragedy

τρά-πεζα *f.* (trapeze; τέτταρες, πούς): table, bank, money changer's

τρεῖς *numeral* (tres): three

τρέπω, *2 aor.* ἐτραπόμην (τρόπος): turn

τρέφω, *fut.* θρέψω, *fut. pass.* θρέψονται, *pf. pass.* τέθραμμαι: bring up, nurture

τρέω, *aor.* ἔτρεσα: tremble

τριᾱκοντα *num.*: thirty. οἱ Τριάκοντα, "The Thirty Tyrants," who ruled Athens from June, 404, to February, 403 B.C.

τρίβω, *aor.* ἔτριψα, *pf. pass.* τέτριμμαι: rub, prepare by rubbing

Τρι-πτόλεμος *m.*: Triptolemus, a mythical hero of Eleusis. He was a favorite of Demeter, and received from her a winged chariot, with which he drove over the earth, making known the blessing of agriculture. **41 a**

τρίτατος *adj.* (τρεῖς): third

τριχῇ *adv.*: in three ways

Τροίᾱ *f.*: Troy, the Troad. **41 b**

τρόπος *m.* (τρέπω): manner, way. παντὶ τρόπῳ, by all means. ὃν τρόπον, in what way, as

τροφεύς, -έως *m.* (τρέφω): foster father, who brought (him) up

τροφή *f.* (τρέφω): food, support, nurture

τρυφή *f.*: luxury

τρωθησόμενος: *fut. pass. partic. of* τιτρώσκω

τυγχάνω, *fut.* τεύξομαι, *aor.* ἔτυχον (τύχη): chance, happen. *With suppl. participle, which often has the greater importance;* τυγχάνει ὄν, happens to be, is. τὰ τυχόντα, chance, common. *With gen.,* happen upon, receive

τύπτω: strike, smite

τυφλός *adj.*: blind

τύχη *f.*: fortune. τύχῃ ἀγαθῇ, God's will be done, as God pleases, "all for the best." This phrase is set at the head of many Attic inscriptions, like Θεοί, "In God's name," "God save the State."

τῷ *encl.*: = τινί, *dat. of* τὶς

ὕβρις, -εως *f.*: insolence

ὑβριστής, -οῦ *m.*: insolent

ὑβριστότατος *sup. adj.*: most insolent

ὑγιεινός *adj.*: healthful, wholesome

ὕδωρ, *gen.* ὕδατος (wet) : water. *Pl.* rain

υἱός, -οῦ: see υἱός, son

ὑμεῖς, ὑμῶν *pers. pron.*: you

ὑμέτερος *adj.*: your, of you. τὸ ὑμέτερον, your work

υἱός, -οῦ *nom. dual* υἱεῖ, *pl.* υἱεῖς, *gen. pl.* υἱέων *m.* (υἱός): son

ὑπ-ακούω, *aor.* ὑπήκουσα : give ear to, listen, *i.e.* answer, open the door

ὑπ-άρχω : am in readiness

ὑπ-εικάθω (εἴκω, weaken): yield

ὑπ-είκω, *verbal* ὑπεικτέοι : yield, as a younger to an older person

ὑπέρ *prep.* (super): *with gen.*, on behalf of, on the part of, in regard to

ὑπ-έρχομαι : creep before, fawn upon, cringe to

ὑπ-έχω : bear, suffer, am subject to

ὑπ-ηρεσία *f.*: service

ὑπ-ηρέτης, -ου *m.*: servant, attendant

ὑπ-ισχνέομαι, *aor.* ὑπεσχόμην : promise

ὕπνος *m.* (somnus): sleep

ὑπό *prep.* (sub): *with gen.*, under, by, because of

ὑπο-βλέπω, *fut.* ὑποβλέψομαι, *aor.* ὑπέβλεψα : look from under the brows, look with suspicion, look askance

ὑπο-δέχομαι : receive

ὑπο-δέω, *pf. pass.* ὑποδέδεμαι : bind under, bind on ; *pf. pass.* am shod

ὑπό-δημα, -ατος *n.*: sandal

ὑπο-λαμβάνω, *aor.* ὑπέλαβον, *pf.* ὑπείληφα : interpose, suppose ; *aor.* came to believe

ὑπο-λογίζομαι : take into account, calculate, consider

ὑπο-μένω, *aor.* ὑπέμεινα : endure, submit to

ὑπο-στέλλω, *aor. mid.* ὑπεστειλάμην : hold back, withhold, dissemble

ὕπτιος *adj.* (ὑπό): supine, upon (my) back

ὕστατον *sup. adv.*: for the last time

ὑστεραῖος *adj.*: later, following. τῇ ὑστεραίᾳ, on the next day, on the day after

ὕστερον *comp. adv.*: later

ὕστερος *comp. adj.*: later

ὑφ-ηγέομαι : lead the way, lead on

ὑφ-ίημι, *aor. opt. mid.* ὑφείμην : yield, concede

Φαίδων, -ωνος *m.*: Phaedo. **57 a.** He was a well-to-do young citizen of Elis, — but was brought to Athens as a prisoner of war, and sold as a slave. Socrates took interest in him and secured his freedom, and he became a devoted follower of Socrates.

Φαιδώνδης, -ου *m.*: Phaedondes. **59 c**

φαίνω, *fut. pass.* φανοῦμαι, *aor.* ἐφάνην : show ; *pass.* appear, am found, seem. οὐ φαίνεται, plainly not

φανερός *adj.*: manifest, seen, open

φάρμακον *n.* (pharmacy): drug, — *eu phemistic for* poison

φάσκω (φημί) : assert, say, declare, claim

φαυλίζω : disparage

φαῦλος *adj.*: worthless, mean, insignificant

φαυλότατος *sup. adj.*: meanest

φαυλότερος *comp. adj.*: of less importance

φείδομαι, *fut.* φείσομαι : spare

φέρω, *fut.* οἴσω, *aor.* ἤνεγκα, *aor. pass.* ἠνέχθην : bear, bring

φεύγω, *fut.* φεύξομαι, *2 aor.* ἔφυγον, *verbal* φευκτέον (φυγή): (1) flee, avoid, shun ; (2) am charged, am defendant in a suit at court, — (*treated as a passive*

verb, am accused, with ὑπό and gen.
of agent); go into exile, am banished

φήμη f. (fama): report, saying (esp.
chance saying)

φημί, inf. φάναι, fut. φήσω and ἐρῶ, aor.
εἶπον, pf. εἴρηκα, pass. εἴρημαι, verbal
ῥητέον: say, assert. οὐ φημι, deny,
say no

φθέγγομαι, aor. ἐφθεγξάμην: utter a
sound

Φθίη f.: Phthia, home of Achilles in
Thessaly. 44 b

φθονέω, aor. ἐφθόνησα: envy, grudge,
begrudge

φθόνος m.: envy, grudge, malice

φιλέω: love

φίλιος adj.: friendly

Φιλό-λāος m.: Philolāus, a distinguished
Pythagorean philosopher. 61 d. Introd. § 6

φιλό-πολις adj.: city-lover, patriotic

φίλος adj.: dear, pleasing, friendly; as
noun, friend

φιλο-σοφέω (σοφός): love wisdom, seek
truth

φιλο-σοφίā f. (philosophy): search for
truth

φιλό-σοφος m.: lover of truth

φιλό-τῑμος adj.: lover of honor, ambitious

φιλο-τῑμότατος sup. adj.: most ambitious

φιλο-ψῡχίā f.: love of life

Φλειάσιοι m. pl.: Phliasians, people of
a small country west of Corinth.
57 a

φλυāρέω: babble, talk nonsense

φλυāρίā f.: babbling, nonsense

φοβέομαι, fut. φοβήσομαι, aor. ἐφοβήθην:
fear, am afraid of, dread

φοβερός sup. adj.: fearful, to be feared

φόβος m. · fear

φοιτάω: frequent, come often

φονικώτατος adj.: most bloodthirsty

φόνος m.: slaughter, slaying, death

φορέω: wear. Frequentative of φέρω

φορτικός adj. (φέρω, φόρτος, burden):
(burdensome), vulgar, commonplace

φράζω, aor. ἔφρασα: point out, tell, declare

φρονέω (φρήν): think. μέγα φρονῶ, am
proud

φρόνησις, -εως f.: intelligence, wisdom,
prudence

φρόνιμος adj.: intelligent, reasonable,
wise

φρονίμως adv.: wisely, sensibly. φρονίμως ἔχειν, to be wise

φρονιμώτατος sup. adj.: wisest, most
intelligent

φροντίζω, aor. ἐφρόντισα, verbal φροντιστέον: think of, consider

φροντιστής, -οῦ m. (φροντίζω): thinker,
speculator, student of. (Followed by
an acc., as if it were φροντίζων.)

φρουρά f.: guard, prison

φυγή f.: flight, retreat; exile, banishment

φύλαξ, -ακος m.: guard, keeper

φυλάττω: guard, watch; mid. guard
(my)self against

φῡλή f.: phyle, tribe, — one of the ten
chief political divisions of the Athenians

φύσις, -εως f.: nature, natural endowment

φυτεύω, aor. ἐφύτευσα: plant, beget. ὁ
φυτεύσας, (your) father

φύω, aor. ἔφυν, pf. πέφυκα (cf. Latin
fui): spring, come into existence,
am born; pf. am, am by nature

φωνή f. (-phone): voice, dialect, speech

Χαιρεφῶν, -τος m.: Chaerephon, a friend
of Socrates. 20 e

χαίρω: take pleasure, rejoice, delight, fare well. *ἐάω χαίρειν*, suffer it to say "farewell," think no more of it

χαλεπαίνω, *fut.* χαλεπανῶ: am angry

χαλεπός *adj.*: difficult, hard, sad, grievous, fierce

χαλεπώτατος *sup. adj.*: hardest, fiercest, hardest to bear

χαλεπώτερος *comp. adj.*: more difficult, harder to bear, worse

χαλκεύς, -έως *m.* (χαλκός): blacksmith

χαλκευτικός *adj.*: skilled in smith's work

χαμ-εύνιον *n.* (χαμαί, εὐνή): ground-bed, i.e. blankets, for sleeping on the ground

χαριεντίζομαι (χάρις): jest, sport

χαρίζομαι, *fut.* χαριοῦμαι, *aor.* ἐχαρισάμην: gratify, oblige

χάρις, -ιτος *f.*: gratitude, favor, thanks. *ἐν χάριτι*, as a favor, to please

χειμών, -ῶνος *m.* (hiems): cold, storm, winter

χειρο-τέχνης, -ου *m.*: artisan, craftsman

χείρων, -ονος (*comp. of* κακός): worse

χίλιοι *pl. adj.*: one thousand

χράομαι, *aor.* ἐχρησάμην: use. φθόνῳ χρώμενοι, through envy, under the influence of envy. χρῶμαι ἐμαυτῷ, do with myself

χρεία *f.*: use

χρή (*sc.* ἐστί): it is necessary, needful, fitting; one must, one ought

χρῆμα, -ατος *n.*: thing; *pl.* property, money. τιμῶμαι χρημάτων, propose a fine

χρηματισμός *m.*: making of money

χρῆν (χρὴ ἦν): it were fitting. χρῆν αὐτοὺς κτλ., they ought, etc.

χρησμός *m.*: response of an oracle, oracle

χρησμ-ῳδέω, *aor.* ἐχρησμῴδησα: deliver an oracle, foretell the future

χρησμ-ῳδός *m.* (ἀείδω): oracle-singer fortune-teller, prophet

χρηστός *adj.* (χράομαι): good, excellent

χρόνος *m.*: time

χρίσεος *adj.*: golden

χρῶμα, -ατος (chrome): color

χωλός *adj.*: lame

χωρέω: proceed, flow

χωρίς *adv.*: apart from, not to speak of

ψευδής, -ές *adj.*: false

ψεύδ. μαι, *aor. pass.* ἐψεύσθην: lie, speak falsely, deceive

ψεῦδος, -εος *n.*: falsehood

ψηφίζομαι (ψῆφος): vote, cast (my) vote

ψῆφος, -ου *f.*: (pebble), vote

ψιλός *adj.*: bare, simple

ψόγος *m.*: blame

ψῡχή *f.*: soul

ψύχ.μαι: become cold

ψῦχ.ος, -εος *n.*: cold, cool

ὠγαθέ: *for* ὦ ἀγαθέ. **24 d**

ὧδε *adv. of* ὅδε: thus, in this way

ὥρα *f.* (hour): season, time

ὡς *adv.*: as, how, that, since. *In* ὡς ἀληθῶς, it is the adv. of the article,— in truth. ὡς with the participle indicates the action as thought or said; ὡς ἐλέγξων, with the expectation that I should prove; ὡς διαφθείροντα, with the statement that I corrupt. ὡς with the superl., like Latin quam, ὡς βελτίστη, as good as possible; ὡς τάχιστα, as quickly as possible

ὥσ-περ *adv.*: as, just as, like

ὥστε *conj.*: with inf., so that; therefore

ὦτα: *pl. of* οὖς, ear

ὠφελέω, *fut.* ὠφελήσω, *pf.* ὠφέληκα: benefit, help, profit, am of advantage

GREEK INDEX

The Indexes have been prepared by Miss Elizabeth Seymour and aim to present the main points elucidated by the editor in the Introduction and Notes; on some of these points further information may be found in the Vocabulary. Light figures refer to pages of this edition, heavy figures to sections of the Introduction.

ENGLISH INDEX